Theatre: a book of words

Other Books of Words from Carcanet

Horse Racing
Gerald Hammond

Fly-fishing
C.B. McCully

Whisky
Gavin D. Smith

FORTHCOMING:

Hunting and Walking, Shooting and Stalking
Michael Brander

Film
Kevin Jackson

Fashion
Helen Maclean

Sailing
Richard Mayne

Music
Brian Morton

THEATRE

MARTIN HARRISON

CARCANET

First published in 1993 by
Carcanet Press Limited
208-212 Corn Exchange Buildings
Manchester M4 3BQ

A CIP catalogue record for this book
is available from the British Library.
ISBN 1 85754 040 9

The publisher acknowledges financial assistance
from the Arts Council of Great Britain

Set in 10pt Plantin by Bryan Williamson, Frome, Somerset
Printed and bound in England by SRP Ltd, Exeter

General Editors' Preface

The *Book of Words* series offers a new conception and analysis of the vocabularies used in our sports, pursuits, vocations and pastimes. While each book contains an essential lexicon of words and phrases – explored historically and in depth – each also contains generous quotation, practical reference, anecdote and conjecture. The result is more than a dictionary: specific, inclusive, thought-provoking, each *Book of Words* offers the past and present through a weave of words, in all their curiosity and delight.

Those intrigued by the language particular to their area of interest will find the relevant *Book of Words* a coherent and challenging treatment of the topic; those interested in the English language itself will find the series yielding significant material on semantic scope and change; and general readers who wish to understand the vocabularies of human endeavour will find the series tracing the necessary but implacable relationships between words and world.

Editors, chosen because of their intimate enthusiasm for their subjects, have been encouraged to be comprehensive in their coverage: vocabularies typically range from the demotic to the esoteric, from slang to the technical and specialised. Within that range, emphasis is also placed on *how* each lexicon developed, and *why* its terms acquired their peculiar descriptive power. These are books to read with pleasure as well as keep on the reference shelf.

Gerald Hammond
C.B. McCully

Acknowledgements

Thanks are due to the following publishers for permission to quote from copyright material: Methuen London Ltd *The Complete About Acting* © 1991 Peter Barkworth, *The Brecht Commentaries* by Eric Bentley, *The Shifting Point* by Peter Brook, *The Semiotics of Theatre and Drama* by Keir Elam, *The Development of the English Playhouse* by Richard Leacroft, *Theatre and Playhouse* by Richard and Helen Leacroft, *Kindly Leave the Stage* by Roger Wilmut; Routledge for *A Concise Dictionary of Slang and Unconventional English* ed. Paul Beale, *A Dictionary of Slang and Unconventional English* by Eric Partridge, *The Art of Coarse Acting* by Michael Green, *Greek Tragedy in Action* by Oliver Taplin; Faber and Faber Ltd for *I Am Hamlet* by Steven Berkoff; Random House UK Ltd for *Beginning* by Kenneth Branagh; Oxford University Press for *The Oxford Companion to the Theatre* ed. Phyllis Hartnoll, *Theatrical Anecdotes* by Peter Hay; Secker and Warburg/BBC for *All the World's a Stage* by Ronald Harwood; Cambridge University Press for *Erwin Piscator's Political Theatre* by C.D. Innes; Phaidon Press for *Stage Management and Theatre Administration* by Pauline Menear and Terry Hawkins; Weidenfeld and Nicolson for *Confessions of an Actor* by Laurence Olivier; Market House Books for *A Dictionary of the Theatre* ed. David Pickering; Harper Collins (Fontana) for *Keywords* by Raymond Williams; Oberon Books for *The Oberon Glossary of Theatrical Terms* by Colin Winslow.

Every effort has been made to contact copyright holders. In the event of any inadvertent omission or error, please contact Carcanet Press Ltd.

I should like to thank the many colleagues and friends who have read sections of the book in manuscript form. Special thanks are due to the General Editors for their support and guidance, especially to my friend Chris McCully, without whose unstinting encouragement and generous assistance I would never have embarked on this project, let alone have finished it in anything approaching an acceptable form. Finally, I must thank my partner, Carol Willis, whose love and consideration have allowed me the time and space to work on this book, despite the fact that it has overlapped with most of Daniel's first four years of life and with Amy's birth.

Introduction

This book is not a dictionary; nor does it pretend to be a comprehensive survey of current English theatrical language. Rather, it samples around 1,200 contemporary and historical theatrical terms, standard and demotic, in the hope of giving the theatre-goer and the general reader pleasure, and the new student of the stage a first glimpse of the theatrical lexicon in all its diversity and complexity. My intention is also that it should encourage the hardened theatre practitioner to examine the familiar and everyday from an alternative perspective, that of words and their derivations. When you pursue a word over two and a half millennia of change and adaptation, it begins to ask its own questions, not merely about itself and its own meanings, but some of those shelved questions about the nature and function of theatre. It may even suggest some answers. By cross-referencing these terms, as the book does, words begin to have dialogues: not witty repartees, perhaps, but exchanges which uncover a number of themes.

My original intention had been to limit this book to words one might reasonably expect to overhear in a theatre bar, but, whilst there can never be too many theatres numerically, there were too many generically to consider in full – and too many bars. There was also a huge range of characters sitting around them in esoteric huddles: *thesps* and *punters*, *technicians* and *critics*, *amateurs*, *walk-ons*, *stuntmen*, *mimes*, Japanese tourists – and it was not always the latter who were the most difficult to understand. Theatre language is not, like *Parlyaree*, a *lingua franca*, though those who speak it share common terms. It has a bewilderingly large number of dialects, some of which – those of dance, opera and music, for instance – I must apologise for dealing with cursorily here: each of those subjects merits its own Book of Words.

I had also intended to limit myself to contemporary usages, but as themes began to emerge it became obvious that would not be possible. The very first term on my tentative alphabetical list was *above*, a stage direction used with two different senses over the last four hundred years. A study of contemporary theatre language must also be a study of the history of that language. And once themes had begun to emerge – the debate over the nice difference between *realism* and *naturalism*, say – it was impossible to ignore small but illuminating digressions. I could not omit the term *cup-and-saucer drama*, for example, theatrical cul-de-sac though that might be, because it rattled around so with *kitchen-sink drama*, another term for a movement of dramatic realism separated from it by a century. I wanted those terms to talk to each other.

But first to the pleasure principle. Readers who enjoy wrestling with words and meanings will find that many of the terms in this book deliver their own condensed narratives. The development of *arena*, for example, Latin for common 'sand', has the logical improbability of a Borges short story: like an illusionist, you pick up a fistful of it from the blood of the amphitheatre, take it into the darkness of an auditorium, open your hand and *voilà!* – it has vanished into an abstract concept, 'an arena for discussion'. *Rostrum*, one of my own favourite words, makes random leaps of sense that transport it from the past-tense stem of the Latin verb 'to gnaw', to 'a beak', to 'a prow', through sea battles and the Roman forum, until, as the result of a passing idea one day in the eighteenth century, it lands, squat, as that unprepossessing wooden box in the corner of the drama studio.

Not all terms are hostages to fortune, though. Some reveal general patterns that fascinate. It is generally agreed that *drama* and *theatre*, both as signifiers and as signified, have prehistoric origins. They come to us direct from the roots of ritual, which can afford to exclude nothing. The language of the theatre excludes nothing. When they appear first in Attica, *drama* is *doing*, *theatre* is *seeing*, and, to confuse, they bring along another key theatrical term, *tragedy*, which is *goat-song*. All three are used to describe some aspect of the representation of reality. When *doing* becomes *pretending*, when *seeing* becomes *participating in an illusion*, when *goat-song* becomes *suffering and purgation*, the audience response is to reappropriate those terms with their changed meanings. Like the dramatist's work, the language of theatre has to be given back, a process we see occurring in this book from Athens to the West End. Because the words are concerned with social identity and role, because they express so vividly conflicts central to our experience – whether that experience be *comic, farcical, tragic* or *absurd* – we reclaim them to help us to understand ourselves, our relationships and our social functions. And then we change their meanings again. Other experiences are *likened* to *pretending*, to *illusion*, to theatrical *suffering*.

Terms for theatre spaces and buildings, too, are eloquent of changing social circumstances and attitudes. The book watches the dismantling of the *proscenium arch* and the complex stratifications

of *boxes* and *circles* and *galleries*. It sees the sudden re-emergence
of the *vomitorium* after an absence of two thousand years. And if
any aspect of this book calls out for further and more detailed
research, it is the role of the ex-sailors who contributed so much
to the physical development of the English stage. Their language
remains – forty-three terms in all in this book – alongside the
practical skills they brought with them into the theatre. Of the
stagehands themselves only a few anecdotes remain, while volumes
are written about Dryden and Garrick. Researching their language
is like joining the boarding party entering the galley of the *Marie
Celeste*: everything is intact, but there's no sign of the crew.

Contemporary usages show the same process continuing today.
I have tried to include technical terms in this book, but I have
become aware, as people attending a first-night party must be
aware, that *techies* are on one side of the room, talking amongst
themselves in unfamiliar terms, whilst everyone is listening to and
praising the *laddies* and *luvvies* on the opposite side, whose names
and language they know intimately from the media. C.P. Snow's
Two Cultures are embedded in theatre and its language. The
eighteenth-century schism between words related to the arts and
those related to science and technology is still apparent today, as
this book evidences. So too, however, are counter signs in the
broadening application of terms like *designer* to *lighting* and *sound
men*, and in the development of performance terms which recognise
a more practical view of art: *workshop, laboratory theatre, studio*.
The language of theatre excludes nothing, including our shames,
and we can watch the *ingénues* and *soubrettes* becoming *actors* and
joining the *feminist theatre*; the *nigger minstrel* escaping the *coon
show* for a *black theatre company*.

It is the energy and unpredictable eclecticism of theatre language
that have made working on this book so enjoyable. It is entertaining
to follow the one-way trading from the subversive, dangerous worlds
of *burlesque, music hall* and *variety*, with their close links with low-
life cant and gangsterism, to the *serious* theatre – the arrival of terms
like *punter* and *fall-guy* and *stooge*, and the huge twentieth century
influx of terms from the United States and cinema and television.
Finally, it is also refreshing to watch the verbal assaults on the
establishment by *new movements*: *the avant-garde* becoming the *fringe*
becoming *alternative, off-Broadway* becoming *off-off-Broadway*.
Applying the tried and trusted Greek test of *drama* and *theatre* and
tragedy, it is perhaps worth ending by remarking that *alternative*
theatre and its language, if it is good enough, always becomes *legitimate*: and you can tell when that has happened when its terms become
firmly established, not only in the theatre but in colloquial speech.

Abbreviations

OE: Old English
ME: Middle English

Fr: French
G: German
Gk: Greek
It: Italian
L: Latin (LL: Late Latin)
OF: Old French
Rom: Romanic

C: century
e: early
m: mid
l: late
Thus: *lC16-eC17* = late sixteenth to early seventeenth centuries.

References to frequently-cited sources, with the exception of
OED: Oxford English Dictionary
OED (Supp): Supplement to the Oxford English Dictionary
are given by the surname of the author: thus Nagler signifies A.M.
Nagler's *A Source Book in Theatrical History* (1952). Full details
can be found in the Bibliography.
We thank Oxford University Press for permission to include material from the Dictionary.

Above A common *stage direction* from Elizabethan times onwards. Its meaning, however, differs significantly according to period. In C16-eC17, *above* described a detail of the physical structure of the stages of most London playhouses. Whilst there is still debate as to the precise structure of these early theatres which were evolving rapidly, (see Leacroft, *English Playhouse*, 25-50), when we read 'Brabantio above, at a window', (*c*.1603, Shakespeare, *Othello*, I.i), we are to imagine the actor standing on the upper stage, a balcony known as the *terrace* and variations on this, which projected, like the first storey of an Elizabethan house, from the *tiring-house* situated at the rear of the main *platform stage*. (For further directions which mirror early theatre forms, see also *within*, *discovered*.)

In more modern texts, 'above' describes a very different stage: the raked stage of many C18 theatres. An actor standing behind an object on a *rake* – that is, *upstage* of it – was literally above it, since the rake sloped gently upwards towards the back of the stage. 'Living room. – Large desk, with a consulting chair above it' (Stage direction for Act I of Ibsen's *Enemy of the People*, French's Acting Edition). As one can imagine, a literal interpretation of this could make for a bizarre opening stage picture. The latter usage remains, though it has generally been replaced in stage directions by upstage, or, as is often the case outside *acting editions*, the *stage direction* has been omitted and the *blocking* left to the director's discretion, the *décor* to the *designer*.

absurd, theatre of the A term first used theatrically in English by the critic Martin Esslin in his book of that name, published in 1962. It refers to a style of theatre (now sometimes abbreviated to *absurdism*) which Esslin saw characterised in the works of Eugène Ionesco, Samuel Beckett (see *Beckettian*), N.F. Simpson and early Harold Pinter (see *Pinteresque*) among others. Anyone familiar with the above playwrights will realise what an umbrella term this is. Esslin claimed that these dramatists' works share certain revolutionary similarities of subject matter and form in response to common mid-20th-century philosophical dilemmas; consequently he borrowed the term *the absurd* from the contemporary European philosophical movement of existentialism. The formal similarities between Esslin's *absurdists* can be briefly

1

characterised as the selection of highly *non-naturalistic settings*, the absence of traditional dramatic structures and plots, inconsistency or absence of characterisation and the use of non-realistic dialogue: as Beckett puts it in *Waiting for Godot*, 'Nothing happens, nobody comes, nobody goes, it's awful.'

The word comes originally from L *absurdus*, 'out of tune', and this sense of dissonance seems to have led to its later development in Latin as 'something contrary to reason', as in *reductio ad absurdum*. This philosophical sense of the word is included in Fr. *absurde*, *(reduire à l'absurde)*, which co-exists alongside *absurdité*, (closer to English *absurdity*). Whilst *l'absurdité* centres on the notion of ridiculousness, *l'absurde* suggests indignation at the preposterousness of things. 'The absurd' to Sartre, Camus and other existentialists was the state of *alienation* in which contemporary man found himself: 'In a universe that is suddenly deprived of illusions and of light, man feels a stranger. His is an irremediable exile . . . This divorce between man and his life, the actor and his setting, truly constitutes the feeling of Absurdity' (1946, Albert Camus, *The Myth of Sisyphus*). The term has not really found a general usage. Whilst situations and conversations can be said to have 'a touch of the absurd' about them, this is usually a reference to their ridiculousness and not their quasi-theatrical form or philosophical content.

accompanist From Fr. *accompagner*, 'to come, go, with'. An eC19 term which can be used in all situations where a musician, usually a pianist, provides musical support (accompaniment) to *singers*, *comedians* etc.: 'The accompanyst played the melody' (1837-9, Dickens, *Oliver Twist*). The term is still in use in all forms of dance and musical theatre, though it does have a rather quaint ring to it: 'Our accompanist was a sweet man, but he had a limited repertoire of tunes. I have nothing against Andrew Lloyd Webber, but nearly three years of "Close Every Door To Me" accompanying what seemed to me impossible movements was more than I could take' (Branagh, 61).

ack-ack The familiar term for a now largely obsolete *lantern*. Although *ack-acks* produced a wide beam of light, they could not be *focused*. It was partially this lack of aim and control as well as the unwieldy appearance of the lantern which led to the borrowing of the term from 'anti-aircraft guns' used in World War II, so-called because *ack* was the abbreviation for *A* in the phonetic alphabet. 'Ack-ack' also relates to this alphabet, being an abbreviation of *acting area lantern*.

acoustics From Gk *akouō*, 'hear'. From the adjective *acoustic*, 'pertaining to the sense of hearing, auditory', *acoustics* refers to the sound quality of any *auditorium*, which is affected by size, design, structure, materials used, the presence or absence of an audience etc. 'Apart from its sublime beauty, as Ralph and I agreed, its wooden interior endowed [the Flemische Schauspielhaus in Antwerp] with the most miraculous acoustic properties' (Olivier, 149). Sound engineers and designers have worked to enhance acoustics from the earliest Greek theatres, where *periaktoi* probably assisted in projecting sound, to modern theatres with their *P.A. systems* and *acoustic shells* – specially-constructed structures, either permanent or temporary, which improve the acoustic properties of a venue.

acrobat A performer in the *circus* or *variety*, capable of feats of great gymnastic skill, working solo, with a team, or with apparatus. The word entered English from Fr. *acrobate*. The earliest OED reference is in *Punch* in 1845: 'And the Clown ... notified the first appearance of the famous Acrobat.' Before that date, although the Greek form *acrobates* was used with reference to antiquity, the English *tumbler*, which is now largely archaic, was preferred in contemporary contexts. (In eC20 slang, according to Partridge, 'acrobat' was also used for 'a glass', with an excruciating pun on *tumbler*.) The word describes the performer's skill (from Gk *akrobatein*, 'to walk on tiptoe, climb aloft', from *akron*, 'summit' + *bainō*, 'walk').

Soon after its arrival in the language, it is found metaphorically: 'Those great little acrobats the Tit-mice' (1859, W.S. Coleman, *Woodland Heaths and Hedges*). An interesting transference from physical to intellectual skill is evident in the common phrase, *mental acrobatics*.

act As both noun and verb, this word and its many theatrical derivatives come from the past participle of the L. verb, *agere*, – *act*, 'to drive, carry on, do, act'. Before dealing in more detail with the English development of the word, it is interesting to consider its development in Latin, where it underwent an extension strikingly similar to that of other key theatre words, e.g. *drama* in Greek, from Gk *draō*, also meaning 'do'. Both words have roots denoting active involvement in the world. Then, at a certain period in each culture's development, these primary verbs were extended to signify the artistic representation of action. There appears to be an underlying linguistic pattern here: primary words are loaned from their everyday contexts for theatrical (and other artistic) uses; later, they are reappropriated into the vernacular with new senses relating to role, identity, simulation and performance. This cross-trading from life to art and back again seems to underline the fact that both doing and pretending are vital human preoccupations, both necessary for survival. Of course, when the same word is extended generally to denote doing and pretending, the dividing line between appearance and reality can easily blur.

As both noun and verb, the theatrical development of *act* in English – and its key variants such as *actor* – is also fascinating. None of these terms appears theatrically until lC16, although when they do appear it is in a rush, which is not entirely surprising given the sudden growth of public performance at that time. It is significant that the terms seem to have developed indigenously, directly from Latin, with little or no influence from French – *actor* for example appears to predate Fr. *acteur* – as would also appear to be the case two centuries earlier with more general usages of act-based words. Even so, the verb *to act* is not preferred to the older synonym, *to play*, and 'actor' is not preferred to 'player' until after the Restoration, when, as can be seen in the emergence or growing popularity of other words – *action*, *cabaret*, *dramatist*, *farce* – continental influences on the returning Royalist exiles had a great effect on London theatre language.

act¹ (verb). As is common with words borrowed from other languages, the verb's entry into English occurred later than that of the noun, on the cusp of C15 and C16 (and more than a hundred years after the poet Henryson used it in Scots). However, its senses, both transitive *(acting a role)* and intransitive *(acting)*, were influenced by the noun's earlier development. The theatrical sense, 'to perform a play', is not attested in OED until 1594, the following being another early example: 'It was never acted: or if it was, not aboue once, for the Play I remember pleased not the Million' (1602, *Hamlet* II.ii). Whilst this verb is now the most commonly used for participation in performance, in C16-eC17 it is less frequently found than 'play'.

A play is said to *act well* if it can be successfully performed on stage. This use of the verb appears to have developed in lC18-eC19: 'My plays won't act...my poesie won't sell (1821, Byron in Trelawney, *Recollections of Shelley and Byron*, 1858).

A logical extension of the sense of pretence inherent in the verb was to lead to one further development of meaning: 'to simulate or feign', recalling the appearance/reality blur mentioned earlier: 'Sunderland acted calumniated virtue to perfection' (1849, OED). Other related common usages such as *acting the fool* have clear theatrical origins, although it is sometimes difficult to decide whether an extension of the meaning of *act* is theatrical or from the word's more general sense of 'to perform, do'.

act² (noun). In general senses, *act* entered English in C14,

possibly from Fr. *acte*, although many of its developments seem
to refer back directly to L. *actum*, 'a deed, a thing done': 'And
all youre actes red and songe' (*c*.1384, Chaucer, *House of Fame*).
By the C15 it had developed the additional sense of 'action', as
in 'The acte of Frenshmen standynge moche in ouer rydynge of
theyr aduersaryes by force of speremen' (1494, OED); it also
gained its parliamentary sense as in 'This was preved acte also in
the perlement' (1458, OED), along with other specialised legal
meanings. By the C16 it had assumed the sense of an ongoing
course of action as in these lines from *The Merchant of Venice*:
'When the work of generation was/Between these woolly breeders
in the act' (I.iii).

Theatrically, it is not attested as 'a sub-division of a text and/or
performance' (compare *scene*) in OED until eC17: 'Some come to
take their ease/And sleep an act or two' (1613, Shakespeare, *Henry
VIII, Epilogue*). This usage appears to occur through direct translation of Latin *actus*, 'an act of a play'. The Romans were greatly
influenced by Greek dramatic theory. As early as the 4th century
BC, Aristotle in the *Poetics* had stated that classical tragedies were
divided into five *acts*, although extant *texts* do not really show this
theory borne out. None the less, Horace, in *Ars Poetica*, restated
this rule and Roman dramatists adhered to it more obviously.
This classical model was certainly known to Elizabethan dramatists (as were the commercial benefits of *intervals*), but the impos-
ition of a rigorous five-act structure on the written text is usually
attributed to that staunch classicist, Ben Jonson. Heminge and
Condell followed suit and arranged Shakespeare's *Complete Works*
accordingly for the *First Folio* (1623), although there is no reason
to believe that he had used the act as a conscious structural unit.
Subsequent generations have redefined the convention of *act division* to their own artistic and commercial tastes. For example,
lC17 to C18 comic playwrights favoured three acts, and there was
a vogue for four acts in C19. Many contemporary dramatists have
abandoned the act and opted for the greater flexibility of inter-
connected scenes (as indeed Shakespeare appears to have done),
though often allowing for a natural break around half-way
through. Whether this is part of the artistic scheme of things or
an awareness that a bar interval is required is open to debate.
(See also *one act play*.)

A further development of 'act', as in *speciality act, routine* or
turn occurred in C19 *vaudeville* and *music hall*, or possibly earlier.
This usage may have developed because the end of each performance by an artiste or group of artistes on a *bill* created a natural
break or interval such as would follow the end of an act in a play;

or act may be used simply as an alternative to *performance*. The term is still common in *variety*: 'Describing herself in her act as "a little torment", she certainly was' (review in *The Stage*, 28 March 1991).

The word has entered into everyday speech in phrases such as *putting on an act*, which carries with it the additional sense of pretence and role-play in real-life situations also found in the verb. It is here that we see, of course, the second half of the transaction described in the introductory remarks: words appropriated by the theatre returning to the vernacular.

actable/actability A play which works well on the stage is said to be *actable*: it *acts well*. This is a C19 term: 'Opinions...as to the actability of certain unacted plays' (1836, *Fraser's Magazine*).

act-drop An *act-drop* was a name for a cloth or *curtain*, lowered as opposed to drawn, at the end of each act in place of the front or house curtain. See *tab*.

act-tune A term used from the Jacobean theatre onwards for the music played between acts in a performance.

acting (See *act* for etymology). The earliest attestation in OED of the verbal noun *acting* to describe the dramatic performance of an actor is from Pepys' Diaries. It occurs in a plural form which sounds awkward to the modern ear: 'The play not good, nor anything but the good actings of Betterton and his Wife and Harris' (1664). Over the next century the word began to replace 'playing' in frequency of usage. 'Acting' used to designate the pastime or profession is a logical extension of this and appears from OED to have been first used in C19: 'Acting was the especial amusement of the English from the palace to the village green' (1856, Froude, *History of England*).

acting area The area of floor, on a stage or otherwise, available for acting. For *acting area* lantern, see *ack-ack*.

acting edition An edition of a text specifically designed for actors, stage managers etc., especially useful for *amateur* companies as it attempts to provide additional help with staging a production by expanding *stage directions*, actors' *moves*, *props* lists, *lighting plots*, *effects plots* etc., not considered in a standard edition. The most famous publisher of *acting editions* is Samuel French Ltd, established 1830. Their initial editions in C19 were based on theatre *prompt copies*; one might describe itself, for example, as 'the only edition which is faithfully marked with the Stage Business and Stage directions as it is performed at the Theatre Royal'.

action¹ The physical *gestures* made by an actor or, as OED would have it, 'the oratorical management of the body and features in harmony with the subject described'! As Shakespeare has Hamlet testify: 'Suit the action to the word, the word to the action; with this special observance, that you o'erstep not the modesty of nature' (*Hamlet*, III.ii). The usage is first attested – along with several other words with 'act' as their root – in lC16: 'Players action doeth answere to their partes' (1579, OED).

In an extension of this sense, *action* is sometimes used – as in 'I enjoyed the action' – to refer to the entire physical dimension of a production, gestures, *blocking*, *choreography*, a sense of the word that incorporates its meaning of 'energetic physical movement', especially in action such as fight sequences.

action² 'The series of events represented in a play'. The term was certainly in use in this sense in eC17 – 'As thou didst live Rome's bravest actor, twas my plot that thou Shouldst die in action' (1606, Massinger, *The Roman Actor*) – but was later to acquire an even more specific sense. *Action* is one of the three *unities* outlined in Aristotle's *Poetics*, written in C4BC: 'Thus, just as in the other imitative arts each individual representation is the representation of a single object, so too the plot of a play, being the representation of an action, must present it as a unified whole.' The classical, Aristotelean idea of dramatic action as a single event or thematic concern which is embodied and worked through to its conclusion in the plot of a play, first appears in lC17-eC18: 'This Action [of an Epic] should have three Qualifications in it. First, It should be but one Action. Secondly, it should be an entire Action; and, Thirdly, it should be a great Action' (1712, Addison, *Spectator*). Whilst the simple definition at the head of this entry remains in use, early definitions such as Addison's, strict and classical, did not bed down well in English theatre and have been lost from the word's usual meaning.

activism A twentieth century artistic movement drawing on *realism* and *expressionism* which concerned itself with the social and political role of theatre. Initially a philosophical term, also used by the end of the First World War to signify 'the policy of those who, by energetic action, seek to fulfil the promises of a political programme'. See also *agitprop*, *Brechtian*, *political theatre*.

actor From L. *actor*, 'a manager, overseer, agent or factor'. It was in translation of this literal Latin sense that the word was first used in English in lC14. These senses, and that of 'a performer of general business' – 'Condemn the fault and not the actor of it' (1603, Shakespeare, *Measure for Measure* II.ii) – remain in occasional, specialist use into the present century, but were rapidly superseded by the meaning first attested in lC15: 'one who personates a character, or acts a part; a stage player or dramatic performer' (OED). For some time, however, as the following early

appearance in Sidney's *Defense of Poesie* confirms, the word was
to contend for dominance, as it does throughout Shakespeare,
with the indigenous word 'player': 'There is no Arte delivered to
mankind, that hath not the workes of Nature for his principall
object...on which they so depend, as they become Actors and
Players as it were, of what nature will have set foorth' (1581).

Since its adoption, the word has been unchanged in meaning,
only gaining increasing respectability as the successful actor's
social status has improved. Following the usual development pattern of key theatre words, *actor* was soon found in figurative contexts, not least in Shakespeare, who had a great fondness for
theatrical metaphors. The following OED attestations demonstrate
the two principal forms of this imagery: 'God sends us not into
the Theater of this World to be mute persons, but actors' (1646).
In that example, we see the common 'All the world's a stage'
metaphor in action. In the next, the equally common trend to see
human behaviour in terms of *role-playing*: 'A Person, is the same
that an Actor is, both on the stage and in common conversation'
(1651, Hobbes, *Leviathan*).

One particular form of C19 *stagese*, still encountered humorously, pronounced the word as a spondee, with an additional
stress on the second syllable. This self-conscious *theatricality* is
captured in the adjective *actorly*, 'of or pertaining to mannered
theatricality' – see also *Macready* – a term which I suspect, without
definite authority, to be lC19.

actor-manager   A self-explanatory term for an actor who is also
manager of his own theatre company. Whilst the pedigree of
actor-managers is long – Shakespeare was arguably an actor-
manager, Garrick certainly was in mC18 – the earliest OED reference to the term is surprisingly and inaccurately late, from *The
Reader* in December 1864, some fourteen years before Sir Henry
Irving acquired his first lease: 'Another mischief-working influence is that of actor-managers and manageresses.' The term was
certainly in use earlier. Thomas William Robertson, writing in
the 1850s, states: 'The actor-manager of thirty years ago was a
man of totally different type to his successor of the present day.
He was an intensely clever, bustling, wrong-headed, highly-
appreciative fellow, fond of his authors, his company, his
orchestra, his scene-shifters, his supernumeraries and all that
belonged to the little world he ruled' (quoted in Nagler, 490-1).
In addition, he was highly industrious:

> On the night of [the] production, attired in his character-dress,
> he would be here, there and everywhere – assisting the actors
> in the adjustment of their wigs, finding fault with the coiffure

of the soubrette, discharging the prompter, imprecating every portion of the anatomy of his stage-manager, helping a carpenter in the 'setting' of a rock-piece, challenging his leading tragedian to mortal combat on the morrow, making speeches to his audience to appease them between the acts... and [thanking] his generous and liberal public for once more cr-r-r-r-owning his humble efforts with their kind approval. (Ibid.)

That final sentence contains an example of a style of delivery predating the Macready, but always associated with this type. Indeed, actor-managers are traditionally renowned for having encouraged large performances: Berkoff bemoans the loss of 'the huge playing we used to have in the days of the actor-manager when the actors were the stars' (p.72).

actress 'A female stage performer', formed simply by adding the feminine ending *-ess* to *actor*. The word was originally coined as an alternative for 'actor' in its general sense of 'agent' or 'doer': 'Opportunity, the chief Actresse in all attempts, gave the Plaudite in Loue' (1589, OED). It seems to have developed independently from Fr. *actrice*, (which during the C18 was occasionally used in English as an alternative to *actress*, cf. *comédienne*.) In C16 and eC17, 'actor' was used for both sexes, there being no great need to make a distinction when no *actress* existed on the contemporary, professional stage (although there were performances by women in *masques*, and theories abound that women may have played in private showings of plays). Even after the first recorded professional performance by a woman – that of Margaret Hughes in *The Moor of Venice* in 1660, in the heady days when theatres were re-opening after a decade of closure under the Commonwealth – Pepys says in a diary entry of 1666: 'Doll Common doing Abigail most excellently, & Knipp the widow very well, and will be an excellent actor, I think.' Actress is first found in OED in a Dryden couplet dating from 1700: 'To stop the trade of love behind the scene,/Where actresses make bold with married men.' One is tempted to ask how the men got there, particularly as Charles II had attempted to forbid audiences access to the *backstage* area. However, from antiquity, actors (and actresses) have had to live with a certain reputation, one which remained in C19 – 'As long as an actress treads the boards, it is impossible to take a worthy view of the theatre' (1882, *Academy* [magazine]) – and, as tabloid headlines reassert at the time of writing – 'Minister of Fun and the Actress' (summer 1992) – one which still persists.

Interestingly, with greater awareness of the need for equal opportunities, many actresses are now choosing to revert to the 'male' title, which, given the fact that doctor, with a similar form to actor, has never spawned doctress, has a strong linguistic as well as feminist justification.

adaptation 'The large companies' biggest successes are interestingly enough the non-actors' plays – adaptations of Dickens or musicals based on T.S. Eliot's plays' (Berkoff, 70). From Fr. *adapter*, from L. *ad*, 'to' + *aptare*, 'to fit', *adaptation* is the reworking of a play from the same or another language, or the translation of an artistic work from one medium to another, an C18 development of the sense of the word. On occasions, it may be regarded as a euphemism for 'plagiarism'. It is a practice 'almost as old as the theatre itself – witness the "identical twins" plot which is found (inter alia) in Plautus, the commedia dell'arte, Goldoni, Dario Fo and Shakespeare (twice)' *(Bloomsbury Theatre Guide)*. The adaptation tends to be the enemy of the new play, particularly in difficult economic climates.

ad lib From L. *ad libitum*, 'to any extent, according to pleasure'. The Latin term is found in English from eC18, the abbreviation following at an uncertain date. *Ad lib* has come to mean 'spontaneous, improvised "scripting" by an actor'. Sometimes this is sanctioned by the author, director or deviser as, for example, in *mystery plays*, as invited in Strindberg's Preface to *Miss Julie* or in some works by modern dramatists such as Dario Fo. Sometimes the ad lib is a cover for an actor who forgets his lines or encounters some other dilemma on stage: 'I dried desperately in the middle of one show and had to walk off while Rupert saved the day with an ad lib – "I think Judd must have a headache or something"' (Branagh, 101). On other occasions, as in the famous cases of Shakespeare's clown, Will Kempe or that of the music hall comic, Max Miller broadcasting on BBC wireless, *ad libbing* is regarded by employers as a sackable offence. See also *extemporise*, *improvise*. The term is now generally used for anyone with an ability to speak effectively 'off the cuff'.

advertisement curtain From Fr. *avertissement*, 'a public announcement, esp. visual', + *curtain*. A curtain bearing the name of the theatre's sponsors, or other organisations which had paid for space, was commonly lowered in front of the safety curtain and the *tabs* in theatres from lC19 and onwards. Now largely obsolete.

affective memory A term used by the *method* school in the 1940s. A variation on *Stanislavski*'s theory of *emotion memory* (whereby actors mime their past experience in order to present 'genuine' emotion on stage). The Russian's phrase, however, is altered in a linguistically telling way. *Memory* remains unchanged, but the qualifying word, *emotion*, is replaced by *affective*, a term used by

C20 psychologists for a specific set of brain functions (in contrast to *cognitive*). Whilst the 'cognitive domain' refers to the conscious areas of the brain, the 'affective domain' relates to parts of the brain related to the autonomic nervous system which controls involuntary functions and the emotions. (The first application of affective in this context is hard to date, but it was certainly used by Bloom in *Taxonomy* in the 1940s.) In the choice of terms, therefore, this American adaptation of Stanislavski's ideas on actor training demonstrates a common mC20 tendency: to borrow scientific authority – compare *laboratory theatre* – or in this case a social scientific authority, to lend additional weight to what are essentially subjective, artistic theories.

afterpiece 'Eight and twenty nights it went without the buttress of an afterpiece' (1806, OED). A descriptive term (see *piece*) for an C18 *playlet*, usually comic or farcical, performed after a full-length tragedy, in much the same way that *satyr-plays* were offered to an audience after the tragic trilogies at the Athenian festival of Dionysus. (See also *anti-masque*.) The *afterpiece* differs in that with half-price admission fees, it satisfied the needs of the working middle-classes who could not make the six o'clock start of the main show.

agent From L. *agens, agentem*, from L. *agere*, 'to act, do etc.' Given the strained relations which sometimes exist between actors and their *agents*, many of the former might find not a little irony in the fact that the root word from which theatrical and dramatic agents receive their name is the same as for actor. Amongst other meanings of 'agent' which entered into usage in lC16 we find 'one who does the actual work of anything, as distinguished from the instigator or employer; hence, one who acts for another, a deputy, steward, factor, substitute, representative or emissary' (OED): 'Being the Agents, or base second means' (1596, Shakespeare, *I Henry IV*, I.iii).

The first professionals with theatrical concerns to assume this title were *literary agents* (or *author's* or *play agents*) in eC19, who sought publishers or *producers* for their clients. The role of actor's agent developed from the consequent involvement of some of these characters in the theatre world. Agents find parts for actors and negotiate contracts, being paid a percentage of the fee they agree, usually 10 per cent. (The old actor's definition of an agent is 'one who resents the fact that an artist takes 90 per cent of his earnings'.) Many also double as *casting agents*, working for producers and thus exerting the power of the intermediary. *Touring companies* employ *advance agents* and *booking agents* to arrange their work and most large theatres will employ a *press agent* to deal with production publicity. In a business beset by agents, even the *theatre-goer* cannot escape: they may have to face independent *ticket agents*, semi-respectable cousins of the *tout*, purchasing blocks of tickets and sometimes selling them for more than the face price.

agitprop theatre A blanket term for a variety of theatre styles all with a common aim: the use of theatre for direct political ends. The name is taken from the propaganda arm of the Russian Communist Party, an abbreviation of the Russian words for agitation and propaganda. See *activism*, *Brechtian*, *political*.

agony From Gk *agon*, 'a contest', possibly gladiatorial. In ancient Greece, *agon* was used to describe the extreme conflict at the heart of the action of any *tragedy*. See *protagonist*, *ecstasy*.

aisle The *gang-way* between seating units in a theatre which, according to the *Licensing Acts*, must be left completely clear during a performance. The number of *aisles* required in any *auditorium* is also set by an agreed formula. The term was appropriated from church architecture and is ME, from OF *ele*, from L. *ala*, 'wing'. Originally, the aisles were the wings of the nave, often divided from the main body by means of pillars. Two confusions occurred, however, in C18: one with *isle*, leading to it being used at times to mean 'a discrete area of a church', and a second with *alley* – L. *ala* being confused with Fr. *allée* – resulting in the present gang-way notion.

alarum From OF *alarme*, from It. *all' arme!*, 'to arms'. A common Elizabethan stage direction indicating a fanfare which would be performed in the musicians' gallery. Like the modern car-alarm, not always a harbinger of doom.

alienation According to Raymond Williams in *Keywords*, 'now one of the most difficult words in the language'. The fact that its most common general use is at odds with the main theatrical sense does not help matters. From OF *alienacion*, from L. *alienare*, 'to estrange or make another's', from L. *alienus*, 'of or belonging to another'. The word has been used in English since C14 to signify a sense of separation from God or society as experienced by an individual or group. It has carried other specialist legal and financial meanings but in lC19 and e-mC20, the concept of political and spiritual estrangement which *alienation* signifies became central to a variety of philosophical movements including Marxism and Existentialism, both of which have had crucial effects on the content and forms of certain genres of C20 theatre (see *absurd, theatre of*).

Alienation includes a range of negative feelings including powerlessness, meaninglessness, isolation and self-estrangement.

The word has entered into everyday speech in ways which are at times bathetic, but as Williams says, 'It is clear from the present extent and intensity of the use of alienation that there is a widespread and important experience which ... the word and its varying specific concepts offer to describe and interpret' (op. cit., 36).

The most common theatrical deployment of the word is in the phrase *alienation effect* or **Brechtian** *alienation*, (also referred to in English as the 'A-effect', the 'V-effect', 'distancing' and variations on these – some measure of the confusion which exists over the concept). Essentially, this English usage is one of the attempts to translate the German *Verfremdungseffekt*, coined in the 1930s by Bertolt Brecht, the German *dramaturge*, to describe a series of techniques employed in the writing and staging of his plays to produce an emotionally-distanced, questioning audience – rather than one which was emotionally involved in watching the performance: 'Alienation is the art of placing an action at a distance so that it can be judged objectively and so that it can be seen in relation to ... the worlds around it' (Brook, 47). Ironically, what he did not wish to produce were any of the negative symptoms of alienation outlined above, which is why this common translation must be considered unfortunate.

alternative theatre 'The alternative R.S.C. [Reduced Shakespeare Company] provided a swingeing counter to bardolatry' (*Plays and Players*, October 1990). From L. *alternare*, from *alter*, 'other', *alternative* is a term which has gained widespread currency since the 1960s in such diverse pursuits as medicine, journalism and rock music. *Plays and Players*, in the edition referred to above, also discussed 'the alternative challenge to mainstream stand-up humour.' It implies a rejection of the structure and values inherent in the traditional manifestations of an art, science or trade and also the offer of new, *avant-garde* approaches to the same concerns.

In theatre the rejection has been focused particularly on commercialism and a perceived lack of willingness in *establishment* theatres to experiment with both subject matter – particularly with regard to political and socio-sexual issues – and form. In Britain, the alternative theatre movement has grown up since the 1950s around theatre *workshops*, the Edinburgh *Fringe*, *arts labs.*, *T.I.E.* companies, Higher Education drama departments etc., and the large number of trained performers *resting*. It has led to the development of a whole host of small alternative *venues*. There is always the danger, of course, that what is alternative today becomes establishment tomorrow (see *off-Broadway*).

amateur theatre The word *amateur* is first attested in English usage in OED in 1784: 'The President will be left with his train of

feeble Amateurs.' It was probably stressed on the final syllable
as in French, from which it is derived – from *amateur*, from L.
amator, 'a lover' – a pronunciation which is still occasionally
encountered. In that first attestation it is used in its literal sense
of 'one who loves or is fond of anyone or anything'. Its first
appearance in its second, more familiar sense, also neatly defines
its main C20 usage: 'Amateur, in the Arts, is a foreign term introduced and now passing current amongst us, to denote a person
understanding, and loving or practising the polite arts of painting,
sculpture, or architecture, without any regard to pecuniary advantage' (*c*.1803, OED).

Amateur can be used disparagingly, especially if directed by
one *pro* at another: 'I used to shuffle backstage, head down, aware
that the word "amateur" was written in neon lights across my
forehead' (Branagh, 61). This pejorative use of the term is by no
means restricted to theatre, and there is probably a combination
of accuracy, inaccuracy and protectionism inherent in all professionals's attitudes towards amateurs. Since the nineteenth century, Britain has been fortunate in having thriving amateur and
educational theatres which have been breeding-grounds for many
professional actors and technicians. Although there are some
amateur groups which indulge in self-congratulation and endlessly offer a menu of *Charley's Aunt*, *The Boyfriend* and assorted
sub-Agatha Christie *whodunnits*, producing disasters memorably
caught in *The Art of Coarse Acting* (1964) by Michael Green, there
are also some extremely 'professional' amateur companies responsible for keeping live, affordable theatre within the local community.

amphitheatre   From Gk *amphi*, 'on both sides' + *theatron*,
'theatre'. Despite the Greek name, the first *amphitheatre* in the
modern sense of the word was built in Rome, primarily as a
popular, human blood sport *arena*. The Colosseum could seat
87,000! These early amphitheatres can be seen, with a little
geometrical licence – they were usually elliptical – as forerunners
of the circus arena and the sports stadium and, with even greater
licence, due to the audience-performer relationship, of *theatres-in-
the-round*. The word has been used theatrically in English since
the seventeenth century, with a sense perhaps based on a misin-
terpretation by Palladio in his design of the Teatro Olympico in
Vicenza which he described, inaccurately, as an amphitheatre. It
is suggested that this 'error' may have been imported by his
admirer, Inigo Jones: certainly, the term was later used to describe
fan-shaped *auditoria* such as that of the Theatre Royal, Drury Lane,
built in 1674. 'The pit, arranged in the form of amphitheatre,

has seats' says Brunet (1676), albeit in translation, in *Voyage d'Angleterre*. Later, the first row of seats in the *gallery* of some theatres came to be known as the amphitheatre. The first English example of a true, purpose-built, though covered-in amphitheatre was the Connaught Theatre in London, constructed in 1867 under its original name of the Royal Amphitheatre, Holborn. (See also *ring*.)

angel The financial *backers* of shows, those who invest money in prospective productions, are sometimes known as *angels*, possibly because, as far as most of those involved in a production are concerned, they are unseen guardian spirits looking after their interests. The term is originally Greek, from *angelos*, 'a messenger'. Later, it was used to refer to Hermes, the messenger of the gods. Subsequently, as the Christian gospel spread in Greek, it was applied to Judaeo-Christian angels. I have been unable to date the first theatrical use of the term, but, were it early, there is a slight possibility that it might also carry a pun on the coin, the 'angel', first minted in 1465, and originally worth 6s 8d (33⅓p), so-called because it bore the image of the archangel, Michael, slaying a dragon.

anger/angry young man 'Suddenly the first "angry young man", Jimmy Porter, was there – we can't throw him off' (Brook, 31). Anger – social and political indignation directed at the Britain of the mid-1950s – was considered to be the driving force behind an ephemeral literary movement taking its name from the title of John Osborne's play, *Look Back in Anger*, (1956), whose hero was the partially-autobiographical Jimmy Porter, recreated by Osborne as a middle-aged reactionary in his 1992 play, *Déjà Vu*. With hindsight, the grouping together of the truculent Osborne, the now-reactionary novelist Kingsley Amis and the still-unrepentant John Arden as *angry young men*, the tag contemporary journalists gave them, seems highly improbable. However, considering the state of the British theatre at the time of Suez, which Arthur Miller described as 'hermetically sealed from reality', their injection of a new realism did make them worthy of some distinguishing label. They ushered in the *kitchen-sink* drama of the late 1950s and early 1960s. The phrase 'angry young man' has stuck in the popular imagination, expressing neatly a sense of the perennial rebellion of youth.

animal impersonator An actor or *variety* performer who dresses as an animal, or, as in the case of the celebrated *speciality artist*, Percy Edwards, makes bird noises etc. (See *impersonator*.) Such performers, who generally wear animal costumes, are consequently also known as *skin acts*. They are now almost solely

used in *pantomime* and *circus*. The man unfortunate enough to
play the back end of a donkey is frequently the butt of jokes. It
has been argued, however, that such performers form an unbroken link with key participants in early fertility *rituals* etc. See
hobby-horse.

anti-masque   Found with a number of variant spellings, the *anti-
masque* is an innovation of Ben Jonson's, which either preceded
the performance of an eC17 *masque* or was performed between
its *acts*. The subject matter of the anti-masque, often a dance by
professional performers, contrasted with the masque proper,
which was often pastoral, (a contrast echoing the function of the
satyr-play attached to Greek tragic trilogies and prefiguring the
afterpiece of the 18th century). The first half of the compound is
punningly ambiguous and probably intentionally so: Gk *anti-*,
'against', suggests opposition to the main theme; L. *ante*, 'before'
(an alternative spelling which is sometimes found), suggests its
occasional position as prologue. It has also been suggested that
because anti-masques contained elements of the grotesque, the
term also conveyed the idea of *antic masque*, from L. *antiquus*,
'old', and this is a spelling used by Jonson himself: 'We may be
admitted, if not for a masque, for an antic-masque (1622, *Masque
of the Augurs*). Antic had come to mean (as in Hamlet's 'antic
disposition') 'grossly comic'.

applaud/applause   It was common at the end of the earliest
Elizabethan *performances* for a member of the cast to request the
audience's approval: 'For Gammer Gurtons nedle sake, let us
have a plaudytie' (1575, *Gammer Gurton's Needle*). *Applaud* and
applause are from L. *applaudere*: *plaudere* meant 'to clap the hands'
(hence *plaudit*), the prefix *ad-*, 'to, towards', having been added
to create the sense 'clap in response to something'. Both words
appear in lC16, probably directly from Latin: however, as Shakespeare makes clear in *Hamlet* (IV.v), the word had already been
extended to incorporate other expressions of public approval:
'Caps, hands, and tongues, applaud it to the clouds.'

apron stage   In a *proscenium arch* theatre, the *apron* is an optional
extension of the stage out beyond the 'picture-frame' of the arch-
way and into the audience; the *forestage*. Clearly, its use enables
more intimate contact between actor and audience: 'It must be
observ'd then, that the Area, or Platform of the old Stage projected
about four Foot forwarder, in a Semi-oval Figure, parallel to the
Benches of the Pit' (1740, Cibber, *Apology*). 'Apron' is from OF
naperon, originally 'table-cloth'; however, by eC14 it had acquired
its most common meaning, 'a garment worn over the front of the
body to protect the clothes whilst working'. From this, the

extended sense of 'a covering' developed. OED clearly demonstrates how it developed a number of specialist technical applications in gunnery, plumbing, engineering, docking, ship-building.
It seems likely that this *nautical* connection explains its theatrical
usage. Smyth's *Sailor's Word-book* (1867) defines 'Apron of a
dock, the platform rising where the gates are closed, and on which
the sill is fastened down.' Interestingly, an additional theatrical
sense is 'a trim under the sill of a flat'.

The structure of apron is interesting in that it was originally a
napron but lost the initial *n* through 'wrong' division. Similar
misfortunes occurred to 'adder' ('a naddre'), and 'umpire' ('a
nonper' = 'non-pareil' = 'unequal').

aquatic drama   A form of *spectacular*, popularised in eC19 Paris,
which involved flooding the arenas of circuses for re-enactments
of great naval battles etc. In the 1830s, no less an establishment
than Sadler's Wells was known for a decade or so as the Aquatic
Theatre when a large water-tank was permanently installed on
stage. Compare and contrast *nautical drama*.

arc   The common abbreviation of *carbon arc spotlight*, (widely used
as *flood*-lighting before the discovery of the electric incandescent
bulb), giving rise to terms such as *arc-lighting*, arc-*lantern* etc.

arena   An interesting example of compounding metonymy. The
basic floor-covering, *[h]arena*, L. 'sand', lent its name to the
central *performance area* of the Roman *amphitheatre*. In turn,
'arena' became the commonly used term for the whole stadium.
In recent times it has partially regained its earlier precision, being
used for the open *acting area* in *theatres-in-the-round*. By eC19, it
had also developed, from its connotation as an area of conflict, a
more abstract sense: 'But dragged again upon the arena stood/A
leader not unequal to the feud' (1814, Byron, *Lara*). In C20, this
sense, too, has broadened out: *arena for debate* refers not so much to
place as to opportunity. Not a bad elevation for a handful of sand.

are you decent?   Once a common phrase spoken at the *dressing-
room* door, the equivalent of 'May I come in?' In days of increasing
openness about matters such as nudity, it is obsolescent.

argument of a play   Often stated in the *prologue* of a play, the
argument is a summary of its subject matter:

> 'And hither am I come,
> A prologue armed, but not in confidence
> Of author's pen or actor's voice, but suited
> In like conditions as our argument...'

(*c*.1601, Shakespeare, *Troilus and Cressida*, Prologue)
'Quarrel' is also used in this Prologue, which leads to the main
etymological interest. The French verb *arguer*, from which the

English verb *argue* (first used in lC14-eC15) derives, appears to have been influenced in its development by two related Latin words, *argutari*, 'to prattle, chide', and *arguere*, 'to prove by reason'. The coexistence of these two meanings in the same word, transferred into English, has itself started many arguments through misunderstanding. The *argument of a play* derives from the second of these meanings.

arras   Arras is a town in Northern France which was renowned for its fabrics. It gave its name to a rich tapestry, often used as a hanging around the walls of great houses, sometimes creating a false corridor round the walls. (Compare another material, *denim*, named after a place: 'de Nimes'. See also *gauze*.) Such hangings may also have been used to divide the *inner stage* from the *forestage* in Elizabethan theatres. Any drape curtain loosely hung across the stage can still be referred to as an *arras*. In *Hamlet*, III.iv, the unfortunate Polonius is stabbed, according to the stage direction, 'behind the arras', possibly giving rise to that phrase's common usage to denote intrigue and secrecy, although the same phrase is used elsewhere in *revenge* drama: 'Why, I would desire but this, my lord: to have all the fees behind the arras...' (1607, Tourneur, *Revenger's Tragedy*, II.ii).

Aristotelian theatre   Any theatre which conforms to the guidelines laid down in Aristotle's *Poetics* (*c*.330 BC), can be referred to as Aristotelian, though the term is also sometimes used to refer to all *naturalistic* drama. Aristotle (384BC-322BC) was a Greek philosopher, scientist and critic. In the *Poetics* he sought to define the mechanics of *tragedy*. During and after the Renaissance his ideas were examined and developed by dramatists seeking a classical model (see *neoclassical*) and adhered to most closely on the continent, where the concept of the three *unities*, held great sway. See also *action, catharsis, hamartia, hubris*.

artist/artiste   Used in English from C16, firstly for a practitioner of any of the liberal arts but almost immediately afterwards for a skilled person in any field of endeavour. *Artist* derives from OF *artiste*, but takes its meaning from the development of English *art*. From C13 to C17, 'art', (from OF *art*, from L. *ars, artis*, 'a skill'), was used to apply to all skills, with no specialist distinctions. In the 18th century a schism occurred, perhaps reflecting the origins of the great divide between arts and sciences discussed by C.P. Snow in *Two Cultures*. It narrowed first to mean 'creative art', and later narrowed even further to 'visual art'; at the same time, the word *artisan* was teased out to be applied to those whose skills were manual rather than intellectual or imaginative. (Compare the development of *technical, technician*.)

Artist as a synonym for dramatic performer is an early C18 development: 'You may often see an Artist in the Streets gain a Circle of Admirers by carrying a long Pole on his chin' (1714, *The Spectator*). It is still used in this sense, particularly for a *variety* performer. However, in eC19, *artiste* was reintroduced, presumably to create a distinction between dramatic and fine artists: 'The German *artistes* who did such ample justice to the choruses of the Freischütz' (1832, *Athenaeum*). Outside of variety circles, this latter term is often used with a degree of irony.

artistic Developing from the C18 shift in the sense of *artist* outlined above, this adjective now has two distinct theatrical senses: i) of or pertaining to critical interpretation and aesthetic judgement: 'artistic questions of promoting another novel adaptation paled into insignificance alongside the pure awfulness of the production' (*Plays and Players'* review of *Treasure Island*, October 1990); ii) as a euphemism for something performed in the nude or with very few clothes on.

artistic director 'God knows what we expected of an artistic director: a nanny/psychiatric nurse/estate agent/mega-talent, that was all' (Branagh, 160). Generally, the *artistic director* is the person with overall charge of the *artistic* policy of a theatre or company. Some companies such as the *RSC* (referred to in the quotation above) use the term for any director of a production. A post-war refinement, following on the English redefinition of *director*. See also *stage director*, *producer*.

ASM The common abbreviation of *Assistant Stage Manager*, which is rarely used in its full form. A verb, *to ASM* is in common theatrical usage: 'I was A.S. Emming on that show.' On a *backstage* flow chart, ASMs should come below the *SM* and *DSM* but above ordinary *stagehands*, in that they constitute an official part of the stage management team. In practice, this is not necessarily the case. Though good ASMs are highly valued, the job is frequently a first rung on the ladder for aspiring actors and directors, those with technical and stage management aspirations, and people who are generally *stage-struck*. Its importance and the precise tasks involved vary depending on the theatre and company: the ASM can be anything from dogsbody to vital member of the production team (see *on the book*).

aside 'An Aside, *scorsim*, is something that an actor speaks apart, or, as it were, to himself' (1727-51, Chambers, *Cyclopaedia*). An *aside* is a line or speech, generally found only in stylised genres such as *Restoration comedy*, *melodrama* and *farce*, delivered directly to an audience or in their hearing, using the convention that the speaker cannot be heard by others on stage. Traditionally,

the aside was *pointed* by the actor using the palm of his upstage
hand or the back of his downstage hand to *mask* his mouth from
them. The aside has been common from the *Elizabethan* theatre
onwards, often being printed in texts as a stage direction. The
aside was particularly favoured in melodrama and the phrase 'little
do they know but . . .', after which the villain reveals his intentions
to the audience was picked up as a C19 *catchphrase*. Asides are
used in everyday humour and phrases such as 'This was delivered
in a cryptic aside' are commonly found.

audience   'The spectators at a performance'. *Audience* has been
in use in English in the sense of 'an assembly of listeners' since
at least eC15, a direct borrowing of F. *audience*, ultimately from
L. *audire*, 'to hear'. Theatrically, it has been used to mean 'the
paying public' since the early days of organised London theatre:
'for by talking and laughing (like a plough-man in a Morris)
. . . you mightily disrelish the Audience, and disgrace the Author'
(1607, Dekker, *The Gull's Hornbook*). Today, it is by far the
commonest way to describe those assembled to 'see a play', which
is odd given that we rarely talk about 'hearing a play'. Its increasing usage over 'spectators' from the C19 onwards must give rise
to speculation. Firstly, it is a collective noun: unlike 'spectators',
it suggests a united body of people rather than a collection of
individuals. However, *auditorium* has also increasingly been preferred to *spectatory*. Could it be that with improved stage-lighting
and more efficient blackout, the tendency of members of the audience to go to the theatre to be seen themselves has diminished?
And could the added darkness provided since mC19 also have
led to increased silence and concentration on the word, and thus
to greater emphasis on the auditory rather than the visual sense?

audition   Only in the eC20 did *audition* acquire its current theatrical sense of 'the trial hearing (and seeing) of an applicant wishing
to perform in a given production, company etc.'. It was a term
borrowed from the world of music – 'When she was nineteen she
was given an "audition" at the Santa Cecilia Conservatoire' (1908,
Evening News) – ultimately from the L. *audire*, 'to hear'. The
first English sense of the word in the C16 was medical, simply
meaning 'the faculty of hearing': 'It draweth all out which is in
the ears, and administreth good auditione' (1599, A.M. Gabel-
houer's *Book of Physic*). In C17, it also came to signify the act of
hearing something and later, in C18, it extended to mean an
auditory hallucination – a vision, as it were, in the ears: 'I went
to hear it for it is not an apparition but an audition' (1762, Walpole).

Auditions remain necessary if not popular; they are employed to help decide on admission to *drama schools*, colleges etc. as well as being part of the vital amateur and professional activity of *casting*. '[Gary Whelan and I] never knew each other until he auditioned to understudy in my play *East*' (Berkoff, 118). In a star-struck, recession-hit world, I am aware of more than one college which, by charging hopeless candidates large sums for a ten-minute audition, furnishes itself with a fairly steady income. At audition, it is normal for an actor to *read* for a part. More unusual forms of selection include the *casting-couch*.

auditorium   The part of the theatre in which the audience is housed. From L.. *auditorium*, neuter form of the adjective *auditorius*, 'of or pertaining to listening and listeners'. Originally an ecclesiastical term – compare *aisle* – as this attestation affirms: '*Auditory, auditorium*...was that part of the church where the *audientes* stood to hear, and be instructed' (1727-51, Chambers, *Cyclopaedia*). It was first used theatrically in the eC18 but until the C19 was still vying in popularity of usage with its anglicised form, *auditory*, and with *spectatory*. See *audience* for further speculation on this point.

author   From AF *autour*, ultimately from L. *auctor* (from *augere*, *auct-*, 'increase, originate, promote'). The word is first attested in English in lC14 with two senses: those of 'writer' and 'agent', occasionally in C15-C16 being found as *actor*, a confusion which, thankfully, was clarified by lC16. *Playwright* and *dramatist* enjoy much greater theatrical usage, but echoes of the cry 'Author! Author!' still ring in the ears, largely, one suspects, fuelled by Hollywood biopics. It is interesting to note that since the 1960s, due to an understandable desire for artistic and critical recognition, film directors have increasingly borrowed for themselves the French designation *auteur* – possibly due to the encouragement of new academic disciplines such as Film Studies. Is this a trend which will extend into theatre?

avant-garde   Also found in the form *avant garde*. From F. 'vanguard, advanced guard': those who dare to lead the rest into battle. In this sense it was appropriated into English in C15 and anglicised, first to *avaunt-guard* and later to *vanguard*. Clearly, the term implies *risk-taking*; in theatrical terms, innovation and experiment. The French form has been reappropriated with this sense in C20. The term can be used approvingly but is just as frequently employed in a dismissive fashion: 'such antagonism in Britain may be rooted in our immunity to an *avant-garde* tradition in European and American theatre' (*Plays and Players*, October 1990). Of course, the ultimate test of all avant-gardes is whether anyone chooses to follow. See also *alternative, experimental, fringe*.

B**aby spot**   A small *spotlight*, usually of less than 500 watts, generally used to light limited areas of the stage sharply. The use of *baby* as an adjective meaning 'small of its kind' is a m-lC19 development. Compare *baby grand* in music.

backcloth/backdrop   'In the trial scene he had a backcloth, like a Longhi picture, with wigged judges, depicted as sheep, painted on it' (Geilgud, 80). These two terms can describe the same stage feature: a large curtain or canvas painted to represent a desired scene, suspended from the *grid* at the rear of the traditional *proscenium stage*. The former term is favoured in Britain but rarely heard in America; both are commonly heard in Britain. Though the two are in practice interchangeable, *cloth* is more frequently applied to *canvas*, *drop* to a *curtain*, (rarely painted): 'Pinned to the black velvet backdrop were two or three dismally dreary-looking wreaths' (Olivier, 54). Since the introduction of the *box set*, the development of the lit *cyclorama* and more. open staging techniques, both features are obsolescent other than in *pantomime* (when often used in conjunction with *gauzes*) or other productions which exploit traditional staging devices for effect, although the terms remain in use: in practice, a *cyc.* might be referred to by either of the terms. They both have long theatrical pedigrees: see *cloth* and *drop*. It is also interesting to note a *nautical* connection: the *back-cloth* is the name given to a piece of triangular material fastened in the middle of the topsail-yard: whether this affected the term's theatrical development is dubious, however. Both have been used metaphorically, certainly in the present century, to describe the physical background to real life events: 'a fitting backdrop for such an historical event' is a common media cliché.

backer   'The curtain fell on the spectacular project...when the backers pulled out last week' (19 July 1991, *Manchester Metro News*). A *backer* is 'one who stands at the back of, supports; financially, one who countersigns, endorses' – a person who puts up the money to finance a production, usually in expectation of a return on their investment: an *angel*. Its sense of 'supporter' has been used since C16; the financial sense seems to be a C19 development: 'When fortune is low and backers scarce' (1838, Dickens, *Nicholas Nickleby*).

backing flat   A *flat* positioned outside a stage opening such as a door or window, usually on a *box set*, to prevent the audience from seeing *backstage*. Since lC18, the verbal noun *backing* has been used for 'material which forms a back or lines the back of something'; in nautical terms it is 'the timber behind the armour plate of a ship' (1867, Smyth, *Sailors Word-book*), a possible source for the theatrical usage.

back projection   See *projection*.

backstage   'Behind the scenes' – once, that part of the theatre which lay literally at the back and sides of the stage, extending from the *wings* to the *dressing-rooms*, *workshops* etc., and finally out to the *stage door*. The opposite of *front-of-house*. The term is probably lC18-eC19. *Backstage* is no longer necessarily a structurally exact term, but refers to all areas which are the province of *theatre-workers* only. For members of the audience *to go (or come) backstage* – unless they are members of the *profession* or close friends of members of the cast etc. – is a privilege, since the separation of backstage and front-of-house areas is usually strictly observed, partly for reasons of security and efficiency, but also to preserve the *illusion* necessary for an audience to believe in what they see on stage: '[Dustin Hoffman] came backstage full of the kind of real enthusiasm that he had not been able to display at any of the other productions he had seen in London' (Berkoff, 30). In the C17, it was necessary for a royal decree to be issued to the effect that 'no person of what quality soever presume to go behind the scenes, or come upon the stage, either before or during the acting of a play'. The common phrases, 'to take a look backstage' or '. . . behind the scenes', imply a privileged glimpse at the way the practitioners of any mystery perform their work. *Backstage drama/comedy/musical* are terms for shows in which the performers play performers, a device which facilitates the introduction of *showcase* devices such as the *play-within-a-play* and the *show-within-a-show*.

balance   Physical *balance*, in the everyday sense, is, obviously, the ability to maintain the body in an erect position and hence to walk and move. Many stylised forms of theatrical performance, not only in *dance* but in other genres of physical theatre require precarious or abnormal feats of balance which make additional demands on the performer's body in terms of the muscles that are required for centring, or holding the centre of gravity. 'It is this extra effort which dilates the body's tensions in such a way that the performer seems to be alive even before he begins to express' (Barba & Savarese, 34).

balcony   The first theatrical usage of *balcony* would appear to be in the term *proscenium balcony*, used after the Restoration for a raised platform with a railing erected over the *forestage*, firstly used as part of the set and secondly as a stage box. It is, however, possible that it was also used for the upper stage of the *Elizabethan* playhouse, though I can find no support for this idea. The usage is probably taken from its first English sense of 'a kind of platform projecting from the walls of a house or room, supported by pillars, brackets or consoles, and enclosed by a balustrade' (OED): 'It was properly a balcone, and so the building it self did jetty out' (1618, Holyday, *Juvenal*). There may, however, also be a nautical influence on the adoption of this term: Pepys, in a diary entry from 1666, under an entry headed 'nautical', talks of 'a very good ship, but with galleries quite round the sterne like a balcone.' Such a 'balcone' was the jutting structure, similar in appearance to an architectural balcony, found on ships of the period. The present meaning always designates an area of seating, today, most commonly some section of the raised area over the rear of the stalls, comprised of the circles and *gallery*.

'Balcony' comes from It. *balcone*, from *balco*, *palco*, 'a scaffold', (see *scaffolding*), itself from Old High German *balcho*, 'a beam', (from which we derive the English 'balk'). Until the early C19, the word was stressed on its second syllable as in Italian, often keeping the final 'e' in the spelling. (To underline the passions that words can arouse, it is worth noting that a spelling in Swift – *balkoni* – induced from Samuel Rogers the comment, '[it] makes me sick.')

ballad/ballad opera   From *ballade* (the same root word as for *ballet*, the ending *-ad(e)* often exchanged for *-et* in C16-C17 France [compare *salad* and *sallet*]), from L. *ballare*, 'to dance', from Gk *ballō*. The *ballad* was introduced to England by the Anglo-Normans, 'and meant a song to which people danced' (1957, Robert Graves, Introduction to *English and Scottish Ballads*). From medieval times onwards, two ballad traditions developed. One was a purely literary form which flourished in England from eC14 to mC17, though often retaining its musical roots with a repeated refrain and envoy. That in this strand of its development it became synonymous with poem and divorced from dance is clear from the occasional translation of the biblical *Song of Songs* as the *Ballad of Ballads*. The second development was through the oral traditions of *minstrelsy* – often with some topical, satirical content – and so-called folk songs which were collected by compilers and scholars from the C18 onwards.

Ballad operas flourished as popular musical drama in the C18, satirising both Italian *opera* and contemporary social and political targets. (See *The Beggar's Opera* and works by Garrick, Fielding and Cibber, amongst others.) Drawing on popular tunes and romantic plots, and combining spoken dialogue and songs, they could also be seen as direct forerunners of the modern *musical*.

ballet Like *opera*, a term which requires its own Book of Words and which, consequently, will be dealt with cursorily here. Like *ballad*, it derives from LL. *ballare*, 'to dance', but this time via It. *balletto*, a diminutive of *ballo*, 'a social ball'. It is an interesting noun in that it can be applied to a highly *choreographed* dance performance and the company which performs it. More significantly, one sees the word for an everyday social activity being narrowed into a term for an art form which then creates a very specialised language of its own. Its common derivatives include the descriptive adjective *balletic* and the noun *ballerina*. A curious theatrical cul-de-sac for the term is found in Strindberg's *Miss Julie*, where it is used, in 1888, as a synonym for *mime* or *dumbshow*.

bally-hoo *To bally-hoo* is to create a spectacular effect, like a night sky during the Blitz, by the random swirling of *follow-spots*. 'Bally-hoo' is an eC20 American *barkers*' term of unknown origin – (ballet, ho![?]) – which OED Supp. glosses as 'eyewash' and which today might be termed 'hype'. However, by extension, as 'barkers' patter' the term has also come to suggest a noisy commotion. The theatrical sense may come from a type of hyping lighting *effect* which often preceded the entry of a *star*.

band From OF *bande*, from medieval L. *banda*, probably from the same Germanic root as *band* meaning a 'strip, strap etc.'. When first used in English in lC15, the word indicated any organised group of people with a common objective, often military or criminal; it has been suggested that this is due to a sash or other piece of distinguishing material such groups would have worn to show their allegiance. The first OED attestation of the term for 'a group of musicians' is also military: 'George Hudson and Davies Mell to give orders for the band of Music' (1660-3, *Warrant Book*). This association is still found in the uniforms worn by many forms of band and, possibly, in the association of many bands with originally martial instruments. The distinct separation of usage between *band* and *orchestra* is intriguing in so far as it exists far more in the language of the audience and critic than in the language of the musician: even 'classical' orchestras refer to themselves as *bands*, and it is certainly by far the common term for a theatre orchestra, giving rise to well-known terms such as *the boys in the band*: 'The big excitement was the arrival of the band. We rehearsed the musical cues out of sequence...' (Branagh, 145). In C20, the term has spread in usage through its adoption by groups of jazz and, later, rock musicians.

banquette   A term sometimes used for a row of seats in a theatre. At Manchester's Royal Exchange Theatre, they are cheap seats on the front row held in reserve for purchase on the day of performance. A French term from It. *banchetta*, a diminutive of *banca*, 'a bench'.

bard   From Old Celtic *bardo-s*, 'poet, singer, minstrel' (now *baird* in Gaelic, *bardd* in Welsh, and *bard* in Irish), or L. *bardus* (derived from the Celtic). Other than with reference to Shakespeare – *The Bard of Avon* (a term which smacks of *stagese*) – *bard* is rarely used for native English writers other than ironically. In fact, it appears to have first been used about Shakespeare by Garrick (in *Works*, 1769): 'For the bard of all bards was a Warwickshire Bard,' with a possible reference to Stratford's closeness to the Welsh borders and the dramatist's Welsh blood. The word was incorporated into Greek and Latin after the Roman conquest of Britain: 'bardus Gallice cantor appelatur, qui virorum fortium laudes canit' ('In Wales, the singer, who extols the lives of great men, is called the bard'). It was first naturalised into Lallans but only used to apply to poets emanating from history, myth or Ireland – 'Sa come the Ruke with a rerd, and a rane roch, A bard out of Irland, with Banachadee!' (*c*.1450, Holland, *The buke of Howlat*) – or to travelling minstrels. The English usage, first attested over a century later, is similar: 'A bard of Ireland told me once, I should not live long after I saw Richmond' (1594, Shakespeare, *Richard III*, IV.ii). The term *bardolatry* – a conflation of *bard* and *idolatry* – is a lC19 or eC20 term for a worshipper of Shakespeare: 'a Shakesperolator' (OED) – 'So much for Bardolatry' (1901, G.B. Shaw, Preface to *Plays for Puritans*).

baritone   A register of tone and musical scale, most frequently used of singers but also used for instruments and the voices of actors. *Baritone* is the range below *tenor* but above bass, usually but not exclusively a male range. From It. *baritono*, from Gk *barutonos* (from *baros*, 'heavy', + *tonos*, 'tone'.

barker   'A *tout* employed by circuses, side-shows and other popular entertainments to attract an audience through oral advertisements.' A term descriptive of style of delivery of the *barker*, (from OE *beorcan*, 'to bark', possibly from *berkan*, a variation of 'to break'). The first attestation with this sense is from lC15.

barn doors   An abbreviation of the lighting term, *barn door shutters*, descriptive of paired *shutters*; often, *lanterns* have two pairs of *barn doors*, one closing in the vertical plane and the other in the horizontal. Adjusting barn doors by opening and closing allows lighting operators to trim the shape and size of the beam of light cast onto the stage.

to barnstorm   'Albert Finney is in superb barnstorming form as Albert [in Ronald Harwood's *Reflected Glory*]' (*The Stage*, 24 March 1992). In the lC19, it was common for travelling companies of actors and, by imitation, local amateurs, to perform in barns and other ad hoc theatres. The type of show they specialised in was characterised by its *melodramatic* content and ranting delivery: as in a military operation, they stormed their venues, plundered and left. *Barnstorming* has come to mean any kind of public performance with more *bravura* than subtlety, hence its frequent application to the performance of politicians on the hustings and in that other, large, undecorous barn, the House of Commons. See *gaff*.

barrack   A term which gained extended usage in Australia meaning 'to heckle loudly, to verbally intimidate', generally referring to the criticism of a group of *hecklers*: 'Those distrusting, suspecting, scathing barrackers' (Olivier, 259). OED Supp. argues that it is a borrowing of New South Wales Aboriginal *borak*: 'barrack – gammon, chaff, banter...*to poke borak*, to make fun of'. An alternative etymology, only found in *Brewer's Dictionary of Phrase and Fable*, argues that in Australia the term is generally used positively and 'stems from the days when army supporters at the Victoria barracks entered the S. Melbourne cricket ground and were greeted with shouts of "Here come the barrackers"' (John Silverlight, *The Observer*, 14 February, 1993). A more plausible etymology, again with a positive sense of the word, is that it derives from Northern Irish *barrack*, 'to boast', introduced to Australia by transported convicts. Certainly, it appears to have first been used in its present sense in Australia in C19 in sporting contexts which, if the Irish origin is accepted, would involve an understandable shift of sense: 'to use a football term, they all to a man "barrack" the British Lion' (1890, *Melbourne Punch*). From there it was transferred to British theatre and other contexts, possibly via the medium of cricket.

barrel   A bar on which *lanterns* or *scenery* can by hung, (*bar* on occasions being an abbreviation of *barrel*). A *lighting barrel* is also known as a *spot bar* in Britain and a *lighting batten* in America. The British and American usages of 'barrel' and 'batten' sometimes overlap, but as their roots suggest, barrels tend to be hollow, for instance internally-wired barrels, which contain a concealed mains electricity supply to lights that can be plugged into them – see also *rain barrel* – whereas battens can be hollow or solid. Most probably a nautical term: the earliest figurative use in OED – for an object which is barrel-shaped – is from *c*.1500 – 'Some pulde at the beryll...Some howysed the mayne sayle' (*Cocke*

Lorelles bote) – where it is 'a revolving cylinder or drum round which a chain or rope is wound ... e.g. ... a capstan, jack, wheel, windlass' (OED).

batten Occasionally abbreviated to *bat*. A word with a long theatrical pedigree and at least three senses: 1) long, narrow piece of squared timber – usually 3″ x 1″ – used in *building* and as a support; 2) a strip of timber attached to the top and/or bottom of a *cloth* to ensure support and a 'good hang'; 3) in *compartment* or *magazine battens* – in the United States, 'strip lights' or 'border lights' – a row of lanterns which, placed as *footlights* or suspended immediately behind the upper *proscenium arch*, are today primarily used for *colour mixing*. (In America, also an alternative for *barrel*).

One might have expected the word to come from F. *baton*, 'a stick', but in fact most sources agree that the active sense implied in the verb (see below) suggests that it comes instead from OF *batant*, 'beating', from the verb *battre*. It appears to be a *nautical* term. Most English-speakers are familiar with the phrase 'to batten down the hatches', meaning to prepare a ship to withstand a storm. Nautical battens were strips of wood, and later metal: 'The battens serve to confine the edges of the tarpaulings down to the sides of the hatches' (1769, Falconer, *An universal dictionary of the marine*). *Battening* is a woodworking principle still familiar to DIY enthusiasts. See also barrel, *boom*.

bay As in *scene bay*: another nautical alternative for *dock*.

beat As a noun, the earliest English theatrical deployments of the noun are musical: either as a drum-beat (1672, OED), the movement of a conductor's baton or, more temporally, the interval between such gestures. It is in this sense of interval that some C20 dramatists, and subsequently actors, have used the term *a beat* as a stage direction denoting a *pause*: '[the sign]/between sentences and words means "pause" or "a beat"' (Barkworth, 11). In extension, *method* acting refined this temporal function in a way succinctly summarised by Barkworth on the same page: 'A Beat is the distance from the beginning of an intention to its end: it is the acting equivalent of a paragraph.'

Beckettian 'Of or pertaining to the works, subject matter and style of Samuel Beckett (1906-1989), Irish playwright, novelist and poet'. Becoming far more frequent with the growth of the Eng. Lit. *critical* industry from lC19 has been the tendency to concoct adjectives from the names of famous *authors* – usually by appending *-ian* (**Chekhovian**) or *-esque* – (**Pinteresque**) to denote peculiarities of their style, content or treatment of content or, secondly, situations in life which seem to echo characteristic incidents or common stylistic occurrences in their work. *Beckettian* traits include a spare but poetic style (often produced by writing in French and retranslating into English), a stoical, Existentialist obsession with the subject of death and a grim, gallows humour. See *absurd, theatre of the.*

bedroom farce   A *genre* of *farce* replete with sexual innuendo rather than explicit sex, found in the works of Feydeau (see *Feydeauesque*), in Whitehall farces, plays such as *No Sex Please, We're British*, and, to a degree, in Alan Ayckbourn's self-consciously titled *Bedroom Farce* (1975).

beginners   The *cue-call* 'Beginners!', the imperative abbreviation of 'Act One beginners, please!' or variations on that, is guaranteed to get the adrenalin pumping through an actor's system: beginners are the actors who appear at the beginning of a show or act of a show.

below   A *stage direction* with two senses, both, not surprisingly, the opposites of *above.*

benefit   Occasionally abbreviated to *ben.* 'The season being ended, his benefit over . . . he made his exit in the Tragedy of "Death," on 17th March, 1798 . . .' (1824, Ryan, *Dramatic Table Talk*). *Benefit performances* were common from lC17 as a means of income supplement for many actors and their dependants and, occasionally, for writers: 'Acted for the Benefit of Mr. Betterton' (1709, Steele, *Tatler*). Ultimately from L. *benefactum*, 'a good deed, a kind action', *benefit* is first recorded as a financial gift in C14. The first theatrical benefit on record was granted to Mrs Barry in 1687, but the system was degrading, financially unreliable, and open to abuse: '[The Commercial Manager] was the original inventor of that wonderful piece of economic meanness, a Complimentary Benefit, which means a benefit for the manager, on which occasion the actors, actresses, scene-shifters, supernumeraries and all give their services gratuitously' (c.1850, Robertson, quoted in Nagler, 492). C20 events staged by the entertainment *establishment* (e.g. the Water Rats) or by *alternative* performers (e.g. The Secret Policeman's Ball) or by both as in the case of Comic Relief have tended to be genuinely charitable successors of the benefit.

bespeak or **bespoke performances**   Meaning 'spoken for beforehand' or 'expressly ordered'; *bespoke*, still common until mC20 in tailoring as 'made-to-measure', refers to a custom similar to the *benefit*, whereby a *patron* or patrons would buy up all the seats for a *command performance*, the proceeds being shared out amongst the company.

between engagements   An actors' euphemism, probably eC20, for being unemployed. Compare the better-known *resting.*

big time, the   An American *vaudeville* term for the larger entertainment *circuits*, possibly so-called because they were successful
enough to *run* two shows daily. Hence, if one *hit the big-time* and
became *a big-timer*, one had achieved success. The term is in
general usage with that sense.

bill/billing   *Bill* is used in a variety of combinations – e.g. *playbill,
hand-bill* etc. – in theatre advertising. From LL *billa = bulla*, 'a
wax seal' (as in 'Papal Bull'), by extension 'bill' was used for any
document conveying authority and, later, information. (The
authority conferred by a wax seal is evident in many meanings,
from the American 'dollar bill' to the English 'draft of a proposed
law to be put before parliament' and 'an account of money owed
for goods or services'.) Such documents, either affixed to posts
(see *poster*) or passed by hand *(handbill)* are first referred to in
C15: 'The scottes made a bylle that was fastnd vpon the chirche
dores of seynt petre (1480, Caxton, *The Cronicles of England*).

The theatrical usage derives from the same origin as a restaurant
'bill of fare': a proposal or advertisement for a service available.
The earliest posters on record – also, to judge by their appearance
for distribution by hand, hence hand-bills – advertise a *variety*
show 'at the Booth at Charing Cross' in 1672. The first such
document for an established theatre is for Drury Lane in 1687.
Playbills (first attested in 1677 [OED]) gradually developed to
include most of the detail we expect on a modern *programme*. By
extension in C19, 'bill', especially in variety, came to mean the
running-order for an evening's entertainment. To *top the bill* or
get top-billing or *star-billing* meant that one's name appeared at the
top of the bill: one had *made it to the top*, or simply *made it*.

Distinctions of usage between Britain and America are particularly complex in the field of advertising. In America, advertising
hoardings are referred to as *billboards* – (first attested there in
1877 [OED Supp]) – more frequently than in Britain and this term
has given its name to the influential American entertainment journal, *Billboard*. In Britain, unlicensed advertising of all kinds is
prohibited, but small-scale productions still persist in illegal bill-
sticking, leading to the ever-popular graffito under the official
notice 'Bill Stickers Will Be Prosecuted' – 'Bill Stickers Is Innocent!'

bio-mechanics   A term coined in Russian and translated into English. It follows a recurring C20 artistic tendency – see *affective
memory* and *laboratory theatre* – to use quasi-scientific terms to
lend authority to artistic theories. Bio-mechanics – from Gk *bios*,
'possessing organic life' + *mechane*, 'a contrivance', i.e. 'machine-
life' – was a system of production and actor-training proposed in

the 1920s by the Russian, Vsevolod Emilievich Meyerhold (1874-1942), an actor and director who was also a favoured pupil of Stanislavski's until the two argued and fell out. Bio-mechanics (and *constructivism*) may in part be seen as a reaction against *Stanislavskian* theatre. Directorial absolutism was demanded alongside the emotional detachment and puppet-like obedience of the actor (compare Craig's *über-marionettes*). The end result is said to have been reminiscent of *kabuki*.

bird, to get the　I had always presumed that *getting the bird* meant that one's performance was met by whistles of disapproval. However, Partridge (who should know about birds) has an altogether more plausible explanation. 'The bird' is an abbreviation of 'the big bird', i.e. the goose, and refers to the audience hissing a performer. In C19 *melodrama*, a villain who *was given the goose* or *the big bird* might take this as a plaudit. However, *the bird's there* was a phrase for an unfavourable reception.

birdie　A lC20 term for a specific theatre lantern: 'the name is a joke on the golf term – [they] are one-below-par-lights' (*Observer*, 3 May 1992). See *par lights*.

bit part　A *bit player* or *bit part player* is a term used, according to Beale, since *c.*1930 for an actor or actress who plays small roles in films. The term is grander than *supernumerary*, *spear-carrier*, and *extra* in that a bit part may involve lines.

biz, the　'I wanted to make the book readable for those not purely in the biz, hence it's a nice anecdotal read' (Ronald Wolfe in *The Stage*, 23 April 1992). *The biz* has been a common abbreviation for *the business* in the United States since mC19: 'I must forth to my biz' (1865, Artemus Ward, *His Book*). The common if *stagey* 'biz' is an American abbreviation of *showbiz*, now common in Britain.

black comedy　A C20 genre of *comedy* which draws humour from the macabre, a term possibly influenced by the French *films noirs* as they became familiar to English-speaking audiences. The British master of *black comedy* was undoubtedly Joe Orton (1933-67), whose life cruelly mirrored his creative art: he was tragi-comically and gruesomely murdered by his jealous, long-term partner on the brink of popular recognition.

black hole (of the auditorium)　A phrase popularised by the translation of Stanislavski's *An Actor Prepares*. The *black hole* to which he refers is the unlit auditorium seen through the *proscenium arch* and the glare of the *footlights* from the actor's standpoint. It was in part to avoid the attraction of playing, unnaturalistically, directly to the audience in this alluring vacuum that led him to develop *psychotechnique*.

blackout A mC19 phrasal verb, *to black out* meant literally 'to obliterate with black' (OED): 'The Russian censor who blacks out all matter that is displeasing to the Government' (1850, General Gordon, Letter). This usage is still current, most frequently as a noun, in media terms such as *news blackout*. In the theatre, the noun *blackout* refers to the effect of creating almost total darkness by the exclusion of natural light and the extinguishing of as much artificial light as possible. (In public theatres, safety lights must remain on in the auditorium by law.) It is also used to refer to the materials – curtains, drapes, and boarding, painting etc. over windows – which produce this effect, sometimes abbreviated to *blacks*. Of course, 'blackout' gained its most widespread currency in British cities during the Second World War – in 'The Blackout': I have been unable to ascertain whether this usage was affected by theatre or *vice versa*.

The term is also widely applied to a range of experiences of loss of consciousness and memory, a term which spread, according to Beale, from RAF usage in the early 1940s. It is now also applied to radio jamming etc, an interesting transference from sight to hearing. An antonym, 'whiteout', has been coined, often to refer to the blinding effects of snow.

'Blackout' is frequently found as a *stage direction* and *lighting cue* in lC20 texts, especially in plays written for production in theatres with no *proscenium arch* or when no *scene-drop* or *act-drop* is desired, a replacement for the more traditional *quick curtain*. See also *DBO*.

blacks Black *curtains* used in the theatre: a *black* for 'a black curtain' is a term used ecclesiastically in the singular (for funerals) since at least eC17. The earliest OED reference to the plural is from 1711: 'The Company of Upholders are not able to furnish Blacks enough for the Deceased' (OED). The precise date of its theatrical adoption is uncertain.

'The black' is also an occasional term for the *apron* and 'blacks' can also refer to stylised black clothing worn by a group of actors or by *stagehands* when used as scene-shifters in view of the audience during a show.

black tat Black waste fabric which finds a variety of theatrical uses, notably to stop unwanted leaks of light. *Tat* has been used for old material (from Standard English *tatter*) since at least eC19: it is now also used generally for anything of inferior value.

black theatre A term coined in America in the 1960s for a theatre movement reflecting the concerns of the Civil Rights and Black Power movements in politics. It was quickly adopted in Britain and now promotes what Yvonne Brewster, a leading figure in the

Black Theatre Forum (a British coalition of Afro-Caribbean and Asian theatre companies), terms 'a black aesthetic'. See also *mixed casting*.

to black up A verb meaning to apply black make-up, usually so that a white actor can play a black role. The opposite, *whiting up*, has been used to satirical effect in films. See *coon show* and *nigger minstrel*.

to blank As all actors know, the statement 'I just blanked' refers to the feeling of bewilderment that comes when they think they know their lines but, through distraction, a lapse of concentration or the effects of *stagefright*, the words are not there *on cue*: they *dry*. The verb is obviously derived from the adjective blank and is probably an abbreviation of the common phrase 'my mind went blank', but I have been unable to find a first usage.

blank verse 'Every subsequent attempt to equal Shakespeare's results by bringing back blank verse has failed' (Brook, 58). *Blank verse* is unrhymed verse – hence *blank* in its sense of 'bare, simple' – written in iambic pentameter, arguably the verse form closest to natural English speech rhythms. Blank verse was introduced *c*.1540 by the Earl of Surrey in his translation of Vergil's *Aeneid* and rapidly became the standard meter for the poetic drama of the Elizabethan and succeeding periods – 'The swelling bombast of bragging blank verse' (1589, Green, *Menaphon*).

bleachers Portable, tiered seating units, generally on wheels, which are particularly useful in flexible spaces, studios etc. First usage of the term appears to be eC20 American, with reference to the cheap seats in a baseball stadium, those in which, it is argued, clothes bleach in the sun. As in Spanish bull-fighting arenas, the more expensive seats were in the shade.

blocking 'A quick reading of the first scene took place round a table, then we went into the blocking or setting of the physical moves' (Branagh, 93). The Standard English verb *to block*, after the meanings of 'to obstruct, to impede with the body', includes the sense of 'sketching in roughly, planning'. (The word derives ultimately, via Fr. *bloquer*, from MDu *blok*, associated with bulky organic and inorganic objects such as logs and lumps of rock.) *To block* in the theatre, and the noun *blocking* derived from it, come from the last sense of the word, first attested in general use in OED in 1585: 'I tuke earnist and willing panis to blok it [this short treatise]' (James VI of Scotland [later James I of England], *The essayes of a prentise, in the divine art of poesie*). Blocking as a rehearsal activity means roughing in the movements of the actors in relation to the set; later, 'the blocking' refers to the agreed pattern of *moves* in a production. Some directors are very prescriptive

about blocking whilst others allow the physical shape of a piece
to develop naturally during rehearsal.

bloodtub   A delightfully descriptive, C19 vernacular term prefiguring eC20 coinages such as 'flea pit'. The word described the
gaffs (or *geggies* in Scotland) which in C19 like the *venues* used
by *barnstormers*, were temporarily converted for theatre use, in
this case for *melodramas*, the violent content of which gave rise
to the name. Originally a theatre in N.W. London, with a rival
in E. London known as the 'Blood Hole'.

blue   As an adjective, '*risqué*', especially with reference to
humour. Probably from the verb *to blue*, a variant of *blush*: 'If a
virgin Blushes, we no longer cry she Blues' (1709, Steele and
Swift, *The Tatler*). '[Max Miller] would offer the audience jokes
from…the white book (clean jokes) and the blue book (risqué
jokes) creating…the feeling that they were getting away with
something a little bit naughty' (Wilmut, 123).

blue, a   A narrow strip of blue curtain hung as a *border*, *top drop*
etc. inside a *proscenium arch* to represent sky. Also known as a
sky border, it serves to *mask* lighting equipment etc. from the
audience's view. Compare *black*.

board   A very common abbreviation of *switchboard*.

boards, the   From the standard sense of 'a piece of sawn timber'.
From medieval *mystery plays* onwards, wooden platforms supported by vertical poles, tie-bars or bracing have been used to
create a stage. In the famous phrase *treading the boards*, 'the
boards' become synonymous not only with the *stage* but, by
metonymous extension, with the very business of being an actor.
It strikes me as significant that the phraseology echoes *nautical*
constructions such as 'crossing the line', 'walking the plank',
'splicing the mainbrace' etc.: given that *boards* also refer to 'the
sides of a ship' and, by extension (in phrases such as *on board*)
the ship itself, the term may have a nautical origin. See *carpenter*,
chips/chippie.

boat truck   A platform on castors which allows entire *scenes* or
sections of scenes to be moved on and off stage. *Boat truck* may
at first seem to be an amphibious term: however, *truck*, too, is
nautical, possibly an abbreviation of *truckie* (from AF *trokle*, from
L. *trochlea*, 'a pulley'). OED defines it as 'a small, solid wooden
wheel or roller…one of those on which the carriages of ships'
guns were formerly mounted', giving the first attestation in 1611:
'Rigolo, a little wheele used under sleds. Gunners call it a trucke'
(Florio).

bomb   In Britain, *to go down (like) a bomb* is to be an explosive
success. In its full form, it seems to be a conflation of *to go like a*

bomb, a World War II RAF term for 'to succeed with precision', and *to go down a bomb*, possibly of the same origin, but in wider general usage. However, in the United States *to bomb* – which, according to Beale, was imported to Britain in the 1970s – means that a show or performance fails ignominiously. Both terms have gained widespread currency on their respective sides of the Atlantic. However, such is the sophistication of speakers of slang both in and out of the theatre, that in Britain the two are used side by side with only minimal confusion.

bomb tank   A tank or drum positioned in a place of safety and specially constructed to withstand the explosion of *maroons* etc.

book¹   The phrase *to be on the book* (see *ASM*) derives from the C16 English theatre when, before the development of advanced reprographics, there was often only one complete manuscript copy of a *script* available to an entire company, (individual actors' *parts* being copied out by hand; see Shakespeare, *A Midsummer Night's Dream*, I.ii). This was the job of the *book-keeper* who also acted as company librarian. The *book-holder*, generally the same man, would act as prompter as well as having charge of all the *props*. After the *Restoration*, elements of these two roles began to be reapportioned as the responsibilities of *prompter* and *stage manager*. It is from the 'foul papers' in the book-holder's possession that Heminge and Condell must have assembled some of the plays in the *First Folio* of Shakespeare.

Today, the book (still in the demonstrative singular) has developed as indicated above into the promptbook, prompt script or prompt copy, which it is the task of a member of the stage management team to draw up during rehearsals in the hope that each performance can be identically smooth. This contains:

– an accurate version of the script, including cuts, rewrites and acting pauses;

– clear and concise blocking;

– all cues – lighting, sound, flys, effects, scene changes – and the details of what each cue does;

– calls for actors and technical stage staff during performance;

– all setting lists, cue sheets, running plot, cast list and charts. (ed. Menear and Hawkins, 31)

book²   The name given to the *libretto* of a *Broadway musical* in contrast to the *score*: the *text*.

book³   As a descriptive adjective applied to certain stage *flats*, *book* denotes the presence of paired or grouped flats joined by hinges, as if the hinge were the spine of a book. So, *book flats* are paired, hinged flats which are safely free-standing when opened at angles of less than about 120°. *Book ceilings*, once an integral part of a *box set* (if the lighting resources of the theatre allowed the set to be roofed) are also hinged, permitting the ceiling to be variously angled, but, more importantly, allowing for easy storage in the *flies*. *Book wings* (also known as *wing flats*) are flats which can be opened or turned like the pages of a book to reveal different scenes: also an American term for a *book flat*.

book⁴/booking 'The bookings for the week ahead were near capacity, there was a great deal of publicity' (Branagh, 213). The verb *to book* is a C19 development – as in 'to book a theatre seat' or, in the case of managements, 'to book an artist, show' etc. It means 'to arrange in advance by payment or promise of payment' – 'I will give them orders to book an inside place for the poodle' (1826, Disraeli, *Vivian Gray*) – and derives from the sense of 'to book' as 'to record by writing in a book' which is found as early as C13. The associated noun, a *booking*, is not attested in OED in reference to tickets until lC19: 'The number of bookings was much larger than . . . last year' (1884, *Pall Mall Gazette*). 'A booking' can be used synonymously with 'job' for a *variety* artist or an actor.

boom From *boom*, a wooden beam. A *nautical* term borrowed from Dutch: English *beam* and Dutch *boom* can both be traced back to the same Germanic root, but whereas 'beam' was used for the timbers from which a ship was built and for its width (hence broad in the beam), 'boom', like *batten*, was used for individual timbers, often unattached at one end. (The sailing phrase that many of us know but few understand, *jibbing the boom*, refers to hanging a triangular staysail from the jib-boom of a large ship to its fore-topmast-head.) Theatrically, both vertical and horizontal *booms* were originally used to denote wooden spars to which scenery, equipment and, latterly, lights could be attached. Today, the term is most frequently used for a vertical pole or pipe situated in the wings. One often sees microphone booms and sound booms – movable poles – dangling into the frame on low-budget film and television.

booth *Booths* are traditionally makeshift canvas shelters and stalls, easily constructed and dismantled, hence their historical use in medieval *passion* and *pageant plays* and their continuing use on fairgrounds and in markets. There are records of Ancient Greek strolling players using such structures and it is more than likely that this tradition was continued in Europe from antiquity. From early illustrations it appears that these booths were sometimes erected on raised platforms and sometimes constructed around an open area which could be used as a performance space.

At times they would have housed the actors and band, on other occasions prominent members of the audience. The term is still occasionally used for the enclosure at the back of the theatre from which a technician operates sound or lighting equipment: a *box*. From Old East Norse *both, boa*, 'to dwell'.

border   A border is a 'top drop' or narrow strip of curtain hung behind the *proscenium arch* to hide lights and equipment. (It can also be used as an abbreviation for *border light*.) *Border* (ultimately from OF *bordure*, 'a boundary or edge') has been used in this sense since at least eC18. Often, borders are named after the scenes painted on them or the things they are supposed to represent: 'an old sky border' (1732, Covent Garden Inventory). See *sky border, blue*.

box   This term was first used in lC16 theatre for a small, private 'room' in a slightly elevated position near to the stage. The builder of the Hope Theatre, Gilbert Katherens, was enjoined in 1613 to 'make two Boxes in the lowermost storie fitt and decent for gentlemen to sitt in; And shall make the particions between the Rommes as they are at the saide Plaie house called the Swan' (quoted in Leacroft, *English Playhouse*, 33). The choice of the term is interesting in that at this date *box* had not yet acquired its present sense of 'a large chest', being used only for apothecaries' pill boxes and jewel caskets: OED speculates that its adoption may be a humorous reference to the priceless value of the people who were accommodated in such boxes. From OE *bux*, from LL *buxis*, 'a box made of boxwood', from L. *buxus*, 'boxwood', a material much favoured by turners and engravers for the ease with which it could be worked.

Boxes were maintained in designs for new entertainment establishments until the eC20, foremost amongst them *the Royal Box; the dress box* was supplied for those who with no right to special seating other than the ability to pay. The latest development of this inegalitarian term came with the corporate *hospitality boxes* of the 1980s. Other extensions of usage have occurred in C20 as the term has been transferred, in phrases such as *lighting box* and *sound box*, to the compartment, usually at the rear of the auditorium, from which *technicians* view a show and operate equipment.

box office   As plans of C17 and eC18 theatres show, customers at early, custom-built theatres paid at the *pay box*. As the booking and renting of the growing number of boxes became a major source of theatrical income in the increasing affluence of C18 London, so the humble pay box was replaced by the *box office*, probably so-called because it was the place from which *boxes* were hired out, though it could also have been an aggrandisement of pay box.

Box office hits, for shows which are *good box office*, are both C20 terms synonymous with viable, commercial propositions in the theatre. Other self-explanatory terms include *box office appeal*, *draw* and *poison*. A *box office plan* is a diagram of the layout of seats in an *auditorium* often seen on display in the box office.

box set *Box sets* were first introduced in England from France in London's Olympic Theatre in 1832 by Madame Vestris, (Lucy Elizabeth Bartolozzi), an English actress who had married and worked abroad. Forerunners of totally *naturalistic* sets, all the walls and ceilings of box sets, contained behind the *proscenium arch*, were created by *flats*, though at this date they might be crudely painted with furniture, utensils etc. as we have come to expect today in *pantomime*. The intention was to create an illusion of scenic reality which lC20 theatre only uses sparingly. In this instance, *box* is simply descriptive of the right-angled geometry of these constructions.

boy At a time when women were not sanctioned to appear on stage, *boy actors* – known simply as *boys* – were common. From C14 onwards the usual company of professional actors was made up of four men and a boy who played all the women's parts. Companies consisting entirely of boys, 'the little eyases' from choirs such as St Pauls, were popular for a time in C16. It was not until the lC17 that the portrayal of women by women was approved (see *actress*) and the transvestite boy discarded. To confuse the issue, the *principal boy* of *pantomime*, perhaps in the tradition of *harlequinades*, was played by a woman from C18 onwards. See also *breeches part*, *drag* and *female impersonator*.

brace From OF *brace*, 'the two arms', especially 'the width of the two arms', from L. *bracchia*, 'arms'. Used since at least C14 in a variety of contexts as 'a device which clasps, supports or secures', *brace* is encountered in the theatre as an abbreviation of *stage brace* – 'a wooden rod, one end of which is hooked to the back of a *flat*, the other screwed in or held firm by a *stage weight*'. A *French brace* is integral to the flat, being a hinged, triangular support which can be folded out and weighted as and if required. 'Brace' would have most obviously been derived from carpentry, where it is, amongst other things, a wooden strengthening-piece; OED also records an entry in Smyth's *Sailor's Word-book* (1867) which suggests it may be a nautical loan. The term has been used since at least eC18: *The Covent Garden Inventory* (1732) lists '12 braces and stays to the round fly'.

bravo From It. *bravo*, 'brave'. *Bravo* was originally used in

in lC16 meaning 'a desperado or murderer': 'Setting on your
desperate bravo to murder him' (1632, Massinger, *Maid of Honour*). The word is first attested as an exclamation meaning 'Excellent!' in mC18: 'That's right – I'm steel – Bravo! – Adamant –
Bravissimo!' (1761, Coleman, *Jealous Wife*.) Its use appears to
have been imported by travellers to Italy; it stuck, presumably,
because of its resounding sound.

bravura   '[His] bravura performance as Comache conveyed the
story beautifully' (*Plays and Players*, October 1990). From the
same root as *bravo*, above, *bravura*, meaning 'bravery' in Italian,
has been employed both nominally and adjectivally since lC18
with reference to a performance which involves either great skill,
spirit or *risk-taking*. It was originally imported as a musical term
but can now refer to any performance: 'In the lofty bravuras she
copies the spheres' (1788, 'Pasquin', *The Children of the Spheres*).

break   Possibly influenced by a *break* in billiards, 'a run of success', *break* (as in lucky break) has been used in America since
eC19 meaning 'a stroke of good fortune'. In theatre it is often
used for a performer's first chance of *stardom*: '[he] is currently
auditioning for a number of roles and is quietly confident that he
will get his second big break soon' (*The Stage*, 28 March 1991).
This term may have influenced later phrases such as *to break into
pictures*, used since the 1920s. Another use of the verb, as in 'Let's
break', or the imperative 'Break!', signifies a pause in a rehearsal
or the ending of the same. The term can also be used for the
accidental omission of *lines* or *business*, (compare *break down*).

break a leg   See *leg*.

break down   An actor's term for 'to fail utterly in a scene, possibly
by drying' – 'I've come in to tell you that I'm going to break
down tonight. I can tell you the very line... I'm going to dry up
– dead' (Ellen Terry, quoted in Robertson, 1931, *Life Was Worth
Living*). The term can also be used with reference to making
props, costumes etc. look old – compare *distress*.

breathing   'I stayed late at college to work on breathing and voice'
(Branagh, 66). *Breathing* in theatre is not merely a vital process:
correct breathing, for the actor as much as the singer, is a vital
skill that must be acquired in order to achieve the control, relaxation, fluency and projection required for public performance in
sometimes difficult acoustics. 'If I kept to [the punctuation marks
in Shakespeare] and breathed with them, like an experienced
swimmer, the verse seemed to hold me up and even disclose its
meaning' (Gielgud, 74).

Brechtian   'Pertaining to or influenced by the works and theatrical
theories of Bertolt Brecht, (1898-1956)', the German Marxist

dramaturge and poet whose writing for and on the theatre has had
a great effect on subject matter and *staging* in British theatre since
1945. *Brechtian* ideas, often mistakenly interpreted as the antithesis of the *Stanislavskian* system, have perhaps had the greatest
impact on *alternative* and *T.i.E.* companies. 'John Doyle...has
moved right back to Brechtian basics:...theatrical illusion is set
aside' (*The Stage*, 28 March 1991). For more details, see *alienation*, *gestus* and *verfremdungseffekt*.

breeches part   A role in which an actress plays a male character.
(From *breeches* as 'male trousers, especially the short ones in fashion in C18, with additional ties below the knee', from OE *brec*,
a plural treated as singular in ME.) One cannot help but wonder
whether the sudden popularity of this device of cross-dressing in
eC18 comedy is related in some way to the demise of the *boy* actor
playing women's roles, which immediately preceded it. The term
is first attested in OED in mC19: 'We do not profess special admi-
ration of ladies in what are technically...termed breeches parts'
(1865, *Dublin University Magazine*), which seems suspiciously
late. See also *dame*, *drag*, *female impersonator*, *queen* and *principal
boy*.

bridge   In the theatre, the *bridge*, sometimes also known as the
catwalk, is a platform above the stage, either fixed or capable of
being raised and lowered, from which work on lighting, scenery
etc. can be carried out. It is most probably a *nautical* term as the
bridge on a ship has been, since at least C19, 'the raised platform
from which ship is directed'; also, the likelier source of the loan,
it is 'a narrow gangway between hatches' (1867, Smyth, *Sailor's
Word-Book*).

bring in a light   A lighting term for introducing a *lantern* not
previously used in a scene. *To bring up the lights* is to increase the
illumination of a scene. The antonym of *to dim the lights*.

bristle trap   A *trap* which works similarly to a *star trap*, except,
as the term suggests, it has bristles attached to the rims.

Broadway   Named after a street which runs through the centre
of the theatre district of Manhattan, New York City, from the
1850s *Broadway* has been synonymous with New York's commercial theatre industry. During C20, the term has come to designate
the lighter end of *show business*. Whereas once 'Broadway' denoted
excellence and innovation in the dramatic and musical theatres,
that mantle has passed to the terms *off-Broadway* and *off-off-
Broadway*, leaving 'Broadway' with associations of commercialism and only the last gleam of its former glitter. In a trend
which the *West End* of London has been in danger of following
since the 1970s, more and more Broadway theatres have gone

temporarily *dark*, closed down completely or turned away from *serious theatre* towards *box office* certainties. It also lent its name to the Broadway *musical*, a term which carries its own ambiguities with it: 'Are musicals the great Broadway art form, America's one truly indigenous contribution to the theatre spectrum? Or are they mere song-and-dance palliatives...? At its best the Broadway musical produces a sense of exhilaration that few creations can match; at its worst...few theatrical genres seem more cynical and more calculated' *(Bloomsbury Theatre Guide)*.

bums on seats   The aim of most theatre managements is to achieve this lucrative coming together of flesh and furniture – *to get bums on seats*. 'Art's fine in its place but it doesn't get bums on seats' (1992, overheard). Consequently, a less than flattering synonym for *audience*. A C20 term, *not* from America, where *bum* is colloquial for 'tramp, hobo' or any person one despises.

built stuff   A term which can include all manufactured three-dimensional props and stage items such as *rostra*.

burlesque   From Fr. *burlesque*, from It. *burlesco*, from *burla*, 'ridicule, mockery'. The word appears to have been introduced in the mass import of Continental artistic terms at the Restoration. 'I shall not here with burlesque penners/Carp at her beauty' (1700, OED). *Burlesque* pervaded all the arts from music to caricature until well into C18 and can be summed up as 'satirical, mock-heroic parody'. In the theatre, Gay and Fielding were perhaps the masters of the art. Later C19 attempts at the *genre* tended to keep the form but lose the satirical edge. By extension, the word became used as a label for any gross mockery of something with higher intentions: 'Why is such a burlesque upon public worship suffered?' (1772, Wesley's *Journal*.) The term was later appropriated for a genre of entertainment show particularly popular in America from 1860s to the 1930s. It managed to live up to its etymology to a degree by including political satire alongside songs, *sketches*, *variety* acts and the essential ingredient for which it was renowned from the 1920s onward – *strip-tease*.

burletta   'A little *burlesque*'. A form of entertainment devised in mC18, continuing into the C19, which, by including at least five songs, managed to get through a loophole in the theatre licensing laws (see *legit*). Most *burlettas*, however, were little more than weak examples of *farce*, interspersed with music.

burnt-cork minstrels   A C19 term descriptive of the materials used by white American artists to *black up* as *nigger minstrels* in a *coon show*.

bus, just got off the   '"Your young lad," he said, sending up some northern actor laddie, "has just got off the bus, as we say in the business. But...he's not half bad"' (Albert Finney, quoted in Branagh, 98). A term applied to a theatrical novice, usually one from the provinces.

business As an abbreviation of *stage business*, the term is applied to any detailed physical *action* or series of actions in a theatrical production; often it is used in contradistinction to dialogue. The earliest OED attestation is from 1671 in the Villiers' *Rehearsal* (III.ii):

'I see here is a great deal of Plot, Mr. Bayes.
Yes...but we shall have a world of more business anon.'

This date, so soon after the Restoration, suggests that *business* may well be a term dating back at least to eC17 (bearing in mind the closure of theatres during the 1650s) if not further.

The other sense of 'business' – as in *show business*, generally abbreviated to 'the business', *showbiz* and often to *the biz* – comes from the general sense of the word as 'an occupation or trade' which dates back to C15, or the sense of 'work as opposed to recreation' which is found in eC14. (For an example of this use of *business*, see the entry under *bus*, above.) For a discussion of the theatrical origins, which are probably American, see *biz* and *show business*.

busk The most common, current sense of *to busk* is 'to perform in the street'. Artists who do so are known as *buskers*: 'Welsh busker-turned-tenor John Corke hired out the London Palladium then disappeared, leaving a trail of unpaid bills' (*The Stage*, 28 April 1992). This term comes from an earlier C19 usage meaning 'to go on tour with minimum technical resources'. From this, an additional sense is now common: 'to run through a scene without rehearsal or prior discussion; by extension, to improvise': 'The brief for the role was Mozart as small, bright, childlike and charming. Bright and charming I could manage, childlike I would busk, but small was tricky' (Branagh, 105). 'Let's just busk it', meaning 'Let's try it out and see what happens' is a common rehearsal term.

The origins of both senses of the term are disputed, some having claimed that *busk* derives from *buskin*, an early term for an actor's shoe or pump. Evidence from Smyth's *Sailors Word-book* (1867), however, which defines 'busking' as 'Piratical cruising: also, used generally, for beating to windward along a coast, or cruising off and on' seems worth pursuing. This term is also used in a figurative extension in *Fraser's Magazine* in 1841 with reference to a certain form of criminal who pawned stolen goods, gave a false address and then disappeared: it was a practice 'for which they had a general term of reproach, viz. "going a-busking".' Contemporary buskers, who play, then change their pitches quickly at the first sign of the law, are, I imagine, obvious inheritors of this sense of the word. (It is interesting to compare this term with another, similar, *nautical* term which suggests dubious or criminal street behaviour: 'cruising' – 'looking for casual or illicit sex'.) The quick-witted improvisation required for success in busking is obvious. If these speculations are accurate, 'busk' is significant as the only example I have encountered of a nautical term used mainly by performers, and not obviously derived from a technical stage term.

Cabaret 'A sophisticated entertainment, usually with music and song, sometimes satirical, performed in bars, restaurants etc.' The origins of the Fr. root are uncertain but it was first used for 'a drinking-house, eating-house or inn', in which senses it became common in lC17: 'In most cabaretts in France they have writ upon the walls *Dieu te garde*' (1662, Pepys). This spelling suggests an anglicisation of pronunciation and according to OED it *was* temporarily naturalised with this French sense (as with other continental words relating to entertainment) after the Restoration, later slipping out of vogue. Its reappearance in lC19 was a second importation, this time with its modern meaning.

The 1930s saw the heyday of the genre, above all in Germany, where satirical, politically-charged cabarets flourished in Berlin and other major cities prior to Hitler's accession to power. This is well reflected in Isherwood's novel *Goodbye to Berlin*, later *dramatised* as *I am a Camera* (1951, Van Druten), which was turned into the *musical*, *Cabaret* (1967, Ebb, Kander, Masteroff), and filmed in 1972. Cabaret strongly influenced the development of *Brechtian* ideas of theatrical structure and presentation. In recent years, there has been a revival, particularly on the *alternative circuit*, along with some strange hybrid forms: 'Saturdays and Sundays offer live entertainment and the occasional Karaoke cabaret' (ad. in *The Stage*, 28 March 1991).

call 'I sat and waited for the first time for my call, praying that my name would be pronounced correctly' (Olivier, 49). The *call* is the traditional name for the order or warning that *actors*, *crew* etc. receive to appear for *rehearsals* or *performances*, for *cues* within a show, or to take a bow – the famous *curtain call*. 'You are cast for Player Queen. Call is for eleven this morning' (1876, OED). Although the latter is the first OED attestation, the term is probably C18.

Theatre time is adhered to strictly and breaches of punctuality are high amongst the sins of the stage for obvious reasons. As the *up* approaches, a *call boy*, or more frequently today an electronic *cue-call*, announces *the half*, *the quarter* and *the five*, sometimes even uttering cinema-flavoured clichés such as 'Overture and beginners, please', before 'Curtain up!' is heard. Personal calls are still a feature in some theatres during the show.

44

call board   A backstage notice-board, traditionally situated just inside the *stage door*, on which *rehearsal schedules*, the *notice* and other information required by *actors* and *crew* can be advertised. From *call*, above.

call book   Whether a *company* employs a *cue-call* system or a *call boy*, it is common practice for a member of the *crew*, in consultation with whoever has been *on the book* at *rehearsals*, to draw up a written schedule of *calls* for a *production*.

call boy   Not to be confused with call girl. A member of the *stage crew*, often, formerly, someone pensioned off from heavier work, whose job is to call the *half*, the *five* etc. and to ensure that people are in place for *cues*. The term appears in Thomas Robinson's articles for the *Illustrated News* in the 1850s, (quoted by Nagler, 490-98), but almost certainly predates this by several decades. Today, the *call-boy* has been largely replaced by the electronic *cue-call*.

call doors   Doors placed in the *proscenium arch* of many older theatres, hence their alternative name, *proscenium doors*. Allowing direct access to the *apron stage*, they received their name because they were often used only by actors *en route* to take a *curtain call*.

cameo   ME from OF *camahieu* (and many variations), of unknown origin – 'a small piece of relief carving in stone (onyx, agate etc.) usually with colour layers utilised to give background relief; design of similar form' (Concise Oxford). First used in English in C13, a fixed form of the word was slow in becoming established. Commonly employed for a brooch decoration with an inlay – often a miniature human profile – by way of design – 'My ryng, wth A white camfeo' (1554, *Bristol Wills*) – the cameo gave its name in lC19/eC20 to any small but detailed characterisation which an author might include in a literary work. It was transferrred to denote any small but exquisitely-played role in which an actor might be cast. It can also be employed (as in the famous cinema example of Hitchcock, who appeared briefly in *cameo roles* in all of his films), as a euphemism for *extra*.

camp   In some contexts, *campness* (see below) and *theatricality* are synonymous, reflecting the enormous role which *gay* men and women have played in the development of the English-speaking theatre: 'visually very extravagant, flamboyant and camp, the company was an inspiration to me' (Branagh, 83).

The origins of *camp* are, Partridge suggests, either the C19-20 dialect word *camp, kemp*, 'uncouth, rough', for which I can find no convincing evidence, or, he hazards vaguely, in French. The Fr. verb *camper*, 'to place, fix, put', is used in French theatrical slang in the phrase *camper un personnage*, 'to play a part effectively'

(Harrap's Shorter French and English Dictionary). In addition, there is the reflexive verb, *se camper*, which means 'to stand in a proud or provocative attitude'. Early English definitions of the word, which do not specifically mention homosexuality, seem related to this latter French meaning. Ware (1909) (quoted in Beale) cites 'camp' in English as 'addicted to actions and gestures of exaggerated emphasis', and Partridge claims that it was current on the streets of eC20 London meaning 'pleasantly ostentatious, or, in manner, affected'.

'Effeminate (for men), butch (for lesbians) and theatrical (for both)' is said by Beale to have been current in the theatre from 1920 and adopted generally by the end of the Second World War. I would suspect, given the French theatrical links, that the word was used by the acting profession much earlier than Beale suggests, from whence it entered social usage. However, along with this acceptance came unfortunate, homophobic connotations: 'camp' is also claimed by Beale to have meant 'objectionable, (slightly) disreputable, bogus', by 1945. A further, extended meaning is demonstrated in this quotation: 'L'Altro is as camp a restaurant as you are likely to find outside a set for a Broadway musical. Slate floor, wrought-iron street lights, mock windows with swooning grille work and distressed friezes contrive an odd little alley fit for Gene Kelly to skip through' (*Independent*, 5 October 1991). Here, we are dealing with a word that signifies 'precious affectation', almost a synonym for *kitsch*. This would appear to be a development from the noun, (see below).

A verb, *to camp*, meaning 'to be homosexual or lesbian or to behave with their (showy) mannerisms', which was common e-mC20, has been surpassed in usage by phrases such as *to camp about*, meaning 'to pirouette and gesture eloquently' (1962, R.C. Cook, *The Crust on its Uppers*), and *to camp it up*, which means in the theatre 'to play (a scene) in an over-the-top (*O.T.T.*) fashion, often unnecessarily', and in broader social terms 'to put in or exaggerate camp behaviour'.

As a noun, 'a camp' for 'a gay person', (which was current eC20), is obsolete. However, 'camp' as a style of performance (and, by extension, everyday behaviour), meaning 'a method of presentation which employs exaggerated, gay speech mannerisms, movements and gestures', has risen to the status of *genre*. Two terms which emerged in the United States in the 1960s, when *campness* – 'the possession of camp qualities, (or *campery*)' – was gaining a higher public profile, (that is, 'coming out'), are *high camp* and *low camp*, the former signifying a stylish, artistically-controlled use of camp and the latter a crude, unaesthetic parody.

canvas   From ME and ONF *canevas*, from OF *chanevaz*, from L *cannabis*, 'hemp plant'. *Canvas* is 'a (piece of) strong, unbleached cloth of hemp, flax, or other coarse yarn' (Concise Oxford) used primarily in theatre in the construction of *flats*: the canvas is stretched over a wooden frame. As in painting, it is ideal on account of its strength and the ease with which it can be decorated with oil-based paints. The fact that many early usages of the word and the material are *nautical* hints that it may have entered theatre from this source.

Captain McFluffer   A lC19-eC20 term, now largely obsolete, found in the phrase *to take Captain McFluffer badly*: to badly *fluff* (stumble over or forget) one's *lines*.

carbon arc spotlight   See *arc*, *spotlight*.

carnival   With true Puritan relish, OED consigns 'to the domain of popular etymology' the notion that *carnival* comes from a Latin phrase translatable as 'farewell to flesh'. In fact, only slightly more prosaically, it is a shortening of med. L. *carnem levare* (It. *carne levare*), meaning 'the putting away or removal of flesh (as food)', a term used for the period immediately preceding Lent, 'theyr Carnoval time (which we call shroftide)', an early English attestation explains in 1549. Lent was a time, according to Evelyn in his *Diary*, (1646), 'when all the world repair to Venice, to see the folly and madness of the Carnavall.' Its first figurative use in English is in lC16: 'The Carnouale of my sweet Love is past,/Now comes the Lent of my long Hate' (1598, OED). In C17 England it came to signify any period of festivity, in which sense it has taken on theatrical significance through the elements of *street theatre* inherent in events such as the Notting Hill Carnival, pale shadows though they are of the epic carnivals of South America.

carpenter   ME, from OF *carpentier*, from LL *carpentarius*, 'a carriage-maker', (from *carpentum*, 'a wagon'). Given the importance of *built stuff* in most *stage design* since Ancient Athens, *carpenters* (see also *chips/chippies*) have played a vital role in shaping the English stage from their shop, or *bay*, as the phrase 'treading the *boards*' suggests. It should not be overlooked that James Burbage, (*c*.1530-67), the first, named *actor-manager* and builder of London's first public theatre, (the aptly-named Theatre, whose timbers were later recycled for Shakespeare's Globe), was a carpenter by trade.

A *carpenter('s) scene*, rarely necessary today given the nature of modern *staging* and machinery, was originally a term used in C19 for a *backcloth*, piece of *scenery* etc. introduced towards the front of a stage whilst a more complex set was being erected out of sight by carpenters or other *stage crew*: 'A Carpenter's Scene is generally a flat in the first grooves consisting of some murky picture or other' (1864, *Graphic*). By extension, it also referred to a scene played in front of such a device: 'The dialogue of a front-scene (known technically as a Carpenters' scene) when your play requires a complicated view to be arranged behind it' (1860, *Cornhill Magazine*). Carpenter's scenes were often *knockabout* or otherwise *comic*.

carpet cut   A descriptive term for a narrow opening in the stage which stretches almost the entire width of the *proscenium* opening behind the curtain. It is used to trap the edge of any *stagecloth*, to prevent the actor from tripping.

carriages   An abbreviation of the phrase 'carriages at (nine o'clock)', *carriages* is a traditional way of referring to the time a *show* ends, dating from C18, based on the time it would be necessary to order one's carriage for the return home . . . or elsewhere.

carriage-and-frame system   Also known as *chariot-and-pole system*. A system for changing the *scenery wings*, devised by the Italian architect, Giacomo Torelli (1606-78), and more common in Europe than in Britain. A series of paired *wing-pieces* are suspended in frames which can be moved on and off the stage on wheeled carriages. Each pair is designed so that as one wing-piece is pulled off by a system of ropes, its partner can be drawn on. Through a shared shaft, the system allows for all the paired pieces in both wings to be moved in unison if so desired.

carrying the book   A phrase meaning to be in the early stages of *rehearsal* when the play is 'on its feet' but the actors still have their *texts* in hand. It is less frequently found in the form *carrying the script*.

cast   As a noun signifying the act of throwing, literal or metaphorical (the latter as in 'a throw or stroke of chance' [ante 1300, OED]), *cast* is long established in English usage. As 'the assignment of parts in a play to actors' or 'the set of actors to whom the parts in a play are assigned', the word is first attested in use in OED in 1631: 'Whimzies: or a new Cast of Characters'. However, none of the earlier meanings listed suggests a clear derivation, though an angling root – as in the cast of a line or net for a suitable catch – is feasible. A verb, *to cast*, is also used, giving rise to the concept of *casting*, 'the art of assigning the correct role to the correct performer'. *Casting directors* of the Hollywood film industry are renowned for having dispensed with the traditional *audition, reading* or screen test for the dubious techniques of the *casting couch*. The duty of finding actors for jobs (as opposed to finding jobs for actors) has this century been taken over by *casting agents*. See also *mixed casting*.

cat-walk   Originally a nautical term, *cat-walk* has been borrowed
by many industries to describe 'a narrow footway along a bridge
amongst machinery or equipment'. In theatre it signifies the *bridge*
above the stage from which *lights* and *scenery* are handled. However, its most common general usage since the Second World
War is for the narrow walkway projecting into the audience on
which models parade in fashion shows. This transfer of meaning
is not entirely logical and one suspects that the word has been
borrowed more for the appropriateness of its imagery than for
precise physical similarities.

catch/catchphrase   Musically, a *catch* was a kind of round for
three or more voices: 'like a singing catch, some are beginning
when others are ending' (1601, OED). *Catch-clubs* were popular
amateur singing and drinking schools in lC18: '[he] was a member
of a catch-club' (1807, OED). From this the term *catchy* is derived
for a song with an insidiously memorable tune, according to Partridge from about 1880. A further OED definition seems to be
related: 'something intended to catch the attention, the popular
fancy or demand', giving rise to *catchphrase* as a name for the
ephemeral phrases of *stand-up comics* in *music hall*, phrases which
were used as a personal signature and which gained even greater
circulation with the advent of radio and television. Few catch-
phrases outlast their own decade.

catharsis   The L. form of Gk *katharsis*, literally 'a physical purging – e.g. a laxative' – from Gk *kathairō*, 'cleanse'. Aristotle first
uses the word theatrically in his treatise on *tragedy*, *The Poetics*
(*c*.330 BC), in an almost spiritual sense, far removed from its
literal meaning: tragedy works on the audience 'by means of pity
and fear bringing about the purging of such emotions' – *catharsis*.
Geilgud (p.113) explains catharsis well when discussing a wartime
production of *King Lear* directed by Granville Barker:

> When people used to come round I would say: "How can
> you stand seeing so agonising a play when such terrible things
> are going on in the world?" and they would answer that it
> gave them a kind of courage. It was catharsis; you felt at the
> end of the play that the old man had learnt something from
> all the ghastly things that had happened to him, and the glory
> of the play and its magnificent poetry took you out of your-
> self.

The word now has the widespread sense '(an outlet for) the release
of intense emotion' in a variety of contexts.

cauldron trap   Named after the famous witches' cauldron in the
opening scene of *Macbeth*, this is one of the simplest of *traps*, a
covered, *upstage* opening worked by counterweights, through

which objects or people can be raised onto or lowered from the *stage*.

ceiling-cloth   A piece of canvas which was stretched over the top of a *box set* and *battened* down so that, like a normal room, it was completely enclosed.

cellar   From AF *celer*, from OF *célier*, from L *cellarium*, 'a store-house'. This is the area below the *stage*, which can be used for storage, the operation of stage machinery and equipment, and for access up onto the stage through *traps*. Now generally known as the 'sub-stage'.

censor   From L. *censor*, 'a Roman government official charged with compiling the census and supervising property, taxation and civil morality'. The latter of these powers led to the theatrical usage. After centuries of *ad hoc* control of the content of English dramatic performances, the Licensing Act of 1737 invested clear powers in the office of the Lord Chamberlain to censor theatrical shows – that is, 'to prevent publication or performance of any text the government deemed unfit for public consumption for whatever reason'. Defending 'civil morality' is easily confused by politicians with protecting the political interests of the government of the day by stifling dissent, as was the intent of the Act. *Censorship* – (the suffix -*ship* denoting status, office, skill and/or honour) – was the province of the Lord Chamberlain from 1737 until the Theatres Act of 1968, which abolished pre-production censorship of texts in favour of the right to prosecute *after* production, thereby replacing overt censorship by a covert brand. Greater linguistic and sexual freedom of expression ensued after the act, but most establishment taboos remained intact.

centre¹   A stage direction (from OF *centre* or from L. *centrum*, 'a mid-point', from Gk *kentron*, 'a sharp point'.) 'Any position along or around an imaginary line (the centre line) drawn upstage to downstage through the centre of a proscenium arch stage'. Often abbreviated to *C* in texts: 'Down C. is [sic] a sturdy dining table and three chairs...' (1956, Osborne, *Look Back in Anger*). Obviously, a position *centre stage* makes a performance the focus of an audience's attention, and it is in this sense that the phrase has entered into common parlance for any social event which places its *protagonist in the limelight*: 'Alan Alda holds the centre of the stage as a wincing, wimpish writer' (*The Stage*, 23 April 1992).

centre²   As a verb, *to centre oneself*, or sometimes merely *to centre*, is an actor's term, by no means universally used and still regarded by some as *avant-garde* and pretentious, for finding a point of physical or emotional *balance*. To do this is *to find one's centre*: 'John Sessions, by far the most easily embarrassed student, would

hide in the nearest coffee bar until we had all "found our centres" '
(Branagh, 59). When this is done, an actor is said to be *centred*:
'The ground opens up and the air seems to cut before you. You
are centred inside yourself and the words have taken you right
there' (Berkoff, 37).

chairman   The role of *chairman* in a *music hall* was similar to that
of *compère* in modern *variety*: that is, he acted as *master of ceremonies*, introducing the acts and, with the use of a gavel, ensuring
that the audience kept order. The function of *concert chairman*
still exists in northern working men's clubs.

channel   The term for a single electric circuit used in a lighting
or sound control system. ME, from OF *chanel*, 'waterway', the
term was transferred to electronics in eC20 from earlier technical
usages in biology etc. as 'a tubular passage used for conduction
(usually of fluids)'; this sense is found in OED in mC17.

character   The word seems to have entered English both from
OF *caractère* and directly from its root, Gk *kharactēr*, 'an instrument for marking and engraving; an impress or brand stamp'. It
was used in this literal sense in eC14, later also coming to mean
'a graphic symbol (as used in writing or printing' (C15), 'a distinctive feature or symbol of any kind' (C16) and 'the essential nature
of any thing' (lC17). Its use in relation to human beings was
initially only as an indicator of external, physical appearance: 'I
will believe thou hast a mind that suits/With this thy faire and
outward character' (1601, Shakespeare, *Twelfth Night*, I.ii). Its
use as 'the sum of the qualities which constitute an individual' is
a mC17 development. The modern literary and theatrical sense
of 'an individual created in a fictitious work' is not attested in
OED until mC18: 'Whatever characters any...have for the jest-
sake personated...are now thrown off' (1749, Fielding, *Tom
Jones*). 'A part played by an actor' is a development of this. If an
actor impersonates effectively, he is said to be *in character*, a phrase
found in general usage in lC18: 'That would be in character, I
should think' (1777, Sheridan, *School for Scandal*, III.i). A further
sense of 'an impudent or eccentric person' developed in m-lC18
– 'A very impudent fellow this! but he's a character and I'll
humour him' (1733, Goldsmith, *She Stoops to Conquer*, II.i). This
led to the term *character actor* in C19 for a performer specialising
in the playing of such quirkily-individual *parts*: '[Sir Herbert
Tree was] famous as an enthusiastic ladies' man as well as a superb
character-actor' (Gielgud, 100). Another well-known term for a
stereotype, a *stock character*, also derives from C19 theatre.

   Characterisation as the art of creation of character (of either the
dramatist or actor) – 'There is a wealth of characterisation in all

the smaller roles' (*The Stage*, 23 April 1992) – is a C19 term: 'A force of characterization worthy of the genius of Shakespeare' (1866, Felton, *Greece, Ancient and Modern*).

checks   *Sound checks* and *lighting checks* refer to the tests performed by the relevant technical members of a *crew* to ensure that such things as lighting *presets* and *sound levels* are in order during later rehearsals (e.g. *the tech.*) or immediately prior to a show. Originally from the chess sense, 'to threaten one's opponent's king', it has come to mean 'to test a situation carefully', especially when skilled technical expertise is involved.

Chekhovian   Of, pertaining to, or influenced by the works of Anton Pavlovich Chekhov (1860-1904). Primarily, the word conjures up a bitter-sweet, *tragi-comic* or elegiac tone, and suggests a *dialogue* rich in *subtext*, spoken by characters created with subtle and detailed observation. It is worth noting, however, that Chekhov himself tended to emphasise the comedy and optimism in his plays when discussing them. For further details of theatrical surnames used adjectivally see *Beckettian, Shakespearean* and *Wagnerian*.

children's theatre   With the exception of companies of performing choristers in the C16, children's theatre companies are very much a C20 development. Largely *amateur*, such theatres have flourished throughout Europe with notable examples being Chancerel's Théatre de l'Oncle Sébastien in pre-war France, the National Youth Theatre in Great Britain and a number of national youth theatres in the erstwhile East European communist bloc. The term is also occasionally used for *theatre-in-education*.

chips/chippie   ' "Chippies" were busy banging away, taking out battens which had been fastened to the floor' (Barkworth, 239). A common name for a theatre *carpenter*, *chippie* is an affectionate development from *chip*, 'a piece of wood split off from a larger timber; a shaving'. According to Partridge, the proverb 'a carpenter is known by his chips' was common from C17-19 and a *chips* for a carpenter was current, especially in the army and navy, from around 1770. It seems possible that the theatrical usage came along the *nautical* route.

choreography   'The arranging and designing of a ballet or any other dance for performance'. This is a modern coining from Gk *khoreia* 'choral dancing to music' (see *chorus*) + *-graphy*, from *graphia*, 'writing'. It was used initially, as the etymology suggests, with the precise sense of 'the written notation of dance': 'Choreography is an art developed about two hundred years ago to delineate the figures and steps of dance' (1789, Burney, *A general history of music*). The noun is used theatrically in this literal sense, the province of a *choreographer* – although until C20, *choreograph* was also preferred as a term for the practitioner. The verb *to choreograph* has come by extension to be used for any piece of physical *stage business* which requires fine tuning and timing to work slickly: 'So we emphasised and almost choreographed the reactions as extra huge' (Berkoff, 122). Like *to orchestrate* and *to stage manage*, it has entered everyday speech, perhaps through journalese, meaning 'to organise a group activity with precise attention to detail'.

chorus   The original *choruses* – from Gk *khoros* – were bands of dancers and singers who performed in religious and dramatic festivals in Ancient Greece; the word also could denote the songs they sang. As interested spectators, the chorus sympathised with and commented upon the actions of the characters. (See *dithyramb*). This usage was taken up in England where the play *Gorbaduc* (1575, Norton and Sackville) boasts a chorus of 'foure auncient and sage men of Brittaine', though the singing and dancing were omitted. The English chorus was rapidly reduced to one actor, as in Marlowe's *Faustus* (1590), for reasons of either economy or artistic preference.

Another C16 use of the word which persisted is as the refrain or burden of a song as in Jonson's *Cynthia's Revels* (1599): 'Chorus. Good Mercury defend us.' The sense of 'a Company of Singers and Dancers, a Quire' (1656, Blount) seems to have been introduced from mC17. The word can still be seen used in this sense in the popular 1970s' Broadway *musical*, *A Chorus Line*. It is not until almost a century later that the additional generic meaning of 'a musical composition' is encountered: 'Would not the words "Tell it out among the heathen that the Lord is King", be sufficient for our Chorus?' (1744, Handel, letter).

Figurative uses of the word in the context of any group of people expressing a common idea, (e.g. the play title, *A Chorus of Disapproval*, 1985, Ayckbourn) or for a commentary on an event in real life have abounded since the first English adoption of the word: 'But yours is pity, a noble chorus to my wretched story' (1634, Massinger, *Very Woman*).

circle   From OF *cercle*, from L. *circulus*, a diminutive of *circus*, 'a ring'. Its theatrical meaning, 'a curved tier of rows of seats', can probably be traced back to L. *circus*, (see below), and was introduced from France (from F. *cirque*) when Henry Holland imported the idea of the horseshoe *auditorium* with cantilevered circles from Parisian theatre design in the rebuilding of Covent Garden and the new Theatre Royal, Drury Lane (both 1794). The 'three circles of boxes' at the former did not meet with universal approval: 'to the people in the pit, those rows of boxes full of company, and having no apparent support, are apt to give an unpleasant sensation' (Ackermann, *The Microcosm of London*). As with most theatrical seating arrangements, differences of status were observed: a *dress circle* is stipulated in the plans for Drury Lane, where the circle above is designated the 'two shilling gallery' and the *upper circle* (or the *gods*) with its precarious situation and vertiginous views is the 'one shilling gallery'.

circuit A group of theatres, usually regionally linked, revisited on a regular basis by *touring companies*, has been known as a *circuit* since C19 as is attested in *The Century Dictionary* (1889). In the case of *variety* and *music hall*, circuits were under the same management, which organised a constant turnover of *artists* and *acts*. The system of theatre circuits began in practice in the C18, and ensured that regional theatres, working wholly or partly as *receiving houses*, could work symbiotically with touring companies for their own and the audiences' benefit. *Doing the circuits*, as variety artists did, often worked similarly, as large managements could ensure protracted periods of work for acts on a touring *bill*. (See *big time*.)

circus The L. *circus*, from Gk *kirkos*, 'a ring or circle' was 'a large building, generally oblong or oval, surrounded with rising tiers of seats, for the exhibition of public spectacles, horse or chariot races or the like' (OED). The most celebrated example in Rome was the Circus Maxima. The modern circus, a circular *arena* which can be permanent but which is more commonly a portable *auditorium* consisting of wooden seating units erected in a large marquee (the 'big top'), dates back to the end of C18. (See also *ring*.) At this time, by a transference of meaning, the word also came to signify the entertainments which took place in the auditorium, namely *variety shows* made up of *clowning*, *acrobatic*, equestrian and other *animal acts*, which also thrived in later *music halls* as *dog dramas*, *equestrian dramas* and the like. As happened with a number of other performance genres which involve a confusion of activity, (e.g. *farce*), *circus* took on an additional, pejorative sense of 'a noisy institution, place, scene, assemblage or group of persons' (Partridge), which in this case appears to be of American origin, introduced into England around 1895.

clap From ME *clappan*, from OE *clappian*, from an Old Teutonic root meaning 'to make a clap or explosive sound'. This word describing the physical action which produces *applause* appears to have become obsolete in Old English but to have re-entered the language from Scandinavia in C14, possibly from Old Norse: all the Scandinavian languages exhibit the exactly same range of

meanings as English: 'Whan this Maister . . . Saughit was tyme he
clapte the dogs . . . keptup a chorus of mingled whining and barking' (1386, Chaucer, *The Franklyn's Tale*). Common as a sign of
approval in all public assemblies, it has given rise to the notorious
and dreaded *slow hand clap*, whose origins as a sign of *dis*approval
are uncertain. (Compare *applause*, the *bird*.)

classic/classics   The *Classics* was a term applied initially in C18
to the body of literature of Ancient Greece and Rome: *Dissertation
on reading the Classics* (1711, H. Felton, [title]). It was used by
Pope in 1736 to refer to any writer of accepted excellence; from
this sense its use developed in theatre for those standard works
in the *repertoire* which had gained an academic seal of approval:
'ballet's most popular classic [Swan Lake]' (*The Stage*, 28 March
1991). *Classic* or *classical* status is being constantly updated so
that, just as Ibsen and Chekhov were assimilated in the eC20, so
writers of the 1950s and 1960s such as Beckett, Osborne, Pinter
and Orton have been accorded such status in record time, possibly
by dint of their frequent appearances on school syllabuses. Like
all superlatives, it has been open to dilution through overuse.
Legit theatre, when it concentrates on the classics, as is the case,
say with the RSC, is often referred to as the *classical theatre* (compare *classical music*). From Fr. *classique*, from L. *classicus*, 'of the
first order, of acknowledged excellence'.

climax   'I am building up to the grand climax and this scene leads
stage by stage to the most inexorable and dramatic series of
climaxes; to an almost orgasmic conclusion' (Berkoff, 145). Gk
klimac developed from common-or-garden 'ladder' into a rhetorical figure of speech 'in which a number of propositions or ideas
are set forth so as to form a series in which each rises above the
preceding in force or effectiveness of expression' (OED). This was
also its original sense in English, as Puttenham makes clear in
English Poesie (1589): '[It] may as well be called the clyming
figure, for Climax is as much as to say a ladder.'
   Theatrically and in common usage, *climax* has come to signify
the dramatic conclusion of a process, series of events or plot; its
pinnacle. However, its most common everyday use (also alluded
to in the attestation above) is as a synonym for orgasm. English
senses of 'completion' or 'zenith' date from lC18: 'In the accom-
plishment of this, they frequently reach the climax of absurdity'
(1789).

cloak-and-dagger play   Sometimes also known as *cloak-and-sword
play*; 'Mr C——, a most solemn and mysterious tragedian of the
cloak-and-dagger school' (1860, Vandenhoff, *Dramatic Reminiscences*). *Capa y espada* plays (a sub-division of the C17 Spanish

genre, comedias de ingenio) were romantic pieces with much disguise, derring-do and duelling. Examples of the genre by authors such as Lope de Vega and Tirso de Molina had some influence on British dramatists in the C19. The English translation *cloak-and-dagger* passed into general use for intrigue and *Machiavellian* plotting in any walk of life, carrying with it *melodramatic* overtones which reflect its theatrical origins.

closet drama   In this context, *closet* (from OF *clos*, from the stem of L. *clore*, from *claudere*, 'to close or shut') refers to 'a small, private room, often used for meetings and interviews', a sense it has had since C14. Its other, less grand senses of 'cupboard, storage recess', and its common later use in the term *water closet* (which now gives *closet drama* a comic ring), are later developments from C17. Plays which fall into the category of closet drama are those intended for private reading rather than public *production*. The genre starts with Seneca and includes many plays written by poets, especially in C19. There is something odd about the concept of private, unacted plays. Currently, closet drama is an obsolete *genre*, though who knows what is happening behind closed doors? Closet, used in this sense, is found most commonly in the term 'closet homosexual': one who has not yet 'come out' (of the closet).

cloth   A piece of material, usually *canvas*, hung from the *flies* or stretched across the rear of the *stage* in the position of a *cyclorama*. Frequently, a *cloth* would be painted. Also known as *drops* (see *backdrop*), cloths are rarely found in modern theatres. Better known in the compound *backcloth*, which suggests a possible *nautical* origin, the word has other specific variations: e.g. *ceiling-cloth*, *cut-cloth*, *sky-cloth*.

clown   'Hats off to Pepe the Clown after he was voted best white-faced clown for the second time at the World Clown Convention in Bognor Regis' (*The Stage*, 28 March 1991). In many N. European languages, there is a word originally meaning 'a lump or clod of earth, a clot etc.', which has also been transferred to mean 'a clumsy, boorish fellow' and variants of that – for example, Dutch *kleun* and Swedish dialect *klunn(s)*. There is no evidence of such a word in OE: *clown* appears to enter English only in mC16 and only with the second sense of the word, referring specifically to someone who lives in the country: 'To brag upon his pipe the clowne begoon...And then to blow the rustick did assay' (1567, OED). The sense of 'professional *fool* or *jester*' is first attributed at the end of that century: 'The roynish Clown, at whom so oft Your Grace was wont to laugh' (1600, Shakespeare, *As You Like It*, II.ii). At this time too the word means a comic

actor: 'Tarlton [who played Touchstone, the character referred
to in the Shakespeare quotation above] clown'd it in a very pleasant vaine Vpon the Stage' according to the poet Rowlands (1600),
who also refers to 'Pope the Clowne'.

   A later development of the word is for the comic performer
elaborated in *pantomime* and *harlequinade* in lC17 who, with his
distinctive make-ups and traditional costumes and mannered, farcical *routines*, grew out of characters in the *commedia dell'arte*.
Joseph Grimaldi, (1778-1837), the clown Joey, is generally credited with having had the greatest influence on the development
of the clown's art. This *genre* of *clowning* is currently very much
in vogue, as are other 'new' *circus* skills. The circus and *children's
entertainments* are the area to which the traditional clown is now
marginalised, although the term is used approvingly of a range
of comic performers: 'I think of him [Benny Hill] is the last of
the great clowns rather than as a comedian' (Harold Berens, *The
Stage*, 23 March 1992). The verbs *to clown about, around* and a
number of variants have, interestingly, succeeded in taking the
word back to its first sense in English.

coach   A specialist teacher, usually privately employed and able
to give individual training in areas of performance skills, such as
voice and *movement*. From Fr. *coche*, from Magyar *kocsi*, itself an
adjective formed from the placename Kocs in Hungary, where
state coaches were built. The first uses of *coach* in English in
mC16 were for privately-owned, horse-drawn carriages and it is
this sense of being privately steered, in relative comfort, from
point A to point B of knowledge that is reflected in the English
development of the word – an eC19 university coining for 'private
tutor', (frequently applied to sport from m-lC19): 'Besides the
regular college tutor, I secured the assistance of what, in the slang
of the day, we irreverently termed "a coach"' (1850, Smedley,
Frank Fairlegh).

coarse acting   A phrase coined by the humorist Michael Green
in his book on *amateur* theatre, *The Art of Coarse Acting* (1964).
Now often used synonymously with all bad acting, essentially
coarse acting is a style which includes all of the most egotistical
and least competent elements of the performer's craft: 'I would
define a Coarse Actor as one who can remember the lines but not
the order in which they come. It is, perhaps, not an entirely
satisfactory definition, and a close friend whom I regard as easily
the most desperately bad amateur actor in West Bromwich
suggests that a Coarse Actor is one who can remember the pauses
but not the lines' (op. cit., 16).

collaboration   From L. *collaborare*, 'to work together', this is a term usually applied to the joint creation of a literary text, borrowed directly from Fr. in mC19, where *collaboration* was in vogue: 'It is plain that collaboration was not less . . . than it now is in France' (1860, Reade, *The Eighth Commandment*). In a sense, all performing artists might be said to be involved in collaboration if not *collective creation* – they are *collaborators*: 'the actor really becomes a collaborator with the author – no longer merely an interpreter but a creator' (Berkoff, 104). Many Elizabethan and Jacobean plays were collaborations, the most famous pairing being that of Beaumont with Fletcher: the latter is also widely believed to have had the honour of collaborating with Shakespeare.

collective creation   The joint creation of a piece of theatre from inception to performance: a *collaboration*. Like 'co-operative', *collective* is a C19 socialist term – 'individual exchange must . . . give place to collective bargaining' (1891, Beatrice Webb, *Co-operative Movement*) – whose left-wing theatrical use was further reinforced by the collective industrial and agricultural projects of the early Soviet Union (and is also found in the *theatre collectives* of mC20). Often, collectively created pieces are devised through improvisation and this method of working, whilst having roots in many international, historical theatre traditions including the *commedia dell'arte*, is one of the hallmarks of m-lC20 *alternative* theatre.

Columbine   A character developed from one of the maid-servants of the *commedia dell'arte*, who made her English début in the earliest *Harlequinades*, from whence she entered *pantomime*. In D'Urfey's *English Stage Italianised* (1727) there is a reference to '*Colombine*, a coquet, in love with every body'; however, more usually she is the daughter of *Pantaloon* and the lover of *Harlequin*. Her name was borrowed from Fr. *Colombine*, ultimately from It. *colombino*, 'dove-like'.

come down, to   A *show comes down*, or ends, when the *curtain* comes down – the opposite of the show starting, or *going up*. This an example of argot which has not as yet gained widespread usage outside the theatre.

comedy   A generic word which could possibly be applied to half the world's known plays. From OF *comédie*, from L. *comedia*, from Gk *kōmōidia*. The latter is in turn derived from *kōmōidos*, 'a comedian/writer of comedy', a compound formed either from *kōmos*, 'a revel' or its likely source, *kōm?*, 'a village', + *aoidos*, 'a singer'. In other words, the original *comedian* was either 'a singer at the revels' or 'a village singer', *singer* also carrying with it the connotations of 'poet, maker'. As with *tragedy*, the etymology alludes to the roots of the genre in pre-Athenian settlements of C6BC and earlier.

The English development of the word is as follows: In C14 it signified 'a narrative poem with an upbeat ending' as in Dante's *Commedia*, written, as he himself commented, 'in the vulgar tongue which women and children speak'. All dramatic usages appear to date from C15-C16. In the eC16, it is attested with reference to *mystery plays* with positive endings; (1538) Bale: 'A brefe comedy or enterlude concernynge the temptacyon of our lorde and sauer Jesus Christ by Sathan in the desart'. With the regrowth in interest in classical plays, it was used to refer to the comedies of the classical era: 'Andria, the first Comoedie of Terence in English' (1588, M. Kyffin), and, as such, arrived with all the associations from that period – it was a catch-all term which included *high* and the *low comic* styles, the *satiric comedy* of Aristophanes, the *comedy of manners* of Menander, and later Plautus and Terence etc. The term is thus applied to indigenous comic writing: 'Our Comedie or Enterlude which we intende to play is named Royster Doyster in deede' (1553, Udall, *Ralph Royster Doyster*, Prologue). The term is also attested very occasionally as 'play' or even 'theatre' in a wider sense, probably in imitation of Fr. *comédie*.

It was not long after this that the word began to be used (and defined) generically: 'The Comedy is an imitation of the common errors of our life' (1581, Sidney, *Apology for Poetry*). Following a pattern noted repeatedly elsewhere, (see *drama*, *farce*, *tragedy*), it soon began to be applied to everyday situations: 'They... can relate straunge and almost incredible comedies of his monstrous disposition' (1592, Harvey, *Fovre Letters*).

A variety of comic sub-genres have flourished: in these cases, it is usual to find *comedy* preceded by an adjective – as in *black comedy*, *low comedy*, *romantic comedy* (see under the appropriate adjective) – or to find it in constructions such as *comedy of character*, *comedy of manners* etc.

comedian   The most common current usage of the term – for 'a comic performer, a teller of gags', as in *stand-up comedian*, is a C19 development, probably concurrent with the rise of *music hall* and possibly an abbreviation of *low comedian*, as in this example: 'Richard Tarlton... was most famous as, what we now call, a low comedian' (1842, Collier, in Armin, *Nest of Ninnies*). However, Sidney, in *Apology for Poetry*, 1581, uses the term for 'a writer of comedies' and it is attested in its more general earlier sense of 'comic actor' by 1601: 'Are you a Comedian?' (Shakespeare, *Twelfth Night*, I.v). Probably influenced by Fr. *comédien*, it was also used as a synonym for *player*, *actor* in the widest sense until well into C18.

comédienne   '[Penelope Keith] is a fine comédienne and a remarkably truthful actress' (Barkworth, 63). This term has been used for 'a comedy actress' since C18. Why French terms have stuck for female performers and roles – compare *confidante*, *ingénue*, *soubrette* – and not for male ones is a question open to dispute, but it may be that the employment of a French term was considered to add a veneer of sophistication to what might otherwise have been considered a rather unfeminine, or *risqué role*.

comic   Adjectivally, *comic*, from Fr. *comique*, from L. *comicus*, has always been preferred to what might be considered a more natural English construction, *comedic*. It is first attested in OED in C14, but appears to have become current in C16, with the rise of public theatres, with the sense of 'of or pertaining to comedy': 'For comick verse still Plautus peerelesse was' (1576, OED). Interestingly, unlike many other major theatrical adjectives, it is not attested in general usage until C18, meaning 'laughable, ludicrous': 'Among the principal of comic calamities, may be reckoned the pain which author...feels at the onset of a furious critick' (1751, Johnson, *The Rambler*). This slow adoption can possibly be accounted for by the development of *comical*.

Theatrically, *comic* is found in a variety of phrases, notably *comic relief*, *comic business* and *comic interlude*.

Used as a noun, it is found historically with the now obsolete senses of 'writer of comedy' (1581) and 'actor of comedy': 'Acting a comicks part upon the stage' (1619, Hutton, *Follies Anatomie*). However, neither of these two terms gained widespread currency, and its most frequent modern usage is as *comedian* – 'the 17-stone comic has a great live act' (*The Stage*, 21 March 1991) – from which sense a more general usage as 'an amusing person' has developed.

comical   The term developed as a concurrent alternative to *comic*, carrying with it all the major adjectival senses outlined above. However, it was adopted earlier into general usage with the sense of 'suitable for comic treatment, laughable, mirth-provoking': 'That it is too light for a Divine, too Comical a subject to speak of Love-Symptoms' (1621, Burton, *Anatomie of Melancholie*). Its frequent use as a simple synonym for 'funny, amusing', may account for the late adoption of 'comic' into general usage.

command performances   Such performances, the result of a direct request or order from a monarch or head of state, reflect a form of patronage which goes back at least to Roman times and which, in English theatrical history, is most commonly associated with Elizabeth I (who is reputed to have commissioned Shakespeare's *Merry Wives of Windsor*), and James I, who by his patronage of Shakespeare's company, The King's Men, justified at least one half of the French king Henri IV's phrase for him, 'the wisest fool in Christendom'. Whilst the practice is ancient, the term would appear to date from C19. In Britain, such events are now limited to an annual Royal Variety Performance and to occasional film *premières*.

commedia dell'arte 'It is very deliberate and performed in a *commedia dell'arte* style...' (Berkoff, 23). A direct borrowing from It., the phrase is now used in such a widespread way in theatre circles that it can be considered to have been naturalised. It has gained additional currency in lC20 in response to a growing dissatisfaction with *naturalistic* theatre. It derives from a *comic genre* developed in Italy in C16, devised largely through improvisation: *dell'arte* means literally 'of the profession', denoting the status of its performers and distinguishing it from *commedia erudita*, the contemporary term for written drama. In this sense, it can be seen, quite literally, as the precursor of *actor's theatre*. Current usage in England is to refer either to the historical tradition or a style of playing which draws on it. For details of aspects of this style, see *pantomime, Harlequin, Pantaloon, Punch, zanni.*

commercial/commercial theatre 'I had decided not to go with *Rebecca* and I told them why: "It's a commercial play, very good for peace-time, but I don't think it's the right thing to do now"' (Geilgud, 107). From L. prefix *com-*, 'with, together' + L. *merx, mercis,* 'merchandise', commerce is found as 'business, trade' from lC16, although *commercial* is not found until a century later. An interesting shift of meaning occurs in mC19, with the coining of the often derogatory term *commercialism,* for 'the commercial spirit' (OED): 'Young men in England with their prurience, their effeminacy and their quill-driving commercialism' (1849, *Fraser's Magazine*). This lent an alternative sense to 'commercial': as well as 'related to trade' it began to be used also as 'motivated by commercialism': thus, *commercial theatre* can be a theatre which takes account of commercial (*box office*) considerations and the audience appeal of plays (as in the Geilgud attestation above), or it can be a theatre motivated solely by the desire for profit, with scant regard for artistic merit. The tension between these two attitudes, the latter often the enemy of the *experimental* and *avant-garde,* is at the heart of current disputes about the health of the *West End* and commercial, unsubsidised theatre in general.

communion 'As I turned to face [the audience], my heart rose to embrace this communion as to the miraculously soft warmth of a rapturous first night of love' (Olivier, 148). *Communion* is a term used to describe a particularly intense relationship either between the actors on stage or between them and the audience. It is based on the spiritual unity integral to the ceremony of partaking of Christ's flesh and blood in the form of consecrated bread and wine, the centrepiece of the Christian mass, in which sense *communion* has been used in English since C14. The quasi-mystical experience which results for some people from this *ritual* was described by *Stanislavski* in *An Actor Prepares*: 'To give or receive from an object something, even briefly, constitutes a moment of spiritual intercourse... Even more difficult is mutual communion with a collective object; in other words, with the public.' Many find this rather grandiose as a concept and would prefer the simpler term 'communication'.

community theatre   This phrase which can mean 'practically all things to all people' *(Bloomsbury Theatre Guide)* is generally taken to suggest a form of socially and politically committed theatre, often *avant-garde* and *agit-prop* in nature, with its focus of attention on a particular audience, a *community*, not necessarily geographically defined, as terms such as *the gay community* illustrate. This is a notion of community which is traditionally to the left and of some influence in Britain at the time the term came into vogue, the late 1950s and early 1960s.

company   ME, from OF *compaignie*, from Rom. *compania*. The original Romanic word *compania – com-*, the prefix meaning 'with, together, jointly', + *panto* from *panis*, 'bread' – suggests the sociable fellowship that is present in the earliest, C13 English usages of the word and still exists to the present day. However, the word as it had developed before its arrival in English included 'a number of individuals assembled or associated together' in ways which also included a working relationship: a retinue or band of retainers could be referred as a *company*. The theatrical sense – 'a group of actors with their (business and technical) associates' – is found early; 'Amonge the saide lordes and the qweene was in order Joannes and his companye, the minstrills if musick, etc.' (1503, Leland, *De rebus Brittanicis collectanea*). The term can also be used adjectivally in a variety of ways, from the self-explanatory *company manager* to more abstract concepts such as *company style*, 'the particular style of performance favoured by a given company': 'Now we have... a coterie of yes-men directors who work with the company style' (Berkoff, 72).

Any group of actors assembled for a production can be referred to as a 'company' and companies vary widely in organisational structure and function. There are *touring companies* which visit *receiving houses* or which set up in an impromptu fashion at *fringe venues*: these have always been a major feature of the British scene, but their number increased with the post-war demise of local *repertory companies*. *Resident companies*, based in a single theatre, are now a luxury which many theatres cannot afford or if they can, only on a temporary basis, taking actors on one *season* at a time.

compère   Literally, in French, 'godfather' from the Romanic *compater*, 'one who stands with or alongside the father'. The *compère* is the **master of ceremonies** at a *variety show* who, like the *concert secretary* at a working men's club or the *chairman* of the *music hall*, is responsible for introducing the *acts* and, in the worst circumstances, keeping order. Its adoption in this context is eC20: 'The genial Davy Burnaby seems to be quite content as a cabaret compère. He has got together a company for the underground grill of the Piccadilly' (1928, *Weekly Dispatch*).

comps   An abbreviation of *complimentary tickets* which theatres have at their disposal to hand out free to a range of VIPs, which usually means anyone who can enhance *box-office* takings: celebrities, *critics* and *reviewers*, a *claque*, or anyone else who can contribute to the theatre's prestige or bank balance. 'RADA was often given complimentary seats for struggling shows' (Branagh, 64). *Comps.* are sometimes also available to the cast of a show or to other theatre staff as a perk of the job. From *compliment*, 'an expression of praise, a formal greeting', from It. *complimento*. OED dates the use of the term to lC19.

composite setting   Formerly called a *multiple setting* and known in the United States as *simultaneous-scene setting*, a *composite set* is one on which several locations are represented on stage at the same time. The technique dates back at least to Medieval times, though the term is C20. From L. *compositus*, the past participle of *componere*, 'to place together'.

concert   When first adopted into English at the beginning of C17, *concert* was confused (as would remain the case until well into the C18) with the earlier word *consort*, meaning, as a verb, 'to bring together, keep company, or agree or harmonize (with)'. In fact, its adoption is from Fr. *concert*, from It. *concerto*, from It. *concertare*, 'to harmonize', whose origins are uncertain. A variety of specific meanings related to harmony, musical and otherwise, or more generally to sound, have given way to the predominant modern meaning of 'a public musical entertainment', although, as in the attestation above, *musical* is frequently dropped from the definition. It is first cited in OED in 1689: 'The Concerts of Musick that were held in Bow-street and in York-Buildings, are now joyn'd together' *(London Gazette)*.

It gave rise in eC20 to *concert party* for a seasonal seaside light

entertainment, often involving *speciality acts*, *pierrots* etc.; this
style was further developed by *ENSA* in World War II: 'At about
the same time – Christmas 1942 – I went with a concert party
company... to Gibraltar' (Geilgud, 68).

confidant(e)   Characters to whom this label is appropriate are,
theatrically, those who are entrusted with the knowledge of the
hero or *heroine*'s private affairs, the term having been in common
usage for 'a bosom friend' in lC17-C18. They are often two-dimensional characters, being a handy means for an unskilful *dramatist*
to convey large amounts of expository detail without the use of
the more subtle techniques of his craft. The word is structurally
interesting in that, although the spelling of Fr. *confident* has been
anglicised, it is still permissible to form a feminine version of the
word by adding a final -*e*. This is probably due to the fact that
usage of the feminine version of the word predominated and by
spelling it with an *a* and keeping a final -*e*, something like the
French pronunciation could be presented graphically and typo-
graphically. See *comédienne*, for a further example of this continuation of French influence. (Ultimately, from L. *confidere*, 'to
trust'.)

conjuring (act)   Our current, residual sense of *conjuring*, a word
which has been used in English since C13, reflects our cultural
development. It originally had a wide range of meanings centred
around the L. root, *conjurare*, 'to publically swear an oath',
including appealing to the antiquated virtue, honour. 'The art of
performing entertaining magic tricks based on legerdemain,
juggling, prestidigitation and the like' (OED) comes from a meaning of the word first attested around 1290: 'Manie deuelene he
coniurede [th]at huy to him wende.' Conjuring devils and spirits
has also gone out of fashion except in limited circles and it is left
to the professional entertainer to carry the word's rather reduced
meaning.

constructivism   A means of theatrical setting devised by the Russian *dramaturge*, Meyerhold (the creator of *bio-mechanics*), which
involved using a variety of materials from which multi-level, non-
representational *sets* were constructed. From Russ. *konstruk-
tivism*, from LL *constructivus*, from L. *construere*, 'to pile, build'.

convention   'Someone afterwards said that Granville-Barker
spoiled my first entrance in *Lear* by ignoring the convention that
the leading character should always come in from the centre'
(Geilgud, 110). Theatrically, a convention is a method, agreed
between writers, performers and audience, by which an element
of writing, performance or audience response which might otherwise be considered unrealistic or implausible is accepted happily.

It is an unwritten theatrical contract, *convention* having been used with this legal sense since C14. The general and literary senses are lC18 developments: 'Every convention of artificial manners was invented not to cure, but to conceal, deformity' (1790, More, *An estimate of the religion of the fashionable world*). 'The willing suspension of *disbelief*', as a result of which, at the most basic level, audiences agree to accept that an actor *is* the *character* he claims to be whilst knowing that he isn't, is the convention on which the success of most theatre depends. From ME, from OF, from L. *conventio*, from L. *convenire*, 'to assemble, agree, fit'.

coon shows/songs The term *coon*, one of racial abuse, was used as a label for black American performers of African origin from at least the eC19. It is probably an abbreviation of *racoon*, 'a nocturnal, carnivorous N. American mammal', from the American Indian language, Algonquian. Because the racoon has white rings around its eyes, it is possible that 'coon' derives from the habit of white performers *blacking up* to play *burnt-cork minstrels*; they would sing black songs in places of legitimate – i.e. white – entertainment before it was acceptable in a racist society for blacks to do so themselves. Such acts were the most popular form of entertainment in the United States from 1840-80. Black artists were gradually allowed to represent their own culture, especially after the emancipation of the slaves. Blacked-up acts remained popular in Britain until at least the 1970s, latterly through the influence of the BBC television variety programme, *The Black and White Minstrel Show*. In use in England by 1860, 'coon' was applied derogatorily on both sides of the Atlantic to any black person.

corn/corny In the theatre, *corn* is used to refer to both certain kinds of subject matter and treatment, and certain styles of performance. However, in general colloquial usage, *corny*, to which it is undoubtedly related, has the meanings outlined in this definition (1959) by a Canadian scholar, Dr F.E.L.P. Priestley (referring to its use by Canadian musicians around 1930): 'It implied old-fashioned and rural; belonging to the Corn Belt [of America] rather than to the city; also applied to jokes and humour.' The traditional association of things rural and rustic with things foolish (see *clown*, for example) and old-fashioned, is perpetuated here. This modern usage is, Beale suggests, a Second World War services' acquisition from N. America, though I feel that, if this is in fact the origin, it is equally likely to have arrived via the cinema. Theatrically, 'corn' comprehends the colloquial meanings but adds an element of gauche, self-indulgent sentimentality into the recipe: 'corny devices such as moving backwards and forwards in time or mixing fact with fantasy' (*The Stage*, 28 March 1991).

to corpse   'I'm going to do everything in my power to make you
giggle and corpse at every performance...and every time you
give way I shall bawl you out in front of the company and staff;
and if nine months of that treatment do not knock this amateurish
smear on your otherwise bright young talent out of you, then you'd
really better start brushing up on some other trade' (Noël Coward,
quoted in Olivier, 68). *Corpsing* is now used almost exclusively
for an actor dropping out of character and laughing in a totally
inappropriate place during a performance. The origins of the
phrase are debatable. Partridge has a reference which he dates to
c.1855 which confuses the issue somewhat: 'To blunder (whether
unintentionally or not), and thus confuse other actors and spoil
a scene; the blunderer is said to be "corpsed"', a definition with
which OED agrees. In the 1950s, according to Beale, *to corpse* was
also *drama school* slang for forgetting one's *lines*. All that can be
said with certainty is that the word is likely to go back at least to
eC19 and has always signified inappropriate and probably unpro-
fessional activity by an *onstage* actor. One possibility given the
etymology – from Fr. *corps* and L. *corpus*, 'the human body', in
English 'a dead body' – might connect the usage with *to die*, 'to
fail ignominiously on stage'. There may also be a connection with
the difficulty for an actor of lying utterly motionless, supposedly
dead, on stage for any length of time, a problem which reaches
epidemic proportions at the end of some *revenge tragedies*.

costume   Fr., from It. *costume*, 'custom, use, wont, fashion' etc.,
from L. *consuetudo*, 'custom'. This word is a post-Restoration
borrowing; even that arch-innovator, Jonson, refers to characters'
costume persistently as 'attires' in his commentaries on his collaborations with Inigo Jones (see *tiring-house*). In fact, the word was
borrowed by English and French in eC18 from its usage by Italian
painters for 'the guise or habit in pictorial represention': 'Not
only the Story but the Circumstances...the Habits, Arms, Manners...and the like must correspond. This is call'd observing *the
Costume*' (1715, J. Richardson, *An account of some of the statues
etc. in Italy*). It does not appear to have been used theatrically as
'the dress or "get-up" of an actor' (OED) until C19 – 'Madame
Judic changed her costume thrice' (1883, *Truth*) – by which time
it was already in use for fashionable dress.

Today, the person responsible for producing *costumes* for a
production, formerly the *wardrobe master* or *mistress* or the *dresser*
(as is still the case in some theatres), is the *costume designer*: 'The
name of the costume designer...should also be spoken about
with contempt...The costumes are an inharmonious rag-bag'
(*Plays and Players*, October 1990). Normally, actors first encounter

their costumes at a *costume fitting*: 'On that first morning I met the make-up and hair artists, and had the first of an endless series of costume fittings' (Branagh, 117).

counterweight system 'A system of lines and weights that permits the raising and lowering of heavy pieces of scenery'. *Counter-*, a prefix formed from F. *contre* and L *contra*, 'against', can denote opposition or reciprocation. In this case the formulation means that the *weights* are balancing each other. The system was used across walks of industry from lC17 – 'Lines, Pullies and Counterweights' (1693, *London Gazette*) – and was probably introduced to theatre via a *nautical* route.

couplet From OF *cople*, *cuple*, denoting a pairing, + -*et*, a suffix suggesting a diminutive, originally used for two pieces of metal hinged or riveted together, later transferred to *verse* as the term for two consecutive line-endings which rhyme: hence, by extension, to the pair of lines itself. The term is first attested in OED in Sidney's *Arcadia* (1580). Some plays, notably in the lC16 and in the post-Restoration theatre, were written entirely or almost entirely in rhyming couplets. More commonly, because of the rather pat, sing-song effect that couplets create, they were saved to point aphorisms or, especially in lC16/eC17 plays, to chime at scene-endings.

cover A descriptive *lighting* term denoting a *wash* of light which *covers* a large area of the stage. *General cover* is standard, performance-intensity lighting of consistent brightness over the whole stage.

credits A C20 term borrowed from cinema and television but now, due to the overlap between people working in the three *media* and, perhaps more significantly, the audience's greater experience of the other two media, in widespread use with reference to the entries in a theatre *programme*: 'acknowledgements of performances and contributions by actors, technicians, designers etc...' By extension, it used to refer to the list and range of a performer's work: 'McKenzie's credits, of course, extend way beyond Sondheim, not least in the musical theatre.' From the phrase *to give credit to*, meaning 'to acknowledge the contribution of', *credit* coming from Fr. *crédit*, from It. *credito* or L. *creditum*, 'belief, trust'.

crew From ME, from OF *creüe*, 'increase', the feminine past participle (as noun) of *croistre*, 'to grow', from L. *crescere*. The original meaning of the word in C15 was for 'a military reinforcement', hence the choice of a word related to growth and increase. By extension, it was applied to any force of soldiers assigned for a particular purpose. The theatrical usage has a *nautical* origin:

'a body of men manning a ship': 'Quarter-gunner, Carpenter's Crew, Steward, Cook' (1692, J. Love, *Marine's Jewel*). The term is found in a variety of phrases for a body of theatre *hands*: *stage crew, lighting crew, sound crew* etc.

crit.   'Those of you who read our stage reviews closely may have been puzzled to find John Mowat's name at the bottom of a recent crit of his show. Gremlins in the works deprived Sidney Vauncey of the credit' (*The Stage*, 21 March 1991). A *crit.* is a common way of referring to a *notice*: a newspaper *review* or criticism of a *production*.

critic   'Most nations can boast a leading light among theatre critics' (Olivier, 211). From L., from Gk *kritēs*, 'a judge', from *krinō*, 'decide'. The judicial sense of *critic* has never become established in English. All moderate-sized dictionaries move rapidly on from general senses including 'censurer', to the specific: 'judge of literary or artistic works, esp. professional reviewer of books etc.; one skilled in textual criticism' *(Concise Oxford)*. The first general usages in English are found from lC16, the specific ones following swiftly: 'Certain Critiques are used to say... That if all sciences were lost, they might bee found in Virgill' (1605, Bacon, *Of the advancement of learning*). *Aristotle's Poetics*, (C4BC), which is generally regarded as being the first great work of literary criticism, concerned itself with the nature of *tragedy*. I think it is worth making a distinction between critics who concern themselves largely with literary, i.e. textual criticism, and those who combine those skills to a greater or lesser degree with those of a journalistic reviewer of new *productions*. Since the war, the greatest exponents of this art in Britain have probably been Kenneth Tynan in *The Observer* and Harold Hobson in *The Sunday Times*. It was the latter who, in the face of a barrage of hostile remarks in the preceding week, wrote in such glowing terms about Harold Pinter's first full-length play, *The Birthday Party*, that everyone felt compelled to look again. This journalistic criticism has hung over *first nights* since the C18. Perhaps the days are gone when, on the strength of one good or bad review by an influential critic, a new *show* can make good or *bomb*, but *notices* are still highly influential in putting *bums on seats* or keeping them off, and collectively, critics have the power to make or break careers and reputations.

crooner   A singer, usually of popular, romantic *ballads*. For many who are old enough, the word immediately conjures up images of Sinatra and Crosby. Corresponding to Middle Dutch *krônen*, 'to lament, mourn loudly' and other Germanic words with senses such as 'to cause to weep', *croon* was a northern, chiefly Scottish dialect word until it was popularised in Burns' *Tam O' Shanter*

(1790): 'Whiles crooning o'er some auld Scots sonnet.' The onomatopoeic suggestions of the word were, I suspect, missed by Dickens: 'Paul sometimes crooning out a feeble accompaniment' (*Dombey and Son*, 1848), but appreciated by George Eliot: 'The cock and hens...made only crooning, subdued noises' (*Adam Bede*, 1859). *Crooner* appears to have first applied to singers in America in eC20.

cruelty, theatre of A direct translation of Fr. *théâtre de cruauté*, an umbrella term for the style of theatre suggested by Antonin Artaud in his seminal work, *Le Théatre et son Double* (1938). *Cruelty* in the lC20 theatre has existed as an influence on a wide range of writers and directors rather than as a *genre*. 'Artaud used the word "cruelty" not to invoke sadism, but to call us toward a theatre more rigorous, or even, if we could follow him that far, more pitiless to us all' (Brook, 56). Artaud was trying to create a *total theatre* in which the spoken word would lose its habitual primacy, and physical movement and gesture, visual images and sound effects, all the resources of a modern theatre would be mobilised to worm into the imagination and sub-conscious of all the participants, actors and audience alike, to strip away conventions and get at the vulnerable, primitive entities beneath.

cue 'The closing word or words of another actor's speech which serve as a signal to the actor that he himself should make an entrance or speak'. Today this can be broadened to include cues given by light changes, sound effects etc. Equally, *technical staff* are *cued* as to when to come in by *lighting cues, sound cues* etc. 'During rehearsal he was criticising an actress for being very slow with her lines in a scene they were playing together. Finally, very worked up, the actress screamed: "If you go on like that I'll throw something at you." Coward replied sweetly: "You might start with my cues"' (1968, Richards, *The Wit of Noël Coward*).

The etymology of this word is uncertain but it is one of the oldest indigenous technical terms in English theatre; it can be traced back to 1553, but was probably used in *ecclesiastical drama*: "Amen must be answered to the thanksgevyng not as to a man's q in a play." This quotation is also significant in that it is from an ecclesiastical work by Strype and not directly from the theatre. Judging by OED entries, it was in frequent use, as much other theatre imagery was, in general writings of the time. This colloquial use of the word has continued: *to take one's cue from someone* and *to come in on cue* are just two phrases of many still in current use.

In the C16 it is spelled either as *q*, *qu*, or *cue*, or in some variation of these. Unhelpfully, Shakespeare uses both: 'Curst be

thy stones for thus deceiuing me . . . Deceiuing me is Thisbies cue;
she is to enter . . .' (1590, *Midsummer Night's Dream*, V.i) and
'Had you not come upon your Q my Lord, William lord Hastings
had pronounc'd your part' (1594, *Richard III*, III.iv). Some
etymologists suggest that it derives from Fr. *queue*, 'a tail', anglicised to *cue*, denoting the tail end of the preceding speech, but
as there is no recording of such a usage in French (where the cue
is logically called the *réplique*, 'reply'), this seems unlikely. However, those who favour *q(u)* argue that it is an abbreviation of L.
quando, 'when', or L. *qualis*, 'of what kind', which was written
in the actors' copies of the play. Other L. possibilities come to
mind – *quis*, perhaps. (In both cases we must remember that
scripts were hand-copied, and it is unlikely that each actor had
the whole play or even scene, for that matter, in his hand, so
signalling the cue clearly on the text must have become doubly
important.) Unfortunately, no helpful actors' copies remain. In
my view, although the Latin explanation seems at first unlikely,
two near-contemporary accounts incline me to give it credence.
'Q, A qu, a term vsed among Stage-plaiers, à Lat. Qualis, i. at
what manner of word the Actors are to begin to speake one after
another hath done his speech' (1625, Minsheu, *The guide to tongues*). 'Q, a note of entrance for actors, because it is the first letter
of quando, when, showing when to enter or speak' (1633, C.
Butler, *English Grammar*).

cup and saucer drama   A term little used today but applied to
the plays of T.W. Robertson (1829-71), a dramatist whose work
was surprisingly contemporary and realistic for its time, set firmly
in the domestic interior of a *box set* and dealing with issues of
social relevance. The phrase may well have influenced the 1950s'
coining of *kitchen sink drama*.

curtain   *Curtains* and other hanging fabrics (see *arras*) have been
used in secular Western European theatre from the point when
it left the confines of the church in C12: 'Let Paradise be set up
in a somewhat lofty place; let there be put about it curtains and
silken hangings, at such an height that those persons that shall
be in Paradise can be seen from the shoulders upward'. This is
a translation of a stage direction taken from the C12 Anglo-Nor-
man *Jeu d'Adam*, probably written by a priest for performance
against a church façade (quoted in Nagler, 45). Undoubtedly
curtains were used to conceal and reveal in *medieval drama*; one
of the earliest known C16 London theatres was actually called
The Curtain. There are a variety of individual terms used in the
theatre: see *act-drop*, *border*, *iron*, *leg*, *safety-curtain*, *scene-drop*,
tabs etc.

The principal theatrical use and usage of 'curtain' which has
appealed to the general imagination – (it has been used generally
as 'a hanging' since C12) – is for the screen separating the stage
from the auditorium: 'Every one cometh there to act his part of
this tragi-comedy, called life, which done the curtain is drawn,
and he removing is said to dy' (1549, Drummer of Hawthornden,
Cypress Grove). Note that here it is also being used metaphorically
at an early date. The word is ME, from OF *cortine, courtine*, from
It. and LL *cortina*, 'curtain': however, the etymological route to
this from classical Latin *cortina*, 'round vessel, arch, circle etc.',
is uncertain.

A plethora of expressions are associated with the word, including *curtain up* (see *up*) – 'I had switched on the lights for the
curtain up...' (Olivier, 58) – and *curtain-fall*. A *curtain-raiser* is
a short play performed before a longer one or before a programme
of *shorts*: 'A new piece put on as a curtain-raiser for "Lady Win-
dermere's Fan"' (1892, *Leeds Mercury*). *Curtain lines* are the final
lines of a play or a scene: 'Ibsen can be melodramatic at the best
of times, but *Ghosts* had more than its fair share of semi-comic
curtain lines' (Branagh, 168). The *curtain call* is the term for the
final return of the cast to the stage, hopefully to receive the reward
of the audience's applause: 'I came straight off from the curtain
calls and was violently sick' (1986, John Neville, quoted in Hay,
Theatrical Anecdotes, 39). Many general usages are, needless to
say, concerned with finality, (compare Drummer of Hawthornden, above), as in the infamous last stanza of Frank Sinatra's
'My Way': 'And now, the end is near,/And I must face the final
curtain...'. The term *curtains* (probably an abbreviation of 'It's
curtains for him') is a euphemism for 'death, the end', which
according to Beale, was a World War II borrowing from American
forces in Europe, with an obvious theatrical source.

cut! As imperative, *Cut!* is an example of a term crossing the
barriers of film into theatre, due to the dual employment of many
theatrical people in both media. Used in film to stop the cameras
rolling, the term is now often used by a *director* in *rehearsals* to
signify that he wants to stop the run of a scene. See also *take*.

An older use of *cut*, however, meaning 'to edit or abridge' or
'an edit', as in *cutting the text* or *'making cuts* in the text for a
performance of *Hamlet'* dates from at least C19: 'In "cutting" an
opera it is not to be supposed that any two persons will agree as
to what should be left out' (1865, *Pall Mall Gazette*).

cycle As in *the Lincoln Cycle* or *the York Cycle* of *mystery plays*,
cycle is a term appropriated by English in eC19, initially used for
a series of poems written around and 'relating to a central event

or epoch of mythic history and forming a continuous narrative'
(OED): 'They formed the basis or nucleus of the epic cycle' (1835,
Thirlwell, *Greece*). The term was transferred later in the century
to other epics such as the Arthurian Cycle and thence to mystery
plays and other *epic* narratives.

cyclorama   The original *cyclorama*, popular from the late 1830s,
was a circular *panorama*, a spectacular scene or landscape painted
on the inside of a cylinder in which the viewer stood: 'The cyclorama [of Niagara] which has "fetched" all London' (1888, *Pall
Mall Gazette*). In the early years of this century, the German
scenic and lighting designer, Mariano Fortuny (1871-1949),
designed an intricate (and prohibitively expensive) system of
lighting inside a *sky-dome* (or *Kuppulhorizont*); this was later mod-
ified for practical theatre usage as the *Rundhorizont*. In Britain,
the term 'cyclorama' was re-employed to describe it. The original
cycs (pronounced *Sykes*), were totally smooth plaster or canvas
walls which curved round the greater part of the stage and which,
when lit, created effects of space and sky. They were, however,
too cumbersome and today have been largely replaced by a variety
of smaller constructions which partially recreate the effect across
the rear walls of stages: some are portable, some permanent; some
are flat, some are curved; they are constructed from a range of
materials; all, however, are commonly referred to as *cycs*.

Dada   A literary and artistic movement which flourished from about 1915-20. Flouting accepted *conventions*, anti-authoritarian, nihilistic and deliberately aiming to shock, *dadaism*, which had its centres in Paris and New York, can be seen as a bridge between the work of Alfred Jarry (1873-1907) and the later *Theatres of Cruelty* and *the Absurd*: '[Arthur Cravan's] art criticism consisted of the most vitriolic attacks possible on all forms of creative work. This was the spirit of artistic anti-art that later fuelled the nihilism of Dada' (*Independent on Sunday*, 10 May 1992). From Fr. *dada*, 'a rocking-horse', the title of a *review* in Zurich in 1916, founded by the Romanian, Tzara, the German, Huelzenbeck and the Alsatian German, Arp. The naïve, childish sound and form of the word, (compare English *dada*, 'father' and *da-da*, an earlier form of *ta-ta*, 'goodbye'), is highly appropriate. The word has spawned the adjectives *dadaist* and *dadaesque*.

dame¹   A female role in *pantomime*, often the hero's mother, traditionally played by a male actor, (c.f. *principal boy*), often since mC19 by a *comedian* who has made his name in *music hall* or *variety* rather than in *straight* theatre. Famous *dames* include Widow Twankey in *Aladdin*, the eponymous *Mother Goose* and the Ugly Sisters in *Cinderella*. From OF *dame*, (from L. *domina*, 'a lady, a mistress'), the term has been used in English since eC14. See also *breeches parts*, *drag*, *female impersonation*.

dame²   The female equivalent of the theatrical *knight* is the *dame of the theatre*, officially Dame of the British Empire, woman Knight Commander etc., etc., a title not without its ironies considering *dame¹*: 'Judi [Dench] had informed me before rehearsals started that she'd just got "a marvellous job for the panto season", which was a delightful way of announcing herself as Dame of the British Empire' (Branagh, 205). The term has been used as a title since C17: 'By custom . . . the ladies that are Knights' wives are in conveyance for the most part stiled Dames' (1611, Selden, *Titles of Honour*).

dance/dancer   As with *opera*, *ballet* and the like, I will only touch fleetingly on this word, being aware that the subject of *dance theatre* is itself worthy of a Book of Words. Dance is found in various forms throughout the Romance languages, the most likely origin being Germanic *dansôn*, 'to draw, to stretch out', 'from which is supposed to have arisen the sense 'to form a file or chain

in dancing' (OED). The term is first attested in English around
1300, directly from OF *dance*. *Dancer*, for the performer of a
dance, is first found in C14. For *dance routine*, see *routine*.

dark *Dark* is an adjective used to describe a theatre which is
closed. It is most frequently used for a *venue* which is closed at
a time it would normally be expected to be open: that is, when
the closure is due to economic recession, lack of *grant* support or
other unforeseen circumstances. The term *dark house* is frequently
found with reference to a closed theatre, and whilst I can find no
early first attestations for the term (suggesting it may be C20), it
interestingly echoes the C16 term for 'a madhouse', a *dark room*
being the proper place to confine a madman (see *Comedy of Errors*
IV.iv, and Malvolio's imprisonment in *Twelfth Night*): 'Love is
merely a madness, and...deserues as well a dark house, and a
whip, as madmen do' (*As You Like It*, III.ii).

darling '[Granville Barker] was quite impersonal, calling everybody by the name of their part or their own surname – none of
the "dears" and "darlings" in which we are so apt to indulge in
the theatre' (Geilgud, 109). From OE *deorling*, as in *dear*, + *-ling*,
(the suffix denoting a diminutive: 'a little dear'). The word is
used for 'one dearly loved' as early as the C9: 'Bi Dauide ðeam
Godes dirlinge' (OED, *c*.897). Along with *love/luvvie*, *darling* is
the most common stylised term of greeting and address in the
theatre, although not always affectionate. The colloquial use as a
common term of general address, particularly in E. Midlands and
S.E., equivalent to other agreeably sociable terms of endearment
such as 'love', 'flower' and 'pet' elsewhere, goes back, according
to Beale, to eC20. In this everyday context, it may carry the weight
of sincere affection or, more usually, be a casual greeting. Theatrically, the usage may go back even longer. By some outside (and
some inside) the *business*, it is regarded as being a rather self-consciously *actorly* or *camp* mannerism, especially when it is repeated
ad nauseam. As with its general usage, it is often applied to total
strangers, and is often used between members of the same sex:
'He'd known my work since I was sixteen, and he was scrupul-
ously honest – no flannel, no "Darling, you were marvel-lous"'
(Branagh, 113).

date A booking, engagement. Originally a *variety* term – 'Remaining dates on Cannon and Ball's tour are at Wolverhampton
(April 25)...[etc]' (*The Stage*, 23 April 1992) – the term has also
spread to *legitimate* theatre, used especially when on tour: 'This
was the set that was to take a slow boat to Chicago for our date
there' (*Plays and Players*, October 1990.) The origin of the term
is self-evident.

dayman   A full-time member of the *stage crew* of a theatre as opposed to those employed only during performances. It dates at least from eC19: 'If he [the stage carpenter] is what, in theatre parlance, is termed a day-man, he reaches the theatre at quarter to ten if the rehearsal be at ten...' (1850s, T.W. Robertson, quoted in Nagler, 496). Etymology obvious.

DBO   An abbreviation of *dead black-out* – a point during a performance when all the lights are suddenly cut for dramatic effect. To achieve this effect in public performance, special dispensation is required from the licensing authority.

dead   In phrases such as *flown in dead, out dead* etc., *dead* signifies a precise, predetermined level to which a piece of scenery should be flown. It has here a meaning developed in C19: 'exact, precise': 'Iron bars cut to a dead length are charged a little more' (OED).

dead-pan   'Eventually she forgot her horrors long enough to notice Miss Merman: dead-pan, fist-on-hip, jaws-slowly-working-gum,,,' (1967, W. Redfield, *Letters from an Actor*). *Dead-pan*, 'blank, expressionless, impassive', is an American *vaudeville* term, derived from *pan* as a slang expression for face (see *pancake*). According to Beale, it entered common English usage via American forces in World War II, as it had already been in general usage on the other side of the Atlantic for some time. It is commonly found in phrases such as *dead-pan humour*, and possibly gained wide circulation through the fame of Buster Keaton, the great *dead-pan actor* of the silent movies.

dead spot   A point *onstage* where vocal *projection* into the *auditorium* is particularly difficult. *Dead* used in the auditory sense of 'silent, muffled'.

décor   Now commonly used to describe domestic interior decorations, *décor* was in fact an early C20 theatrical borrowing from the Continent (compare 'art deco'), where it is used for 'stage *scenery, set*': 'Despite the producer's hortatory notes, the ingenuity of the décor and some very clever acting...' (*Observer*, 5 June 1927). As with some other C20 continental borrowings such as *mis-en-scène* (though contrast *dénouement*), it may be considered rather pretentious to employ a foreign term in place of a perfectly serviceable indigenous one.

delivery   From Standard English 'uttering of speech': 'the vocal quality of an actor, including *projection, diction, timing* etc.'. 'Entertainer J.P. James is a very talented young man with an excellent singing voice and a good delivery in comedy' (*The Stage*, 28 April 1991).

dénouement   'The resolution of the *plot* of a play; in *tragedy*, the catastrophe'. *Dénouement* was an eC20 borrowing which added to

literary and theatrical vocabulary the sense of the unravelling of
the threads of plot and *sub-plot* etc., coming from Fr. *dénouer*, 'to
unknot'. It can also be found in general usage, meaning 'outcome'.

dep   *To dep* is a common theatrical abbreviation of *to deputise*. It
is most often used by stage crew and technicians; also by orchestra
members; *depping* for someone is functioning as a *stand in*.

design/designer   'The visual *interpretation* of a production, usually manifested in *set, scenery, costumes, lighting* etc.' The root
word here is L. *designare, dissignare*, 'to mark out, trace out,
denote'. A range of English senses of *design* including 'to plan,
develop a scheme' were borrowed via Fr. *désigner* in C16. However, the Italian verb *disegnare* underwent a key development in
the Renaissance, taking on the sense of 'draw, paint, embroither,
modle, pourtray' (1578, Florio, *Firste fruites. Also a perfect induc-
tion to the Italian, and English tongues*). It is first attested in English
with an added artistic sense in eC17, once again arriving via
changes to the sense of Fr. *désigner*: 'A good invention, well
designed and seasonably coloured' (1638, Junius, *The painting of
the ancients*). Around the same time, *designer* also takes an added
artistic meaning: 'Where the workman is not an accomplished
designer' (1662, Evelyn, *Sculptura*). It is from a combination of
this sense with the earlier English meanings that the theatrical
usage of English 'design' develops with overtones of 'creating
(and putting into effect) an artistic plan', the word being capable
of conveying both the prior artistic concept and that concept
embodied in the finished product.

The role of the *scenic designer* has differed in importance according to period. The first great and influential representative of the
skills in England was Inigo Jones, who co-operated with Ben
Jonson on the lavishly-designed *masques* of the Jacobean period:
'So much for the bodily part. Which was of Master YNIGO IONES
his designe, and act' (1605, Ben Jonson, quoted in Nagler, 144).
However, the designer is generally and very unfairly expected to
be a discreet figure in the background, whose major role in the
success of a production is rarely given due credit. Often, the
designer plays a vital role alongside the director in the conceptual
plans for both the *interpretation* and *staging* of a production. When
the designer *does* come to the fore, the literary and directorial
egos can by put severely to the test: 'Although I have loved working with designers, I find it is terribly important in Shakespeare
in particular that I design myself' (Brook, 91). And in Jonson's
'Expostulation with Inigo Jones' (1631) we find:

> To plant the music where no ear can reach,
> Attire the persons as no thought can teach

> Sense what they are: which by a specious, fine
> Term of [you] architects is called Design;
> But in the practised truth, destruction is
> Of any art beside what he calls his.
> Whither, O whither will this tireman grow?...
> He is, or would be, the main *Dominus Do-*
> *All* of the work...'

The word itself has been extended in C20: not only are there *costume designers* and *set designers*, but also *lighting* and *sound designers*, rightly reflecting the artistic role which people who would once have been termed *technicians* play in the artistic *design* of a show.

detail scenery 'Small pieces of scenery, usually *built stuff*, which are brought on *set* during the course of a *production*.' From Fr. *détail*, from *détailler*, from *dé-*, the prefix here suggesting *removal*, and *tailler* 'to cut': 'to cut away; to remove an item from the whole', hence 'one item from a whole' + *scenery*.

deus ex machina Latin for 'the god from the machine'. Although a Latin phrase, this harks back to a rather facile means of achieving a neat *dénouement* to certain Greek *tragedies*, (*satirised* at the time by Aristophanes), whereby a god from Olympus is introduced into the final scene of a *tragedy* by means of a *machine* or crane – (Gk *mechane*) – to omnisciently and omnipotently tie up all the plot's loose ends. It was an ending favoured particularly by Euripides. The phrase is generally used today for anyone whose surprising arrival at the eleventh hour resolves a dilemma. It has a literary use as any means by which a hard-pressed writer manages to resolve a recalcitrant plot. *Brecht* parodies the technique amusingly in his comically-improbable last-minute reprieve of MacHeath in *The Threepenny Opera*.

deuteragonist See *protagonist*.

devised theatre A common term in lC20 for *collective collaboration*. *Devised shows*, created by the group, are a feature of *T.I.E.* and other *fringe* work. The verb to devise, in use since 1400, arrived with 'to plan' among its many senses, but it does not appear to have been used with reference to the performing arts until C18: 'Of patient Grissel I devise to sing' (1714, Gay, *The Shepherd's Week*).

dialogue 'The dialogue pulls no punches and is not for the faint-hearted' (*The Stage*, 28 April 1991). As a term for 'conversation', *dialogue* (from OF *dialoge*, from L. *dialogos*, ultimately from Gk *dialegomai*, 'to speak alternately') is found in English from eC14. However, it is used earlier (from eC13) in the sense of 'a literary work in the form of a conversation' (as in *Platonic dialogues*). It does not appear to have been used theatrically, however, (as 'a conversation between actors on stage') until C18: 'The diction . . . is too luxuriant and splendid for dialogue' (*c*.1780, OED).

diction   By *diction* an actor means 'elocution, clarity of pronunciation', a development of the earlier English sense of 'choice or selection of words and phrases' or 'Elocution: By which they always meant, what we call, Diction; which consists of suiting our Words to our Ideas, and the Stile to the Subject' (1748, J. Mason, *Elocution*). The meanings of both *diction* and *elocution* have gradually shifted in emphasis from choice of vocabulary to manner of *delivery*. The word can be traced back to L. *diction -em*, carrying the sense of 'word' in LL.

die, to   An abbreviation of the expression to *die the death*: 'to meet a complete lack of response from the audience' (Beale). The shortened version may only date from mC20; its origins appear to be in *variety*: Beale traces the usage back to *comics*, *c*.1940: 'My gags didn't mean a thing [to the audience]. I died' (Richard Merry quoted in Beale). However, it may be earlier. Compare *corpse*.

digs   'Lodgings', a word particularly used for boarding-houses (see *landlady*) frequented by actors and *variety acts* on tour, and which entered general usage from the theatrical in C19. 'LIVERPOOL CENTRAL, best theatrical digs. B&B, dinners or supper, all facilities' (Ad in *The Stage*, 28 March 1991). To quote another advertisement in the same edition, digs are often 'run by *theatricals* for theatricals'. The word is an abbreviation of the American *diggings*, which can be traced back in this usage to the 1830s, though the reasons for its adoption are uncertain. (In Standard English, *diggings* as 'gold-field' with *digger* as 'miner' can be found as early as the 1530s. It may thus be that it became a frontier term for temporary accommodation near a mine.) It was first anglicised in its unabbreviated form in lC19, the earliest reference I can find showing it already in general use: 'You may see his diggings from your daughter's bedroom window, sir' (1884, Clark Russell).

dim   A *lighting* term: 'to decrease the intensity of lighting *onstage*, generally slowly'. Strangely, the verbal phrases *to dim in*, or *dim up* mean 'to increase the lighting intensity'. See *dimmer* for an explanation of this.

dimmer   A *lighting* term. Originally, a control device consisting of a coil of electrical wire wound round insulating material: 'Each spotlight is controlled by a *dimmer* . . . an apparatus consisting of a coil of wire wound round an insulating material. A slide contact runs over the entire length of the coil and connected in circuit

with a lamp it increases or decreases the amount of light radiated'
(Baker, 181, 188). In practice today, the term has been transferred
to refer to each control slide on a *dimmer board* which permits an
individual *luminaire* to be *brought up* or *brought down*, or often,
on modern computerised *boards*, to a press-button which controls
a pre-programmed *fade*. The old term for the lighting-control
board, *switchboard*, has largely been replaced by *dimmer board*,
itself abbreviated to *dimmer*: hence, the control device for a *single
lantern* has given its name to the larger control system.

Dionysiac/Dionys[i]an   'Of, or pertaining to Dionys[i]us'. From
L. *Dionysius* from Gk *Dionusos*. Dionysus was a vegetation god
from Asia Minor, also known as Bacchus or Bromius, appropriated by the Greeks (see Euripides *The Bacchae*) as a deity of
fertility, annual resurrection, mystical possession, license and,
later, of the theatre. The Festivals of Dionysus in Athens developed from intense *rituals* into week-long theatrical competitions
for which the city suspended normal life and, to some degree,
rules. *Dionysian* can relate to all or any of these references but,
at its simplest, it is used as a synonym for 'orgiastic' or 'alcohol-
ically self-indulgent'.

diorama   'The Diorama, invented by Daguerre and Bouton, was
first exhibited in London, 29th Sept. 1823, the building being
erected in Regents Park' (OED). A large-scale *peep-show*, a variation of the *panorama*, which, by using cut-out *scenery*, transparencies and other special visual *effects* including *lighting*, attempted
to create an illusion of three-dimensional scenic realism. There
were attempts to use these techniques theatrically, which contributed to the development of the modern *cyclorama*. A modern
coining from Gk *di-* 'through', + *horamo*, from *horaō*, 'see'.

dips   Small *traps* in the stage floor containing electrical sockets
for use with lights, *mikes* etc. The verb *to dip* is, alongside other
meanings, 'to go below any surface or level'; it is also a *nautical*
term for lowering and raising sails, masts, flags etc., which may
well explain its theatrical appropriation: 'The men who dip the
sail should stand on the lee side' (1882, Nares, *Seamanship*).

director/direction etc.   'It is indeed hard to define what *directing*
really is...' (Geilgud, 86). Not until 1956 was it officially agreed
that, to avoid confusion, British theatre would adopt the American
term *director* for the person with overall artistic and interpretative
responsibility for a production; formerly, *producer* was the more
frequent term. In the eC19, this role had been taken by *actor-
managers*, leading actors, *stage managers*, prompters, *authors* and
the like: the gradual shift towards what is termed *director's theatre*
in the English-speaking world began, perhaps, with Madame

Vestris (see *box set*) in Britain and David Belasco in the United
States in m-lC19, a movement reinforced by the influence of continental *régisseurs*.

The role of the director differs from person to person and company to company, as do the techniques they employ, though it
generally demands a great ability to understand, co-ordinate and
control the *text*, the *design* concepts of a production, *actors* and a
whole range of *technical* considerations. Many actors, (including
Geilgud, above), might be tempted to side with Noël Coward:
'Noël Coward once said that the only real use of a director was
to stop the actors from bumping into each other' (Olivier, 210).
However, here is one of the pre-eminent voices of director's
theatre: 'A director can treat a play like a film and use all the
elements of theatre, actors, designers, musicians, etc. as his servants, to communicate to the rest of the world what he has to say'
(Brook, 5).

The term is ultimately from L. *dirigere*, 'to direct', and whilst
it has been used generally in English since C15 for 'one who
directs, rules, guides', an artistic usage does not appear to have
been employed until C19, probably via Fr. *directeur*, from a musical term equatable with *conductor*: 'In 1769 Mozart was appointed
director of the archbishop of Salzburg's concerts' (1839, *Penny
cyclopaedia*). The explosion in theatrical usage is C20, from the
United States.

Director's theatre, which stresses the director and his *reading*
of a text rather than the actor and his performance is coming
under fire currently from those (mainly actors) who favour what
they term 'actor's theatre'. See also *artistic director*, *stage director*,
producer.

disbelief, willing suspension of   A phrase coined by the poet and
critic, Samuel Taylor Coleridge, in relation to poetry: 'That willing suspension of disbelief for the moment, which constitutes
poetic faith' (*Biographia Literaria*, Ch.14). It is used in the theatre
to denote the occasions when the audience enters into an unspoken
contract with author and/or performers, ignoring features of performance that would be unbelievable in real life and immerses
itself wholeheartedly in the theatrical illusion. It is the central
and essential theatrical *convention*.

discover[1]   ME, from OF *descovrir*, from LL *dis-*, + *cooperire*, 'to
cover': 'to uncover'. The literal theatrical sense of the word derives
from the structure of Elizabethan/Jacobean outdoor public
theatres: *characters* could be *discovered* or revealed to an *audience*
by the opening of the *curtains*, *arras* or door which concealed the
inner stage below the balcony of the *tiring-house*. 'The entrance of

the Cell opens, and discovers Ferdinand and Miranda playing at chess' (1612, *The Tempest*, V.i).

discover² A second theatrical sense of *discovery* comes from its use as the accepted translation of Aristotle's concept of *anagnōrisis* in *The Poetics*, a recognition by the *hero* or *heroïne* of a play of something of great importance hitherto unknown or neglected, frequently occurring in the *dénouement*: for example, the hero's discovery in the final scene of *Othello* that Iago has been lying to him about Desdemona's behaviour throughout their stay in Cyprus.

disguise As a technique, *disguise* (whereby a character within a play assumes another role, usually involving a change of *costume*) was rife in the plots of Elizabethan and Jacobean plays, particularly in *comedies*. Although it has many antecedents in classical theatre, this was probably in large measure the result of sheer pragmatism on the part of dramatists which was then turned to artistic advantage. By allowing a character to 'cross-dress', the playwright also allows his *boy actor* the opportunity to play a role in which he can exploit his true sexuality. In turn, it allows for the development and exploitation of the theme of mistaken identity, so central to *comedy*. The popularity of disguise may also owe something to the C15-eC16 *entertainment* known as a *disguising*, a form of costume entertainment with music and dancing which involved the participants dressing up in elaborate costumes, an earlier form of the *masque*. ME from OF *desguis*, from Rom *dis-*, + (probably) *guisa*, 'external appearance; assumed appearance'. The term is first found in general use in lC13-eC14.

distancing Along with *alienation*, an English attempt to translate Brecht's concept of *Verfremdungseffekt*, itself derived from the Russian Formlist concept of 'defamiliarisation'. It is the attempt to create a *critical* distance between *audience* and *performance* which will lead to an intellectual rather than emotional response. Like most theoretical statements on theatre practice, it is open to interpretation: 'Brecht's use of "distance" has long been considered in opposition to Artaud's conception of theatre as immediate and violent subjective experience [see *Cruelty, theatre of*]. I have never believed this to be true' (Brook, 47). From OF from L *distare*, 'to stand apart'.

distress *To distress* props is to make them look older or more worn by a variety of artificial means. A playfully metaphorical use of the word's standard sense.

diva '[My] performance . . . resembled Benny Hill crossed with a manic opera diva' (Branagh, 35). *Diva* has been used in English since lC19 for 'a great woman singer', (based on the Italian usage, from L. *diva*, 'goddess'). It is now at times used in a rather *camp* way for any great female performer.

dithyramb   An Ancient Greek theatrical *genre* which is possibly a transitional form between early *Dionysian* rituals and the tragedies of the Festival of Dionysus; in its early, pre-literary form, the *dithyramb* was probably sung by a *protagonist* and a large *chorus* as a hymn in honour of the god. From Gk *dithurambos*, of unknown origin.

DLP   An abbreviation of *dead letter perfect*: an hyperbolic actor's version of being *word perfect* – fully in command of his *part* in the *script*. As in *DBO* – 'dead black out' – *dead* is used here in its colloquial sense of 'complete', on this occasion adverbially.

dock   As in *scene-dock, prop dock* etc., any area in which *scenery* and equipment can be stored and/or worked on. Ideally, the *dock* is chosen for easy access to both the stage and the street. A *nautical* term, used since C16 for a natural or artificial basin in which ships could be anchored, the term was borrowed from Dutch *docke* (modern Dutch *dok*), and the reasons for its use in theatre are obvious from this source. The origins of *docke* are uncertain, though it has been suggested that there may be connections with Icelandic *dōkk*, 'pit, small pool', Norwegian *dokk*, 'hollow, low ground' and med. L. *doga*, 'ditch, canal'.

documentary drama   A theatrical *genre* inspired by the success of film documentaries, which were able to support a thesis with 'real' celluloid proof (compare *projection*). The first exponents of this style were the Federal Theatre in the United States, who, in the mid-1930s, attempted to use cinema-inspired techniques in their Living Newspaper shows which were copied in Britain in the Second World War for both *propaganda* and adult *education*. Later, politically-inspired shows such as Joan Littlewood's Theatre Workshop's *Oh, What a Lovely War!* (1963) and the RSC's *U.S.* (1966) used some of the same presentation techniques which still flourish on the Fringe and in *community theatre*. From *document*, 'writing or inscription which furnishes evidence', from L. *documentum*, 'proof', + *drama*.

dog drama   A form of theatre particularly popular in eC19 which included roles written specifically for canine performers. The most famous of these works is said to be Pixérécourt's *melodrama Le Chien de Montargis, ou La Fôret de Bondy* (1814). As with *equestrian drama*, *aquatic drama* etc., such entertainments enjoyed a limited afterlife in *circus*.

door slam   The common term for sounds from a *practical* door, fully-equipped with locks, bolts etc., formerly situated in the wings during appropriate productions to give the *sound effect* of an *offstage* door.

double, to   For an actor: 'to play more than one *part* in a given *show* or *production*'. (*Double* is ME, from OF *dobler, dubler*, from LL *duplare*, from *duplus*, 'double'). Partridge dates this term back to *c*.1800, which suggests that it was probably current before that date. The general term for employing this kind of *casting* is *doubling* or *doubling up*, both of which have entered into common usage. 'Early West End assignments either found her replacing performers into the run...or *doubling* as a chorus girl and the fiancée from Darien in the Ginger Rogers *Mame*' (of Julia McKenzie in *Plays and Players*, October 1990). *Artistic doubling* is the exploitation of this expedient – (usually resorted to because *companies* cannot afford to pay the required number of actors for a show, especially when on *tour*) – to comment on the themes of a play. For example, it is common to cast the same two actors in the roles of Hippolyta and Titania, and Theseus and Oberon in productions of *A Midsummer Night's Dream* on the pretext that the latter fairy characters are somehow projections of the former Athenian rulers into the world of magic, dream and the id.

double act   A *variety* act, usually *comic*, featuring two *performers*, one usually presenting the funny lines whilst the other acts as his *straight man, feed* or *stooge*. Although the term itself is probably only eC20, the comic tradition is long:

> Even in the classic Greek and Roman drama of about 300 BC there were often comic servants who argued with their masters; and in Shakespeare's *Comedy of Errors* a master and servant amuse themselves by putting on a couple of ex tempore double act routines. [Act II.ii and Act III.ii.] This pattern of serious or 'straight man' trying to cope with the vagaries of a comic servant set the pattern of the principal type of double act as it flourished in the first half of this century. (Wilmut, 53)

Famous acts included Clapham and Dwyer in the 1920s and 1930s and Flanagan and Allan in the 1930s and 1940s. Here is a sample of another, Naughton and Gold's double act on BBC Radio (October 1, 1943):

GOLD: If I asked you to have a drink, what would you say?
NAUGHTON: Milk and Soda.
GOLD: So you know about milk?
NAUGHTON: I wrote three columns in the paper about milk.
GOLD: And they published the three columns?
NAUGHTON: No – they condensed it...I really drink beer.
GOLD: You really drink beer? Why?
NAUGHTON: Because I'm thirsty.
GOLD: Then you should drink milk. Milk makes blood.
NAUGHTON: Oh, I'm not *blood*thirsty...

and so on. This sort of *corny*, *gag*-laden *patter* is a far cry from some of the relatively sophisticated, character-based material of Morecambe and Wise, who flourished from the 1950s to the 1980s.

Colloquially, *double act* can now be used for any two people who either work well together or who are inseparable. In the 1920s, *to do the double act* was a colloquial term for 'getting married'.

double bill The presentation of two plays on the same bill, as this quotation somewhat mathematically demonstrates: 'One Step Theatre Company, the first resident company at the Green Room, Manchester, has lined up six one-act plays in three double bills which will each play for a week . . .' (*The Stage*, 21 October 1991).

double masque See *masque*.

double-take An actor's term (from *take*, 'a pointed look which *takes* the audience's attention'): a *double take* is 'a second look, because the first is not credited'. With the correct *timing*, the double-take (which must have existed as a basic tool in the comedian's *repertoire* for centuries) rarely fails to get a laugh. It has been in general usage since the 1940s at least.

down An abbreviation of *downstage*.

downstage A *stage direction* denoting the area of a *proscenium arch* stage nearest to the audience: the area at the very front, directly behind the *apron* or above the *orchestra pit*. The choice of the term *downstage* is explained by the fact that lC17 and eC18 stages were *raked*, a slope running from the rear of the stage (known as *upstage*), downwards towards the *pit*. In texts, it is almost always abbreviated to *down*, or *D*. 'On the gas-stove a statue of Buddah. Down R., a fireplace' (1960, Harold Pinter, *The Caretaker*).

drag A *drag artist(e)* is a male performer who specialises in female roles: a *female impersonator*. Although the term is C19, the art of female impersonation is almost as long as theatrical history: see *boy actor*, *dame*, *principal boy*, *queen* etc. Recent masters of the art have included Danny la Rue, and Barry Humphries in his incarnation as Dame Edna Everage. A woman's costume worn by a male actor was referred to as a *drag* as early as the 1880s. In the London underworld in 1850, the phrase *to go on the drag* – 'drag' being Cockney for 'street', (in all likelihood from the word for a carriage driven by four horses) – was 'to wear women's clothes for immoral purposes' (Partridge). The still-current phrase *in drag* was already in use at that time. The term *drag queen* has been current since 1930.

drama The distinction of definition between *theatre* and *drama* is a nice one. According to the semiotician, Keir Elam, 'Theatre is taken to refer here to the complex of phenomena associated with the performer-audience transaction...By "drama", on the other hand, is meant that mode of fiction designed for stage representation and constructed according to particular ("dramatic") conventions' (p.2). Whilst this might be useful for his own purposes, his working definition of 'drama' is in conflict with both classical etymology and current English usage.

Firstly, if one looks at the word's origins – from Gk *drama*, 'deed, action; thence, a play', ultimately from *draō*, 'do' – one starts with a verb and then a noun, both denoting active involvement in the world. 'Deed' suggests a real task completed or to be completed, 'action' a fluid process of activities which may or may not amount to a completed deed. Only in the 5th century BC, with the emergence of the *Dionysian* competitions in Athens, was the word transferred to 'a play'. As with other key theatrical terms which originate in ancient Greece and Rome – *theatre, acting* etc. – the linguistic roots involve a primary verb, in this case, 'to do'. And as soon as the word's sense includes 'a play', it comprehends 'the actor-audience transaction'. Oliver Taplin's definition of 'drama' in 5th-century Greece gets to the sap of the root: 'something that is acted out, a communication through action' (p.2). Elam's relegation of 'drama' from complex interaction on a communal level to literary blueprint is incomplete.

Although found in its Latin genitive form in the earliest published Elizabethan plays in the term *Dramatis Personae*, ('characters of the play'), 'drama' was slow to find currency in English, the indigenous 'play' being preferred. It first appears in its French form. Throughout the 16th century, its rare occurrences retain ambiguity: the precise definition is unsettled though it does at this stage appear to denote a literary form, the single play: 'Such rascal drames promoted by Thais, Bacchus, Licoris, or yet by Thestalis' (1515, Barclay, *Eclogues OV*). When it first appears as 'drama', it continues to carry a short *a* on the first syllable, as was probably the case until C18, a pronunciation still found in some accents in Scotland and Northern Ireland: 'Neither are Dramma's of this nature so despicable' (1636, Heywood, *Love's Mistress*). Jonson's use of it in 1616 is interesting: in 'Epigram CXII, To a weake Gamster in Poetry', the poet and playwright attacks an annoying imitator who copies every literary form Jonson himself essays: 'I cannot for the stage a Drama lay,/Tragick or Comick; but thou writ'st the play.' It appears likely that Jonson is using 'drama' and 'play' synonymously here, although the couplet could be read as making a distinction between drama, the idea behind a play, and the play itself. If, however, the terms *are* used synonymously, the suggestion must be that no distinction is made between text and performance, as is the case with 'play' itself.

When the word becomes more common in mC17, it has developed its own sense discrete from 'play': as a generic term for theatrical literature, probably derived from the adjective *dramatic* or, possibly, from the growing tendency from this period onwards to study subjects and categorise their elements in a quasi-scientific manner. 'His drollery yields to none the English drama did ever produce' (1661, Bullen, Pref. to Middleton's *Mayor of Queenborough*). By 1711, Addison is referring in *The Spectator*, in typical Augustan style, to 'the received Rules of the Drama'.

Its meaning as a generic term, however, has altered in C20, as many who have studied Drama as a subject will know. It now comprehends not only dramatic literature, but also many other aspects of the *Performing Arts*. In these usages, 'drama' denotes a process, a series of activities which may not include text at all. Much of this work is *improvisation*-based. *Educational drama* is seen by many teachers, not as an end in itself, but as a means to an end, a teaching tool which uses *role-play* and *simulation* techniques to deliver skills in a range of subject areas. In addition *drama therapy* and *psychodrama* have developed, using drama games, trust exercises etc., devised in *warm-ups* in the professional *rehearsal room*, or as teaching techniques in schools and *drama schools*, for social and medical purposes.

It is noticeable that in lC20 England, 'drama' in this educational sense is a term which is going out of fashion: along with elements of music and dance, it is being subsumed by the label Performing Arts; technical aspects of production and performance can be also found under the heading Media Studies. Coming to Britain from the United States, this trend seems to stem in part from the desire to rationalise educational subject boundaries in response to training needs and technical developments, but also from the belief that portentous-sounding, quasi-scientific titles add a kind of spurious respectability to the arts, a tendency similar to that found elsewhere in the adoption of terms such as *experimental* and *laboratory* theatre.

But to return from speculation on current trends to history, in eC18, 'drama' was extended metaphorically to mean a series of actions 'having a unity like that of a drama, and leading to a final catastrophe or consummation' (OED), following a pattern common with major theatrical terms (see *farce, theatre* etc.). In 1714, J. Sharpe could refer in a sermon to 'the great drama and contrivances of God's Providence.' It was inevitable that this change of usage should bring with it all the trappings of conflict, excitement and suspense for which audiences flocked to plays. When Burke at end of C18 refers to 'the awful drama of Providence now acting in the moral theatre of the world' (*Two letters on the proposals for peace with the regicide directory of France*), the phrase is full of theatrically-baited breath.

It is in this sense that the word is now most familiar to us in the media, etiolated by tabloid over-use as *tragedy* has been. 'Real life drama is how, late in C20, we receive and interpret contemporary events. We are all playgoers now' (Mark Lawson, *Independent on Sunday*, 16 August 1991). The most minor local news stories are heightened to 'drama' and this usage also has general currency in expressions such as 'There's no point making a drama out of it'.

drama schools See *RADA*.

dramatic 'Foure sundrie formees of Poesie dramatick...to wit, the Satyre, olde Comedie, new Comedie, and Tragedie' (1589, Puttenham, *English Poesie*). This OED attestation of *dramatic* as 'of or pertaining to drama', prefigures the later generic development of *drama* itself in mC17 and may well have contributed significantly to that development. Its other major sense, 'characteristic of, having the sensational attributes of drama' develops in line with the development of 'drama'.

dramatics 'I'd clearly let school dramatics go straight to my head' (Branagh, 32). Also found in the term *amateur dramatics*, this word (comparable to *theatricals*) is a C19 development for non-professional drama, formed from the adjective *dramatic*: it seems to imply that such endeavours display the characteristics of the real thing but somehow never quite become it.

dramatise/dramatize 'At an early stage, Bryden hit on the idea of producing a play which would dramatise life in the communities which dedicate themselves to shipbuilding' (*Plays and Players*, October 1990). 'To convert into a drama', a term first attested in OED in lC18 and neatly exemplified in this: 'They are busy dramatizing the Lady of the Lake here in Dublin' (1810, Scott, *Familiar Letters*).

dramatist 'They...impatiently cry out against the Dramatist, and presently deplore the Plot' (1678, Cudworth, *The true intellectual system of the universe*). The late date of the first attestation of this term for 'playwright' in OED is no surprise, considering that *drama* itself was much overshadowed by the indigenous *play* until this period. Its adoption was probably hastened, as that of so many other foreign terms were at this period, by the return of Royalist exiles and the consequent upsurge in European artistic influences.

dramaturge/dramaturgy A rare alternative to 'playwright, dramatist', though its modern usage extends beyond this. *Drama-turgy* is most frequently encountered as 'dramatic writing' or 'the art of dramatic writing'. From Fr. *dramaturge*, from Gk *drama-tourgos, dramaturge* is a term much more highly favoured in continental Europe, particularly in Germany. Although it is encountered in lC19 – 'Schiller was starving on a salary of 200 dollars per annum...which he received for his services as "dramaturg" or literary agent' (*The Times*, 17 November 1859) – the term has gained greater vogue in lC20. Its popularity may be put down to its all-embracing vagueness: Gk *-ergos* denotes 'a worker', therefore 'dramaturge' is literally 'theatre worker'. As such, it has become favoured by those on the left on account of its democratic non-specificity – it can be applied to anyone working in theatre. In addition, it is also much favoured by those who consider themselves to be theatrical jacks-of-all-trades. Many feel it has rather too pretentious a ring about it to be taken seriously.

drapes ME, from OF *drap*, from LL *drappus*, 'cloth'. Referring to curtains as 'drapes', in the home as well as in the theatre, tends to be an American usage, though *draper* was once commonly found; in Britain today, however, *drape* is found theatrically: 'Tabs, Legs, Borders & all Stage Drapes – Hire & Sale' (Ad. in *The Stage*, 28 March 1991).

drawing-room comedy A dramatic *genre* much favoured by *dramatists* from the lC19 to mC20: plays set in a middle-class drawing-room, ideally suited to re-creation by a *box set* on a *proscenium arch stage*, with all the limitations of subject matter that suggests, have gone rapidly out of fashion since the 1950s. The term is now used derogatorily to suggest a form of theatre which is both conservative and passé. *Drawing-room* is an abbreviation of *withdrawing-room*, found in C16 but much more common in C17; originally for a private room attached to a more public one, it was later adopted for domestic use: 'The king...is very cheerful, and by the bawdy discourse I thought I had been in the drawing room' (1642, Lord Sunderland, *Letter to Wife*).

dress As a noun, *dress* has been used as 'clothing' since lC16 and is used theatrically as a synonym for *costume*. Its adoption can probably be accounted for by the fact that it initially denoted clothing worn for a specific function such as a ceremonial. It is now most frequently encountered in the terms *dressing-room* and *dress rehearsal*, or, with reference to the audience, in the *dress circle*: it is rare to refer to an actor's *dress*.

As a verb, however, 'dress' has two more specific senses, the first dating back at least to eC18: 'Scenes affect ordinary minds as much as speeches; and our actors are very sensible that a well-dressed play has sometimes brought them as full audiences as a well-written one' (1711, Addison, *The Spectator*, quoted in Nagler, 245). *To dress a set* is to scenically decorate it. The term is most likely a *nautical* one: *to dress a ship* is to array it with flags; to decorate a stage with the appropriate *cloths* etc., would be a natural transference for early *crews*. *To dress a character* is to furnish them with a costume (see *dresser*): 'I can't do this part unless you let Cosprops dress me' (Patience Collier, quoted in Barkworth, 208).

dresser Today, *dresser* is largely used for someone who assists with dressing before, and *costume* changes [see *quick change*] during a *show*; the dresser also takes care of the general condition of those costumes. 'Mike Maloney, Julian Glover and I present our dresser with a birthday present – he glories in the name of Black Mac the Bastard' (Tim McInnerny, *Guardian*, 24-25 October 1991). The term is much better known generally in its more outdated sense, almost equivalent to 'personal valet', a sense in which it has been used generally since C17: 'Command my dresser to adorn her with/The robes that I gave command for' (1631, Massinger, *The Emperor of the East*, II.i). Many actors of the old school employed their own personal dressers, a relationship notably explored in the play *The Dresser* by Ronald Harwood, (1980), reputedly based in part on his experiences as actor and dresser with the *actor-manager* Sir Donald Wolfit in his Shakespeare Company.

dressing-room 'Each evening, the broom-cupboard office becomes dressing room number one. Dressing room number two is two portable *pissoirs* into which is jammed a primitive make-up table' (Michael Coveney on the Gate Theatre, *Observer*, 3 May 1992).

In 1666, *dressing-rooms*, the rooms *backstage* where actors dress and make up, were still referred to as *tiring-rooms*: 'my business here was to see the inside of the stage and all the tiring-rooms and machines' (Pepys, *Diary*); however, the first general OED attestation of *dressing-room* also comes from around this time: 'I...was made free of their society and dressing-rooms for ever hereafter' (1675, Wycherley, *The Country Wife*, IV.iii), It would appear that here we are on the cusp of the two usages.

droll A *comic* extract from a longer play, often accompanied by a *dance*; used during the outlawing of the theatre in Commonwealth England as a means of presenting a brief *entertainment* which, because of its simple *staging*, might elude detection and prosecution. From Fr. *drôle*, perhaps from Middle Dutch *drolle*, 'a little man'. The word had originally entered English as a synonym for 'jester', and gave rise to the general adjective meaning 'amusing, (usually in an odd sort of fashion)'.

drop   A term for a *cloth*. See *back-cloth/back-drop*. This is probably a *nautical* term since a '*Drop* of a sail, [is] a term sometimes to courses and topsails instead of depth' (1794, *Rigging and Seamanship*).

drugget   A form of floor-covering, usually either of matting or carpet, which is placed around the performance area to deaden *offstage* noises. From Fr. *droguet*, *drugget* was initially used for a blended material used for clothing, but it gradually came to be applied solely to carpet material. It is first found in English in lC16: 'Ane pair of droggat courtingis' (1580, Lady Errol, Letter). One line of speculation, that it derives from the placename *Drogheda* (cf *arras*), although appealing, is largely rejected for lack of evidence. It is more likely to come Fr. *drogue*, with its sense of 'a stuff of little value'.

dry   To forget one's lines or *business*, the common theatrical abbreviation of the more general phrase *to dry up* – 'to run out of things to say' – itself probably of theatrical origin, which has been in general usage since mC19. 'He suddenly dried up as he noticed the ominous expression on the great man's brow' (1888, Rider Haggard). It has been suggested that this usage of the verb, which according to Partridge is of American origin, arose as a colloquial antonym of the verb 'to babble'. He also claims that a *dry-up*, now obsolete, was used in the C19 for 'a theatrical failure', though the only noun now in use, *a dry*, which seems to date from mC20, simply denotes the state of being at a loss for one's lines: 'It [a role] grew wooden and heavy and my concentration wavered in performance until I dried desperately in the middle of one show' (Branagh, 100).

dry ice/dry ice machine   *Dry ice* is frozen carbon dioxide, which, when dropped into heated water in a *dry ice machine*, produces a misty or smokey effect which tends to lie near to the stage floor: 'each one had ordered his cannisters [sic] of dry ice for the Ghost scene where it would roll into the audience who suspected they were being gassed' (Berkoff, 171).

drum-and-shaft system   A Renaissance system for moving a number of pieces of *scenery* simultaneously, which, though now abandoned, remained in use in some theatres until this century. Above the stage, a central drum controlled by a single rope, would lever a series of shafts which moved the scenery pieces.

DSM   A deputy stage manager. *DSMs* hold the position of *stage manager's* right-hand man or woman, a ranking higher than that of *ASM*, for whom they are sometimes responsible.

dumb show   'The groundlings...for the most part are capable of nothing but inexplicable dumb-shows and noise' (1612, Heywood, *Apology for Actors*). An early theatrical term for a scene in *mime*, usually used as a shorthand means for conveying plot information, particularly of a sensational kind, hence Heywood's rather scathing reference. *Dumb shows* were particularly favoured in Elizabethan or Jacobean revenge drama and could be quite macabre.

dummy, ventriloquist's   From *dumb* (from OE from OHG *tumb*, 'stupid'). From a C16 sense of 'deaf-mute', *dummy* followed a common linguistic pattern by taking on the connotations of 'half-wit and simpleton' by C18. It also came to cover a variety of people or objects, in each instance standing in place of a 'real' or 'normal' one. In lC19, a dummy was another of the many names for a *supernumerary* or extra, but its lasting theatrical sense is as a form of puppet characterised by a *ventriloquist*, a form of *variety entertainer* who gained in popularity in C19.

duo   A pair of *variety artists* who regularly perform together, especially found in the phrases a *comedy duo* (see *double act*) and a *singing duo*. From It. *duo*, 'two', later 'duet'. Musically, the term has been in use since C16: 'Songs for 2 voyces, of the which some be plaine and easie...the rest of these Duos be made for those that be more perfect in Singing or Playing' (1590, T. Whitehorn, *title*).

duodrama   A piece of theatre for two speaking characters. A *two-hander*, A development from *monodrama*.

duologue   A development from *monologue*: a part of a scene, an entire scene, or, occasionally, an entire play in which the speaking parts are played by two actors. (See *two-hander*.) Alternatively, the term can be used for a scene where other actors are on stage but, by *convention*, only two can be heard in conversation, the others acting in *dumb-show*. It is also occasionally used in place of *dialogue*. This is a C19 term: 'The dramatic monopolists...are now taking steps to stop a "duologue entertainment" at Weston's Music Hall' (*Home News*, 19 December 1864).

Edinburgh A shorthand way of referring to the *Edinburgh Festival*, the prestigious, annual, international arts *festival* held, since 1947, for three weeks in August in Scotland's capital. Its greatest contribution to theatre and its language is the *Fringe*.

effects ME, from OF, or from L. *effectus*, (from *ef-*, a variation of the prefix *ex-* [before *f*], denoting movement away from our out of, + *ficere, -fect*, a variation of *facere*, 'to make'): to produce something as a result or consequence of something else. Such *effects*, an abbreviation of *special* or *stage effects*, (abbreviated in *lighting* to *specials*), contribute greatly to the acoustical and visual elements of a *production*. They are usually created and controlled nowadays by sophisticated electronic equipment, though such work was once the business of the *props* department. Although now largely redundant, until relatively recently an *effects man*, positioned usually in the wings, could make a variety of *live* effects: acoustically, he might use coconut shells for galloping horses, rusty hinges for creaking doors; he would control the *bomb tank*, too. Effects men have a long and not always glorious history: one of their number was responsible for burning down Shakespeare's Globe when firing a cannon during a performance of *Henry VIII*. An *effects wheel* is a disc placed in front of a lantern which, when it revolves and the lantern is lit, can produce effects such as clouds passing, snow falling etc. It has now become common to abbreviate *effects* to the phonetically inexact *FX*.

electrics Frequently abbreviated to *LX*, this is the term for the staff employed by a theatre company to handle electrical supply and distribution and to ensure the safety of all electrical equipment. They are generally quite distinct from production specialists such as the *lighting* and *sound crews*, though there can be some overlap, especially in smaller companies.

elocution From L. *elocutio*, from *e-*, the prefix in this case denoting 'out' + *loqui, locut-*, 'to speak': to speak out, declaim'. The art of public speaking, with particular reference to *delivery*, pronunciation etc. The term has been used in this sense since eC17: '*Elocution*, good vtterance of speech' (1613, OED). In a modern context, the word is applied to a form of *voice coaching*, most frequently undertaken by children and adolescents in their free

92

time, which places great stress on correct *voice production* and the development of accent, often stressing the particular need to master Received Pronunciation. Compare and contrast *diction*.

emote, to   To act or behave emotionally; to artistically imitate emotional behaviour. '"No, no, no, no. I want to do it again. *Please* Mr. Forman, I can emote more. *I can emote more.*" A great deal of emoting went into this plea...' (Branagh, 107). The verb *to emote* is a C20 coining, probably American, from the noun 'emotion'. In theatrical terms the word means to emphasise the emotional temperature of a performance or scene, to play it with intensity. There is a stereotyped image of an intense *Stanislavskian* director in rehearsals passionately exhorting his actors to 'Emote! Emote!' A term generally used with a degree of irony.

emotion(al) memory   Alternative translations (from the Russian) of a phrase coined by the *director* and theatre *practitioner*, Konstantin *Stanislavski* in his seminal handbook for actors, *An Actor Prepares* (1936). A part of his acting system, *psychotechnique*, in essence it requires an actor who has analysed their character's *motivation* in a given scene to plunder his or her personal memory story to find the same or an equivalent emotion to the one the character is imagined to be experiencing. The circumstances of that feeling, Stanislavski claimed, should be thoroughly visualised and explored so that the actor can re-experience the emotions at will and 'lend' them to the character.

encore   'Whenever any Gentlemen are particularly pleased with a Song, at their crying out Encore... the performer is so obliging as to sing it over again' (1714, Steele, *Spectator*, No. 314). Contrary to popular belief, there is no evidence that this exclamation was ever used in a French theatre, (nor that the Italians ever used *ancora*): in both France and Italy the equivalent term is *bis!* None the less, the term clearly comes from Fr. *encore*, 'still; yet; again (occasionally)', and its adoption would, consequently, appear to be a rather pretentious affectation on the part of lC17-eC18 audiences. The noun *encore* used as 'a repeat rendition' dates from mC18 but its common theatrical sense, as in the phrase 'taking an encore' is to take additional *curtain calls*.

end-of-the-pier   The pier became a prominent feature of many English holiday resorts in C19, not least because of the popular *entertainment* provided in its theatres. *End-of-the-pier* show is a phrase which evokes a now-dated form of *variety* entertainment: shows of good humour but dubious quality. An *end-of-the-pier joke*, likewise, suggests *corn*, and, occasionally, *risqué*, picture-postcard vulgarity. See also *concert party*.

ENSA   'It was really the Variety and theatrical profession at large being recruited by ENSA' (Michael Standing, quoted in Wilmut, 152). Many successful actors, musicians and artistes of the era succeeding the Second World War received their training in ENSA: the Entertainments National Service Association, which worked out of Drury Lane Theatre in close conjunction with the NAAFI (the Navy, Army and Air Force Institute). Many others, who had established their reputations previously, were also involved in providing the broad spread of entertainment it offered, from *classical* music and drama to *variety concert parties*.

ensemble   Fr. from LL *insemul*, from L. *insimul*, 'at the same time'. *Ensemble* has been used in English to mean 'together' since mC15. It would appear to have entered theatrical usage from music. It is only since lC19 that it has been used to denote 'a performance company', especially in *music hall* and *variety*. C20 continental usages – Brecht's *Berliner Ensemble*, for example – have contributed further to this usage in *straight* theatre. It is attested in OED as meaning 'the united performance of all voices and all instruments in a piece of concerted music' since mC19: 'It was really possible for five principal vocalists to achieve a perfect ensemble' (*Musical Examiner*, 28 September 1844). The sense of 'harmonious playing' inherent in this usage has probably contributed to the common contemporary theatrical term, *ensemble playing*: 'the quality of performance of a company of actors performing with and for each other; teamwork': 'This is truly ensemble playing at its best – not one weak performance' (*Plays and Players*, October 1990).

enter   'Enter Kent, Gloucester, and Edmund' (1605, Shakespeare, *King Lear*). Alongside its antonym, *exit*, this is probably the most common *stage direction* for an actor: it tells him when to make his *entrance* on to the *stage*. It is found in a variety of combinations in *acting editions*: *enter stage right*, for example.

entertain/entertainer   ME from Fr. *entretenir*, from Rom. *inter-*, the prefix denoting a mutual or reciprocal arrangement, a joint participation in something, + *tenere*, 'to hold'. Amongst a list of now largely obsolete transitive senses revolving around 'maintaining, sustaining and occupying', *entertain* as 'to receive a guest, show hospitality' is found from lC15: 'I haue them not onley receyved, but entreteyned, furnyshed and systeyned' (1490, Caxton, *The boke yf Eneydos*). The sense of *entertainer*, likewise, is a social one around this period: 'She was content to be talkatiue with a straunger, & wax a proper enterteiner' (ante 1535, Thomas More). However, the sense of an entertainer as 'someone or something which amuses' does not develop until lC18: *Wonderful Magazine and Marvellous Chronicle or new weekly entertainer* (1793,

title). 'Entertainer' as 'professional performer' and the general
sense of *entertainment* solely as 'amusement' are surprisingly late,
C19 concepts.

entr'acte   From Fr. *entre*, 'between', + *acte*, 'an act': a C18 borrowing. Quite literally, an *entr'acte* was a *performance*, often of
music and dancing, which took place between the *acts* of a play,
although later it also came to signify *'interval'*. Occasionally anglicised: 'Play...is only the "inter-acts" of other amusements
(1750, Chesterfield, Letter). See also *entremès*.

entrance   *Entrance* is the theatrical antonym of the noun *exit*, used
since at least C16 – 'They have their exits and entrances/And one
man in his time plays many parts' (1600, Shakespeare, *As You
Like It*, II.vii) – 'the moment at which an actor *enters* onto the
stage'. An *entrance round* describes a round of *applause* received
by famous actors on their entrance. In general terms, it is regularly
found in expressions such as 'she loves to make a dramatic entrance', possibly a reference to renowned *up centre* entrances of the
actor-managers and *stars* of C19.

entremès   Spanish version of *entr'acte*. Ironically, from Fr.
entremets, from *entre*, 'between', + *mets*, 'dishes'. *Entremets* can
still be used in English as 'a sweet dish, a side dish', but as the
etymology suggests, it harks back to performances in banqueting
halls and the like in medieval times. Compare *entr'acte*.

epic   A term borrowed from classical literature in the 1920s by
the German *dramatists* and *dramaturges*, Piscator and *Brecht*. The
origins of *epic* evoke the ancient roots of oral poetry, as the etymology suggests: from L. *epos*, from Gk *epos*, 'a word, story'. This
was the *genre* that *Aristotle* considered second only to *tragedy*, and
its characteristics – a tale of great import to its mother society,
the outcome of which is probably already known by the audience,
told by a *narrator* in the past tense and in the third person –
appealed to Brecht and Piscator's aims, namely to fashion an
objective *political theatre* for the C20. Its current theatrical usage
comes from German.

epilogue   'No epilogue, I pray you; for your play needs no excuse'
(1594, Shakespeare, *A Midsummer Night's Dream*, V.i). From Fr.
epilogue, from L., from Gk *epi-*, the prefix denoting 'in addition',
+ *logos*, 'speech': 'that which is additional to the text of a play'.
The *epilogue* is an afterpiece in verse or prose, the former traditionally being the more common, used in English for 'the concluding
part of a literary work' since at least mC16. In a play, it generally
occurs outside the *plot* proper, after the *dénouement*, and may be
spoken in role by a *character* or by the *chorus*, or by an actor out
of role. On occasions, it is used by the *dramatist* as a commentary

on the preceding action or to contain a summary of his argument.
Contrast *prologue*.

epithalamion   'A song or poem in celebration of a marriage; a
nuptial hymn'. Whilst many individual plays contain *epithalamia*,
(or *epithalamiums* – both plurals are acceptable), there are also
entire plays which are deemed worthy of the title: it is widely
believed from the internal evidence that *A Midsummer Night's
Dream* (1594, Shakespeare) was written to celebrate a noble
marriage. From L., from Gk *epi-*, the prefix denoting 'in addition',
+ *thalamion*, from *thalamos*, 'a bridal chamber'.

equestrian drama   A popular theatrical form in the C18 and eC19,
equestrian dramas, (from L. *equestris*, from *eques*, 'a knight or
horseman', from *equus*, 'a horse', + drama), provided opportunities for the demonstration of fine horsemanship in all their
plots. They were primarily staged at Astley's Amphitheatre and
at Covent Garden and Drury Lane, and the popular remains of
the genre can still be witnessed at *circuses*. (See *ring*).

Equity   Both British and American Actors' Equity Associations
are trade unions which negotiate and protect actors' salaries and
conditions of employment, whether they work on the stage or in
any of the other of the performing media. The British union was
founded in 1929. The literal meaning of *equity* is 'fairness;
recourse to principles of justice to correct or supplement law...'
(Concise Oxford: ME from OF *equité*, from L. *aequitas*, from
aequus, 'fair'). Membership of the union – *having Equity* – involves
getting Equity – being accepted as a member, which often leads
young hopefuls into a protectionist, Catch-22 situation: 'The
Catch 22 of Equity was infuriating: no card without a job, no job
without a card...' (Branagh, 76).

establishment   The *theatrical establishment*, strongly fulminated
against by *avant-garde* members of the *fringe* and *alternative*
theatre communities, is that body of people who represent covert
authority and influence in theatre. The word has been borrowed
from that for the legally-established position of the Church of
England in the State, and from the word for a body of men maintained for a specific purpose, such as the army, navy or civil
service. As the following etymology indicates, there is an inherent
conservatism in all establishments: from OF *establir*, from L.
stabilire, from *stabilis*, 'stable'. The term was used ironically in
the name of the 1960s' satirical *revue* club, The Establishment.

exit   *Exit* is the third person singular of L. *exire*, 'to go out': that
is, 'he/she goes out'. As a *stage direction*, (plural *exeunt*, 'they go
out'), its etymology is obvious. Its theatrical use in England dates
at least from C15: 'Tunc exit Iohannes; et dicit Petrus' (1485,

Digby Mysteries). Its most famous manifestation must be in Shakespeare's *Winter's Tale*, 'Exit, pursued by a bear' (III.iii). The noun, 'an actor's departure from the stage', dates back to at least C16: 'Keep some state in thy exit, and vanish' (1588?, Shakespeare's *Love's Labours Lost*, V.ii). It is commonly found in the well-known phrase *to make an exit*: 'never making an *Exit*, but that she left the Audience in an Imitation of her pleasant Countenance' (1740, Cibber, *Apology*). From this, the word was transferred metaphorically to any departure, including death – 'He scorn'd an Exit by the common means' (1661, Felton, *On Sir R. Cotton*) – and to any place of departure – 'They might find an easie exit...almost everywhere' (1665, Glanvill, *Scepsis scientifica*). Theatrically, the term for actors' *stage exits* was extended to refer to the doors and passages leading from the *auditorium* into the *foyer* and later to legally-required *fire exits*, terms which have been borrowed for all public buildings and, in mC20, via America, for the slip-roads leading from motorways. Phrases such as *making a hasty exit* have entered common parlance, as has the verb with its grammatically curious past tense: *he exited hastily*. An *exit line* is used for a character's parting shot before leaving the *set*.

experimental 'A season of new and experimental work at The Place' (*Plays and Players*, October 1990). Theatrically, this is a term for *avant garde* theatre work which gained a widespread currency in mC20. For a discussion of the implications of the use of this quasi-scientific term, see *laboratory* and *workshop*. *Experimental* comes from med. L. *experimentalis*, from L. *experimentum*, from *experire*, from *periri*, 'to try'.

exposition 'The revelation of vital elements of the plot of a play; also, the introduction of characters and themes'. Ultimately from L. *exponere*, 'to put forward, propose etc.', *exposition* entered English from Fr. as early as C14 as 'a statement in which any matter is set forth in detail'. Its literary and critical (and, hence, theatrical) usages are C19, borrowed from either music – where it signifies the introduction of a musical theme – or from philosophy – where it signifies the initial expostulation of a rhetorical thesis.

Expressionism 'Expressionism...is a violent storm of emotion beating up from the unconscious mind' (1923, MacGowan and Jones, *Continental Stagecraft*). This was an initially German, anti-*realistic* movement embracing all the arts which, whilst it had its roots in C19, was at its zenith in the period 1910-25. Such work, epitomised in theatre by Georg Kaiser, Ernst Toller and the early Brecht, expressed an intensely personal vision of individual and social life, expressed through a violent distortion of the objective

world and bold stylisation: often, characters were anonymous
types, dialogue was fragmentary or exclamatory, and, in design,
much use was made of masks and highly non-representational
sets.

extemporise   To *improvise, ad lib*. From L. *ex tempore*, literally
'out of the time', *extempore* has been used adjectivally and adverbially since at least mC16: 'Yes and extempore will he dities com-
pose' (1553, Udall, *Ralph Roister Doister*). The verb *to extemporise*
is a lC17 coining: 'The Extemporizing Faculty is never more out
of its Element, than in the Pulpit', (1692, South, *Sermons*).

extra   A supernumerary: an actor with no lines, used in crowd
scenes etc. Extra, 'outside, beyond' is rarely found in classical
Latin although the adjective *extaordinarius* was common. OED
considers it highly likely that English *extra* is from an C18 abbreviation of *extraordinary*, 'beyond, more than usual etc.'. The term
experienced a considerable vogue on both sides of the Atlantic in
C19. The theatrical term was probably coined in America in C19
as the following attestation on transport hints: 'Mr. Howel
informed him that an extra in America meant a supernumerary
coach...' (1838, J.F. Cooper, *Home as Found*). Its use in film
and television further supports this view.

extravaganza   From It. *extravaganza*, 'an extravagance', the term
has been used in English since lC18 for any extravagant or fantas-
tic artistic composition or performance. Theatrically, it is often
used for productions which have huge amounts of cash lavished
on their *design* and visual elements.

Fact, theatre of A form of *documentary drama* epitomised in the works of Rolf Hochhuth and Peter Weiss in the 1960s and early 1970s.

fade A C20 *lighting* and *sound* term: to *fade in* and *fade out* is 'to gradually increase or decrease lighting and sound *levels* – i.e. effect a change in brightness or volume'. Compare *dim*.

fake/fakey Used theatrically with the sense of 'false, insincere': 'the real reason why I couldn't get it was that it's a fakey scene' (Berkoff, 106). An actor who *fakes* an element of a role achieves his ends through *technique* alone, without belief. *Fake* has been used generally with this sense since at least eC19, coming originally from one meaning of the London underworld slang term, *fake* – 'to tamper with for the purpose of deception': 'to *fake a screw*, is to shape a skeleton or false key, for the purpose of *screwing* a particular place' (1812, J.H. Vaux, *A New and Comprehensive Vocabulary of the Flash Language*). For another underworld term used in theatre, see *drag*.

fall-guy In general usage, 'a scapegoat' – one who 'takes the rap' for someone else's shortcomings. Often, the word carries the sense of someone who is deliberately set up by others. In theatrical terms, a *stooge*; the *straight man* who is the butt of the *comic's gags*. According to Beale, the English usage, which he claims is as recent as the 1970s, is an adaptation of American underworld slang, where the word means 'a victim', i.e. one who falls down dead. From OE *.f(e)allan*, + American *guy*, probably from Yiddish *goy*, 'a Gentile', (which was anglicised by eC20).

falling flaps Key elements in the *transformation scenes* which are one of the hallmarks of English *pantomime*. *Falling flaps* were *hinged flats*, scenically decorated on both sides. One side would be shown to the audience, then, at the release of a catch, they would fall under their own weight and immediately present a totally different scene.

false proscenium A construction of *wings* and *borders* which effectively reduces the size of the *proscenium* aperture.

falsetto A high-pitched, male singing voice, imitative of the effects of the female voice in its higher register. Like other such terms, it is also used for the quality of an actor's voice: '[The Player Queen] begins the text...in a high-pitched falsetto'

(Berkoff, 125). From It., diminutive of *falso*, 'false', first used in English in mC18.

fan effect   A particularly spectacular domino technique of *scene changing* employed during certain *transformation scenes* in *pantomime*, whereby the *set* would collapse laterally, like a folding fan.

farce   From Fr. *farce*, 'stuffing'. This genre of *comedy* which relies heavily on improbable plots, unlikely coincidences, split-second *timing* and *slapstick* action has a venerable pedigree in folk tradition which may stretch back beyond the Greek satyr-plays and Roman comedies which are its antecedents in the 'respectable' theatre. The irreverence of the word's etymology is apt. In C14 England and France, L. *farsa* or *farsia*, from *farcire*, 'to stuff', were terms applied to phrases which priests interpolated into the middle of religious formulae such as the *kyrie eleison*: 'Kyrie, genitor ingenite, vera essentia, eleison' (OED): i.e. 'waffle'. (It may be of interest that C20 ecclesiastical historians have insisted on referring to this habit with an alternative spelling, *farse*.) Comic actors in French *mystery plays*, like all comedians, also had a tendency to improvise on the script, sometimes encouraged by the authors; their gags and business also came to be known as *farce*: 'Cy est interpose une farsse' (ed. 1837, *La Vie de St. Fiacre* in *Mystères Inédits du 15me Siècle*).

In C16, farce was used occasionally for a colloquial form of low comedy: 'Such as writte farcis and contrefait the vulgare speche' (1530, Palsgrave, *Lesclarcissement de la langue francoyse*). After the Restoration, however, English tastes which had been refined on the Continent made farce socially respectable: 'To the King's House, to see the first day of Lacy's "Monsieur Ragou"... a farce' (1668, Pepys, *Diary*, 31 July). It was at this period that farce achieves the status of *genre*. It has always been good *box office* but has rarely won critical acclaim, as Dryden's Epilogue to Etheredge's *Man of Mode* shows: 'Those Nauseous Harlequins in Farce may pass,/But there goes more to a substantial Ass' (1676). Following the trend that can be observed with other generic theatrical terms, 'farce' then underwent a metaphorical extension; it was applied to events in real life which are considered to be as ridiculous as theatrical farce: 'What should be great you turn to farce' (1704, OED). And later, 'These delegates... duly went through the farce of selecting and voting for persons already determined on by the King' (1888, Bryce, *American Commonwealth*). Today, as any sports' fan can testify, 'farce' can also carry with it the sense of a travesty of justice: 'The result was a farce' (1991, overheard, Old Trafford, Manchester).

It has also given rise to the terms *Feydeauesque*: *Aldwych farces*,

the inter-war work of Ben Travers (1886-1980); *Whitehall farces*.
The more radical end of the tradition is kept alive in Europe by
the Italian socialist *farceur*, Dario Fo (1926-   ), who argues that
satirical farce is the true theatre of the people and that the condes-
cending attitude shown towards it by the theatre establishment
is an expression of the distance between *legitimate* theatre and the
popular audiences who stay away from it in droves.

Faustian   'Of or pertaining to either the *character*, Faust, in the
eponymous plays (Parts I and II) by Goethe, (eC19) or to Dr.
Faustus in the lC16 play by Christopher Marlowe; or to the
character's situation in either of two plays; or to the style of
Goethe's play: written in a variety of verse forms, with radical
changes from high *tragedy* to low *farce*'. A C20 coining. The crux
of all the many dramatisations of the Faust legend is his pact with
Mephistopheles, to buy knowledge and worldly power for a
limited period at the end of which his soul is to belong to the
devil. Marlowe's version ends tragically, Goethe's with Faust's
redemption. One takes one's pick.

fauteuils   'Theatre seats resembling armchairs'. This term for
those rare commodities, comfortable theatre seats, is from Fr.,
from OF *faudestuel*, from the West Germanic *faldistōl*, as in 'fold',
+ 'stool': *faldstool* is still used in English for a bishop's backless,
folding chair.

feast of fools   See *fool* and *misrule*.

feed   'In America I was attacked after every rehearsal by desperate
actors asking "What is this character *about*?"... "It's about being
a good feed to Hamlet"' (Geilgud, 70). A *feed* was originally the
support artist or *straight man* who supplied the principal *comic* with
cues for his *gag-lines*; sometimes, the *stooge*. From the verb *to
feed*, as in *feeding lines* to the comic. It is a *variety* and *music-hall*
term which Partridge dates back to *c*.1890, and has transferred
to *straight* theatre. A *feed-line* is a line of dialogue immediately
preceding a *laugh-line*.

female impersonator   'A male actor who impersonates a woman
on stage'. The phrase became popular as an umbrella term for a
variety of styles of performance in lC19, and was used as a rather
formal euphemism in *music hall* and *variety*. See *boy actor*, *dame*,
drag, *principal boy*, *queen*.

festivals   '[A]n opportunity... to read and perform one-act plays
along the lines of the festival work I'd done while at the RSC'
(Branagh, 188). *Festival* is a noun formed from an adjective: ME,
from OF, from med.L. *festivalis*, from L. *festum*, 'a feast'. In
relation to religious feast-days, this term has been used adjectivally since at least eC14, but its employment for an organised

artistic celebration seems to derive from C19 musical celebrations such as the three-yearly *Handel Festival*. See *Edinburgh*, *fringe*, *carnival*.

festoon A *stage curtain* which, by means of attached *lines*, hangs in attractive swags. From Fr. *feston*, 'a festoon', probably so-named due to its decorative function at feasts. The term was first used in painting and architecture in C17. A row of coloured light-bulbs on a cable is also called a festoon.

Feydeauesque Of or referring to subject matter and style of the plays of George-Leon-Jules-Marie Feydeau (1862-1921), the pro-lific French *farceur* whose plays were renowned for their slick critiques of bourgeois hypocrisy, especially as regards sexual mores.

finale '*Fin*, *Finis*, or Finale, is the End or last note of a piece of music' (1724, *A short explication of such words as are made use of in the musick books*). Starting as a musical loan-word from Italian for 'the last movement of a piece of music or the piece which brings any of the acts of an opera to a close', *finale* was transferred for 'the last scene or closing section' of any public entertainment by lC18-eC19: 'It doubtless gratifies me much that our finale has pleased, and that the curtain drops gracefully' (1814, Byron, Let-ter). Around the same time, the word was transferred metaphor-ically to signify 'conclusion'. It is commonly found theatrically and generally in *grand finale*: 'the dramatic climax of a perfor-mance or series of events'.

fire regulations Fire is an enormous risk in the theatre, as it is in all indoor public meeting-places, seriously heightened by the amount of combustible material both *onstage* and *backstage*, and by some of the *dramatic effects* required in the staging of texts. The destruction of Shakespeare's Globe by a spark from a *sound effects* cannon during a production of *Henry VIII* graphically demonstrates this danger. Both Covent Garden and Drury Lane theatres have also twice burnt down and in the greatest ever theat-rical fire disaster, 1,670 members of an audience were killed in China in 1845. Hence the massive precautions taken, only partly to comply with government *fire regulations*, and the regular visits to theatres of local fire officer who ensures that the requirements of the 1968 Licensing Act are being complied with, especially the provision of adequate *fire exits*, *safety lights* etc. Electric lighting and more advanced fireproofing techniques and sprinkler systems have greatly reduced the dangers that were inherent in candle-light.

first night 'The first night, on 2 February 1933 at the new Theatre, did not seem to be particularly successful...' (Geilgud, 85). A self-explanatory alternative to *opening night*, *première* (see *night*). It gives rise to the common theatrical and general expression, *first-night nerves*, to describe apprehension before the opening of a new show or prior to any new experience. Also, *first night party*.

fit up   The setting up of *scenery*, *props* etc. for a show is termed the *fit up*. In the case of a touring company, this would also be the *get in*. A nautical term dating from at least mC17: 'The Dutch ...do fit up more Ships to Navigation, and cheaper than the English' (1670, Coke, *A discourse of trade*). The term *fit up company* can still be used: it was particularly common in C19 to describe a *barnstorming touring* company who erected their own stage at every *gaff* in which they performed.

five, the   A *call*, usually for members of the *cast*, given five minutes before a *show* is due to *go up*, or commence.

five and nine   The abbreviation given to Leichner *greasepaint* sticks nos 5 and 9, which, whilst now largely replaced by water-based *make-ups*, were traditionally combined to create the standard foundation for a basic, Caucasian, flesh-coloured make-up.

flash box   A descriptive term for a metal box or other container in which material to be detonated to produce a stage flash (usually, in pantomime, accompanied by a puff of smoke) is stored for safety reasons. Compare *bomb tank*, *maroon*.

flats   '(*Flats in the Scene Room*.) Cottage and long village, Medusa's cave and 3 pieces, Grotto that changes to a country house...' (1743, *Covent Garden Inventory*, quoted in Nagler, 352). *Flats* are *scenery* pieces traditionally constructed by stretching *canvas* over a wooden frame, though some flats are now constructed entirely of hardboard. The choice of canvas is due to the ease with which it can be scenically painted. Flats come in all shapes and sizes but the most common in a large theatre are rectangular, measuring roughly 6 metres by 3 or 4 metres, an ideal size for their primary function, the enclosing of a *box set*. They are usually supported by *flippers*, *stage braces* and *stage weights*. See also *backing flat*, *book flat* and *French flat*. Clearly, the term is descriptive of the object's shape, but its origins are unclear. There is a possibility that it is a nautical term: '*Flats*, in ship-building, the term given to all the timbers in midships' (1815, Falconer, *An universal dictionary of the marine* [ed. Burney]).

flexible staging   A C20 system of *staging* which allows marked variation of *acting areas* from one *production* to another within the same space or theatre. *Flexible staging* has replaced the *proscenium arch stage* as the most popular system in theatres constructed since the late 1950s.

flier   (Also found as *flyer*). A small poster – a *fly poster* – or leaflet used for publicity purposes. The term probably originated in America in C19: 'Inserting gaily-coloured advertising fliers in the body of the magazine' (1889, *The Literary World*).

flies *'(Flats in the Top Flies.)* Shop Flat and Flats in the shop…' (1743, *Covent Garden Inventory*, quoted by Nagler, 352). The *flies* is the name for the area of a theatre building above the stage from which *scenery*, *lighting equipment* and so on can be hung, and, if so desired, raised or lowered: that is to say, flown. The flies can also be used as a storage area. Undoubtedly, the term is *nautical* – for more details see *fly¹*.

flipper A wooden support for a *flat*, to which it is often attached by hinges. The *flipper* is designed to give support by standing at a 90-degree angle to the flat. It probably gets its name from its appearance: cut out like a piece of profile *scenery*, it resembles the flipper of a marine animal, a term not attested in OED until eC19. The animal's flipper derives from the verb *to flip*, probably from *fillip*, in its sense of 'a sudden jerk or blow'.

float An occasional synonym today for *footlight*, which it pre-dates. *Float* describes a means of *lighting* which preceded gas and electricity: illumination supplied by wicks, *floating* in oil.

floods 'From either side of the proscenium arch, two floodlights played upon the actors' (1925, A.E. Newton, *The Greatest Book in the World*). A C20 *lighting* term; an abbreviation of *floodlights* (or *flood-lights*). Floods are *lanterns* which, due to their intensity and the diffuseness of their beams, are capable of giving *general cover* over a wide area of the stage, or *flooding* it with light. Outside the theatre, floodlights are frequently used for outdoor illumination, notably for sports *arenas* and for large work areas such as dockyards, but this abbreviation appears to be restricted to specialist theatre use. The use of liquid terms for lighting is particularly common.

floor cloth Another term for a *stage cloth*: a sheet of painted canvas covering the floor of the stage.

floor plan See *ground plan*, *stage plan*.

floor show A C20 *cabaret* entertainment, often involving dancing of an exotic nature, so-called because it tends to occur in and amongst the audience, seated at tables, or on a dance floor surrounded by the audience. In phrases such as *I enjoyed the floor show* it can be used ironically for an unintentional entertainment supplied by the behaviour of others at any social gathering.

flourish An Elizabethan/Jacobean stage direction, signifying a point at which there is to be a trumpet fanfare. 'Flourish. Enter Gloucester, with France and Burgundy; Attendants' (*King Lear*, I.i). There is something elaborate or showy about a *flourish*; when

Lear enters earlier in the scene, Shakespeare gives the *cue*, "Sound a sennet", suggesting a more austere signal. Frequently in his plays he opts for the general direction "A trumpet sounds". From ME verb, from OF *florir*, from L. *florere*, from *flos, floris,* 'a flower'. The expression *to do something with a flourish*, whilst it may originate from ostentatious or flowery physical gestures rather than from the theatre, captures the spirit of the word.

fluff 'If, in rehearsal, you have fluffed a line several times, or if you fear you might fluff it...it's worth taking it out of context and practising it over and over again like a tongue-twister...The most noticeable mistake an actor can make is a fluff' (Barkworth, 57). Partridge dates the term back to *c*.1880 as 'lines imperfectly learned and delivered'. However, it is also used as a mistake in other areas, noticeably sport, as in *to fluff a shot*. The origins are uncertain, but there is possibly an obscene connection with *fluff* as 'the female pudend', to use Partridge's coy terminology.

fly¹ *To fly* is a nautical term, used originally with reference to hoisting a sail: 'Flying of sails, setting them in a loose manner; as royal sails without lifts' (1794, *Rigging and Seamanship*). Theatrically, it has been used since lC17-eC18 with reference to anything which is raised or lowered from the *flies*. It was this skill which led to the employment of sailors and ex-sailors in the theatre. The method employed to fly in a theatre is known as its *flying system* which is housed in the *flying gallery* or on the *flying floor* over the stage. The area available in the *fly tower* is known as the *flying space*. The system is operated by the *flyman*: if scenery is being lowered, it is attached to a *fly line* or *flying line*. If actors are being *flown*, they are attached to a leather *flying harness*.

fly² '[W]hen there's a very sympathetic audience or for whatever reason, I feel I begin to fly. We none of us know why it happens, do we? But new things which happen on those nights can be incorporated into future performances' (Prunella Scales, interviewed in Barkworth, 222). When *fly* is used metaphorically by actors, it denotes an inspired performance, one in which everything not only goes according to plan but, as if miraculously, the sub-conscious introduces new and highly appropriate elements into a role.

focus 'David Leveaux is characteristically calm and calming as he focuses everybody for the hours ahead' (Tim McInnerny, in the *Guardian*, 24/25 August 1992). L. *focus*, 'hearth, fireplace' (see *foyer*), was first transferred for use with reference to vision by the scientist Kepler in 1604, probably because the focus of a glass lens is the point at which it pin-points the rays of the sun to burn a piece of paper. It is from this sense that the term is used in *lighting* for adjusting and concentrating the direction of the beams of a *lantern* on a particular area of the stage. In other metaphorical usages in C20, it has come to mean 'the focus of (a person's) attention, concentration', another sense in which it is used theatrically. This sense has replaced an earlier one quoted by Bowman and Ball: 'to turn to face another actor, an object etc.'. Today, when actors are fully prepared for performance, they refer to *being focused*.

F.O.H.   The commonly-used abbreviation for *front of house*.

folio   The ablative case of L. *folium*, 'a leaf', referring to the format of a book. A *folio edition* was one produced in the largest possible format, by folding the large sheet of paper with which the printer worked, once, to produce two leaves (or four pages). (*Quarto* is folded twice.) The term has been used since at least eC16. In theatre terms, the word is used most commonly with reference to the *First Folio* of Shakespeare's *Complete Works*, published by Heminge and Condell in 1623, an attempt to draw all his extant theatre writings together; previously, only certain individual plays were available in quarto editions. This concept of a folio edition of a dramatist's work was borrowed from Ben Jonson who, conscious of his own status as a serious writer as opposed to a theatrical jobber, was keen to preserve his own work in his own lifetime.

follow spot   A *spotlight* whose directionality can be controlled by hand. Its beam follows a performer as they move so that it is particularly useful for lighting *variety acts* such as *singers* where the intention is to keep the audience's attention focused on the artist. See *spot* and *limelight*.

fool   A *stock* character of the C16 English drama. Although *fool* entered English from OF *fol*, it can be traced back ultimately to L. *follem, follis*, 'a bellows': its usage for a foolish person is thus connected in sense with modern English 'wind-bag', especially appropriate considering the tendency to verbosity of most theatrical fools. While such characters occur in ancient *comedy*, the English fool is a descendant of the professional fools (see also *jester* and *clown*) resident in large households, some of whom were wits, others of whom were harmless simpletons: 'Lyke a fole and a fole to bee,/Thy babule schalle be thy dygnyte! (1370, OED). The theatrical fool inhabits the ambiguous border territory between wisdom and madness, both perceptive and unfathomable, most conspicuously in his greatest incarnation, Lear's Fool. See also *misrule*.

foot   As in *to foot a flat*, a term used by *stage crew* meaning 'to prevent a flat from slipping when being moved by judicious use of the foot'.

footlights 'Unhappily on the first night the sand blew across the footlights, spraying the orchestra pit and the occupants of the first ten rows of the stalls' (Geilgud, 94). *Footlights* is a descriptive term referring to a *batten* of *lanterns* or some other source of illumination situated *downstage*, at, or more usually below, stage level, providing low-angle *lighting*; sometimes also referred to as *floats*. Their effectiveness is usually enhanced by some form of reflector. Footlights, originally positioned for concealment, an early nod towards *naturalism*, were in use on the Continent by the 1620s and had reached England by the Restoration, although the term would appear to be eC19: 'The foot-lights have just made their appearance' (1836-9, Dickens, *Sketches by Boz*). Because of the unnaturalistic shadows thrown by them, they are rarely used other than in combination with other lights in modern, realistic productions. (For a critique of their effects see Strindberg's *Preface* to *Miss Julie*.) Their once widespread use is immortalised in phrases such as *the lure of the footlights, the smell of the footlights* and in the name of the famous Cambridge University revue club, The Footlights, founded in 1883, which has produced several generations of influential comic actors and writers. In the C19, footlights could be lowered into the *cellar* by means of the *footlights trap*, either for trimming or, during a show, to reduce the intensity of the light cast on the stage.

fop A *comic*, dandyish figure; a *stock* character, particularly of *Restoration Comedy*. The term used simply as 'fool' in C15, but came to mean 'a foolishly dedicated follower of fashion' by m-lC17, a sense in which it is still occasionally used: 'some foolish fluttering fop or another' (1681, Otway, *The Soldier's Fortune*). *Fop-doodle* was also common in C17 as was the term *Fop's Corner* for the corner of the *pit* nearest the stage – an ideal place in which to be seen and from which to be heard. The fop's desire for attention was also reinforced in the name *Fop's Alley* for the *gangway* between the *stalls* and the *pit*.

forestage A term used nautically from C14-15 as an abbreviation of 'a ship with a forestage', *forestage* being synonymous with *forecastle, (fo'csle)*. 'Thei sey, there shulde come in to Seyme CC. gret forstages out of Spayne' (1462, *Paston Letters*). Sometimes still known as an *apron*, this is in the fact the residue of Restoration apron stage found in front of later, C18 *proscenium* stages. Whilst it is sometimes used for earlier stages, this is a retrospective usage.

formal stage (setting) Used for a *scenic setting* which, with the possible exception of *detail scenery*, remains fixed throughout a show.

Formalism Russian Formalism was a movement which saw

literary language (and by extension, every element of a *dramatic production*) as self-referential: it drew attention to its own formal, structural features rather to an external world, in some senses a prefiguring of post-modernism. In theatrical terms, its prime movers were the directors, Akimov and Meyerhold, the latter of whom formulated *bio-mechanics* and *constructivism* as means of achieving his *formalist* ends.

fourth wall   'My favourite version, though, which I can't use too often, is what I call the "fourth wall version", when I spend the entire performance shutting out the audience...as if I'm in a room, alone' (Alec McCowen, interviewed in Barkworth, 173). The *fourth wall* is an imaginary structure which the actor constructs in his mind when playing on a *proscenium arch* stage: by mentally closing up the proscenium aperture, he creates a fourth wall between himself and the 'black hole of the auditorium' (1936, Stanislavski, *An Actor Prepares*).

fox wedge   A wooden wedge designed to fit underneath the lower frame of a *flat* to compensate for the *rake* of a stage. *Fox* is possibly used here, as it is in other words and terms, because the ingenuity of the device reflects the animal's traditional craftiness.

foyer   A room or hallway *front-of-house*, designated for audience use prior to a show and during the interval; a 'crush-room' or 'crush-bar'. In many theatres, the *foyer* is the area just inside the main entrance doors, near the *box office*, though foyers can be found at any level of a theatre building. The word comes from Fr. *foyer*, 'a hearth, home', probably from Gallo-Romanic *focarium*, from L. *focus*, 'the fireplace' or simply 'the fire'. For obvious reasons, the *focus* was the pivot of the life of a Roman household. The transference from the home to a public room occurred in French and was borrowed by the English theatre at the Restoration.

freeze, to   'On the appointed night I walked to the little 100-seater theatre which was on the edge of the Reading University campus. And then I froze' (Branagh, 33). The word has two theatrical meanings, both hinted at above in an everyday situation. The first, to stand motionless, frozen like a statue, is an obviously descriptive actor's term. The second is allied: when an actor not only *blanks* but also finds himself incapable of movement, perhaps through *stagefright*, he is also said *to freeze*. A similar use of the word can be traced to soldiers in the First World War: 'When a blasted shell comes screaming...I don't move at all, just lie perfectly still and "freeze", waiting' (Soldier's diary entry from 1915).

friends in front/out front   A common actor's term for having friends or relations in the auditorium. This is often a cause for concern, even for the most experienced actors: 'on those nights when you have to be careful, like First Nights, or friends in front. Do you like to know when friends are out front?' (Barkworth, 183).

French brace Unlike the *stage brace*, which is a separate unit, usually attached to a *flat* by means of a hook, the *French brace* is an integral, triangular structure of wood, hinged to the back of a flat, which can be pulled out to lend support when required, either by being weighted or screwed down. The origins of the 'French' reference are uncertain.

French flat/Frenchman A term used for a large *flat*, or several large flats attached in a *run*: often used when they are to be flown in and out. The origin of the term is uncertain. One possible reason is that there is some unflattering *nautical* connection (a 'Frenchman' being a term for a French ship).

French's Acting Editions See *acting edition*.

fresnel The name given to a soft-edged *spot(light)*, i.e. one whose beam, whilst giving dominant, focused light to a specific area of the stage, is diffused so as to give no clearly-defined outline. Such *lanterns* are generally used in combination. From Augustin Jean Fresnel, (1788-1827), the French scientist who invented the concentrically-grooved lens which characterises this light. (Pronounced without the *s*).

the Fringe/fringe *The Fringe* is the name which was given in the 1950s to events held during the Edinburgh Festival which were not part of the Official Festival. Such events tended to be *alternative* and *experimental*; consequently the term *fringe*, used adjectivally without a capital F, soon became generic for such work not only in Edinburgh but throughout Britain. The term now covers a wide variety of performance arts from *straight theatre* to *stand-up comedy* and more exotic *acts*. Relations between the two halves of the festival have tended to be strained: 'All week Edinburgh seemed to be debating the Fringe. Third-rate circus or artistic engine-room? The truth surely is that it is a bit of both: in an unregulated market, hyped baloney inevitably exists cheek by jowl with genuine innovation' (Michael Billington, *Guardian*, 26 August 1991).

Today the term has been extended for use in other contexts: for example, unofficial meetings held during the round of party political conferences each autumn are referred to as *fringe meetings*. *Beyond the Fringe* was the name of the highly-influential joint Oxford and Cambridge *revue* which brought Alan Bennett, Peter Cook, Jonathan Miller and Dudley Moore to public notice.

frocks A familiar theatrical term for *costumes*. In C14, *frock* was

used for male outer garments, ecclesiastical, military or peasant;
since eC16 it has gradually been transferred in general usage to
the clothing of children and young girls. (*Frock* is still used for
a woman's dress.) Its theatrical use may be nautical, however;
'*Frog*, an old term for a seaman's coat or frock' (1867, Smyth,
Sailor's Word-book). Alternatively, and more probably, it may be
a playful term.

front of house   The term applied to those parts of a theatre which
are open to the public; that is, not *onstage* or *backstage*. *Front of
house staff*, including *programme* sellers, *usherettes*, *box office* staff
etc., perform managerial or ancillary duties in a theatre, under
the supervision of the *front of house manager*. See *house*.

full up   When the lights are *full up*, they are providing the brightest
lighting possible. This leads to the term *F.U.F.* – abbreviation
of *full up to finish*: increasing the brightness of the illumination a
few bars from the end of a musical *number* is supposed to encourage increased applause.

funambulism   One of several grandiose alternatives for *speciality
acts*, in this case *tight-rope* walking (see also *prestidigitation* and
légerdemain); it is a literal composite of L. *funis*, 'rope' and *ambulare*, 'to walk'.

Futurism   An eC20 artistic movement which believed in rejecting
traditional forms and *conventions*, preferring to place its faith in
technological developments. The emphasis the movement placed
on dynamic growth and energy led to its identification with proto-
Nazism, but not before its experiments with fragmented dramatic
form and dialogue, and its innovative staging and lighting techniques had created considerable opposition and interest. The term
(It. *futurismo*) was coined in 1909 in a manifesto by the Italian,
Marinetti, entering English from this or from F. *futurisme*.

FX   The common abbreviation of *effects*, or *special effects*, (a crude
approximation of the sound of the word), used for any unusual
visual and/or auditory requirements in a show, from a simple
door-slam to a complex *transformation scene*.

G **aff** A C19 term for a building temporarily given over for use as a theatre, usually for *music hall* or *melodrama*; often referred to as a *penny gaff* on account of the low admission fee. In the mC18, a *gaff* was a fair and the theatrical usage is probably derived from the fact that the earliest penny gaffs were also travelling shows. Additionally in C19, 'gaff' began to be used for any place of public entertainment; in C20, it has assumed the additional sense of 'home' (particularly in low slang) and 'street market'.

gaffer[1] An abbreviation of *granfer*, itself from *grandfather*. *Gaffer* has been used generally and affectionately for 'an old man worthy of respect' and as 'master, employer, boss' since at least C16. By the 1840s it was in use amongst navvies to refer to a 'foreman', and was also used in nautical terminology for 'the captain of a ship'. Slightly later it is recorded as a 'fairground master', possibly from the different origin, *gaff*, above. Its theatrical usage as 'boss of a theatrical department' is occasional, and is possibly borrowed from film where it means 'foreman electrician'.

gaffer[2] A common *stage management* abbreviation for *gaffer tape*, a strong, thick, adhesive tape which is used in theatre for sticking down material (such as cabling) and for masking and marking. Etymology uncertain, although it may be derived from one of the senses in *gaff* or *gaffer*[1].

gag 'a joke, a *punchline*'. Standard English *gag*, 'something placed in the mouth to stifle or prevent the subject's cries' (from ME verb *to gag*, probably imitative of a choking noise), was extended in eC19 to mean 'a hoax, a witty deception'. It is from this that the theatrical sense of *comic effect*, *business* or *dialogue* developed, at first as a collective noun: 'Mr. Augustus Harris pointed out that... actors and singers were continually introducing comic gag into their business' (1890, *Pall Mall Gazette*). By far the most common usage today both inside and outside the theatre is as *a gag*: 'a single, usually verbal, joke'. 'Stan & Ken Warby Scripts. 150 snappy gags, 150 one-liners, £2' (Ad. in *The Stage*, 28 March 1991).

gala (performances) '[W]e were delighted that he [Prince Charles]...could attend a Royal Gala Preview of *Twelfth Night*' (Branagh, 199). Ultimately from It. *gala*, 'festive dress', *gala* was

111

used in its Italian sense from eC17, later being extended to mean
'a celebration' in C18, and 'a special event or performance' by
e-mC19.

galanty show   A *shadow play* popular in C19, in which the sil-
houettes of *puppets* were projected onto a screen. From It. *galanti*,
plural of *galante*, 'gallant', due to the romantic subjects of the
Italian shows.

gallant   Man of fashion and pleasure, a ladies' man, lover. The
term has been used in this sense since C14 (from OF *galant*, the
participle of *galer*, 'to make merry'): 'Galauntes [are] purs penyles'
(1388, OED). The *gallant* was an Elizabethan/Jacobean stereotype
common both as a character on stage and as a member of the
audience of contemporary plays.

gallery   The original galleries in public theatres – internal seating
platforms in a theatre – developed druing the Renaissance, probably from the balconies of the noble courts or from the structure
of church interiors or inn courtyards from which many of the
players had graduated. 'Necessarie seats to be placed and sett...
throughout all the rest of the galleries of the saide howse' (1599,
Henslowe and Alleyne's contract with the carpenter of the Fortune theatre, quoted in Nagler, 118-19). These tiered platforms
which project from the inner walls to provide extra room for
spectators have remained a feature of most traditional theatres. In
lC17, the *gallery* became the name for the topmost *balcony* only,
where the cheapest seats – often backless benches – could be
found. In mC18, the term *The Gods* was first applied to the occupants of the gallery on account of their elevated position (and,
possibly, their constant interventions and interpolations into the
stage *action*), a formulation which, in the phrase *up in the Gods*,
can now be applied to the gallery itself. *Playing to the gallery*, a
phrase first recorded in mC19, is now used generally in many
walks of life for those who consciously seek popular attention and
adulation. One of the most charming, theatrically self-conscious
exploitations of this location is in the *Music Hall* song 'The Boy
I Love Is Up In The Gallery', traditionally addressed to an imaginary beau in the cheapest seats.

games, drama or **theatre**   It has become commonplace during
the second half of this century for actors, during the *warm-up* for
a rehearsal or performance, to participate in exercises or *games*
which will focus their attention on particular skills or elements
of ensemble playing required for the task in hand. Many of these
games are now also used in educational theatre. Some of the more
searching, *experimental* work which can be done in these sessions
falls under the heading of *psychodrama*.

gang show   A *show* designed and performed by Boy Scouts since e-mC20, often in the form of a *revue*. Because of its boisterous amateurism, use of cheap jokes and enthusiastic *choral* singing, the term is often used as a pejorative comparison for other, apparently more professional shows.

gauze   Like *arras*, this is another name for a material derived from its place of origin: in this case, via F. *gaze*, from *Gaza* in Palestine. It is a transparent fabric, originally of silk or cotton, which can be used in manufacturing *costumes*. However, its foremost theatrical use is in heavier duty versions (the word can even refer to a fine mesh of wire) as a *gauze-cloth* or *transparency*, a form of netting which can be painted like a normal stagecloth and which is opaque when lit from the front but almost transparent when lit from beind. Because of these properties, it is frequently used for quick scene changes, particularly magic *transformation scenes* in *pantomime*. A *gauze* is also known as a *scrim*, particularly in the United States.

gay theatre   It has been suggested that the adjective *gay*, meaning 'homosexual', originated in America or Australia in the 1940s, being appropriated in Britain in the following decade. The word's original meaning, 'light-hearted, disposed to mirth' etc., is a ME acquisition from OF *gai*, of unknown origin. However, its alternative use would appear to have a much longer pedigree than those who complain about its new sense might choose to accept. According to OED, *gay* was used for 'of loose or immoral life' by mC18: 'The old gentleman... had been a gay man, and was well acquainted with the town' (1754, *The Adventurer*). It was used as an underworld euphemism for both bought and casual sex as early as the lC18/eC19, which, given transportation, may strengthen the case for its modern usage having initially been Australian. According to Partridge, it was found in phrases such as *to feel gay*, 'to feel amorous or randy', *a gay girl* or *bit*, 'a prostitute', and *to feel gay in the arse or groin or legs*, 'to be loose, or easy'. The existence of Fr. *avoir la cuisse gaie*, also meaning the latter, suggests a possible origin. Unlike *camp*, which may well have a theatrical origin, *gay theatre* is an appropriated term for groups created either to cater for gay interests or to work in an *agit-prop* fashion to advance the gay rights movement.

gels   An abbreviation of *gelatines*: 'colour filters', sheets of transparent, coloured plastic which, when secured in a *gel frame* or holder in front of a *lantern*, colour the beam it produces. They can also be used effectively in combination with *gobos* and *colour wheels*. The word, (from Fr. *gélatine*, from It. *gelatina*, from *gelata*, 'jelly'), points back to a pre-synthetic age when lighting

and photographic gels were produced from that colourless, taste-
less, water-soluble, setting substance also used in food preparation
(hence 'jelly') derived from rendered-down animal skins, liga-
ments, tendons etc.

general cover   A lighting *cover* which gives an even distribution
of light to the entire *set*.

genre   A particular category of dramatic work, usually characterised by the nature of its subject matter or its style of performance.

'What is most fascinating about [Shadwell's *The Virtuoso*] is
the way it prefigures, in a way other Restoration comedies do
not, a broad *genre* of English comedy that manifests itself in the
Crazy Gang and the Carry On films' (*The Stage*, 23 April 1992).
Critics from *Aristotle* onwards have attempted to categorise works
of literature, a tendency satirised by Shakespeare, through
Polonius, in *Hamlet* (II.ii): 'tragedy, comedy, history, pastoral,
pastoral-comical, historical-pastoral, tragical-historical, tragical-
comical-historical-pastoral . . .'

Genre is a French term meaning 'a type or kind', from OF
gendre, (from which *gender* is derived), from L. *genus*, 'birth, race,
stock', a term which has been used for classification in logic,
biology etc. 'Genre' as a *critical* term has gained in currency since
the 1960s due to the influence of Structuralists such as Roland
Barthes, who conceived of genre as a set of *conventions* and codes
which alter from age to age but always imply an implicit contract
between *writer/performer* and *audience*.

gerb   A C20 term for a device which, when detonated, produces
a large flash and explosion. Etymology uncertain.

gesture   'This filling-in by highly charged facial expressions and
gestures of human detail seems to have been the characteristic of
C19 playing . . .' (Brook, 17). A *gesture* is 'an expressive movement, particularly of the arm', used by an *actor* to emphasise the
thought or feeling contained in a word, phrase or even a moment
of *silence* on stage. ME, from med. L. *gestura*, from L. *gestus*,
from *gerere, gest-*, 'to weild'.

Gestus   A word much favoured by Bertolt Brecht (see *Brechtian*)
as an alternative to the standard German *Geste*, or 'gesture', often
translated as *gest* (from the obsolete English word meaning 'bearing, carriage, mein'. *Gestus* was meant to contain both the ideas
of 'gist' *and* 'gesture': it referred to the attitude of a *character*
towards a given circumstance. 'Each single incident has its basic
gest' (1948, Brecht, *A Short Organum for the Theatre*). For an
actor, the Brechtian Gestus is the sociological significance of a
scene, in radical contrast to the complex, individual, psychologi-

cal motivation preferred by adherents to the *Stanislavski* system and the *Method*. A *social gest* can be clearly distinguished from an individual gest: 'One's efforts to keep one's balance on a slippery surface result in a social gest as soon as falling down would mean "losing face"; in other words, losing one's market value' (mid-1930s, Brecht, *On Gestic Music*). The adjective (coined by the critic Eric Bentley) is *gestic*.

get-in, get-out, the   These nouns, formed from the simple verbal phrases *to get in* and *get out* are the jargon employed by *touring companies* to describe the act of getting their scenery and equipment etc. in and out of a *receiving house* or other *venue*. Because of their architecture, some theatres are notorious for creating *difficult get-ins*, where access to the stage with bulky scenery is problematic.

get on, off   'During the performance the time passed in a whirl of worrying about getting on and off' (Branagh, 210). Self-explanatory actors' terms for *getting on and off the stage*.

ghost glide   An alternative, descriptively exact, term for the 'Corsican Trap', (so named because it was originally devised in 1852 to solve a stage problem in *The Corsican Brothers* by Dion Boucicault). This most sophisticated of traps allows an actor to be drawn along a narrow *stage cut* by means of one of a variety of forms of tracking, giving the impression that he is moving supernaturally.

ghosts   There is a long tradition of theatre ghosts in England, usually claimed to be the spirit of some deceased actor associated with any given *venue*. In a highly superstitious profession, ghosts are generally regarded as good luck omens.

   Ghost is also a term used to describe the accidental spillage of light to a place on the *set* where it is not wanted.

   The phrase 'Has the ghost walked?' means 'Has the manager come round with the pay?' The origin of this, according to theatre lore, is that Shakespeare, who is reputed to have played the Ghost in *Hamlet*, paid the cast's wages during the long wait between this character's *entrances*; alternatively, though slightly less appealingly, it is claimed that the job of going round with the wages tended to be given to the actor playing that role.

gig, a   Originally a jazz musicians' term dating from the 1930s for a one-off performance or one-night-stand. The term has passed to the theatre through obvious channels: it is now the classical musician's term for a *concert*, too. The etymology is uncertain – it possibly comes from a confusion with *jig*, 'a dance'.

glass crash   A *sound effect* from the days prior to the *Revox* (tape recorder), usually created by pouring broken glass and crockery from one tin bucket to another. *Crash*, like many other imitative words in English, is of ME origin.

glove-puppet In all early societies from Japan to Western Europe, the *glove-puppet*, composed of a firm head made out of carved wood or a substance such as papier mâché, with an attached, loose, open costume beneath it, was the most rudimentary form of *puppet*. (Contrast *marionette*.) It is worn with the index finger controlling the head and the first and second fingers in charge of the arms. See also *Punch*.

go In a variety of specialist theatrical usages, the verb *to go* is associated with the onset of actions. A show *goes up* rather than simply begins (see *curtain*). A somewhat curious noun, *the go*, also exists as the *cue* for the opening of the show. The imperative *Go!* can also be used as a cue, as in *Go lights!* – 'Bring the lights up now' etc.

gobo A device, usually a metal disc, which masks part of the beam of a *lantern*, so that the light cast from the lantern corresponds to an image cut out of the disc: a *template*, a term by which it is sometimes known in America, alongside *pattern*. If one wanted to flood the floor of the acting area with the effect of light spilling across a church floor from a stained-glass window, a *gobo* could be cut to represent the shape of the window surround and the leading, the gaps filled with variously-coloured *gels*. I have tried in vain to discover the derivation of this term. Certainly, it was already in use in the film industry in late 1930s, for a *pattern* used in front of a lantern, but even the manufacturers I have contacted seem unsure of its etymology. Several acronyms have been suggested – 'gel over black-out', for example – but all are unconvincing, as is the desperate suggestion that an early lighting operator using the device was called Bo (or Beau), and used to receive the shouted instruction, 'Go, Bo!'

gods[1] OE. A jokey term coined in the mC18 referring to the occupants of the theatre *gallery*. Farmer and Hensley in *Slang and its Analogues* (1890-1904), quoted in Partridge, claim that it was 'Said to have been first used by Garrick because they were seated on high, and close to the sky-painted ceiling', but the existence of the analogous Fr. *paradis* underlines the unlikeliness of Garrick's being the author of the term.

gods[2] OE. A term used for *theatrical backers* or *angels*. This is probably an abbreviation of *godfather*, a term used from C18 for someone 'who pays the bill or who guarantees the rest of the company' (Partridge).

going round Used in this shorthand form, it is an abbreviation of *going round* to see an actor in the dressing-room, sometimes before but more commonly after a show.

gopher   Sometimes also found as *gofer*, a term used in many industries including the theatre for 'a dog's-body', someone who can be asked to *go for* this and *go for* that. Often a junior *ASM*. Probably an American term, from a play on the name of the small American mammal.

goliard   Originally, a medieval drop-out scholar or cleric who joined bands of travelling *players* and provided the strong satirical, anti-ecclesiastical element of their shows. The name comes from their protested allegiance to the fictional Bishop Golias. In the later Middle Ages, *goliard* became merely a synonym for *jongleur* or *minstrel*. See *guillare*.

Grand Guignol   A largely French theatrical *genre* characterised by its *melodramatic* treatment of subject matter which included murder, rape, suicide, the supernatural etc. In English, the word is generally applied in passing to works which display one or more of the excessive tendencies of the French genre. Guignol is a French Mr *Punch*, an C18 Gallic improvisation on the theme of Polichinelle. In C19, his name became associated with *cabarets* in the Montmartre district of Paris, such as the Théâtre du Grand Guignol, where the genre grew up.

grave trap   Named after its suitability for use in the so-called Gravediggers' Scene in *Hamlet*, (Act V.i), this *trap* is a rectangular box situated *centre stage*: the term is found in *the Covent Garden Inventory*, (1743, quoted in Nagler, 355), and its use probably predates this by several decades.

grease-paint   Grease and other oils had sometimes been used in solution with earlier powder *make-ups* in the theatre, but theatre *grease-paint* in the form of numbered sticks was invented by Ludwig Leichner, a Wagnerian opera singer, in the 1860s and marketed in England a decade later, becoming regulation equipment before the turn of the century: 'He only used materials that [are] in every actor's make-up box – grease-paint, rouge, lining pencil and powder' (*Pall Mall Gazette*, 1 September 1888).

green   According to Beale, the *stage* has been referred to as *the green* by actors since at least eC20. He suggests that this is from 'greengage', Cockney Rhyming Slang for 'stage'. However, see *green room*.

green room   'I would see actors come on and feel the green room being brought on with them; I can almost sense the tea and fags' (Berkoff, 150). A *backstage* rest room for the cast. The original Restoration *green rooms* – the first attestation is in Shadwell's *A True Widow* (1678), were places where actors and actresses could receive their audience, with whatever entertainment that entailed.

The etymology is uncertain. It is possible that the name comes prosaically from the colour the rooms were painted, as was certainly the case in The Theatre Royal, Drury Lane, as green is supposedly restful. There are others who claim that, since an alternative Restoration name was 'scene room', 'green room' was a corruption of this. However, were the traditional actor's term *green* already in use for the stage, this might also account for the name.

gridiron or *grid* 'Mrs. Clive was one night seen standing at the wing, alternately weeping at and scolding Garrick's acting. Angry at last at finding herself so affected, she turned on her heel, crying "D--- him, he could act a gridiron"' (C19, Russell, *Representative Actors,,* quoted in Hay, 10). Originally a framed arrangement of joists, rafters, beams etc. – later girders and battens – high above the stage, from which scenery was suspended and by means of which it could be raised and lowered. A *nautical* term: *gridiron* is also the name for the frame of parallel beams used to support a ship in a dock. Grid can now also be used synonymously with *rig* to describe the structure on which *lanterns* are hung. A further use of the term is for the sectioned, scale plan of a stage which a *lighting designer* might draw up to aid his design. From ME *gredire*, (a variation of *gredil*, 'a griddle'), the second syllable later being replaced by *iron* because of the sound similarity.

groundlings 'O, it offends me to the soul to see a robustious periwig-pated fellow tear a passion to tatters, to very rags, to split the ears of the groundlings, who for the most part are capable of nothing but inexplicable dumb-shows and noise' (1600, *Hamlet*, III.ii). The name for the members of the *audience* in an Elizabethan/Jacobean theatre who occupied standing positions around the *stage*.

ground plan Stage plan: a scale drawing of the *stage* showing the precise location of *set, props, lights* etc. for a given *production*. The term has had a general architectural usage since eC18.

groundrow This word now means any piece of *scenery* which stands on the floor of the *stage*, though in C19 it was a descriptive term for a long, low, cut-out piece, often depicting some natural feature such as foliage or rocks, (known in C18 as a *ground piece*), placed to mask another stage feature also called a *ground row*: a strip of gas lights illuminating the *upstage area* or the *backcloth*.

groupie A 1960s term, borrowed from the teenage fans of rock musicians who followed their idols around and went to great lengths, often including the offering of sexual favours, to show their appreciation. Theatrical groupies are descendants of the C19 *Stage Door Johnny*. The phrase is also frequently used humorously: 'After two productions at the National Theatre ("I'm a Peter Hall groupie") the parts are more important than the place' (1979, actress Maria Aitken in the *Telegraph Sunday Magazine*).

guillare An Italian version of *goliard*, repopularised since the early 1970s by the work of the satirical *farceur*, Dario Fo.

Half, the   Like *the five* and the *quarter*, a *cue-call* signifying the amount of time left before *curtain up*, the *up*: that is, half an hour to the opening of the *show* – according to cautious *theatre time*, thirty-five minutes.

halls, the   An abbreviation of *music halls*. The expressions *working the halls* and *on the halls* were common in the lC19 and eC20, the earliest attestation of the use of this expression in Partridge being prior to 1887.

hall keeper   A now largely defunct term for the *stage door-keeper* (or *-man*), whose job it was to man the area just inside the *stage door*.

ham actor   As noun, adjective and verb and in all its variants, 'ham is hollow' (Brook, 53). *Ham actors*, or *hams*, usually fail due to a tendency to *ham it up* – that is, to overact and to play up the dramatic and emotional content of a role in an exaggerated or *camp* fashion. They use the *stock techniques* and tricks of C19 *melodrama* rather than searching for the truth of a character or dramatic situation. This rather cruel snippet from a review of an *adaptation* of *Treasure Island* on the 1990 *Edinburgh Fringe* captures the spirit of the term nicely: 'Hamming there was a-plenty, with a cast of jolly tars in designer sea-rags yo-ho-hoing, singing and calling for rum to their hearts' delight' (*Plays and Players*, October 1990). *Hammy* is also found: 'The orchestra takes up the sound of the ghost...it's deep in the throat, a sound that could be hammy in the wrong hands' (Berkoff, 6).

The origin of the term is disputed: that it is an abbreviation of Hamlet, drawn from the temptation to bleed dry the opportunities of that role, is one rather weak suggestion. There are other dubious suggestions – one which claims an English origin for the term suggests that it comes from Ham House, near Richmond, a building renowned for being over-decorated and baroque.

The most plausible derivation, with a more detailed and credible etymological story, is that in C19, before the invention of *Leichner* make-up, powder make-ups were combined with some form of grease or oil before application. *Amateurs*, or actors on a low income – that is, those who tended to be inferior – were forced to employ cheaper substances (rather than the professionals' sophisticated oils) to apply their make-up, hence the nicknames *ham-bone* and *ham-fat(ter)* from the fact that they used ham-rind and other unpleasant greases as a medium. *Ham-fatter* may come directly from a *negro minstrel song*, 'The Hamfat Man'. This was abbreviated to 'ham'. Thus it was only a matter of time before it began to be used pejoratively for any amateurish (i.e. old-fashioned, melodramatic) performance. It is generally agreed that the term was adopted in England from the United States just after the First World War, which makes this suggested etymology the most likely. Today, the term *you old ham* can be used quite lightly, almost affectionately between friends who are actors, but this lightness does depend on context and is not to be recommended for general use.

It is from the theatrical sense that the term *radio ham* is alleged to have developed for an amateur radio operator, again in America in the 1920s and 1930s, though others argue that it is merely a corruption of *amateur*, with an appended aitch (another of the less plausible contenders for the theatrical etymology, too, incidentally).

hamartia   The loosely-translated 'fatal flaw' which leads the *tragic hero* to his downfall in the *Aristotelian* definition of tragedy: a more accurate translation of the Gk would be 'error of judgement'. See *hubris*, the most common example of *hamartia*.

Hamlet wait   Any prolonged period which an individual actor spends *offstage* between his last *exit* and his next *entrance* in a show. The phrase derives from the *wait* the actor playing Hamlet endures between IV.iii and V.i of *Hamlet*. In fact, it is not that long: 'At the matinée I would sleep on my sofa for ten minutes during Ophelia's mad scene, which is the only wait Hamlet has...' (Geilgud, 66-7). For a longer *wait* for an actor in this play, see *ghost*.

hand   As in *stage-hand*, a term for a member of the stage crew, often an unskilled one like a *scene-shifter*. A *nautical* term for any sailor, the entire crew being referred to as *all hands*: 'Come aft all hands' (1669, Sturmy, *Mariner's Magazine*). Interestingly, it is one of the very few nautical terms to have been transferred to performance (see – *hander* and compare *busk*).

hand-bill   A *hand-bill* – as in 'pressing handbills on harried passers-by' (*Plays and Players*, October 1990) – is a small advertisement to be thrust into the hand of a pedestrian, tucked under a driver's windscreen-wiper or nonchalantly scattered over all the tables in a bar, restaurant etc. A C18 term: 'Who make their appearance either in hand-bills or in weekly or daily papers' (1753, *The World*, No. 1). See *bill* for further details.

-hander   As in *a one-hander* or a *two-hander*, these are compounds which denote the number of actors (or *hands*) required to play in any given production or scene from a production. Thus, Act I.i of *Macbeth*, in which the First, Second and Third Witches meet on a heath, is a *three-handed* scene or *three-hander*. Pinter's one-act play *The Dumb Waiter*, with only two actors, is a *two-hander*. It is interesting to compare this formulation with the famous *single-handed ocean races*, more obviously connected with their *nautical* roots.

hand-worked house   Also known as a *rope house* or *hemp-house*, this is a largely anachronistic term used to refer to a theatre which had not installed a *counterweight system*, but had retained the traditional technique of raising and lowering *scenery* by means of *lines* from a *grid(iron)* or *fly-floor*.

happening, a   a word appropriated by hippies in the 1960s – part of the *arts lab.* movement – signifying theatrically either 'a *multimedia* event' or, generally, a social party. *Happening* was taken from the jargon of drug-addicts and jazz musicians in the United States, where it meant 'a spontaneous eruption of feeling or display' (Beale).

Harlequin   Arlecchino was one of the *zanni* of the *commedia dell' arte*, traditionally costumed in a black mask and multi-coloured suit of diamond-shaped patches. He was borrowed and renamed *Harlequin* in C18 by the English tradition of the *harlequinade* in which he is the lover of *Columbine*, and the forerunner of the *principal boy* of later *pantomime*.

harlequinade   A popular tradition of romantic and *comic entertainment* which caught on in eC18: 'He formed a kind of harlequinade, very different from that which is seen at the Opéra Comique in Paris' (1780, Davies, *Memoirs of the Life of David Garrick*). Its romantic elements, based on the music, *mime* and *disguise* of the characters *Harlequin* and *Columbine*, were to remain but be gradually subsumed into the *comedy* surrounding another character, *Pantaloon*, as the harlequinade evolved into *pantomime*.

heads!   A warning cry from members of the *crew* issued either when something has been accidentally dropped from a ladder or from the *flies* or when something is being lowered to *stage* level.

heavy father, woman   Two of the *stock characters* of C19 *repertory* in which an actor might be typecast. In this sense, *heavy* means 'sober, serious', a usage dating from eC19 which appears to have originated in the theatre: 'The regular dramatic performance was thought too heavy a business for the evening' (1829, Disraeli, *Vivian Gray*).

heckling   'For the first time I confronted an audience who talked loudly all the way through, who heckled and threw things'

Branagh, 230). *Heckling* is unwanted and hostile audience inter-
ruption during the course of a dramatic performance or public
speech. *To heckle* is a variant of *hackle*, ultimately from Germanic
hakila, (from *hak*, 'a hook'), either 'a flax-comb' or a name for
the long feathers on the neck of the cock and certain other birds.
These feathers rise in a hostile display then the bird is preparing
to attack a rival or intruder, and thus we get both the expression
with one's hackles rising (or *up*) for a person who is spoiling for a
fight, and the verb *to heckle*.

hemp house   See *hand-worked house*.

hemps   The name given to un-counterweighted *flying lines* made
of rope, so-called because, before the adoption of manila ropes
from the Philippines, all available rope was made from the cortical
fibres of the *hemp* plant, which had originated in India. The name
of this plant, *Cannabis sativa*, gives us the word *hemp* in the following way: Gk *kannabis* becomes Germanic *hanipaz* which
becomes Old Swedish *hanap*, Old Norse *hampr* and, eventually,
OE *henep*. It is intriguing to note that *canvas* has the same root.

hero/heroine   '[Hamlet] is also their hero; the reason for coming
out on a wet night' (Berkoff, 8). *Hērōs* was the term conferred by
the Ancient Greeks on those men who were in some way supernaturally gifted. The word was adopted in English in this sense
in C14, acquiring the metaphorical sense of 'a man of exceptional
valour' in C16 and 'a man exceptional in any field of endeavour'
by C17, general usages which remain. The literary usage as the
protagonist of a fictional work, from the sense *epic hero*, 'the subject
of an epic', however, is a post-Restoration development, probably
borrowed from Fr. *héros*: 'His Heroe falls into... an ill-tim'd
Deliberation (1697, Dryden, *The Works of Virgil*). The literary
heroine, again probably from Fr. *héroïne*, develops alongside, or
(given the nature of socio-linguistic sexism) just behind the male
form, being attested as 'the chief female protagonist in a literary
work' by eC18: 'The other Saints have regard only to the Heroine
of the Picture' (1715, OED).

heroic   'An heroic play ought to be an imitation, in little, of an
heroic poem, and consequently... love and valour ought to be
the subject of it' (1672, Dryden, *The Conquest of Granada*). A
minor English dramatic *genre* drawing on the Greek sense of *hero*
and introduced at the time its first adoption of 'hero' into English
(see above).

high comedy   (See *comedy*). *High*, here, is used in its early, C9
sense, 'of exalted dignity': in modern terms, 'sophisticated'. This
sense of sophistication refers to both the setting and subject of
high comedy (contrast *low comedy*). Its characters are usually of

high social standing, preoccupied with concepts such as honour and idealistic love – and speak in a highly articulate, informed and witty manner, provoking what George Meredith terms 'intellectual laughter' (1877, *The Idea of Comedy*). Examples might include Shakespeare's *Much Ado About Nothing*, much *Restoration Comedy*, and, later, works by Wilde and Coward.

high-wire   A taut, elevated wire or *tight-rope* in a *big top* or other *circus venue*, along which specialist *artistes* perform balancing *acts*. See *acrobat, funambulism*.

history plays   *Histories* (as they are referred to in abbreviated form) belong to a *genre* which became popular in the patriotic fervour which followed the defeat of the Spanish Armada in 1588. Such plays, which deal with English national history and most commonly chart the reign of a particular monarch (although the term is also used for any play based on historical fact, such as Jonson's *Sejanus* and, in recent times, Robert Bolt's *A Man for All Seasons*) were called chronicles in C16 and eC17: they were based on a rearrangement of material from works such as Raphael Holinshed's *Chronicles*, works which belong to a prose and verse tradition dating back in English at least to the C9 *Anglo-Saxon Chronicle*. The term *history* for a chronicle play would appear to have become established in critical tradition due to Heminge and Condell's decision to divide the *First Folio* of Shakespeare's Complete Works (1623) into *tragedies, histories* and *comedies*. Ultimately from Gk *historia*, 'finding out, narrative, history', (from *histōr*, 'learned, wise man'.)

histrionics   Even more than *thespianism, histrionics* is an archaic, self-conscious term for 'the profession or activity of acting'. Today, its primary usage as a noun is metaphorical, extra-theatrical, and usually derogatory, suggesting the *dramatic* pretence of non-existent emotion, or the self-indulgent exaggeration of emotions. From LL *histrionicus*, from L. *histrion -em*, 'an actor', the word is occasionally found adjectivally from mC17 with the sense of '*stagey*'; it has only been used as 'of or pertaining to actors, dramatic', since mC18 and has never been fully assimilated into theatre language.

hit   'I had been reading plays for a theatrical manager until I realised that four of the biggest hits in London were all plays I had recommended' (Margaret Ramsay, *Guardian*, 24/25 August, 1991). A hit is used of a show or production which has proved itself a great *box office* success. As a colloquial term for 'success' it can be traced back to the eC19, along with its antonym, *miss*. See *smash* for details of its sporting origins.

hobby horse   Reduced by the lC18 to a character in mummers' plays (see *mumming*) and to a child's toy – a wooden pole with a horse's head at one end – the *hobby horse* made frequent appearances in much early European drama. The actor playing it would be dressed in a horse-shaped wicker framework like a one-man *skin act*, and was probably acting out the vestigial rites of an earlier, animal-worshipping culture. Probably due to its phallic appearance, by lC16, 'hobby-horse' was also used to refer to a prostitute. Its current sense of an obsessional interest, as in the phrase 'You're on your hobby horse again', would appear to be a development from the other Standard English meaning of *hobby*: a favourite subject or occupation which is not one's main business. From *hobby*, *hobyn*, *hoby*, familiar forms of Robin (as, interestingly, is one of the other traditional names for a horse, *Dobbin*). The name Robin is traditionally associated with characters who are left over from older, indigenous religious traditions such as the Robins Goodfellow and Hood. It is also echoed in *hobgoblin*.

hoist   American name for a *slote*. From the verb meaning 'to raise', a C16 alternative of *hoise*, from C15 *hysse*, probably of Germanic origin.

hoofer   A professional dancer. This American term, from the verb *to hoof*, most frequently applied to members of the *chorus line* but applicable to both sexes, has its origins in *vaudeville*. Its English usage can be traced back to the 1920s: 'Mr. Tommy Nolan proposed to his partner, Miss Annie King. She accepted him, and they planned their wedding and honeymoon while "hoofing"' (*Daily Express*, 2 July 1928).

hook clamp   A *clamp* used to attach a *lantern* to a *lighting bar*, so-called because of its shape and function.

hot-seating   A common *drama game*, often used in educational drama and as an actors' *rehearsal* technique, whereby an actor or student, often in role, is placed on a single chair in front of a group of others who question them. The technique is frequently used to explore either a character's *motivation* or the *subtext* of a script. The phrase *to be in the hot seat*, meaning 'to be in a difficult or responsible situation', was borrowed from America *c.*1950, *the hot seat* (or *hot squat*) being a long-established term for the electric chair. However, it is highly likely that the theatrical term crossed the Atlantic in its specialist sense.

house¹   as in *hemp house* or *receiving house*, 'a theatre'.

house²   as in *a good house*, 'the audience'.

The relationship between these two senses of *house* is intimate, as the expression *a full house* – 'a theatre in which all the seats are taken' *or* 'a capacity audience' exemplifies. In the C16/eC17, the word was used to refer to whole theatre building: 'The frame of

the said howse to be set square... with a good suer and strong
foundation...' (1599, Henslowe and Alleyn's contract with the
carpenters of the Fortune theatre, quoted in Leacroft, 33). *Public
house, eating house* and *whorehouse* are other places of public 'entertainment' which share this development of originally-domestic
OE *hūs*. Those, like Shakespeare, who owned all or part of the
building were referred to as *house-keepers*, and, as such, were
entitled to a percentage of the takings on the door. In the lC17,
'house' began to be used more predominantly for those areas of
the theatre which would now be called *front-of-house*: i.e. those
which are not *backstage*, including the *auditorium*, passages, lob-
bies and *foyers*, the bars and refreshment rooms, cloakrooms and
box-offices, under the care of the *front-of-house manager*. Consequently, such terms as *the house lights*, (which illuminate the
auditorium), and the *house* (or *front*) *curtain* or *tabs* (which separate
backstage from front-of-house) have developed. *House seats* refer
to a limited number of *complimentary* seats set aside at each performance. Common phrases include 'there wasn't a dry eye in the
house', to describe any event which has a profound emotional
impact on those who witness it.

hubris   The most common form of *hamartia*, or 'fatal flaw' in a
tragic hero or *heroine*. Hubris (a Greek term) is now generally used
in the sense 'an overweening pride or presumption which leads
to a person's downfall', but in the precise, *Aristotelean* usage it is
a character's blind self-confidence and self-absorption which leads
them to disregard divine laws and warnings in the pursuit of a
personal objective, thus bringing about their own *nemesis*.

hurry music   Sometimes abbreviated to *a hurry*: the music commonly associated with scenes of chase or haste in *melodrama* and
silent movies. 'The wrongful heir comes on to two bars of quick
music (technically called a hurry)' (1835, Dickens, *Sketches by
Boz*.) *Hurry* is a C16 coining, presumably imitative of the action
or state it describes.

ice-breaker *Ice-breakers* or *ice-breaking exercises* are *warm-up* techniques employed in the early stages of rehearsals (and a common feature of *group-building* in much educational drama, their aim being to inspire trust and co-operation amongst groups of relative strangers. 'Judi saw the need for an *ice-breaker*, and once the Company had been finalised she had the inspired idea of holding a Company party in her country home' (Branagh, 202). The term is C19 (from ships developed for Arctic conditions) and its theatrical employment is C20.

illusion¹ 'We can...abandon ourselves to the illusion or refuse it' (Brook, 57). One of the basic aims of *naturalistic* theatre is to make the audience believe in the dramatic *illusion* represented on stage. *Illusion* is from Fr., from L. *illudere*, 'to mock', but was in use with its present sense of 'something that deceives by creating a false impression' by C14, although its sense at that time did not take into account the *convention* of the audience's 'willing suspension of *disbelief*'.

illusion² A *conjuring* trick such as 'sawing the lady in half', in which the audience's perception of reality is actually duped, (see *illusion¹*). *Artists* specialising in such *acts* are known as *illusionists*. 'As well as escapes, Houdini also presented more ordinary illusions, and was also able to simulate many effects presented by the so-called "mediums" at séances' (Wilmut, 175).

impersonate One element of the actor's art is to imitate actuality and to *impersonate* a fictional character: 'to portray a character dramatically; to act'. (This is not so, however, in the cases of the *variety* performer, the *impersonator* or *impressionist*, who *takes off* living characters in an amusing or satirical way; nor is it the case with doubles, people who make a living out of their physical resemblance to the famous – such as Jeanette Charles, who has made a mint out of her uncanny resemblance to Queen Elizabeth II.) The term is a C17 coining following a Latin form and is first attested in use (metaphorically) in relation to performance in eC18: 'The Master and Disciple of the Dialogues often think fit... to impersonate other more surprizing Actors' (1715, Davies, *Athenae Britannicae*). The term is often used in a slightly negative fashion, as if *impersonation* were a poor relation of real *acting*: 'There's much more to it than mere impersonation' (David Calder, discussing his role as Gorbachev in *Plays and Players*, October 1990). In a review in the same edition of the periodical: '[They] brought the incomparable double act to life with a skill that went beyond mere impersonation'.

impresario   'I think we agree that all forms of theatre are going through a deep crisis:... is it the commercialising influence of the impresarios... ?' (Branagh, 202). From It. *impresa*, 'an undertaking', *impresario* denotes 'the undertaker of any business', but has been used since its adoption in C18 largely in relation to entertainments: 'We have operas... the Prince and the Lord Middlesex *Impresarii*' (1746, Walpole, *Letters to Sir Horace Mann*). The impresario of a show is the person responsible for organising the finance and practical arrangements of its presentation, a role similar to that performed in cinema by the producer. It may also be used to refer to a show's *angel* or *backer*, as this function overlaps financially with that of the impresario.

impressionist   'Alastair McGowan... is a witty impressionist who can reproduce the voices of people as diverse as Julian Clary, Antoine de Caunes and Rolf Harris with little difficulty' (*The Stage*, 28 March 1991). An *impressionist* is a *variety entertainer* who specialises in *impersonating* – doing impressions of or mimicking – other well-known entertainers or public figures. Many such performances are affectionate and welcomed by their subjects, but others are savagely satirical. Surprisingly, the first English usage of this word is in C19 with reference to the French painting movement, *Impressionism*. From L. *imprimere*, 'to press', the word had been used in Latin by Cicero as 'a mental impression', a sense which was adopted in English by C14. Theatrical impressionists, who create mental impressions of other characters, have only been known by the term from e-mC20.

improvisation   'Ten years ago, to get a group of English actors to improvise on any theme would be difficult; the most prominent thing you'd come up against would be the English actor's unwillingness to throw himself into something uncharted' (Brook, 62, writing in 1966). *Improvisation* is unscripted *performance* which relies on the artist's ability to *extemporise*: that is, to create spontaneously either in rehearsal or in front of an audience. (See also *ad lib*, *busk*.) *Improvisation* as a tradition in English theatre dates back at least to medieval *mystery plays*, (see *farce* as an example), but fell out of favour under the influence of what might be termed the writer's theatre that predominated from C16-mC20. Improvisation has been gradually reintroduced during the C20, as a means of exploring text in rehearsal, as a creative technique in *collective collaboration* and as a teaching methodology in drama schools and in educational drama and drama therapy, particularly through *role-play* and *simulation* in the latter cases. In the 1960s it began to be pursued for its own sake, as a performance genre in *happenings*, and its popularity with certain audiences has led to the growth of performances based on *impro*, or *improv* (both accepted abbreviations), at a range of *fringe* and *legit* venues.

The verb *to improvise* comes from Fr. *improviser*, from It. *improvvisare*, from *improvviso*, 'extempore'. Improvisation is not encountered in English until lC18-eC19: 'The flexibility of the Italian and Spanish languages... renders these countries distinguished for the talent of improvisation' (1811, Scott, introduction to *Don Roderick*).

incidental music   Music written expressly for, or previously written and performed during, a dramatic performance. Whilst it contributes to the overall mood or provides the setting for a song, it is not intended in itself to be a central part of the performance as, say, music in *opera*. An obvious example of the employment of *incidental music* in Elizabethan theatre is found in the opening lines of *Twelfth Night*: 'If music be the food of love, play on,/Give me excess of it...' As with most incidental music, no clue remains as to the music played at the first production of this play. The adjective (which is not found until e-mC17) derives from a now rarely-used sense of *incident*, 'a subordinate or accessory event'. ME, from med L. *in-*, the prefix here denoting 'in', + *-cidere* = *cadere*, 'to fall' – i.e., 'to occur casually'.

in dead   A fixed position or level for a *flown* piece of *scenery* when it is lowered to the stage: i.e. it is *flown in dead*. This use of *dead* to mean precise or exact, as in other phrases such as 'dead cert' or 'dead heat', appears to date from lC18 or eC19. See *dead*.

in it   'I just said to myself that old cliché, come on, be "in it" a bit more' (Wyn Jones, interviewed in Barkworth, 190). An actor's term for being fully involved with the flow of a show.

ingénue   'When attacked sometimes Becky had a knack of adopting a demure *ingénue* air, under which she was most dangerous' (1848, Thackeray, *Vanity Fair*). The feminine form of Fr. adjective *ingénu*, from which *ingenuous* is derived: 'artless, unsophisticated, simple'. The French term was adopted in C19 for 'a young naïve girl': in theatre terms, a young female role or an actress specialising in playing such roles. (For the use of other French terms for female performers see *comédienne*, *confidante*, *soubrette*.)

inner stage   In Elizabethan theatres, the *inner stage* was, arguably, – for much debate still rages about the exact structure of these buildings – the interior *performance area* set into the *tiring-house*. It is generally believed to have been concealed from the main stage, when not in use, by a door or *curtain* (see *arras*). Actors might be *discovered* here during the course of a *performance*. However, the term would appear to have been coined at a much later date.

inset A design term for a piece of *scenery* concealed within a larger piece, enabling quick *scene changes* to be effected. An *inset scene* is a small scene played within the larger stage setting. Used architecturally (as 'a recess') and in art as 'a smaller picture inserted within a larger one', it is a C19 term.

intercom An abbreviation of *intercommunication*, used for public address systems in theatres and for the *tannoy* which enables those *backstage* to hear what is being spoken *onstage*. An e-mC20 coining.

interlocutor A modern L. coinage (based on med. L. *interlocutorius*, 'a dialogue, conversation'), from *inter*, 'between, among', + *loqui, locut-*, 'to speak': someone taking part in a conversation or *dialogue*. In *negro (nigger) minstrel shows*, the *interlocutor* was the central figure or *compère*, who introduced items and, in that sense, held a dialogue with the audience.

interlude A word with a surprising range of meanings. In lC13-eC14, *interludes* were brief, humorous *sketches* performed between the acts *mystery* and *morality* plays or between other items during an evening's entertainment: 'Entyrludes or syngynge,/Or tabure bete or oþer pypynge' (1303, Robert Manning of Brunne, *Handlyng Synne*). Following a pattern that was to be repeated with later theatre terms (see *drama, theatre*), by lC14, 'interlude' was in use metaphorically for any event that might be likened to a play: 'Now may ye heir...Interludys and Iuperdys, þat men assayit on mony vis Castellis and pelis for till ta' (Barbour, *The Bruce*). Under the influence of the Players of the King's Interludes (first referred to in 1493 in Henry VII's reign) and later under the dramatist John Heywood (*c.*1497-1580), the interlude became a dramatic *genre* in its own right. By mC17, picking up on the idea of a break between sections of an entertainment, 'interlude' was used for '*interval*', a sense which was to lead to its more general usage as 'any intervening space (of time) between actions'. Also in C17-C18, harking back to its medieval sense, it was used colloquially as a synonym for 'stage play', especially if the subject matter was humorous. The final major sense of the word – 'an instrumental piece between verses of a psalm or secular song' is a C19 development. The sense of the word – from med L. *interludium*, from *inter*, 'between, among', + *ludus*, 'play' – was probably influenced by It. *tramesso*, which was an entertainment during a banquet, which in turn spawned the *intermezzo* (and later

Fr. *entremède* and Span. *entremès*), which were also short pieces between the *acts* of a longer play (see *entr'acte*).

intermezzo   A light, often *comic entertainment* between the *acts* of a more serious play in lC15-eC16 Italy. Like its English equivalent the *interlude*, it also developed a musical meaning, in this case a short movement linking two longer movements in a musical work. A translation into Italian of L. *intermedium*, 'an intermediate thing', from *inter*, 'between, among', + *medius*, 'middle': 'that which is in the middle'.

intermission   The literal meaning found since C16 is 'a pause; a cessation of activity'. Although it also is used for 'a break in any activity' from the same time, OED does not record the term theatrically formalised as '*interval*' until C19: 'At the intermission many strangers flocked around me' (1854, OED). It has also been used occasionally for the music performed in an interval (compare *interlude* and *intermezzo*). From L. *intermissio*, from *inter*, 'between, among', + *mittere, miss-*, 'to let go'.

interpretation   'Pip Broughton's interpretation of F.G. Lorca's characters allows each an independent existence' (*The Stage*, 28 March 1991). To *interpret* a *text* is to explicate its possible meanings by a deliberate emphasis in *production* on certain features of the play's genre, themes, characterisation etc., an *artistic* decision generally made by the *director*: his *reading* of the play. Such a slant will ideally be the product of detailed analysis and is known in literary circles as *hermeneutics*. *Interpretation* is conveyed to an audience by focusing their attention on aspects of the play through its design concept, the style of playing, individual performances etc. Even the *blocking* can be used to highlight certain characters at certain times, much in the way a film director might use a camera. From OF *interpreter*, or from L. *interpretari*, 'to explain, translate' – the noun *interpres, –pretis* originally meaning 'an explainer'. The term is first found in English in C14.

interval   'One of the most interesting things in the production is the interval, when Paul Slack continues with his building and two Palestinian actors give a wonderful song and instrumental recital that is too good to miss' (*The Stage*, 23 April 1992). An *intermission*: a break between the *acts* of a play which allows time for the *set* to be changed and for the audience to take refreshments etc. Ultimately from L. *intervallum*, from *inter*, 'between, among', + *vallum*, 'a rampart': the change from a physical to a temporal space occurred in Latin. The word is first attested in a general sense (from Fr. *intervalle*) – 'a pause, break' – in 1300, though the word is rarely encountered before C17. The theatrical usage may well be a Restoration borrowing from French: 'I . . . talked to them all the intervals of the play' (1667, Pepys, *Diary*).

in the round   See *theatre in the round*.

irradiation   A term with which the rational might take issue. It is a translation from Stanislavski's Russian to describe the way in which he believed an actor's emotional charge could be communicated to other performers and to the audience when he felt a particular emotion strongly and concentrated on transmitting it: akin to the way a fire transmits or *radiates* heat: 'During that pause, I was conscious of you sending out rays...It is like an underground river, which flows continuously under the surface of both words and silences and forms an invisible bond between subject and object...In our slang, we call that *irradiation*' (1936, Stanislavski, *An Actor Prepares*). Compare *communion*.

iris   A *lighting* term for an adjustable, circular shutter consisting of overlapping metal plates which can be used to vary the size of the *beam* from a *profile spot*. It is an abbreviation of *iris diaphragm*, a C19 coining used in a variety of contexts relating to lenses, based on the iris, the membrane behind the cornea of the eye which contains a circular opening, the pupil, at its centre. From L. *iris*, from Gk *iris*, '(goddess of the) rainbow'. It assumed its physiological meaning in Greek.

iron   A fireproof *safety curtain* directly behind the *proscenium arch*, the ultimate barrier between the stage area and the auditorium, so-called because of its manufacture. Today it usually consists of a strong framework containing panels of steel and asbestos. See *fire*.

IWB   An abbreviation for *internally wired barrel*: a lighting bar which contains an inferior electricity supply, so that lanterns can be conveniently plugged into sockets without the need for yards of *tripe*.

Jack-knife stage   A method of *staging* which employs *rostra* which are pivoted on castors at one corner so that they can be swung quickly on and off stage. *Jack-knife* is descriptive of the folding action of the large clasp knife of that name, so-named since at least mC18 and here defined in Smyth's *Sailor's Word-book* (1867): '*Jack-knife*, a horn-handled clasp-knife with a laniard, worn by seamen'. *Jack* (as in *jack-tar*) was a common term for a sailor and may well be the origin of the term. It has been used as verb since at least mC19.

jester   The word comes from the noun *jest*, which originally meant 'a deed or exploit' rather than its later, more specialised meaning of 'a piece of foolery, a joke'. This can be seen from its derivation: from OF *geste*, from L. *gesta*, from *gerere*, 'to do'. Originally spelt with a *g* (see *Gestus*), by the C14 the word carried its present sense of a professional maker of amusement, especially one employed by a prince or nobleman, alongside the now obsolete sense of a professional reciter of romances. By the C16 it was also in metaphorical use: 'I heare the Parson is no Iester' (1598, *The Merry Wives of Windsor*, II.i). See also *fool, clown*.

jig   A C16 word of unknown origin, denoting a lively, jumping dance and by extension the music that accompanied it, which was usually in triple time. The most famous early theatrical exponent of the jig, which commonly followed every public performance (along with a prayer for the queen), was Shakespeare's *clown*, Will Kempe, possibly the original Falstaff. After leaving the Lord Chamberlain's Men in 1599, he performed (and recorded in print) *Kemp's nine daies vvonder*, by dancing a jig (referred to as a *morrice*) from London to Norwich. Today, the jig still has folk overtones suggested in its most famous musical echo, the *Irish jig*. See *gig*.

Johnny, stage-door   A common name for the male stage-doorers who hung around backstage or at the *stage doors* of C19 theatres, waiting to talk to or proposition the *leading ladies* or *men*. *Johnny* was common in the sense of 'fellow, chap' from C17, probably because it was the most common name for a male child. Compare *groupie*.

jongleur   'It was that of the Troubadours, or Poets, who composed sonnets in praise of their beauty; and of the jongleurs who sung them at the courts and castles of the great' (1778, Alexander, *The History of Women*). *Jongleur* is a term originating in Norman French which was in currency throughout late medieval Europe for a type of *minstrel* or *travelling player* of either sex, usually a *solo performer* who was adept at a range of performance skills from music to tumbling. Although it later came to be synonymous with *minstrel*, it may be a variation of Fr. *jougleur*, 'a *juggler*'. Those *jongleurs* who composed their own material were known as *trouvères*. The word entered (or re-entered) English in C18, in historical usages, though it is now coming back into vogue with *improvisation* groups.

juggler   'One swallowed a large knife, and another walked a tight-rope at a perilous height, while another did a juggling act with countless balls' (Berkoff, 78). Probably because of the trading and overlapping of roles and skills between members of medieval *travelling companies*, there seems to have been an exchanging of terms, too. Just as *jongleur*, which came to mean *minstrel*, may well be from Fr. *jougleur*, a *juggler*, so this term for a person skilled in *conjuring* tricks, and, more commonly, feats of manual dexterity (such as tossing several objects up in the air and catching them in repeated sequence), comes from L. *joculator*, 'a joker, a trickster', from L. *joculus*, a diminutive of *jocus*, 'a jest'. It is recorded in English as a term for a general entertainer, often with strong overtones of disapproval, from eC12. The verb *to juggle*, first attested in C15, has gained a variety of Standard English meanings through metaphorical development, most of them associated with dexterity in handling a range of tasks, though the element of trickery can still be detected in some usages.

juvenile   This adjective, from L. *juvenilis*, meaning 'a young man', or, as an adjective, 'of or pertaining to youth', from *juvenis*, 'young', was used in two theatrical contexts in C19. *Juvenile drama* was an alternative for *toy theatre*, children's models with cardboard sets and movable cardboard actors. It is more commonly known from the phrase *juvenile lead*, abbreviated to *juve lead*, or *juve*, the term for the young actor in a *stock company* who specialised in playing the youthful heroes and lovers around whom so many plots revolve: 'In juvenile parts I was inclined to be an exhibitionist and for a long time my ambition was to be frightfully smart and West End, wear beautifully cut suits, lounging on sofas in French window comedies' (Geilgud, 65). The term can still be used, generally ironically, for a young actor. Part of the irony used to reside in the fact that many juve leads went on beyond their sell-by date, putting off the day when they would be judged on acting ability alone.

K **abuki** A form of Japanese popular theatre which evolved at the beginning of C17 from the *Nō*, Jōruri and Bunraku traditions, encompassing subject matter as diverse as history and domestic drama. 'The kabuki plays... have no particular literary value, being frameworks for the display of technical accomplishments by the actors...' (ed. Hartnoll). *Kabuki* is derived from the Japanese characters *ka*, 'song', + *bu*, 'dance', + *ki*, skill/art/acting'. The word at first appears to be self-descriptive, but the emphasis in performance – and traditional Kabuki performances last *at least* half a day, the audiences eating, drinking and talking during the boring bits – is on *stylised, bravura* acting. Kabuki has exerted considerable influence on a range of Western practitioners in C20.

karaoke 'Portable karaoke is here. World's first portable, hand-held, professional sing-along machine' (ad. in *The Stage*, 28 March 1991). *Karaoke* is a popular entertainment form which originated in Japan and caught on in America and Europe in the mid-1980s. Like *cabaret*, it thrives in bars and restaurants, the essential difference being that in *karaoke cabaret*, the audience are also the performers: a backing-tape of pre-recorded music is played and members of the audience are invited – for prizes, kudos or humiliation – to do the rest. From the Japanese *kara*, 'open, empty' – (as in *kara-te*, fighting with 'an *empty hand*') – + *oke*, an abbreviation of the loan word *okestra*, 'orchestra'.

kill The theatre sense of *to kill* is 'to remove, subdue, lessen'. It can be applied in a variety of contexts: for example, *to kill a light* is to switch it off; *to kill a chair* is to remove it from the set, to *lose* it. For an actor *to kill a gag* or even *a scene* is to diminish its effectiveness, perhaps totally, 'to *murder* it'. In the case of *killing a light*, which means 'removing its energy', the term can be compared with 'killing a ball' in sport, a usage attested in OED from late C19. *Killing a chair* etc. would appear to be unique to theatre. In the case of *killing a scene*, compare *corpse, die*.

king of misrule See *misrule, lord of*.

kitchen sink drama A catchy but possibly derogatory phrase coined in the late 1950s (and rapidly popularised by the media) for the works of such diverse dramatists as Shelagh Delaney, David Storey, Harold Pinter and Arnold Wesker (who in 1959

135

wrote a play entitled *The Kitchen*), many of whom might well have preferred to be labelled, if at all, as '*New Wave*' social realists or *angry young men* and women rather than *kitchen sink dramatists*. The interest of some dramatists of the 1950s in *realistic*, working-class settings (in reaction to the armchairs, anti-macassars and upper-middle-class values of *drawing-room comedy*) and a determination to use everything *including* the kitchen sink as subject matter and *props*, led to the popular adoption of this phrase which bears an interesting resemblance to *cup-and-saucer drama*, coined in the 1860s.

kitsch From German *kitschen*, 'to throw together, possibly hastily', this term has been embraced by all the arts to describe any work which might be regarded as lacking in artistic value due to its pretentiousness or the poor or dubious taste inherent in it; '*tacky*'; '*naff*'. The word is now familiar in this sense throughout Europe; it appears to have first been used widely in English in literary, musical and artistic circles in America in the mid-1960s, whence it was imported to Britain.

knockabout comedy A descriptive phrase for physical or *slapstick comedy* and low *clowning* of the type epitomised in *pantomime*. 'Classic knockabout film routines were seamlessly recreated' (*Plays and Players*, October 1930). The phrase appears to date from the 1880s or earlier (Partridge) and is from the colloquial verb *to knock about*, 'to beat up, maltreat', (as in the *music-hall* song 'One of the Ruins that Cromwell Knocked About a Bit').

knight of theatre Since Sir Henry Irving was knighted by Queen Victoria 'for services to the theatre' in 1895, for the first time demonstrating that actors had arrived as *bona fide* bricks in the *establishment* wall, it has become traditional for the *leading men* of their theatrical generation to be honoured in this manner; the phrase has gained widespread usage, ironic though that usage may be in some circles. Base camp in the actors' ascent of the social ladder was shifted even higher when Laurence Olivier became Baron Olivier of Brighton in 1970. *Knight* is from OE *cniht*, 'boy youth', the formal recognition of *knighthood* as a rank conferred by the sovereign having been instituted in C16.

Kuppelhorizont The name given to the *scenic designer* Mariano Fortuny's 'sky-dome', (the German meaning literally, 'dome horizon'), a 1902 forerunner of the present *cyclorama*.

L **aboratory theatre** A term related to *experimental theatre* and the 'arts lab.' movement of the 1960s, which (like *workshop* etc.) is typical of a linguistic tendency of the C20 theatrical left to relate theatre work to both science and industry (compare *affective memory, workshop*): '[Grotowski] calls his theatre a laboratory. It is. It is a centre of research . . . In Grotowski's theatre as in all true laboratories the experiments are scientifically valid because the essential conditions are observed' (Brook, 37). From med. L. *laboratorium*, from L. *laborare*, 'to work'.

ladder Although conventional ladders are used in theatre, often referred to as 'steps', this ladder is not to be climbed, being a metal structure, ladder-shaped, hanging in the *wings*, supporting *lanterns* used for *side lighting*. (Compare *tower*.)

laddie 'In those days [1921] the company had been full of the sort of old actors you read about in Dickens. I was terrified of them because they were real old "laddies", rushing off to the bar every five minutes and using awful language' (Geilgud, 62). Like *darling* and *luvvie, laddie* is a much-satirised, traditional, *actorly* form of address. The above attestation shows it already in ironic usage. Whilst the peculiar theatrical use of 'laddie', which takes no account of age, dates back to the *stagese* of mC19 (Partridge) or earlier, it is traceable as 'a term of endearment, chiefly Scottish' (OED) to C16.

lake The name given to a thin, reddish stick of *Leichner greasepaint*, often applied with a stick or very thin brush, to give a bloodlike or veined effect to detail *make-up* or, if *worked in*, to lend its particular shade to a make-up.

> Barkworth: Did you have a red nose? Was that because of drink?
> Petherbridge: Yes . . . no, it was because of a little bit of lake I put there . . . yes, [Newman Noggs] was described as having a red nose.'
> (Interview with Edward Petherbridge, Barkworth, 176.)

From the pigment *lac*, from Hindu *lākh*.

lamp Like *lantern* and *luminaire*, an individual item of stage lighting equipment which the layman would probably refer to as a *light*. From OF *lampe*, ultimately from Gk *lampas*, 'a torch'.

landlady, theatrical From the early days of *circuits* and *touring*

137

companies, a wealth of comic lore has accrued around the figure of the *theatrical landlady* and her *digs*. 'I was directed to a desolate-looking house, which styled itself a Temperance Hotel, and after some persuasion, the landlady consented to take me in... "Ye'll no raise the blinds, nor come out of the room, until the kirk is over. I wouldna hae the neighbours ken I had a low play-actress in ma hoose"' (1926, Constance Benson, *Mainly Players*). Landlady is a term found from eC16, from *land* in the sense of 'property, dwelling'.

lantern   Like *lamp* and *luminaire*, an individual item of *stage lighting* equipment. *Lantern* (and sometimes *haystack lantern*) is also used for the skylight or air-vent in the roof of a theatre above the *grid*. From OF *lanterne*, from L. *lanterna*, from Gk *lamptēr*, 'a torch, lamp', ultimately from the same Gk root as *lamp*.

lashline   A largely American alternative to *throwline*. From the ME verb *lash*, probably imitative, 'to make a sudden, violent movement of the limbs', + *line*. To *lash up* is to fix something together with rope: 'For *Hiawatha* [the set] had been a bamboo lash-up job' (*Plays and Players*, October 1990).

last night   The final *performance*, or *night*, of a *show*, probably most famously in *the Last Night of the Proms*, the *finale* of the Sir Henry Wood Promenade *Concerts*. *The last night party* is a revered and generally very *Dionysian* theatrical tradition.

laugh   From OE *hlaehhan, hleihhan*, 'to laugh'. *A laugh* – an audible, physical response from the *audience* – as opposed to the alternative noun *laughter* – is the primary aim of the *comedian* or *comic actor*. It is now in general use in phrases such as *playing for laughs* – 'you mustn't play this line for laughs since it holds up the flow of the scene' (Berkoff, 121). – *strictly for laughs*, and *going for* and *getting laughs*: 'Shocking place to get a laugh, I know, but I think it can be justified since Hamlet's mind is already unhinged...' (ibid., 48). One of the arts of comic acting is to learn to *ride a laugh* which, rather in the way a surfer rides a wave, means to use instinct and experience in one's *timing* in order to get the laugh, pause for long enough to let the audience enjoy it, then carry them on to the next *laugh-line*. *To tread* or *stand on a laugh* (along with variant verbal phrases) is to *kill* it.

laugh-line   A *line* in an actor's part which is expected to *get a laugh*. 'Remember that when you have a *laugh-line* you are not only inviting the audience to laugh but you are inviting them to laugh at a particular moment...that moment, usually the last word of your line, could do with a little extra punch' (Barkworth, 63).

lazzo   A *comic* embellishment on the text or *plot*, *improvised* by the players in the *commedia dell'arte*: *lazzi* (the plural) might include bits of *business*, displays of personal skills, tricks and verbal *ad libs*. There appears to be no comprehensive translation for the word and no obvious etymology.

leading role 'During the thirties and forties [Godfrey Kenton] notched up 32 leading roles for the RSC in Stratford and London' (*The Stage*, 24 April 1992). The *principal* male and female performers in a *show* have been referred to as the *leading man* or *leading lady*, or, asexually, the *leading roles* since C18. In abbreviated form, these are known as the *male* and *female leads*. 'How many of you can remember actors standing at the back for countless minutes in a Shakespeare revival while the *lead* speaks?' (Berkoff, 159). The term is usually employed only for experienced actors, and seems to come from a military metaphor – *leading one's company* (as into battle). By the 1880s, *leading heavy* was the term for the serious middle-aged female character in a play.

left A *stage direction*, as in *stage left*, (abbreviated to SL in *acting* copies of play-*texts*); also known as *prompt side*. *Left and right* in theatre terms are always referred to from the actors' viewpoint, therefore, if a text says 'There is a large window L with a desk placed in front of it...' (1981, Willy Russell, *Educating Rita*, *French's Acting Edition*) the audience would see it on the right of the stage.

légerdemain From Fr. *léger de main*, 'light of hand', i.e. dextrous, *légerdemain* is 'sleight of hand', the art of the *conjuror*, the cardsharp and the *juggler*. It is curious to note that many theatrical acts which involve trickery aggrandise themselves through their names. Compare *ventriloquy*, *conjuring* and the synonym for this word, *prestidigitation*.

leg A *leg* is a long strip of cloth or a narrow *flat* at the side of a *proscenium arch stage*, which, often in conjunction with a *border*, serves to *mask* the *wings* from the audience's view. The phrase is, with an effort of the imagination, descriptive, but its origin may be nautical, *leg* being a term for both 'a short rope' and a shipbuilding term for 'a supporting pole'; in addition, a sailing ship which was overmasted could be referred to as being *all legs and wings*.

leg, break a The traditional way of wishing a fellow-performer 'good luck'. Theatre superstition has it that wishing people 'good luck' directly might actually bring them bad luck. This phrase which wishes obvious bad luck on the performer it is addressed to, is now, like *toi, toi, toi*, in use throughout the European theatre, and is generally said to have its origins in the United States.

legitimate (legit.) theatre A term used to refer to performances of the classics and *straight*, contemporary drama as opposed to *musical theatre*, *variety* etc. It can also be used for the performers: 'Ours was the straight act on the bill – and the comics and trick-cyclists, all the most brilliant talents imaginable, would gather in the wings to watch the "legits", greatly and reverently impressed' (Olivier, 47). The origins are C18, when any play that was per-formed in a *venue* without a *licence* – i.e. not in a *patent* theatre – was required to contain music in order to avoid breaking the law: thus, most performers worked outside the *legitimate theatre*. This decision was made partly on moral grounds, but more impor-tantly as a means of political *censorship* (see also **Lord Chamber-lain**). In the C19, the phrase was sometimes abbreviated to *the Legitimate*; it is now colloquially known as *legit. theatre*. *Comedians* who go *straight* might equally say that they are *going legit*. From med. L. from L. *legitimatus*, from *lex, legis*, 'law'.

leg show   A lC19 term used for a *variety* or *musical show* which strongly featured a female *chorus line* or dancers wearing costumes designed to show off their legs: in occasional but rare use today. The term appears to date from about 1890, succeeding the previ-ously popular *leg-drama* (1870) and *leg-piece* (1880). Theatres which specialised in such shows were known as *leg-shops*, possibly influenced by the term *leg-business* for dancing, which could have evolved as an unflattering pun on an earlier sense of that phrase meaning 'sexual intercourse'.

Leichner   'Taking my small suitcase containing my ready-made dinner jacket, shirt, shoes, studs etc., and a tin with a few sticks of Leichner greasepaint in it, a tin of Cremine, a towel and a piece of soap, I went to the topmost floor to dressing-room No. 12...' (Olivier, 49). *Leichner* was and is the most famous proprietary name for *greasepaint*, invented in the 1860s by Ludwig Leichner, (1836-?), a Wagnerian opera singer. 'He opened his first factory in 1873, and his round sticks, numbered and labelled from 1, light flesh colour, to 8, reddish brown for Indians, (later increased to 20, and by 1938 to 54) were soon to be found in every actor's dressing room' (ed. Hartnoll). The two shades most frequently used for basic make-ups have been *five* and *nine*. See also *make-up* and *ham*.

leko or **Leko**   A largely American term for a *profile spotlight*, based on a trade name.

leotard   'There was a whole selection of dazzling leotards and a few "pros" had sweatbands on every available area of exposed skin' (Branagh, 43). A *leotard* is a one-piece body-costume worn by dancers during practice, though in the 1980s, due to the popu-larity of aerobic exercise-dancing, it became generally fashionable.

Leotards are named after the celebrated French *acrobat*, Jules Léotard (1830-70), about whom the famous *music-hall* song 'The Daring Young Man on the Flying Trapeze' was written. Instead of the glittery costumes favoured by other contemporary *trapeze artists*, he wore a plain, one-piece affair.

level   A term used in *lighting* to refer to the degree of intensity of a given *lantern* or circuit and in *sound* for the recording or playback volume of an *effect* or, as in *checking the levels*, for the sound balance of live instruments, amplified voices etc. in a musical performance. The origins probably lie in radio broadcasting. By extension, the term is now used in relation to *performance*, where *the level* can refer to the degree of emotional as well as auditory intensity. From OF *livel*, from Rom *libella*, a diminutive of L. *libra*, 'scales, balance'. In *staging*, a 'level' can be used as a synonym for a *rostrum* or any raised area of the stage, the sense of 'level' coming from the unequal height of the two scales on a balance.

libretto/librettist   'If the Libretto, as they call it, is not approved, the Opera... will be condemned' (1742, Richardson, *Pamela*). The *lyrics* and *text* of a *musical show* or *opera*, regardless of whether they are spoken or sung, are referred to as the *libretto*, the music being contained in the *score*. A diminutive of It. *libro*, 'book': i.e. 'a little book'. 'Vaughan Williams' libretto is founded on John Bunyan's allegorical work and... is so rich in every sense that it is a wonder that it is still so rarely performed' (*The Stage*, 23 April 1992). Italy being the home of modern opera, the loan of this Italian term which entered English in eC18 is hardly surprising. *Librettist* for the author follows naturally, although it is not attested in OED until mC19. Usually a librettist works in close co-operation with the *composer* of the music. Many successful C19 and C20 librettists, such as W.S. Gilbert (of Gilbert and Sullivan), are almost inseparable from their partners in public utterance; others, such as Stephen Sondheim (who wrote the libretto for Leonard Bernstein's *West Side Story*) are more famous for individual creative endeavours.

licence   Since the Licensing Act of 1968, which ended the absolute *censorship* powers of the *Lord Chamberlain*, all public performances in England and Wales, whether *professional* or *amateur*, have needed to be authorised by a licence issued by the local authority, in according with statutes first set out in the Theatres Act of 1843. ME, from OF, from L. *licentia*, from *licēre*, 'to be lawful'. See also *fire*.

life mask   A plaster cast taken from a performer's face, used as a foundation on which a more complex *mask* can be built or upon

which a *prosthesis* can be modelled. The term is in direct contrast
to the gruesome *death masks* which it was the fashion to have
made of the faces of fresh corpses in C18-C19.

lifts   Worn inside the heels of a performer's shoes, *lifts* are wedge-
shaped inserts, formerly of leather but now most frequently of
cork, used to give the illusion that they are taller than is actually
the case. The term is probably American.

lighting   In the Renaissance, indoor theatres were *lit* by candle-
light, and in England after the Restoration, chandeliers above the
stage and lamps in the *wings* became the norm. Significantly,
from the outset, artificial *lighting* was exploited for effect, candle-
light sometimes being transmitted through coloured glass or
enhanced by water *reflectors*. Major lighting developments have
been the introduction of *footlights* (after the Restoration), gas lighting and *limelight*, (1810-20), the dimming of the auditorium
(mC19) and electric lighting (1870s). The traditional term for
those in charge of *lighting a show, lighting man* – 'Wayne Dowdeswell, the RSC's Swan Theatre's lighting man is anything but
bland' (*The Observer*, 3 May 1992)' – is now giving way to the
more status-conscious *lighting designer*: 'Lighting designer ... may
sound like a vain euphemism for engineer, but, in 1992, lighting
design is almost as diverse as stage design ... Designers ... can
make scenery out of light, furnish a stage with it, even make light
a prop for performers to carry round' (ibid). See also *birdie, board,
circuit, cover, gel, gobo, fade, ladder, lamp, lantern, levels, limelight,
parcan, switchboard* and others.

limelight/limes   *Limes* is the common name for *calcium oxide*. First
used in the theatre in 1816, calcium flares, or *limes* – (lime heated
in a cylinder in an oxyhydrogen flame) – gave off an intense white
light which could be used for certain *naturalistic* effects. However,
since the beam was manually-directable, *limelight* was also ideal
for what soon became its primary use in the mannered and *melodramatic* companies of the day: *spotlighting* the *principal actor* and
following them around the stage, giving rise to the phrase *in the
limelight*, still in common use for 'being the centre of attention'.
'Now I cannot go to the theatre because I believe there has been
a conspiracy by directors to steal the limelight' (Berkoff, 72).
Follow spots are still commonly called 'limes'. Interestingly, *lime-
juice* was a common alternative name in the theatre for 'limelight'
by 1875, suggesting that *juice* for 'electrical current' (and later
'petrol' and other fuels) first attested in use in 1903, may well
have a theatrical origin.

line(s)[1]   The two immediate sources for ME *li(g)ne* can both, ultimately be traced back to L. *linum*, 'flax'. 'We've learned our lines

inside out, but the ritual of going through them every time is hard to lose' (Tim McInnerny, in the *Guardian*, 24-25 August 1991). *Lines* are the words in the script to be spoken by an actor in performance; his *part*. In the singular, a *line* is used to denote a single piece of spoken dialogue, as in '*delivering* a line'. The term has gained wide currency in phrases such as *forgetting* and *losing one's lines*, where the suggestion is that something learned or *rehearsed* in advance has been forgotten, or, conversely, 'you've certainly learned your lines!' The word originates from the days before printed *scripts*, when the actor would be handed his part along with his *cues* in a hand-written copy. These lines would often literally be lines of *verse*. A *line rehearsal* is one which concentrates on dialogue.

line(s)² A rope or cable attached to or suspended from the *grid*. See *fly-lines*. A line can be used in many contexts where rope or other fastening materials are being used – for example, as 'a length of *sash cord* used to cleat a *flat*'. The theatrical use of the term is from the *nautical* term for 'rope': 'The seymen... thair lynys kest, and weytit weyll the tyd' (*c*.1470, Henry, *The actis and deidis of... Schir William Wallace*). It was largely due to their skill with *lines* that sailors were employed in the post-Restoration English theatre.

lion comique A male comic singer of the *music hall* era, often specialising in performing aristocratic, alliterative characters such as Burlington Bertie and Champagne Charlie. From C19 habit of using the term *lion* for any celebrity or person of high social standing, as in 'a social lion'.

literary Ultimately from L. *littera*, 'a letter', *literary* is found as 'pertaining to the letters of the alphabet' from eC17, but its present sense of 'pertaining to literature' does not occur until mC18: 'A man of literary merit is sure of being caressed by the great, though seldom enriched' (1759, Goldsmith, *Miscellaneous Works* [1837]). Sometimes, 'literary' is used disparagingly by theatre people, as in 'a too literary production': one in which the full exploitation of a work's *theatricality* is sacrificed in favour of a concentration on language or ideas. However, the term is also found with less judgemental senses. A *literary agent* is one who helps a writer find a publisher, or often in the case of theatre, a *producer*. A *literary manager* is the person in a theatre responsible for the *repertoire*, including reading and suggesting new plays – though this is not always the sum total of his job: 'Simon Reade, the literary manager, goes off to clean the toilet with a toothbrush' (Michael Coveney, discussing The Gate Theatre, *Observer*, 3 May 1992).

live 'The 17-stone comic has a great live act as customers at

Warner's, Bembridge, quickly found out' (*The Stage*, 21 March 1991). Since lC19, *live* has been used for any piece of electrical equipment attached to and switched on to an electrical circuit. This is a logical development of an earlier and still current sense, 'containing unexpended energy': 'A quantity of six-inch live shells fired' (1799, *The Naval Chronicle*). The phrase *live theatre*, which is in common use today, was coined in eC20 to create a contradistinction between traditional theatre and the new cinemas. By extension, it has gained a further sense through television: a performance or event occurring simultaneously with transmission.

loading floor/gallery   A *platform* or *gallery* at the side of the stage above the *fly floor*, used for loading weights in the *counterweight system*.

lock off   A *lighting* term. A safety precaution, *to lock off a lantern* after focusing is to tighten the screws used to adjust its angle. As the preposition 'off' often suggests in phrasal verbs, *locking off* is a sign that the job of focusing has been completed (compare 'tie off' and the tautological 'finish off').

Lord Chamberlain   From the *Licensing* Act of 1737 until the Theatres Act of 1968, the *Lord Chamberlain* was the official responsible for all dramatic *censorship* in England. 'The abolition of the Lord Chamberlain's powers certainly brought new subjects to the fore' (*The Stage*, 28 March 1991). In preceding centuries, the Lord Chamberlain of the Household had been an official with a range of responsibilities covering the general management of the royal household, which included entertainment; prior to their appointment as the King's Men, Shakespeare's company had been known as the Lord Chamberlain's Men. *Lord*, from OE *hlāford* = *hlāfweard*, meaning literally 'warden of the loaf'; + *Chamberlain*, from OF, from Frankish *kamerling*, from *kamer*, 'room', + *ling*, 'a person connected with'. See also *licence*.

lose   To decommission a stage item during a show: therefore, *to lose* a light is to switch it off; *to lose a prop* is to remove it from the *set* and so on. Often found in the *stage manager's* imperative 'Lose table!' etc. The verb has been used with the sense of 'to get rid of' ('occasionally', says OED) since C17: 'To lose/In sweet forgetfulness all pain and woe' (1667, Milton, *Paradise Lose*, Bk II). Compare *kill*.

love/luvvie (and variant spellings)   Perhaps the most common and certainly one of the most *camp* theatrical endearments; like *darling*, used between *actorly* actors regardless of sex. 'Rehearsal room revelations, psychological detail, conversations with prospective monarchs are all out of window while the old pro inside you is screaming, "But how do I get off, love?" ' (Branagh, 146). *Luvvie*,

first found around 1730, was a Standard English endearment until
around 1820 from whence it became increasingly low colloquial
and, as implied here, theatrical. *Luvvies* seems to have replaced
lC19-eC20 *laddies* as a collective term for self-consciously theatrical people. A *luvviedote* for 'an anecdote recounted by a luvvie'
is a term attributed to the actor John Sessions in *Private Eye* (30
July 1992).

low comedy/comedian   The term *low comedy* is used occasionally
to indicate the social milieu in which a piece is set, but more
commonly it refers to a genre of *comedy*, the antithesis of *high
comedy*. Low comedy has no pretensions to subtle *characterisation*,
wit or intellect, relying instead on *knockabout*, *farce*, *gags* and
clowning for its effects; as such, it can be traced back to the *satyr-
plays* of Ancient Greece. 'Low' with its sense of 'coarse, vulgar,
undignified', is a usage which can be traced back in literary references to C17: 'Never did any author precipitate himself from such
height of thought to so low expressions as he often does' (1672,
Dryden, *Essays* [1700]). *Low comedians*, (or *low-comedy merchants*
as they were known in the m-lC19, sometimes abbreviated to *low
comedies*), were actors and *comics* in *stock companies* who
specialised in broad, farcical roles.

luminaire   A *luminaire* is the internationally-recognised term for
a unit or instrument of theatre lighting such as a *lamp* or *lantern*,
adopted in mC20. In practice, it is rarely used. From Fr.
luminaire, 'light'.

luvvie   See *love/luvvie*.

LX   A common abbreviation of *electrics*, which, as opposed to the
more general *electricians*, is the name given to the *lighting* and
electrical staff employed by a theatre. Although the term would
appear to derive from simple sound abbreviation, it is interesting
to note the merely coincidental fact that *lx* is also a common
shortening of *lux(es)*, a term in physics for a unit of illumination
equivalent to one *lumen* per square metre, from L. *lux, -lucis*,
'light'.

lyric   The most general use of *lyric(s)* today is as 'the words of a
song, the *libretto*', (*lyricist* for 'song-writer' first being attested in
18802). 'Your concentration level has to be such that you can't
let up for a second because of the lyrics and the speed of the music
but particularly the lyrics, which are very complex' (Julia McKenzie, *Plays and Players*, October 1990). 'Lyric' reached English
both from Fr. *lyrique* and from direct translation of L. *lyricus*,
from Gk *luricos*, the adjective meaning 'of or pertaining to the
luros, "lyre",' with the sense of 'designed to be, or fit to be sung'.
By lC16, in the phrase *lyric poet*, it had come to refer to a writer

of verse prone to the composition of personal pieces in a short stanza form. The adjective *lyrical*, however, still carries with it overtones of its Greek origin, suggesting not only words which lend themselves to song, but words which are also romantic, Arcadian and possibly rather emotionally overcharged (hence the common term 'waxing lyrical' about something).

Machines, machinery The stage equipment used for changing scenery, such as *revolves* and *boat trucks*, or for the equipment for creating sound and optical effects such as sound horn or *trap door*. *Machine* is derived – via L. *machina*, from Gk *makhana* and Doric *mēkhanē*, (from *mēkhos*, 'a contrivance') – from the term for equipment used in Ancient Greek theatre, for example the crane in the theatrical device of the *deus ex machina*.

The main use of *machinery* throughout Europe in medieval times was for *liturgical drama*, where a series of extremely complex contraptions were created to facilitate the display of supernatural happenings: 'On high was a Heaven full of living and moving figures, and a quantity of lights which flashed in and out. I will take pains to describe exactly how the apparatus of this machine was devised, seeing that the machine itself is destroyed, and the men are dead who could have spoken of it from experience' (mC16, Giorgio Vasari, *Vitae*). A fascination with elaborate stage machinery developed through the *masque* in Italy where, in C17 Italy it was to continue under the influence of *opera*, beating a continual path to England. More complex machinery remained in use due to the sensational effects required in popular genres such as *melodrama*, *pantomime* and, later, *musicals*. Any presentation which relies heavily on machinery can be referred to as *machine theatre*.

Macready Named after the noted Victorian *actor-manager* William Charles Macready (1739-1873), a *Macready* is a stylised *pause* or loud inhalation delivered for effect at a dramatic point in a speech, regardless of the text's sense or punctuation. It was a hallmark of Macready's style, and an example of *melodramatic* acting or what Stanislavski was later to term *mechanical acting*.

magic act/magician '*Mod. Adv't.*, Professor ---'s Home of Magic and Mystery' (OED). *Magicians* are *conjurors* or *illusionists* who entertain by means of *legerdemain*, although the term does not appear to have been transferred to this usage from its C14 sense of 'sorcerer, magus' until lC18-eC19: 'Even the most ignorant beholder regards the modern magician as an ordinary man' (1831, Brewster, *Letters on Natural Magic*). The same late transference applies to *magic*, the title of Brewster's book (above) being the earliest OED attestation of the modern sense.

make a break In acting, to accidentally omit *lines* or *business*: i.e. to break the flow of the performance.

make it To be a success, especially in respect of the *box office*. Appropriated from America in the 1930s, the term can in fact be employed for success in any walk of life, but the constant repetition in the media of phrases such as *making it big* and *making the big time*, from which the term probably derives, has ensured it is most commonly associated with *show business*.

make-up Given modern, sophisticated theatre *lighting*, the contemporary view is that *make-up* – 'the application of greasepaint, water-based paints, false facial hair, prostheses etc. to alter the appearance of an actor's face' – should be subtle, *naturalistic* and minimal, just adequate to suggest the peculiarities of the *character* played.

The origins of theatre make-up lie in *ritual*: one can still observe the use of elaborately-stylised make-up, sometimes accompanied by the use of *masks*, in tribal ceremonies around the world. In these contexts, make-up is intended to transform the individual, to translate a man into a god or an animal, or into a cipher for something infinitely beyond himself. As such, it tended to be bold and anti-naturalistic. The idea that theatrical make-up should aim at verisimilitude can already be seen in the *Dialoghi* of Leone di Soni (1527-92), the *dramaturge* of the Mantuan court:

I strive as much as I can to transform each one from his usual appearance, so that he will not readily be recognised by the audience, which sees him daily. I do not, however, want to make the mistake the ancients made, who, in order that their actors should not be recognised, painted their faces with wine sediment or with mud. I find it enough to disguise them, without changing the appearances of their faces, doing my utmost to make them appear new persons... in order that [the audience] may believe as long as is possible that everything we present is really happening.

The English verb *to make up* had a much broader definition in eC17, meaning 'to dress appropriately for a given occasion': 'Wat Terrill, th'art ill suited, ill made vp,/In Sable collours' (1602, Dekker, *Satiro-mastix*). The theatrical usage appears to have developed in C18, gradually losing the association with *costume* and becoming standard by eC19: 'I made myself up with the barber's aid... as a sort of middle man between Don Caesar and Gil Blas' (1809, Malkin, *Gil Blas*). The noun, *a make-up* – 'He [Ralph Richardson] always took great pains with his make-up' (Geilgud, 74) – is derived from this, as is *make-up artist* for the person who specialises in applying make-ups.

malcontent   A *stock character* of Elizabethan and Jacobean *revenge tragedy*: a discontented person; one inclined to rebellion. The *malcontent* was usually an educated man with no visible means of support, whose intelligence and ingenuity could thus be bought by those of greater means and lesser morality. 'There's hope in him, for discontent and want/Is the best clay to mould a villain of' (1605, Tourneur, *The Revenger's Tragedy* IV.i.) Frequently the malcontent faced a moral dilemma: the necessity to act against his conscience in order to ensure his own survival; although others such as Shakespeare's Iago are arguably inspired by 'motiveless malignity' (Coleridge). The term is now archaic in French, its language of origin (from *mal-*, used here as a negative prefix, + *content*, 'happy, contented'), but is still used occasionally in English in a political and social context due to the influence of revenge plays.

manager, management   The verb *to manage* was borrowed by English in lC16, influenced both by It. *managgiare*, 'to handle, train', applied expecially to horses and Fr. *ménager*, 'to manage carefully, husband' (from *ménage*, 'a household'). This latter source was to have the greatest influence on the development of the word which, in the following decades, was transferred to the handling and conducting of other, more general affairs, by mC17 more and more frequently to financial business. *Manager* was in common usage before the end of the century: 'Her Estate therefore requir'd both a discreet manager to husband it, and a man well furnished with money' (1670, Cotton, *Girard's History of the life of the duke of Espernon*), leading to its theatrical usage for the person charged with running a theatre or theatre company. For example, after 1710, the Theatre Royal, Drury Lane was managed by three *actor-managers*, one of whom, the Poet Laureate Colley Cibber, set down their duties in his *Apology*; these included, if Cibber's account is to be believed, those of *dramaturge, producer, artistic director, house* and *stage manager, impresario* etc. This extract gives a flavour of the tone: 'A Menager, is to direct and oversee the Painters, Machinists, Musicians, Singers, and Dancers; to have an eye upon the Doorkeepers, under-Servants and Officers, that without such care, are too often apt to defraud us, or neglect their Duty . . .' The functions of theatrical *managements* (an eC18 term) in the commercial and subsidised theatres are intricate and depend on the structure of the theatre or company, with *tour managers, front-of-house managers, catering managers* etc. all being responsible for their separate departments in large companies. It is likely that there will always be some tension between artistic and managerial interests in theatre: 'Wherever we did this

play there was an outcry, and in London theatre managers hur-
riedly discovered reasons for preventing our having a stage'
(Brook, 36).

manet A *stage direction* (plural *manent*) directly from L., he/she
stays, (contrast *exit*), indicating that a character remains on stage
when others leave, often to deliver a *soliloquy* or, as below with
Deflores (a *malcontent*), in Middleton and Rowley's *The Change-
ling* V.i. (1621 or 1622), to deliver a parting shot in *aside* to the
audience:

VERMANDERO: Deflores call upon me.

ALSEMERO: And upon me, sir.

Exeunt. [Manet Def.]

DEFLORES: Rewarded? Precious, here's a trick beyond me.
I see in all bouts of sport and wit,
Always the woman strives for the last hit.

Exit.

Many examples found in old texts are the work of later editors,
however.

Marie Tempest A device to keep an *onstage* door open or closed.
Properly, a metal hinge with a screw lever adjustment is fixed to
the door; however, a simpler arrangement – attaching one end of
a length of string or cord to the door and the other end of it to a
stage weight – can also be called a *Marie Tempest*. The device is
named after the actress of that name, who is reputed to have
requested that such hinges be fitted to the doors of a set on which
she was playing. According to Geilgud, who worked with Marie
Tempest in the 1930s when she was reaching the end of her career,
she was 'an enormously skilled little lady with superb technical
accomplishments...a rigid disciplinarian [who] worked like a
demon all through rehearsals' (p.89).

marionette Although *marionette* is now generally used to refer to
any *puppet* worked by strings, those used in the heyday of the
marionette's stage popularity, from the Restoration well into the
C18, were full-sized puppets managed from above the stage by
means of rods or wires fixed to the centre of their heads. The use
of strings was probably developed by the Italian Fantoccini in
the lC18. 'The standard marionette, which is usually made of
papier-mâché, has nine threads, one to each arm and leg, two to
the head, one to each shoulder, and one to the back. These are
gathered on a "crutch", or control, held in one hand by the man-
ipulator, while with the other he plucks at the strings' (ed.
Hartnoll). Marionettes (from Fr., from *Marion*, the diminutive
of *Marie*, + suffix *-ette*, meaning literally 'little Mary') have their
origins in southern European folk tradition. They probably

achieved their British theatrical apogée either in the Puppet Theatre of Martin Powell, the dwarf marionettist situated below the Piazza in Covent Garden (1710-13) or in their satirical use slightly later that century by Samuel Foote and Charles Dibdin. (The use of puppets in creating caricatures for satire continues, of course, in the currently popular television programme *Spitting Image*). A brief resurgence occurred under the influence of Gordon Craig and his theories of the actor as an *über-marionette* in eC20, otherwise they have been relegated to a position well down the *bill* in *variety*. The term can still be used to refer to a form of cold, stylised playing: 'The Queen is played as a slightly marionette-like figure' (Berkoff, 124). Compare *glove-puppet*, *puppet*.

mark[1] An indicator on the stage floor – usually made with adhesive tape, although paint, chalk etc. can be used – to allow the exact positioning of a piece of furniture or scenery. A *mark-out* or *mark-up* is a scale outline of a set marked on the floor of a *rehearsal room* with tape or paint. Occasionally in theatre and more commonly in film, marks are used to direct an actor as to where to stand on set in order to be in the exact position to be correctly *lit* or to comply with a set-up camera shot. The phrase *to hit your marks* is used in relation to this: 'Always be sure you can hit your marks by pacing your walk up to them, like bowlers do to the wicket' (Samuel West, interviewed in Barkworth, 227).

mark[2] *To mark a scene* is to rehearse it by *walking through* it: i.e. rehearsing it to conserve energy, without full use of the voice or physical apparatus. Referring to a television rehearsal, Barkworth (p.70) has this advice: 'If it's a rehearsal, don't try to do it well ... If you do it well, you'll think, damn, I'll never be as good when we record it, and you'll probably be right. Just "mark it" as Ralph Richardson used to say: just go through the motions.' Compare *line rehearsal*.

maroon An electronically-operated explosive device, usually detonated *offstage*, imitating the noise of a large explosion. For reasons of safety it is usually set off in an iron container known as a *bomb tank*. From Fr. *marron* or It. *marrone*, 'a chestnut', probably on account of the way chestnuts explode when toasted in front of a fire.

mask *Mask* is from Fr. *masque* (first found in C16), but its earlier origins are disputed, the two most likely contenders being Sp. *máscara* or It. *maschera* (possibly from Arabic *maskhara*, 'a laughing-stock, buffoon'), though there may also be a link with med. L. *mascus*, 'a mask, spectre'. The term is first found in English as 'a facial covering with eyeholes, a disguise for the face' in 1534: 'The vices that they brought [from Asia] to Rome... The patriciens bearyng Measques and the Plebeyens usynge smelles, and the emperours to weare purple' (Berners, *The golden boke of Marcus Aurelius*). Although the term was then new, replacing the previous, less specific term, *disguise*, the custom of mask-wearing in the theatre has its roots in early *ritual* and became a vital accessory in Athenian drama (see *persona*). Since C16 masks have had their periods of theatrical vogue in Western Europe, most notably in the *masque* proper, the *commedia dell'arte*, and, sporadically this century, through Eastern influences on writers such as Yeats, Brecht and O'Neill.

The verb *to mask*, 'to conceal from view', is a development of the above (or a borrowing from Fr. *masquer*) first found in lC16. Theatrically, one actor *masks* another by standing in front of him, thus blocking the audience's view. Avoiding such problems is one of the fundamental tasks of the *director*, with his external view of rehearsals. *Masking* is an abbreviation of *masking piece* – a piece of scenery such as a *backing flat* used to conceal or mask part of the stage from the audience's view. *Masking-tape* is used to conceal joins in material etc.

masque/masquerade   'The king and xi. other were disguised, after the maner of Italie, called a maske, a thynge not seen afore in Englande' (1545, Hall, *Chronicle*). From the same root as *mask*, above, (Fr. *masque* only being preferred, probably due to its use by Jonson [see below] in eC17), the sophisticated *masque*, which was to become a *genre* in its own right, was a development from earlier folk traditions and court *disguisings*. It began to be refined in Italy in eC16, where the social, masked ball was embellished by poetical, allegorical drama, increasingly complex and lavish costume and *set design* and ever more intricate *machinery*. In Jacobean and Caroline England, the great influence on design was Inigo Jones and the greatest scripter of masques (excluding Milton, whose later *Comus* has little in common with the masque in its hey-day) was his collaborator Ben Jonson. In many ways, the masque is the forebear of *opera*, another form which was imported from Italy. *Masquerade*, from Sp. *mascarada* (see *mask*) and Fr. *mascarade*, is a more plebian, social form of disguising which has lent its name by figurative extension to the verb *to masquerade*, 'to counterfeit, (sometimes ludicrously)'. See also *anti-masque*.

master   An abbreviation of *master switch* or *master control* – a *lighting* and *sound* term for a device which can control all (or a selected group) of the electrical circuits in a theatre by overriding their individual switches and controls. Adjectivally, *master* has been used as 'controlling' (as in the 'master-beam' of a building) since at least C17.

master of ceremonies Frequently abbreviated to MC or *emcee*. In American *vaudeville* and less frequently in British *music hall* (see *chairman*, *compère* and *concert secretary*), the MC was the person whose duty it was to announce or introduce the *acts*. Often, he was something of a *star turn* himself. By the 1950s in Britain, the verb *to emcee* was also in common use by function-organisers, journalists etc., probably from America. During the late 1980s' craze for scratch and rap music, again emanating from the United States, MC was taken as a title by many of the chief performers, notably, in terms of general public recognition, M.C. Hammer.

material *Stand-up comics* refer to the content of their *acts* – *the gags* and *business* – as their *material*, probably in the sense of the raw material from which the performance is fashioned. Compare the use of 'stuff' in *strut one's stuff*. 'When you are under pressure to find new material, you need support' claimed an article in *The Stage* (23 March 1992), referring to the high incidence of stress-related illnesses amongst comics.

matinée An afternoon performance. Theatrically, Fr. *matinée* meant an early or, literally, morning performance, (from Fr. *matinée*, 'morning', usually preferred to the simpler *matin* in cases where a duration of time is involved, e.g. *Je ne l'ai pas vu de toute la matinée*, 'I haven't seen him all morning'). In C19, (and, dare one say, occasionally now), matinée performances and their audiences tended to be looked on as inferior to evening ones, hence the advice about when to try out new *business*, *try it on the matinée dog*, which Partridge claims was current from 1885-1915. Barkworth quotes Edith Evans, hinting at this attitude: 'Always do your best at every rehearsal, at every performance (including matinées)...' (p.78). And of course, matinées are tiring: "I soon began to dread *Richard*, particularly the double dose on *matinée days*" (Olivier, 167).

A *midnight matinée* is a performance in the very late evening, when other theatres are closed: 'Several actors who were in shows had rung to ask would I do a *matinée* so that they could see it' (Branagh, 129). The phrase *matinée idol* for a handsome actor popular with these audiences not necessarily for his acting skills alone, dates from 1920s and gained a continued currency in cinema, which borrowed *matinée* for its own use.

MC A common abbreviation for *master of ceremonies*.

MD An abbreviation of *musical director* – the person with overall responsibility for the music in all theatre shows with sufficient musical content to merit their appointment.

mechanical acting Translated from the Russian, a term coined by *Stanislavski* and used in *An Actor Prepares* (1936) to describe the clichéd conventions of an acting style dating back to and probably predating *melodrama*, a style still visible in early silent movies. According to Stanislavski, *gestures* include 'rubbing the brow with the back of the hand in moments of tragedy', 'spreading your hand over your heart to express love', 'tearing your hair when in despair'. Vocal embellishments include 'exaggeratedly high or low tones at critical moments of the role, done with specifically theatrical "tremelo", or with special declamatory vocal embellishments'. (See *Macready*.) 'There is nothing more boring than mechanical acting: the only thing that is interesting, for an audience, is to be in the presence of people who are thinking and feeling and not just going through the motions' (Barkworth, 254).

medium   An abbreviation of *colour medium*, a *gel* or piece of glass used to transform white light into coloured light.

melodrama   Sometimes found originally as *melodrame*. From Fr. *mélodrame* – or from its appropriation into German – (from Gk *melos*, 'music' + Fr. *drame*, 'drama'.) The first play in English to be labelled a *melodrama* was *A Tale of Mystery* by Thomas Holcroft (1802), based on *Coelina, ou l'Enfant de Mystère* by the Frechman René-Charles Pixérécourt, who, along with the German August Kotzebue, is regarded as one of the founders of the *genre*. (The earliest OED attestation of the use of the word is by Southey in 1809: 'They have made a melo-drama out of "Mary the Maid of the Inn".')

It was music that gave the genre its name. In German in lC18, *melodrama* meant dialogue delivered to musical accompaniment (see *singspiel*); in France, *mélodrame* was the musical *accompaniment* to a *dumb-show*. However, it is the content and style of the plays that the word tends to refer to, now: melodrama is highly romantic and sentimental, crammed with sensational, sometimes horrific incidents appealing violently to the emotions; it is packed with *stock characters* – the wronged maiden, the mercilessly evil *villain*; it is prone to mawkishly happy endings, and above all, it is played in an exaggeratedly stylised fashion.

As early as 1814, in the private diary of Sir R. Wilson, the OED has the word used in a general sense: 'The world will approve the catastrophe of the melodrama which metes out signal punishment to Joachim the first in the last act of his life.' *Melodramatic*, referring to general demeanour, is also widely used as the *Observer*, in a rather satirical piece about rural violence in England (10 May 1992) illustrates: "'There are traitors here, you know. Traitors everywhere... Tell the world what is happening.' In Newborough, it was difficult to pass of the words of a melodramatic old woman."

member   In Elizabethan theatres, a *member* was a 'sharing actor' in a company who took his agreed share of the receipts, in contrast to a 'hireling' (a man hired on a temporary basis) or 'apprentice', both of whom were employed by the company on negotiated wages. Although this specific sense fell out of use, the word has remained in the phrase *member of the company* for any acting employee of a theatrical company, and in the phrase *member of the cast* for anyone taking part in a given production. From Fr. *membre*, ultimately from L. *membrum*, 'a limb, a part of the whole'.

memory board   A *lighting-board* with a computerised memory which can be pre-programmed to hold all the *lighting cues* for a show, bringing in and taking out the correct *lanterns* and fixing their *levels*. *Memory* is a general term in computing and information processing for the ability of machines to store information which can be retrieved by the user. 'In all but the tiniest theatres, lights are computer-controlled' (*Observer*, 3 March 1992).

Theoretically, after a successful *technical rehearsal*, a simple show could be run with a relative novice *on the board*, given that they had a working knowledge of the *production* and a good *cue sheet*. One of the many advantages of computerised or memory boards is the *slow fade*, which can be set to occur gradually over an entire scene, as subtly as the fall of dusk itself.

men aside   '[T]he men in the stage departments working on each side of the stage are described as a certain number of *men aside*' (Baker, 327). Whilst I can find no definite evidence, the term has a ring to it which suggests a nautical origin.

merciful darkness   A dimly-lit scene, particularly a boring or badly-performed one, is shown in *merciful darkness* in the parlance of *lighting crews*.

Method, the   'To rouse your sub-conscious to creative work, there is a special technique' (Stanislavski, *An Actor Prepares*, 1936). *Stanislavski's* own system of actor *training* is occasionally referred to as *the method*, but, more properly, *method acting* is applied to systems of training based on his ideas (especially those involving the internal, mental processes of creating a role – see *psychotechnique* and *emotion memory*) – which were elaborated in the United States. Richard Boleslavski began to explore ways of teaching and using Stanislavski's ideas on inner *motivation* at the Laboratory Theatre in the 1920s, ideas developed in the 1930s by Lee Strasberg among others at New York's Group Theatre. See *affective memory*. The method was brought to public notice, however, by the success and influence of some of the alumni of the Actors' Studio (founded in 1947 by Elia Kazan and led from 1950 by Strasberg). The Method has attracted controversy:

My opinion of [Strasberg's] school is that it did more harm than good to his students and that his influence on the American theatre was harmfully misapplied. Deliberately anti-technical, his Method offered instead an all-consuming passion for reality, and if you did not feel attuned to exactly the right images that would make you feel you were actually *it* and *it* was going on, you might as well forget the scene altogether' (Olivier, 220). Rightly or wrongly, it was the intense introspective brooding and the mumbled *diction* of Marlon Brando and James Dean and the controversy which surrounded some of their early cinema roles which placed method acting firmly in the public imagination and in everyday vocabulary.

metteur en scène   French 'theatre (or cinema) director', occasionally used in English for no immediately obvious reason other than that it sounds grand. However, it means literally, if awkwardly, *putter-on-stage* and therefore combines the role of artistic director with wider production responsibilities. In this sense, it is perhaps closer to the former English sense of *producer*, which was abandoned in the professional theatre in favour of *director* by general agreement in the post-war period. See *mis(e)-en-scène*.

mic/mike   Dating from *c.*1927, according to Beale, these are variant abbreviations for the *microphone*, so-called because it amplifies small sounds: from Gk *micros*, 'small', + *phōnē*, 'voice, sound'. 'Performers warned as DTI clamps down on illegal mics' (headline in *The Stage*, 23 April 1992). Whereas everyone is familiar with the singer's wired *mike*, either sitting on its stand or wielded as a hand-prop, many modern shows use small, wire-less, *radio microphones* attached to the body to amplify even the actor's spoken voice. Whilst such devices add greatly to an artist's mobility, many purists bemoan the way they act as a disincentive to young performers mastering traditional skills of voice *projection*.

milk   To *milk a scene* or *to milk it dry* is an actor's description of working hard to extract the maximum response from an audience. It is most common in *comedy* where *comedians milk laughs*. '[Albert Finney] shamelessly and joyfully milks the role for all, and possibly more, than it is worth' (*The Stage*, 23 April 1992). The theatrical use is a metaphorical development from the primary Standard English meaning of the word.

mime   From Fr. *mime*, from L. *mimus* and Gk *mimos*, *mime* was originally used in English as a noun to describe those often scurrilous Greek and Roman *farces* which were based on physical action, mimicry 'and the ludicrous representation of familiar types of character' (OED); it was also applied to the actors who played in them. 'Scaliger describes a Mime to be a Poem imitating any action to stirre up laughter' (1642, Milton), and 'The antient mimes were so expert at the representation of Thought by Action' (1748, OED). As Milton suggests, dialogue was present in these shows, but action was primary: sensational presentations of indecency and violence – including on occasions real executions – were what packed in the audiences.

'Mime' is still used to signify both *genre* and *performer*: 'We did a very stylised mime which Kemp and I worked out in great detail... I hastened to offer all my credentials as a mime' (Berkoff, 36). The sense of the word had narrowed in French by C18, however, having come to mean an *entertainment* without words and its performer, whose *gestures* and expressions are used in place of dialogue. Aspects of the *commedia dell'arte* were metamorphosed into the *pantomime* of Debureau's *Pierrot* who began a tradition which has spawned great C20 mimes such as Barrault, Marceau and Le Coq. As the interest in *physical theatre* is growing in England, so artists like Lindsay Kemp and Steven Berkoff, who have studied under Marceau and Le Coq respectively, are greatly adding to the prestige of mime by broadening its theatrical base and adding to its vocabulary.

minstrel From OF *menestral*, 'servant, entertainer', from Provençal *menest(ai)ral*, 'official, officer'. As is the case with many medieval terms for 'performer', until C16, *minstrel* (which also occasionally meant 'servant' in English in C13) could denote a person with a range of performance skills from singer and storyteller to *juggler*. The later narrowing of the term is accompanied by a gradual romanticisation of the image of the minstrel, as in Scott's poem, 'The Lay of the Last Minstrel'.

In the C19, a further shift of sense occurred in America, where 'minstrel' came to signify 'a performer in a minstrel show', which, in terms of general entertainment, took the term back closer to its medieval meaning. The immense popularity in the United States of white *vaudeville* artists *blacking-up* to perform black music (see *coon show*) began with Thomas Dartmouth Rice under his soubriquet Jim Crow in the 1820s. His success led to a craze to see *burnt-cork minstrels* (so-called because of the use of burnt cork and glycerine for *make-up* before the advent of brown *greasepaint*). In addition to music, the shows featured *comic patter* between two characters, (Mr) Interlocutor and (Mr) Bones, known as the 'end-men'. Although white artists were gradually replaced by black ones, to many there remains something offensive and patronising about this form of entertainment. There were revivals in the C20, notably, in Britain, television's *Black and White Minstrel Show* with George Mitchell's Minstrels, which was hugely popular well into the 1970s, but the hey-day of the minstrels was over by the early C20.

miracle play A form of medieval drama, in part synonymous with the *mystery play*, but differing in that *miracle plays* celebrate the lives of the apostles and saints and the miracles associated with them as well as recounting stories from the Old and New Testaments. They were known simply as *miracles* in lC13-eC14: 'þat make swiche pleyys to any man/As myracles and bourdys' (1303, Robert Manning of Brunne, *Handling Synne*). *Miracle* comes from OF, from L. *miraculum*, 'a thing of wonder', from *mirus*, 'wonderful'.

mirror scrim A mirror of flexible plastic, used on stage similarly to a *gauze*, of which it might be considered a hi-tech version: that is, in one *lighting state* it can be transparent, in another opaque, thus rendering it particularly useful in *pantomime*, *transformation scenes* etc. See *scrim*.

miscast To *cast* an actor in a role for which they are unsuited, for whatever reason. 'Every actor feels he is born to play it . . . You cannot be miscast for *Hamlet* – "*fatally* miscast" as one critic called me in fact – since he too had *his* version of Hamlet fixed in his head' (Berkoff, vii).

mis en scène Sometimes found as *mise-en-scéne*: a mC20 borrowing of a French formulation for the director's realisation on stage of all the elements of his production such as performance, set, *lighting* etc. Elements of theatrical *production* and *direction* overlap in *mis en scène* but it still carries 'un-English', slightly *avant garde* associations: 'When one creates a mise-en-scène which is imaginative or recognises the wandering mind of the spectator, the production is curiously called "European". Here in England we are used to a kind of dullness . . . a safe representation and "natural" reading' (Berkoff, 60). See also *metteur en scène*.

misrule 'To Ringley, lorde of mysrewle, vpon a prest, £5' (1491, *Excerpta historica*). In C15 and C16, a Lord, King or Abbot of Misrule was appointed each Christmas at Court, and also in some colleges and schools to oversee the seasonal entertainments and festivities. He was a form of *master of ceremonies*, presiding over a controlled breakdown of order and normal conventions. This tradition probably descended from the clerical Feast of Fools which originated in C12 France, overseen by a junior clergyman appointed King or Boy Bishop. Such entertainments, which involved dramatic presentations, may well have their origins in Roman traditions and echo the importance of the shadowy figure of *Dionysus* at the dawn of European drama.

mixer A contraction of *mixing board* or *mixing desk*, a machine which allows *sound technicians* to mix vocal, musical and other more complex *FX* sounds from more than one source, and to doctor their respective volumes, tones, frequencies etc. The *mixer* can be used either during a live performance or in advance of performance to produce a sound tape for a show.

mixed casting A contraction of *mixed race casting* (see *cast*), whereby actors of different ethnic origins are used in a production. This can sometimes be done 'artistically' to point an issue in a text: for example, I have seen a production of Lorca's *Blood Wedding* at Contact Theatre in Manchester (by the Yvonne Brewster Company touring for the *National*, [1991]) set in Cuba with black actors as the members of the Bridegroom's family and white actors as members of the eventually antagonistic Bride's family. Four years earlier, in the same theatre, the resident company directed by Tony Clarke performed the same play, again with a *mixed cast*, but on this occasion the actors were divided between the families regardless of race. The latter might also be termed 'integrated casting'. Carelessly handled, this can cause problems of under-standing for some members of an audience. Both terms seem to have first been employed in the late 1970s - early 1980s as theatres began to become more actively aware of the lack of opportunities for actors from minority social groupings. (See *black, gay, feminist theatre*). As *Plays and Players* said of the casting of the Coventry Mystery Cycle in 1990: 'Moreover, and thank goodness, casting reflects the cultural diversity of the Midlands.'

model An abbreviation of *set model*: a detailed scale model of the *stage setting* constructed by the *designer* from sketches to demonstrate the design scheme to the *director*, *lighting designer* and other members of the *production team*. Usually built of a light wood such as balsa, or of card, the normal scale of a model is about 1cm to 15cms. Amongst the items listed in the Covent Garden Inventory (1743) is 'a large modell of the Stage not finished', suggesting that the use of models in design is at least three centuries old.

modern dress 'Vanya was immediately followed by the high com-ical role of Parolles in a modern dress *All's Well that Ends Well...*' (Olivier, 71, referring to a production in the 1920s). Nowadays, productions which use contemporary dress, even for the classics, are so common that they do not provoke much comment (except from inexperienced theatre-goers). The phrase *in modern dress* became current, however, in the eC20 as the result of some desig-ners' and directors' artistic decisions to *costume* the classics, parti-cularly Elizabethan and Jacobean drama, in contemporary cloth-ing rather than in *period costume*, at the time to some an expression of the most outrageous excesses of the *avant garde*. This was largely done to point the contemporary relevance of plays and to encourage audiences to focus on the central concerns of a production rather than on its trimmings. It also had the authority of costuming in the Elizabethan theatre, which paid less heed to historical authenticity.

modern theatre Whereas 'contemporary theatre' is generally considered to be that produced within five to ten years of the date of reference, *modern theatre* is usually said to have begun in the early 1870s, at the period when Ibsen began writing the enormously influential, *realistic* plays of his middle period. However, as with all attempts to label and date historical movements, the final decision on where to draw a dividing line between periods depends on individual judgement. (See *medieval*). Doubtless, as the decades pass, *modern* and *contemporary theatre* will be subdivided into a variety of as-yet-undreamed-of generic labels.

monodrama Strictly, a *monodrama* should differ from a *monologue* (though the terms are often used synonymously) in that monodrama only applies to a play – usually short – or an extract from a play, in which one actor appears alone on stage throughout; the meaning of 'monologue' is broader. 'I had taken with me Tennyson's *Maud* which he referred to as a "monodrama"... The word "monodrama" had appealed immediately to my actor's instinct for one-man show or audition material...' (Branagh, 113). A vogue for monodramas in lC18 Germany caught on in England, the first OED attestation being in a letter written by Southey in 1793 in which he refers to 'monodramas, comodrams, tragodramas, all sorts of dramas.' The term is occasionally applied more specifically to a play which is supposed to occur inside the head of a single character (such as *Beckett's Not I* or *Krapp's Last Tape*), but even in these specific cases 'monologue' is more commonly if less accurately found.

monologue In a play, a long speech by a single character. 'This was a classic monologue; a prostitute talking to the audience as if to a passer-by, assuming our complicity in her situation' (review in *Plays and Players*, October 1990). The *monologue* differs from a *soliloquy* in that other actors may be present on stage when it is being delivered. In general usage, someone who bores others with their garrulousness can be accused of *delivering a monologue*. The term is also used synonymously with *monodrama*, as with Harold Pinter's short play entitled *Monologue* which was premièred on BBC Television in 1973): 'Man alone in a chair. He refers to another chair, which is empty.'

'Monologue' can, however, also be used for a *recitation*, often in verse, popular in *music hall* and *variety*. '[Stanley Holloway] was perhaps the last major *artist* working in this sort of style, presenting rhyming narrative monologues spoken with a simple piano accompaniment... "[Ernest Hastings] used to perform monologues, playing for himself at the piano, and one he did was *And Yet – I Don't Know*. That was the first one I did as my party piece"' (Stanley Holloway quoted by Wilmut, 29).

morality play A late form of medieval drama which, through allegory, focused on moral teaching through characters personifying abstract virtues and vices. Whilst *moral* and *moral play* are found in C16, the terms *morality play* or simply *morality* are C18 coinings, first attested in OED in the title of J. Skot's 1773 edition of '*Everyman. A Morality*', a borrowing from French literary historians, *moralité* having been used in France in C16. A further justification for this choice lies in the C16 usage of 'morality' for a piece in prose or verse with a moralising content: '*The moralite of the hors, the goose, and the sheepe, translated by Dan Johne Lidgate*' (*c*.1430, Lydgate, *Minor Poems* [1911]). Despite their didactic intent, many of the later plays, developing as they did out of the *mystery* tradition, had their humorous moments. Their lasting significance is that they were instrumental in both the secularisation of drama and the establishment of professional acting companies. Notably examples of the genre are *Everyman* and Skelton's *Magnyfycence*.

morgue Especially in America, a theatre showing an unsuccessful show was referred to in lC19-eC20 as a *morgue*, for obvious reasons. The name is also sometimes applied to a theatre company's archives with their yellowing cuttings and production records.

morris dance Found in lC15 as *morys*, *moreys* and variants, *morris* is a corruption of *moorish*. Such dances were common throughout Europe in late medieval times – compare Flemish *mooriske dans* and Fr. *danse moresque*. *Morris dancers*, sometimes accompanied by a *hobby-horse* and characters from the Robin Hood legend, have their antecedents in folk *ritual*. The term probably derives from the powerful Moorish influence in Spain and Southern Europe throughout the medieval period (see *mask*). See also *mumming*.

motivation '[Judi Dench] questioned not only the motivations of her own character but of all the other parts, and at all times wanted to know how the play was shaping up as a whole' (Branagh, 184). Arguably, every effective actor from *Thespis* onwards has searched in his own way to identify with the essence of the *character* he is playing, to find what *Stanislavski* would call 'the inner life of a character', hidden behind words and actions in the *subtext* of a play. *Motivation* is the term employed by actors to describe the fundamental driving forces behind a character: why they do what they do, say what they say. A character does not, however, have one single motivation or even a bundle of fixed motivations: they may be predisposed to certain responses but each new situation encountered elicits a fresh response which, in Stanislavskian terms, gives rise to a new motivation, to a new 'creative objective' for the actor.

The term is probably American, influenced by Stanislavski but not directly from him. 'The American cast did not appear to understand very much of what I was trying to do. All they seemed to want was motivation. Unfortunately, the Method does not work for Shakespeare' (Geilgud, 70). From OF *motif*, in the sense of 'that which causes a person/thing to move', the word's root can be traced back to L. verb *movēre*, *mot-*, 'to move': at the heart of 'motivation' is a fluidity, a sense of change and development in response to changing circumstances.

motley   A coarse cloth used to make the costume of Elizabethan and Jacobean *fools* and *jesters*: 'A noble fool,/A worthy fool! Motley's the only wear' (1600, *As You Like It*, II.viii). This sense could be transferred to a fool himself, as Shakespeare illustrates in Sonnet 110: 'Alas! 'tis true I have gone here and there/And made myself a motley to the view.' It is generally thought that such costumes were multi-coloured, or at least patched with materials of various colours, but the original sense, from ME *mottelay*, perhaps from Anglo-French *motelé*, refers more to the rough texture of the material: from *mote*, 'a particle of dust', (corresponding to Dutch *mot*, which also means 'sawdust'), famous from the reference in Matthew 7:3 – 'Why beholdest thou the mote that is in thy brother's eye, but considerest not the beam that is thine own eye?'

The current theatrical usage of the word is for stage *costumes* generally, leading to the famous if rather ironic phrase *on with the motley!*

mount   *To mount a show* is to stage it: to put it on public view with all the financial outlay and attention to organisation which that entails. *A dictionary of modern slang, cant, and vulgar words* (1874, ed. Hotten) defines *mount* as 'in theatrical parlance, to prepare for production on the stage'. Possibly the term has its origins in the *gaffs* of touring companies, where the stage needed to be erected, or mounted, at every stop.

mouth   *To mouth one's lines* is to deliver them in an exaggerated way; to *ham it up*. The verb is Standard English, obviously descriptive of the physical appearance of the person mouthing. The usage can be traced back at least to Hamlet's instructions to the players: 'Speak the speech, I pray you, as I pronounc'd it to you, trippingly on the tongue; but if you mouth it as some of your players do, I had as lief the town crier spoke my lines' (1600, *Hamlet*, III.ii).

move A stage *movement* made by an actor during a show, which has been planned in rehearsal, or *blocked*. 'Sometimes called "Blocking", "Plotting", "Seeing What Happens" or – Barry Davis's favourites – "Busking", "Bluffing", or "Finding Your Feet".' (Barkworth, 25). Such *moves*, when decided, are generally recorded by whoever is *on the book* at the rehearsal and also marked in the actor's *text* or committed to memory. 'I can't bear being given arbitrary moves arbitrarily preconceived by the director. Only sleepless nights and awkward arguments ensue, for such a director discards one of the most precious ingredients in the making of a play: the actors' instincts.' (Barkworth, 26). The verbal phrases *to move on, off, up* and *down* also exist, corresponding to those prepositional *stage directions*, with the exception that *moving on* may be applied to an actor already *onstage* moving nearer *centre stage*, and *moving off* may involve a movement towards the *wings* but not necessarily an *exit*.

movement *Movement* can be used for a stage movement or *move* (see above), but is now far more commonly used with reference to the *movement exercises* and *movement classes* which are part of the training of most actors, and a feature of much educational *drama*. 'The first class [at RADA] was Movement, in room ten, directly opposite the locker-room' (Branagh, 52). Movement may involve dance but need not: it is essentially a way of training the actor's physical apparatus to increase their body and spatial awareness, strength and stamina, suppleness, physical and emotional trust in others etc.; it should also help to improve *breathing* and relaxation skills. For actors in performance or rehearsal, movement exercises often play a vital part in *warm-ups*. 'I am perhaps less fanatical about it now and didn't precede each rehearsal with an hour's obligatory movement which would have exhausted both me and the cast' (Berkoff, 80).

mugging Partridge has the verb *to mug*, 'to assume exaggerated facial expressions', as a theatrical term which became general in about 1880. For obvious reasons, *mugging* tends to be a *comedian's* term (otherwise it is used pejoratively), and the nouns *mug* and *mugger* were applied to comics who had a tendency to exploit facial expression. It is at least an eC19 term and may predate this: 'The low comedian had "mugged" at him...fifty nights for a wager' (1855, Dickens).

multiple set   A C20 term for a *stage set* (also known as a *composite set* and, in America, as a 'simultaneous-scene setting') in which three or more *sets* are constantly on view to the audience. This was how much medieval drama in continental Europe was staged, the presentation of a variety of scenes in different areas of a church being preferred to the English use of ambient *pageant wagons*, pausing at agreed sites. *Multiple sets* can be found on *proscenium arch stages*, and in C20 have sometimes been deliberately exploited by dramatists: Alan Ayckbourn's plays *How the Other Half Loves*, *Bedroom Farce* and *Absurd Person Singular* are examples. One frequently finds the use of multiple sets at *perambulatory* (or *promenade*) shows, where the audience walk from set to set, much as the medieval European audiences did in church. American terminology for this system is closer to Fr. *décor simultané* and German *Simultanbühne* (alternatively *Standortbühne*).

mumming   The precise origins of the English and Scottish *mummers' plays* are in doubt although clearly they are part of a European-wide tradition of folk drama closely connected with fertility *rituals*. The most commonly-repeated variant – and the earliest extant texts only date back to C18 – follows the pattern of a resurrection myth: St George, killed in combat by the Turkish Knight, is revived by the Doctor. Casts in mummers' plays were all-male, roles sometimes being handed through generations of the same family, the only payment being some token in money or kind. For excellent descriptions of C19 *mumming*, see Hardy's *Return of the Native*. *Mummer* is ME, from OF *momeur*, from *momer*, 'to act in dumb-show', from Middle Low German *mummen*. Like *hum*, this word obviously has the same phonaesthetic origin as the interjection Mum!, 'Silence!' (as in 'mum's the word'), and the adjective 'mum' (as in 'keep mum'). *Mummer* is now occasionally used pejoratively, or with jocular affection (compare *thespian*) of all actors, most frequently by actors themselves.

murder   In a phrase which could be misinterpreted (compare *bomb*): a *hit show*, especially in America, is said to be *murder at the box office*. (Also contrast *corpse*, *kill*.)

muses, the   Greek mythology has supplied actors with two *muses*, or sources of divine inspiration: Thalia, the Muse of Comedy and Melpomene, the Muse of Tragedy. From Gk *mousa*, 'muse' (see *music*).

music   Like *ballet*, *dance* and *opera*, music, though it has played such a vital role in almost every stage of the development of theatre, is taken here as a separate topic worthy of its own Book of Words, and so the history of the term and its associated theatrical senses will be dealt with very briefly.

Music derives ultimately from Gk *mousikē*, 'the art of the Muse', (from *mousa*, 'muse'), and could be applied to all the arts, though it was used more specifically with reference to music. It is first attested in English in C13, via OF *musique* and L. *musica*: 'Wit of musike, wel he knew' (*c*.1250, *The Story of Genesis and Exodus, an early English song* [E.E.T.S. 1865]). It is also used quasi-adjectivally from eC17, as found theatrically in terms such as *music cue* and *music hall*. *Musician* is first found in C14: 'Also, Musice maketh musiciens as phisike maketh phisissiens' (*c*.1374, Chaucer, *Boethius*). The adjective *musical* is found in eC15. Theatrically, it is found in a number of major terms – e.g. *musical director* (see *MD*), *musical comedy*.

musical comedy/musical   *Musicals*, an eC20 American abbreviation of *musical comedies* are the *box office hits* which keep *Broadway* and the *West End* financially buoyant. Their origins are found in m-lC19. Essentially, musicals combine a strong, often romantic plot and contemporary dialogue with memorable songs and spectacular *dance routines* to create lively popular entertainment. It is argued that the American musical play, *The Black Cloak* (1866) was the first *musical comedy*, drawing on *burlesque, melodrama, dance* and *opera* to create a new, indigenously American theatrical genre; however, from the late 1870s, the London *operettas* of Gilbert and Sullivan also contributed an influence on the later style of musical comedy. According to *The Concise Oxford Companion to the Theatre*, 'the first English musical comedy was *In Town* (1892), staged at the Prince of Wales's by George Edwardes'.

music hall   The British forerunner of *variety, music halls*, (or *the halls*, as they came to be known), flourished from mC19-eC20). They developed from the *song-and-supper rooms* of lC18-mC19 and from organised sings-songs in pub tap-rooms. The first purpose-built music hall was The Canterbury, built in 1851 opposite a pub of the same name in Lambeth, which had been bought three years earlier by Charles Morton, specifically for the presentation of popular singers, comedians and *speciality acts* which characterised the form. See also *burlesque, chairman, variety, vaudeville*.

mystery plays   It has often been mistakenly presumed that because the medieval *mystery plays* were performed by guilds of tradesmen whose specific skills were also known as *mysteries*, there must be a connection between the two terms. There is not. 'Mystery' is in fact a translation of Fr. *mystère*, a term applied to the French *miracle plays* (from med. L. *misterium*) of the late Middle Ages, appropriated for English use with reference to indigenous miracle plays in C18 (compare *morality play*): 'The mysteries only represented in a senseless manner some miraculous History from the Old or New Testament' (1744, ed. Dodsley, *A select collection of old plays*). The distinction between the 'miracles' and the 'mysteries' is a nice one and in a sense one manufactured for critical convenience: essentially, those plays termed 'miracles' include stories of the apostles and saints, whereas 'mysteries' tend to be devoted entirely to biblical stories: but, since both terms are modern, how much would this have meant to a medieval tradesman?

N **aff** Of low quality; contemptible; lacking in all aesthetic value. *Naff* has synonymous links with both *tacky* and *kitsch* but is more contemptuously dismissive than either of those terms. '[A certain performer] has a mania for the lowest kind of show business, for things which are tacky, and, to use the old trouper's term, "naff"' (*The Observer*, 24 September 1978). 'Naff' would appear to have entered theatre language from *Parlyaree*, an infiltrator like other such terms along the *'camp* connection'. (One etymological suggestion which Beale quotes – that it is a World War II naval acronym for 'not available for fucking' – has the same fanciful ring as the chestnut that *wog* is an acronym for 'Western oriental gentleman': I suspect both of these acronyms were coined after the words were in common naval usage.) Beale also received a definition from Kenneth Williams, who defines 'naff' as 1960s' gay jargon for 'unlovely; a gay denigration of someone was *naff omi*, "a dreary man".' By the late 1970s, the word was in general usage in all walks of society, surpassing *kitsch* as the latest vogue term of dismissal for what is 'Non-U' (as described in the 1950s by Nancy Mitford).

name A *name actor* is one who has been sufficiently successful for their name outside the theatre and on publicity material to attract an audience when their *name is (up) in lights* outside the theatre. Likewise, if an actor is *playing a name part*, they are playing the eponymous central character in a show whose name inevitably appears on all the publicity material, for example *Hamlet* or *Hedda Gabler*. Other usages, especially in the United States, where the term originated in e-mC20 include *name act, name billing, name star*. See also *title*.

narrative/narrator The *narrative* aspects of a play or a production (from L. root word *narrare*, 'to give a continuous account of events, to tell a story') are those which concern themselves with unfolding and advancing the *plot*. This, perhaps, is why many in an audience go to the theatre: 'There is a lot to be said for a play with a strong narrative line... It is a long time since I went to the theatre wondering what was going to happen next – a reversion to childhood, maybe, but that must be in part Ayckbourn's intention...' (*Plays and Players*, October 1990). Many dramatists with an axe to grind, (among them, on his own assertion, *Brecht*), are

167

suckers for the storyline. As the same issue of *Plays and Players* quoted above says in a review of a contemporary play: 'It seems ironic that for all the script's anti-populist posturing, the writing is better at sheer narrative propulsion, the stuff of soaps, in fact, than any of the ideas [the dramatist] wishes to be seen to be fighting for.' The term has been used in English since mC16.

In theatrical terms, a *narrator* is that person on stage, (not always a *character* or active participant in events), whose function is to fill in details of the plot, (the narrative), not described by the play's action, or to comment on events in the way a *chorus* might. In C20 theatre, this function has been much exploited in the *epic* theatre of Bertolt Brecht, based as it is centuries-old narrative traditions dating back to before Homer: the use of a narrator, (in the example below from Scene One of *The Caucasian Chalk Circle* he is called The Singer), is also, almost incidentally, a vital part of his theory of *verfremdungseffect*:

THE EXPERT: How long will this story take, Arkadi? I have to
              be back in Tiflis tonight.
THE SINGER: It's actually two stories. A few hours.
THE EXPERT: Couldn't you make it shorter?
THE SINGER: No.

the National   The common abbreviation amongst theatre people and playgoers of The Royal National Theatre, now housed in a three-*auditoria* complex on the South Bank of the Thames in London. The idea of establishing such a theatre was mooted as early as C18 but no action was taken until the establishment of a Shakespeare Memorial National Theatre Committee in 1907. This was followed, after a delay of two world wars, by the first building work in 1951: 'On 13 July the first foundation stone of the National Theatre was laid, somewhat inauspiciously in the wrong place . . . It had ultimately to be removed for the Queen Elizabeth Hall and the Purcell Room complex' (Olivier, 189). In 1962 a National Theatre Board was created, with Laurence Olivier as *artistic director*. Not until 1976, after a period in residence at the Old Vic, did the company move to the present building (designed by Sir Denys Lasdun) as The National Theatre Company of Great Britain. *Royal* was appended in 1988.

nativity play   In Britain, the most immediate associations of this phrase are with those tiny, public acts of devotion and disaster made by young children in school halls and on Sunday-school stages each year around Christmas. The *nativity play* must provide most people's first experience of *treading the boards*, and many people's last. In fact, the nativity play as a devotional tradition dates back to medieval liturgical drama. It was originally performed in church, in Latin, before the adoption of vernacular presentation.

naturalism   The current theatrical usage of *naturalism* might be summarised as 'a theory of theatrical performance which believes that an accurate external presentation of human behaviour should be presented on the stage'. However, achieving a distinction of meaning between *naturalism* and *realism*, two words which are often used synonymously, is no mean task. (For a detailed analysis of the development of both words beyond their theatrical contexts, see Raymond Williams, *Keywords*, [1976, Fontana].)

In brief, 'naturalism' was first used in English in eC17 in a philosophical sense, in contrast to 'supernaturalism': 'those blasphemous truth-opposing Heretikes and Atheisticall naturalists' (1612) were people who based their moral ideas on the empirical study of nature and human nature rather than on divine teaching. From the sense of external observation suggested by this, later in C17 the sense of 'natural philosopher, scientist' developed, which has narrowed since to 'natural scientist', and at its narrowest to 'botanist' (as in Seamus Heaney's poem, 'Death of a Naturalist'). Modern artistic applications of the word appear to stem from the French school of *naturalisme*, which included the novelist and dramatist Émile Zola, a post-Darwinian movement that believed in applying the scientific method (and up-to-date theories such as natural selection) to literary observation and expression. When Strindberg calls *Miss Julie* 'a naturalistic tragedy', he is not only discussing the style summarised at the top of this entry. For him naturalism is Darwinian (with a large dash of Nietzsche): whereas realism is a question of theatrical practicalities – 'when one has only one set, one is entitled to demand that it be realistic' – he sees naturalism as more complex: '[the modern, woman struggling for emancipation] is a tragic type, providing the spectacle of a desperate battle against Nature – and tragic also as a Romantic heritage now being dissipated by Naturalism, which thinks that the only good lies in happiness – and happiness is something only a strong and hardy species can achieve' (1888, Preface to *Miss Julie*).

Returning to its current sense, theatrical naturalism needs to be limited and edited on stage by artistic judgement. A totally naturalistic production based on a totally naturalistic text, written and performed in the arduous, arbitrary and detailed way that everyday events occur (granted that such a thing were possible), would certainly lack dramatic urgency.

An anti-naturalistic movement is now in full swing in the theatre: 'John Hurt told me this morning that he's sick of naturalism.

"We are entertainers, after all" he said, "and we need a sort of heightened naturalism"' (Barkworth, 215). 'The fondness for naturalistic gestures has afforded us some awful Hamlets and I have seen the worst. The very worst. The most worst. The utmost, boring, uncut versions...' (Berkoff, 15). Despite the above distinctions, however, it must be admitted that in everyday theatrical practice, 'naturalism' and 'realism' are used virtually synonymously.

nautical drama Not to be confused with *aquatic drama*, where the water in the production was real, *nautical drama* was merely a form of *melodrama* which took sea-faring men, their ships, lifestyle etc. as its subject matter, a notable example being Douglas William Jerrold's *Black-Ey'd Susan* (1829). Gilbert and Sullivan's *H.M.S. Pinafore* (1878) could be seen in part as a parody of the genre.

The term was coined in C19 from *nautical*, (from Fr. *nautique* or from L., from Gk *nautikos nautēs*, 'sailor', from *naus*, 'ship'.

nautical influences on theatre language There are over forty entries in this book in which I have detected what I have termed a *nautical* influence behind the adoption or development of a theatrical term. Most concern the staging and the mechanics of staging, but a couple – see *busk* and *-hander* – also encroach on performance. Arguably, the most important theatre term introduced by them is *set*. One obvious reason for this the nautical influence is that in the first decade C18, more complicated systems of *flying* were introduced above the London stage, requiring operation by men skilled in handling ropes. As a great port and ship-building centre, the city had a plentiful supply of skilled labour on offer, in the form of sailors and shipbuilders. However, ropes and lines had been used much earlier on the English stage, as had machine rooms – there is evidence of those above the Elizabethan stage (see Leacroft, 34). Given the proximity of these theatres to the river, it is possible that the nautical connection could be over a century older than the first estimation. In fact, James Burbage, the founder and builder of the first purpose-built London theatre, The Theatre, in Shoreditch, was a carpenter.... but here speculation is running away with itself. The fact is that these unknown figures and their successors have contributed hugely to theatre language: see *apron – back-cloth – backing – barrel – batten – bay – boards – boom – bridge – busk – canvas – catwalk – chips/chippie – crew – dips – dock – droop – fit-up – flats – flies/flying – forestage – gridiron – hand – -hander – line – men aside – pilot – platform – rail – rig – sand bag – set – stand by – strike – stringers – toggle – trestle – walk (a flat) – work (a show) – workers.* (See also Introduction.)

neoclassical drama   An eC19 term applied to the C17 and C18 European-wide movement back to *classical* – i.e. Greek and Roman – principles of dramatic composition and presentation, or to misconceived principles based on a limited understanding of classical practice. The adoption of the *Unities* and formal *act divisions* were permanent developments of *neo-classicism*. See *Aristotelian*.

night, the   A common abbreviation of *opening night*, as in the traditional comment on bad late rehearsals, 'It'll be all right on the night'.

nō theatre   (Also found in the anglicised form *noh*). A form of Japanese classical drama developed in C14 from a fusion *Dengaku no Nō* ('field music performance') and *Sargaku no Nō* ('monkey-music' or 'scattered music'), forms refined from local entertainments and Shinto ceremonies respectively. In Japanese, *Nō* is a loan word, written with a Chinese character meaning 'to be able', the Japanese at that time having a penchant for giving their artistic vocabulary a Chinese air. 'It signifies "talent"; hence "an exhibition of talent" or "performance"' (Arthur Waley, *The Nō Plays of Japan*). The staging of the developed Nō play – on a highly-polished wooden platform below a pagoda-style temple roof, with the audience on two sides – and the positioning of the actors – entering down a forty-foot corridor to assemble with a ten-man chorus to the leading actor's left, a four-man band and two conventionally-invisible stage-hands to his rear – make the 'rules' of European *neoclassical drama* seem alarmingly lax. Certain elements of *nō*, such as the use of *masks*, ritual music and dances, the elaborate costumes and stylised *delivery* have made a big impact on western *dramaturges* from lC19 onwards, their interest popularising the term. Whilst there has been little direct imitation, selective borrowing has occurred frequently. (See *kabuki*).

noises off   A term covering all sound effects used in the theatre which are produced *offstage*, or, as it is abbreviated, *off*. (See *effects, FX*.) The term is also used as a *stage direction*, often to indicate some commotion unseen by the audience, and is the title of a play by Michael Frayn (1982).

notes   A term used for the comments given to *cast* and *production team* by the *director* both during the *rehearsal period* and, periodically, during the run of a show, so-called because they are often culled from the hasty aides-memoires jotted down in a *run-through*, frequently in the dark, to be delivered afterwards: 'I have never liked giving notes after a run-through while the actors gather like schoolchildren waiting for approval or criticism, which, though meant to be helpful, being given publicly is always felt to be personal. I would rather wait until the next rehearsal and approach them individually before it starts, or merely rehearse the bit that wasn't working' (Berkoff, 114). Others also use this approach: '[Michael Rudman's] best notes were his last ones; maybe for other actors it would have thrown them, that he would suddenly come up at the last minute and say, "You do not need that pause, you don't need to strive so hard for that effect, you don't need to make that point so clearly, trust this, trust the other." He was so marvellously selective. And very sensitive' (Alec McCowen, interviewed in Barkworth, 170). Branagh also gives an example of Sir John Geilgud delivering his notes on the 'rogue and peasant slave' soliloquy in *Hamlet*: 'Well done. There are some good things there, but you're really trying too hard. Don't over-colour the early section. You can be much straighter. Give yourself a breather in the middle. Don't stress "I *am* pigeon-livered" when "pigeon-livered", is much more juicy' (p.67). From Standard English *note* as 'a brief written record'.

notice The common theatrical term for a *press review*. 'On the way back Ralph bought *The Guardian*; I must admit that I had forgotten about such things as notices...I looked over Ralph's arm to see what I could of the notice he was reading, and what my eyes saw made them smart with displeasure' (Olivier, 144). It has been used as 'information, intelligence, warning etc.' since lC15 and with the sense in question since mC19: 'Before you write that brilliant notice...of some book of verses' (1872, Holmes, *The poet at the breakfast table*). From L. *noticia*, from *notus*, 'known'.

In addition, the way in which *theatre managements* formally announce the end of a *run* is by placing details of the show's closure on the *call-board* in the form of a *notice*. It has been in this sense – 'the intimation of the termination of an agreement' – since eC19: 'All I've come about is just... to give my governor's notice' (1837, Dickens, *Pickwick Papers*).

Theatrically, a *notice-board* is a much less common alternative to call-board, though it is found frequently in general usage. 'Notice-board' was used, however, from eC19 for an *onstage* display board used to communicate dialogue and other information to the audience in theatres which, due to the tightness of the *Licensing Act* (see also *legit.*) were unable to function in the normal manner.

novelty act In *variety*, a portmanteau term for any act specialising in the unusual – for example, seal acts, memory man etc. – a *speciality act*. The term originated in *vaudeville* and *music hall*, from ME, from OF *novelté*, 'a new thing', in use since C14.

number   As in 'a nice all-round singer of ballads and up-tempo numbers' (*The Stage*, 28 March 1991), *number* is now most frequently found as a *variety* term for an individual song. It was used in *music hall* in lC19 to refer to any act or *turn* and also to refer to an individual song or a distinct segment of a production such as a *dance routine*. This is in line with the standard sense of 'one of a collection of songs and poems' (OED) – 'there was a number in the hawker's collection called *Conscrits Français...*' (1878, Stevenson, *An Inland Voyage*) – and 'a division of an opera' (1881, OED), both of which may well derive from the C16 senses of 'a group of notes' or 'a metrical unit of verse' (hence 'a line or a stanza').

Objective (creative) Translated from the Russian, this is the agreed English term for an element of the *Stanislavski* system of actor training, *psychotechnique*. When a *super-objective* for a production has been decided on and the actor has decided on his own *through-line*, he is advised to break the part down into discrete units of action which may be several scenes long or consist of only a few lines. Whilst the unit of *text* may be summarised in a noun clause, the actor's creative *objective*, which must be found within the unit, should be expressed in a sentence which contains a verb: 'Every objective must carry in itself the germ of action...Try sitting on a chair and wishing for power *in general*. You must have something more concrete, real, nearer, more possible to do. As you see, not any verb will do, nor can any word give an impetus to full action...It is important that an objective have the power to attract and to excite the actor' (1936, Stanislavski, *An Actor Prepares*). The actor's creative objective, therefore, corresponds to the character *motivation* within the *sub-text* of the role.

For example, before her first entrance in Strindberg's *Miss Julie*, a Stanislavskian leading actress must obviously decide on her creative objective. From the opening lines, it would appear that she has entered the servants' quarters to request something from the cook, Christine, but the actress is likely to infer from the subject that she has really entered to flirt with the servant, Jean. The actress may therefore light on the objective: 'I want my every action to be so attractive and provocative that Jean falls under my power'.

off An abbreviation of *offstage*. (See *noises off*.) *Off* can also combine with other verbs to produce *stage directions*: *to move off*, for example, is to move towards the *wings* from a position nearer the *centre line*. (See also *go off*.) An actor can be said to be *off* if he has missed his *entrance cue*: i.e. he is offstage when he should be onstage. (Contrast *on*.)

off-Broadway, off-off-Broadway *Off-Broadway* is a term used for professional theatres in New York City which are not situated in the main *Broadway* theatre district. The term was coined in the 1950s, when disenchantment with the artistic quality of Broadway shows and their unwillingness to take on contemporary issues

174

and formal experiments was widespread; following the success of Tenessee William's *Summer and Smoke* at the Circle-in-the-Square in 1952, an *alternative* set of venues began to develop off Broadway – hence, the name – linking up with other venues and theatre companies across the States.

Commercial realities meant that many of these alternative theatres, too, were unwilling to take sufficient artistic risks to satisfy the *avant garde* and by the mid-1960s, a new range of alternative venues was developing under the logically-appealing label *off-off-Broadway*. The later development of *off-off-off Broadway* is not much used but does exist. Doubtless *off^n-Broadway* has been used, denoting true alternative status. These mid-C20 developments can be compared with the growth of *fringe* theatre in Britain.

offer up   Any member of a theatre's *technical crew* might be asked by to *offer up* a *prop*, a *lighting state*, a *sound effect* etc.: what is being asked for is a demonstration of the particular component of the production *in situ*. ' "Offer up the yellow ambers" means to bring in the pale amber light circuit' (Baker, 327). OED has no phrasal verbs connected with *offer*, but OED Supplement has *offer up* as a modern usage meaning 'to put (a part of a structure' in place to see how it looks or whether it fits properly' and offers this example: 'Well, mate, it's no use looking at it, we can't tell without offering it up.'

off-set   A piece of scenery at an angle to another is said to be *off-set*. Alternatively, there are those who claim that the phrase should only refer to a piece of scenery which is set at a right angle to the *centre line* of the stage.

offstage   (Also found in the forms *off stage* and *off-stage*, and frequently abbreviated to *off*.) Sometimes the word refers specifically to the part of the stage not visible to the audience. 'But we go offstage, or off to the side' (Berkoff, 49). Sometimes, confusingly, as the second part of that attestation indicates, to *move offstage* may mean merely to walk away from the centre of the stage. And the word can be even less geographically specific: 'How important do you think the offstage life of an actress is?' (Barkworth, 167).

There are a legion of related terms which are self-explanatory. (See also *noises off*.)

old stagers   Like *old pro* and *old trouper*, a term used to refer to a veteran actor, with a pun, obviously, on the stage. Its origins, however, are probably not theatrical. It has been borrowed because of its appropriateness. Partridge, defining it as 'a very experienced person', finds its earliest colloquial usage in 1711, originally meaning someone who frequently travelled by stagecoach and who was, as such, experienced in the ways of the world. An alternative view explored in OED is that the term comes from OF *estagier*, a translation of L. *stagiarius*, used in English monastic records for an old monk who was lodged permanently in the infirmary. It is certainly the better story and, since the first attestation is from 1570, more likely to be true: 'They betook them to theyr legges... resembling in some part a spectacle not much vnlike to the old stagers of Oxford, worse feared then hurt, when as the Church there was noysed to be on fier' (Foxe, *The Book of Martyrs*).

on/onstage   A common abbreviation of *onstage*, as in *to be on*. It is found in a variety of phrases such as *to go on, to walk on* and *to move on*, the latter also capable of meaning 'to move further towards centre stage' for an actor who is already *on*. (Contrast *off*.)

on the book   When used in relation to a performance, being *on the book* means to be acting as *prompter*. I would speculate that the phrase dates back at least to C17, although I can find no attestation for this: but note how it implies that there is only *one* book, *the* book. The rest of the cast were given hand-written copies of their own *lines or parts*.

A member of the stage management team 'on the book' at a modern *rehearsal* has the onerous task of cutting up a copy of the text of the play and, in a loose-leaf notebook or ring-file, sandwiching each leaf of the text between sheets of blank paper to produce a *prompt copy*, known as 'the book'. Notice how the definite article lends authority to this copy over all other copies of the *text*. That is because it is in the book, during rehearsals, that the *ASM*, *DSM* or whoever will be expected to record all the show's *entrances, exits, moves*, alongside *lighting* and *sound cues*, actors' *calls* etc. (See *book* and contrast *carrying the book*.)

on the road   On tour. Whilst there is something grand about being 'on tour' (with its echoes of the Grand Tours of the leisured classes of preceding centuries), this C19 term for taking a show around the country has overtones of both the rough-and-ready and the glamorously romantic. It suggests both highwaymen ('knights of the road' and 'gentlemen of the road') and tramps (also latterly 'gentlemen of the road' and, in C19, 'roadsters') and Jack Kerouac's cult, autobiographical, beat novel of the 1950s, *On the Road* (also, incidentally, Australian slang for being given the sack [like 'down the road' in N. England]). It seems aptly chosen, probably from the jazz musicians who also used the term. 'Let's get the show on the road', now a common expression, meaning 'Let's get moving', captures some of the restless energy of the enterprise.

on tour   See also *on the road*. Companies have gone *on tour* since the earliest recorded times, and it is likely that travelling players were on the road keeping theatre alive even in the so-called Dark Ages. The London companies of the Elizabethan era toured, too, partly to escape the ravages of the plague in the city. The tradition continued in the C18 and C19 (see *circuit, barnstorm*) and has been particularly prevalent since the decline of *rep*, with a number of companies (for example The Prospect Theatre Company and, amongst *alternative* groups, Red Shift) being set up solely as *touring companies*.

one act play   Also known as a *one-acter*: '"The Burglar and the Judge", the very clever one-acter by F.C. Phillipps and C.H. Brookfield' (*Pall Mall Gazette*, 11 October 1895). A play consisting of only one *act*. Generally, these plays tend to be relatively short; they are produced either as lunchtime shows, as *curtain-raisers* or on a *double bill*. They are also generally concentrated and economic in their use of detail: they are short stories to the full-length play's novel. Modern examples include Beckett's *Krapp's Last Tape* and Pinter's *The Dumb Waiter* (both 1958).

one-hander   A common theatrical term for a *monodrama*. See *- hander*.

one-liner   '150 *one-liners*, £2' (Ad in *The Stage*, 21 March 1991). As this suggests, the *one-liner* is the staple of the *stand-up comic*, a brisk *gag*, containing its own *feed-line* and *punch-line* along the lines of Groucho Marx's 'I never forget a face but in your case I'll make an exception' (quoted in the *Guardian*, 18 June 1965). Early *music-hall* comics tended to favour character-based routines; quick-fire humour based on one-liners as the basis of an act appears to have been imported from American *vaudeville* in the e-mC20, catching on first in the South of England: 'The northern comic would tend to build a situation rather than going for the one-liner...Northern audiences prefer the warmth of northern comedy to the hustling attitude of southern comics' (Roger Wilmut discussing the stand-up comics of the 1940s in *Kindly Leave the Stage*). Like many other *variety* terms, it has now entered the jargon of the *legit. theatre*.

one-man show   (sometimes found as *one man show* and *one-man-show*). 'Shortly before leaving home for the Antipodes we had been to see Danny Kaye in his wonderful one-man show at the Palladium' (Olivier, 167). Unlike *one-hander* and *monodrama*, which tended to be dramatic terms, most *one-man shows* were originally *showcases* in which individual *variety artists* would display the full range of their skills. Due to the shift to non-sexist language over the last decade, they are now becoming known as 'one-person shows: 'One-person shows seem ever more popular' (*Plays and Players'* review of the Edinburgh Fringe, October 1990). This last remark reflects the ever-increasing cost of mounting a show with a large cast. The term, like many others from *variety*, has now entered the language of the dramatic theatre, with such 'serious' pieces as Alec McCowan's dramatisation of *The Gospel According to St Mark* in the early 1980s being referred to as a 'one-man show'.

one-night stand   Originally, a *music-hall* term for a single night's engagement, a *stand* being a stop on a *circuit tour*. The term had certainly entered the vernacular by the 1930s meaning 'a night of illicit or casual sex', due to the pun on 'stand', which has been a colloquial term for the male erection since at least the C16. Of course, it is quite possible that that or a similar phrase existed colloquially much earlier, rendering variety the borrower.

OP/OPS   A *stage direction*, abbreviation of *Opposite Prompt Side* – i.e. *stage right* (from the actor's standpoint when facing the audience). See *Prompt Side*.

open   '*Romeo and Juliet* opened at the Royal Shakespeare Theatre, Stratford, on Thursday' (*The Guardian*, 24 August 1991). When a *production* is first performed or is first performed at a new *venue* it is said to *open*. At the *Restoration*, when an area of the stage was revealed by the wings being pulled apart, the set was said *to open* and it is from this idea of revelation, possibly also influenced by the opening of the *curtains*, that the term is derived. (Compare *go up, down*). *Shows* also *open* each night, rather than *begin*, and they commence with an *opening scene*: 'His opening scene is revelatory' said a *Plays and Players notice* of Brian Cox's Lear in October 1990.

A play that *opens* in the *West End* without a preliminary *provincial try-out* is said to *open cold*. In the United States, the same term is used on *Broadway*.

The *opening night*, sometimes abbreviated to *opening*, is an alternative to *first night*. '. . . After almost four weeks and with the opening night looming closer, I began to be nervous that the occasion would be a shambles' (Olivier, 210).

An *opener* is another name for a *curtain-raiser*: a short piece played before the main play, or the first in a series of *shorts*. In actors' terminology, however, *an opener* can be an alternative for an individual actor's *opening scene*, not necessarily the *opening scene* of the play: 'I would praise Laertes for a good opener' says Berkoff (p.170) of directing *Hamlet*.

Both doors and windows on a set may *open on* or *open off*, depending on whether, when opened, the hinges swing them *onstage* or *offstage*.

Variations in the sense of the verb occur in actors' terminology: *to open out a speech* is to give it more breathing space by slowing the *pace* and allowing the pauses to work rather than giving it a hurried *delivery*, which is often a sign of nerves and lack of relaxation. *To open (up)* the body is to present it front-on to the audience, whereas *opening up a prop* is to draw the audience's attention to it by, say, touching it, picking it up etc.

An *open rehearsal* is one at which either invited friends or the general public are invited to watch a show in preparation, (compare *preview*).

Open time describes dates when an actor or company are available to take *engagements*.

open air theatre   An outdoor theatre, or a generic term for theatre performed in the open air. Of course, all the earliest theatres, including the Greek and English C16 Bankside theatres were, at least in part, open to the elements. In Britain, the tradition is occasionally revived, but due to the climate there are few solely outdoor sites, one notable exception being the Open Air Theatre in Regent's Park, London, which was first established to play *summer seasons* of Shakespeare in 1900, from which date this formulation would appear to derive.

open stage   An alternative name for a *thrust stage*: a performance space (usually but not obligatorily a raised platform), located against one wall of the *auditorium* and thrusting forwards so that the audience surrounds it on three sides. Due to its similarity to Jacobean and Elizabethan stages, it is highly suited to the performance of lC16-eC17 plays.

opera   A dramatic composition for the stage in which all or most of the lines are sung, or (with a distinct difference of emphasis) a musical drama more sophisticated than a *musical comedy*. Like *ballet, dance* and *music, opera* is a performance genre with a vocabulary that merits its own Book of Words (largely in Italian). Here I will deal only with the etymology of the word and a limited number of associations.

From It. *opera*, from L. *opera*, 'labour, exertion', hence 'a work produced', (the plural of L. *opus*, 'work'), it is first attested in OED in 1644: 'It is a work of Bernini...who, a little before my coming to the citty [Rome], gave a publiq opera (for so they call shews of that kind) wherein he painted the scenes (etc.)' (Evelyn, *Diary*, 19 November). Opera has never truly become an indigenous English theatrical form, though it has gone through periods of great fashion: 'Some years ago the Italian opera was the only fashionable amusement among our nobility' (1759, Goldsmith, *The Bee* [No. 9]). The term *operatic*, 'of, pertaining to, or similar

in certain features to opera' is first attested in mC18. A form to
which English writers and composers can lay greater (albeit
second-hand) claim is the *operetta*, 'short, light and often humorous operatic entertainment', a term first found in mC18 but a
form which only truly burgeoned, if at greater length, in the
hands of Gilbert and Sullivan in lC19. It is considered by some
to have given rise to the *musical comedy*.

opposite   As in *OP(S)*, opposite was occasionally used as a stage
direction to denote 'the opposite side of the stage'. Its main contemporary use, however, is in the related phrase *to play opposite
someone*: '[Godfrey Kenton's] broadcasts have included Robert
Browning opposite Peggy Ashcroft in *The Barretts of Wimpole
Street*; the lover opposite Marlene Dietrich in *The Child...*' (*The
Stage*, 24 March 1992). This term is derived from the habit that
developed in C19 or earlier, whereby the *leading man* in a show,
usually the *actor-manager*, would be granted, or demand, his own
side of the stage in order to dominate proceedings and stay in the
limelight. A co-star would be granted the *opposite* side of the stage,
though not necessarily for their sole use.

orchestra   From L. *orchestra*, from Gk *orkhēstra* (from *orkheomai*,
'to dance'). The Ancient Greek orkhēstra was a circular or semicircular space in front of the *proscenium* where the *chorus* performed, both singing and – the element which gave rise to the
name – dancing. However, like *skēnē*, it was to undergo striking
changes. In Roman times, the orchestra was used as a seating
area reserved for VIPs. The re-introduction of the term in lC17-
eC18, brings with it a range of new meanings: '*Orchestra*, is that
Part of the Theater where the Musicians sit with their Instruments
to perform' (1724, *A short explication of such foreign words as are
made use of in musick books*). This area is still also known as the
orchestra pit, the area immediately below the stage: 'Unhappily
on the first night the sand blew across the footlights, spraying the
orchestra pit and the first ten rows of the stalls' (Geilgud, 94).
(Such seats are still known as the *orchestra stalls* [compare the
Roman usage].) 'Orchestra' was also transferred to mean the band
of musicians, themselves: 'But hark! the full orchestra strike the
strings' (1720, Gay, 'To W. Pulteney'). The adjective *orchestral*
followed in eC19, as did the verb *to orchestrate*, first literally and
later with its extended sense of 'to organise a complex procedure'
(compare *to stage manage*).

OTT   The common abbreviation of *over the top*, in widespread
general usage since the early 1980s for any extreme reaction or
behaviour.

out   If an actor claims to be *out*, he has *blanked* completely, forgetting his lines and everything about the scene or even the play he is in. This expression can be traced back directly to the Elizabethan theatre, thanks to Coriolanus:

> '.....Like a dull actor now,
> I have forgot my part, and I am out,
> Even to a full disgrace.'
>
> (1607, *Coriolanus*, V.iii)

The phrase is probably an abbreviation of a phrase with similar construction to 'out of sorts', possibly along the lines of the modern 'out of character': when an actor slips, falls or *drops out of character* in a scene, he is shattering the illusion by intruding personally into the action.

out front   Originally, the American term for British *in front*, but now widely used in Britain: 'in the auditorium', i.e. in American English, *out front* of the *proscenium arch*. 'We had hard wooden chairs at rehearsal and no-one warned us it would be like this... Anyone fool enough to go out front and watch will know how completely thrown I am' (Barkworth, 157). (See *friends in front*.)

'Does playing out front present any problems to you?' (Barkworth interviewing Prunella Scales, 222.) *To play out front* is to perform directly to the audience, (through the *fourth wall* in a *proscenium arch* theatre), whether it be in a *soliloquy* or *aside* or simply through the angle of the body and eye contact. In *realistic* drama, it is not generally to be recommended: 'He had major notes about my relationship with the audience. "Don't do so much out front. You're speaking to the other character, not the audience"' (Barkworth, 263, on advice from playwright Simon Gray).

out-of-town   (Sometimes found as *out of town*). Used in phrases such as *out of town* and *out of town try-out*, the phrase refers to London-based actors and companies working outside the capital. Compare *provincial*. Londoners, like all other inhabitants of towns, have always tended to refer to London as *the* town, or simply *town*, as if no other existed: 'The kyng sent for all his Lordes...thenne beyng in Towne' (1450, Rolls of Parliament).

overact   To try too hard in a role; as a consequence, to give a performance which is over the top and *stagey*; to ham it up. A synonym for *overplay*, just as *act* and *play* are synonymous. See *over-parted* for an attestation.

overlap   An *overlap*, an abbreviation of *overlapping dialogue*, describes the technique of one actor beginning a speech before another has finished his, a natural feature of some colloquial conversation, and therefore potentially useful in *realistic* acting. Overlaps must, however, be used with extreme care so that a) they do not stop the audience from gathering vital information and b) so that they do not *throw* other actors on stage. Whilst realistic, overuse of overlaps can appear mannered. 'Used sparingly, I like overlaps...I like them even more since I saw that great production of Eugene O'Neill's *Long Day's Journey into Night* by Jonathan Miller in 1986, which, because of extreme use of overlaps, shortened the play by a reputed 40 minutes' (Barkworth, 54).

overnight (success) 'You can't expect to rush on stage and become a big star overnight. You've got to "pay your dues"' (*The Stage*, 23 April 1992). *Overnight success* is a term applied to a performer who gains recognition suddenly, often very early in their career. The term comes from good *notices* building up the performer's reputation: 'overnight' describes the time between the performance ending and the newspaper notices being published.

over-parted An actor's term for being *cast* in a role which is beyond their skills or technical capabilities: Kenneth Branagh says of his RSC début, playing the title role in *Henry V* in 1984, 'Some critics thought I was over-parted, and some thought I over-acted, but several thought I was good...' (150).

over the top 'One of the things I liked about working with Guthrie was that he had a real sense of fun and he would prod us all to go over the top which is one of the things I usually don't like doing. I like restraint. It's been the undoing of me a lot of the time.' So speaks Edward Petherbridge in an interview with Barkworth (p.177), isolating the lack of restraint which is one of the characteristics of *over the top* performances, and part of the legacy which C20 *actor-managers* such as Guthrie handed on directly from their C19 predecessors. Their performances were highly exaggerated, close to the *melodramatic*, especially in their portrayal of emotional states; OTT acting can be extreme, big and *hammy*, though Berkoff offers a rider to this: 'Now in acting you can go *over the top* and be an embarrassment, but with a little conviction you can get away with it' (62).

The term is undoubtedly C20. Beale suggests that it comes from RAF pilots in the late 1930s, meaning 'flying above the clouds or above bad weather', soon taken up to mean also 'flying over Iceland and Greenland on trans-Atlantic flights'. (It may also, I would suggest from what follows, have referred to flying over enemy ground fire.) Beale also claims that the phrase did not come into use in the sense of 'highly exaggerated' until the early 1980s. However, common sense suggests that it echoes the practices of First World War trench warfare, when *going over the top* was very extreme: heading for no man's land and the enemy batteries with an extremely limited chance of survival. If the theatrical usage is not from this time, it perhaps emphasises how some horrors remain in the collective imagination.

overture   The introductory music played before the beginning of a performance. From OF *overture*, (Fr. *ouverture*), 'an opening', the term has been used in English with a variety of senses since C14, only coming to mean 'an orchestral piece opening or introducing a longer work', in 1617: 'While the overture is playing, the curtain rises' (1667, Dryden and Davenport, *The Tempest*, I.i). In this sense, it was borrowed from Fr. C17 theatrical usage in the way that many terms were at the Restoration. For the famous 'Overture and beginners, please', see *call*.

P **ace** 'Under the sure direction of Mollie Guilfoyle the pace, which was inevitably slow as befits the subject, crackled with electric intensity and pathos' (*The Stage*, 28 March 1991). *Pace* is the speed at which a performance is played. An actor who is gabbling may be told to watch his *pacing*. Compare *tempo*.

pack A group of *flats* piled together for storage either in the *wings* or in a *scene dock* is referred to as a *pack*. From the Standard English sense of 'a tied bundle', (from ME, from Middle Low German *pak*, of unknown origin). However, if a show is *packing them in*, it is playing to full or *packed houses*. If one wants to fill the theatre by handing out *comps.*, or to invite an audience of friends or pay a *claque* in order to ensure that a show gets the desired reception, one is said to be *packing the audience*. Compare *paper (the house)*.

pad (out) *Padding out* – adding lines and business in order to extend a performance – can occur because an actor has missed a *line* or *entrance cue* and others are covering, because the length of a scene of an individual actor's role needs to be increased, or merely to extend the length of a short show so that the audience feels it is getting value for money. The verb, from the Standard English sense of *pad* as 'cushion or stuffing-material', (probably of Dutch or Low German origin) dates back to at least eC19: 'His [Johnson's] constant practice of padding out a sentence with useless epithets' (1831, Macauley, *Critical and miscellaneous essays*).

pageant Contemporary pageants are generally spectacular, festive, outdoor entertainments, often processional, with imaginatively-costumed members of a community involved in local celebration. *Pageant*, however, (from ME *pagyn*, of unknown origin), originally signified the portable wagon on which much medieval liturgical drama was performed, and which would put most modern floats to shame. It is worth quoting a first-hand description of the Chester pageants left by Archdeacon Robert Rogers (d. 1595) at some length, as it describes their detail and function much more effectively than any paraphrase could:

> [These] pagiants weare a high scafolde with two rowmes, a higher and a lower, upon four wheels. In the lower, they apparelled them selves, and in the higher rowme they played,

184

beinge all open on the tope that all behoulders might heare
and see them. The places where they played them was in every
streets. They began first at the abay gates, and when the first
pagiant was played it was wheeled to the highe cross before
the mayor, and so to every streete; and soe every streete had
a pagiant playinge before them at one time, till all the pagiantes
for the daye appointed weare played: and when one pagiant
was neere ended, worde was broughte from streete to streete,
that soe they mighte come in place thereof excedinge orderlye.
(Quoted in Nagler, 49)

paint shop, frame, bridge   *Painters* are permanent employees of
many large theatres, kept on the payroll to decorate *flats*, *sets* etc.
Their backstage workplace is known as the *paint shop*, or occasionally *paint room*, as has been the case since at least eC18, as these
items from the Covent Garden inventory (1732) illustrate: '*Wings
in Great Room*), Eight moonlight. (*Do. in Painters Room*), 2 of
Ariodante's pallace, but are rubbed out and not painted. (*Do. in
the Shop*)...'. When large pieces of scenery are being painted,
they can be held by a wooden support known as a *paint frame*.
The *paint bridge* is a construction of adjustable height which permits the painters to cover the scenery on the frame with relative
ease.

pan   In C19, used merely as an abbreviation of *panorama* (much
more frequent than the occasionally-used *pam*). A second and
much more widespread use of the abbreviation however, has been
appropriated by cinema from theatre, from *panorama*. When a
movie cameraman *pans*, he is moving the camera lens smoothly
through a wide, horizontal angle, thus creating the effect of a
panorama. *Panning* in theatre was an earlier *lighting* term which
involved swinging a *lantern* through, or back and forth across, a
horizontal plane: clearly, this action applied most frequently to
a *follow-spot*, for which it is still used.

Used as a verb, if critics *pan a show*, they are holding it up to
severe criticism, sometimes verging on ridicule. This usage,
adopted in England in the late 1940s, originated in America in
eC20 and may be related to an earlier phrasal verb, *to pan out*, 'to
speek freely', attested in OED Supp: 'I'm panning out about this
because it seems so deuced interesting, (1914, W.J. Locke, *Jaffrey*).

pancake   Water-soluble *make-up*, so-called either because it is
purchased in small, flat, circular containers which, with a degree
of imaginative effort, resemble small, fat pancakes – a term used
according to OED for flat objects since mC19 – or because it is a
cake of make-up designed to be used on the *pan*, an American
slang term for 'face' (see *dead-pan*).

panorama (Sometimes also abbreviated to *pan* and, rarely, to *pam*). From Gk *pan*, 'everything, all', + *horama*, 'view' (from *hora⁻*, 'see'): literally, 'the whole view'. Rarely used now, a *panorama* was a landscape painted on a continuous length of canvas and wrapped around two drums situated at either side of the stage; when the drums were turned, the scene changed. An early forebear of the modern *cyclorama*.

Pantaloon An anglicisation of It. *Pantalone*, a character incorporated into the English *harlequinade* and early *pantomimes*. *Pantalone* was a character of the *commedia dell'arte*, the father, guardian or husband of *Columbine*. He was presented as the stereotypical old man, the authority figure, presented alternately as cunning and avaricious, then as amorous and absurd; ultimately he was a character to be challenged and duped by *Arlecchino (Harlequin)*. He was generally portrayed as a Venetian merchant and it is likely that his name is taken from San Pantaleone, a saint once widely revered in Venice. The name was anglicised by C16, and in *As You Like It* (1599), Shakespeare in Jacques' Seven Ages of Man speech (II.vii) uses it as a common noun signifying an old man:

The sixth age shifts
Into the lean and slippered pantaloon,
With spectacles on nose and pouch on side
His youthful hose well sav'd, a world too wide
For his shrunk shank; and his big, manly voice
Turning again towards childish treble, pipes
And whistles in his sound.

pantomime Also commonly known as *panto*. Today, *pantomimes* are seasonal family entertainments, ostensibly targeted at children, with a loose *narrative* structure based on a nursery story; usually their main romantic plot and comic subplots provide an excuse for song and dance routines, audience participation, *slapstick set-pieces*, scenic spectacle, and *gag*-telling liberally spiced with contemporary references. In some cases, they have deteriorated into vehicles for pop stars and television celebrities. However, the word goes back to antiquity: the Roman *pantomimus* was a high-grade *mime* (from Gk *pas, pantos*, 'all' + *mimos*, 'mimic actor'), who danced, masked, to musical accompaniment, playing all the characters in a narrated dumb-show based on stories from history or mythology. The modern English form was developed out of the C18 harlequinade, probably by John Rich (1681-1761), to attract audiences to his theatre at Lincoln's Inn Fields, borrowing the name from the C18 French *ballets-pantomimes*, themselves loosely and inaccurately based on the Roman model:

Rich created a species of dramatic composition...which he

called a pantomime: it consisted of two parts, one serious and the other comic. By the help of gay scenes, fine habits, grand dances, appropriate music, and other decorations, he exhibited a story from Ovid's *Metamorphoses*, or some other fabulous writer. Between the pauses or acts of this serious representation, he interwove a comic fable, consisting chiefly of the courtship of Harlequin and Columbine, with a variety of surprising adventures and tricks... such as the sudden transformation of palaces and temples to huts and cottages... (1808, Thomas Davies, *Memoirs of the Life of David Garrick.*)
See also *dame, principal boy, transformation scene.*

paper (the house) A largely obsolete term for filling the house to capacity, producing a *paper house*, by issuing free admission slips or *papers*. (For other publicity frauds, compare *claque*.)

paradise A largely American term for the topmost seating area in an *auditorium*, based on a pun on *the Gods* (known as *paradis* in French). For similar reasons (and because of the cheapness of the seats) this area was once also offensively known as *nigger heaven*.

par lamps Very bright, powerful *lights* which contain their own optical system designed to produce an almost parallel beam of light: hence the abbreviation, *par*. The lamps are housed in cylindrical containers known as *parcans*. '"Par lights are a sort of cylindrical tin with a car headlamp inside. Very punchy," says Wayne Dowdeswell [a lighting designer]. "Terrific with strong colours, designed specifically for rock 'n' roll touring"' (*Observer*, 3 May 1992). See *birdie*.

parlyaree (Also found as *parlaree, parlary, polari* and a range of variants.) From It. *parlare*, 'to speak', most of the vocabulary of this international language, much spicier than Esperanto, was Italianate. *Parlyaree* is claimed, (see Beale, *Here, There and Everywhere*, 1949), to be the *lingua franca* of C18-C19 non-*legit* performers; later, through commerce, it became current in the mC19-20 London underworld – the world of costermongers, criminals and the sexually excluded, including the gay community. Parlyaree *may* provide an historical link between theatre and the *camp* world (see *drag, queen* and especially *naff*), although certain experts, including Beale, argue that the choice of *polari* as a term for gay slang since about 1970, may well be an affectation. The main speakers in the early stages of its history were *circus* entertainers and other artists whose profession involved foreign travel; by mC19 it had become more widespread, though never respectable. See also *pong*.

parody From LL *parodia*, or from Gk *parōidia*, 'burlesque poem'.

A *parody* involves imitation of the content or, more frequently, the style of another work or artist, usually in order to ridicule or satirise the original. A *classic* example in English is Shakespeare's use of the players in *Hamlet*, which is not only a clever plot device but also allows him, through his hero acting as amateur *dramaturge*, to present a brief, partially satirical treatise on acting. It is likely that Shakespeare knew the word when writing *Hamlet*, as the first OED attestation is from his colleague Ben Jonson in *Every Man in his Humour*, (1598): CLEM: (reads some poetry) 'How? this is stolne!...A Parodie, a parodie! to make it absurder than it was.' See also *send-up*.

part   Both the modern senses of *part* – i) an actor's role and ii) an actor's *lines* – were certainly in use by 1594 when Shakespeare wrote *A Midsummer Night's Dream* (I.ii):

BOTTOM: Ready. Name what part I am for, and proceed...
SNUG: Have you the lion's part written? Pray you, if it be, give it me, for, I am slow of study.

Although Bottom's usage is now standard, it is none the less logical that Snug's gives the clue to the term's etymology. Before easy reprographics, that *part* or section of the *script* of a play which an actor needed to learn, including his *cues*, would be copied out and handed to him for learning and *study*, *part* deriving from OF, from L. *pars partis*, 'a part, a section of a whole'. If an actor was illiterate or could barely read, as we guess from the *subtext* is the case with Snug, giving him a written part would arouse the fear he expresses here. (See *prompt*.) It can be said with some confidence that a 'part', in English, requires a literate actor, an illiterate one with friends, or a very tolerant director. (It is worth noting that a number of modern actors who are dyslexic – Susan Hampshire being a celebrated example – or who have other difficulties with *sight-reading*, are enormously disadvantaged when *reading for a part* at auditions.)

participation   *Audience participation* is a C20 term but by no means a modern concept, since all performance from early *ritual* onwards has required some involvement from the audience – empathy, intellectual engagement etc. – in varying degrees; however, most also requires a degree of separation between audience and performer. It is this separation that direct audience participation seeks to break down. The conjurer picking a *punter* from the audience to act as his *stooge* has been a common variety trick; to invite the whole audience to come up and dance on stage in the *finale*, encouraging them to strip off their clothes, as in the 1960s *musical*, *Hair*, is a different matter, though it may, in fact, echo some ancient rituals.

pass A *pass door* is a side door, generally fire-proofed, between the *stage* and the *auditorium*, for use during performances only by authorised personnel. *Pass* is probably used here with its Standard English sense of 'permit': formerly, a *pass* was also used for a permit to let someone into an audience without a ticket. A *passout* is a term for a member of the audience who leaves the theatre temporarily during a show, and the written authorisation they receive.

passerelle A *catwalk* in front of the *orchestra pit*, running the full width of the stage. *Passerelles* are often used in *variety* shows to bring showgirls tantalisingly close to the *punters* (see *floor-show*), and for effect are often lit from below. Since the term is merely French for 'cat-walk' or 'gangway', I would suspect that it was adopted, in mC20, either because its use developed in the Pigalle or because the use of French adds extra glamour and spice to a fairly prosaic construction.

Passion play Sometimes abbreviated to *Passion*. A *passion play* is a religious drama concerned with the events surrounding the crucifixion: Christ's Passion (ME, from OF, from LL *passio -onis*, from L. *pati pass-*, 'suffer'). The German, Swiss and Austrian *Mysterienspiel* emphasised the Passion (and other sensational incidents such as Hell's Mouth) to a much greater degree than the English *mystery play*, which took a broader spread of subject matter for presentation. Such plays are still to be found in Germany today, notably at Oberammergau. There is no evidence that the term was used in English in the Middle Ages; rather, it seems to be a modern critical tag, used retrospectively: 'There were performances of Passions in Reading in 1508, in Dublin in 1528...' (E.K. Chambers, *The Medieval Stage*).

pastoral *Pastoral* subject matter was particularly popular in mC16-C17 with playwrights including Lyly, Fletcher and Daniel, (and part-exploited, part-satirised by Shakespeare in *As You Like It*). It reflected an urban myth that the rural life of nymphs and shepherds was idyllically blessed with peace, love and plenty. The *genre* was initiated in Greece by Theocritus (C3 BC) and later imitated by that grand model for the Renaissance, Virgil, in his *Eclogues*. ME, from L. *pastoralis*, from *pastor*, 'shepherd' (from *pascere past-*, 'feed, graze').

patch *To patch* is a lighting term for linking *dimmers* to their electrical circuits. A *patch board* or *panel* is the most effective and flexible way of doing this: through a plug and socket system it is possible to link any of a theatre's circuits to any individual dimmer. This C20 electrical term is derived from the Standard English sense of *to patch*, as to piece together.

patent theatres   The *patent* referred to here was the royal license granted only to certain, selected London theatres granting the right to perform *legitimate* drama in the period 1660-1843. The two great patent theatres were Covent Garden and Drury Lane. The term comes from *letters patent*, from Fr., from L. *litterae patentes*, literally 'open letters', which, from eC13 are recorded in use to grant some form of authority, proof, right, privilege etc.

patrons   A dying breed. The first British theatrical patrons were people of royal and noble birth who gave financial support and protection to specific companies; for example Shakespeare's company, the King's Men, until the accession of James I had been the Lord Chamberlain's Men – the Queen's Men may not have sat well with Elizabeth I, the Virgin Queen. The term has been used in this sense since C14. Such functions still exist, but much more nominally than in C17: 'This production was also the first occasion on which our Royal Patron could be present. I had had the gall to invite Prince Charles to become Patron, making my initial approach in a letter typed from a hotel bedroom in Egypt' (Branagh, 199). Perhaps the modern equivalent is the corporate sponsor of a production.

A more general sense has developed, with any supporter of the theatre or, for that matter, any spectator, now being accorded the title of *patron*. Whilst the term is used as 'supporter' in C17, the sense of 'paying customer' appears to be a C19 development: 'The Proprietor...thanks his Patrons for the support they have extended to him for the past 11 years' (*Falkirk Herald*, 18 July 1891). ME, from OF, from L. *patronus*, 'a protector' (in a range of senses, many of them legal and financial), ultimately from *pater*, 'father'.

patsy   An alternative name for a *fall-guy* or *stooge*: a stage assistant, sometimes a *feed*. The butt of the comic's *gags*. An early C20 American term, probably based on the fate of a specific hoodlum of Irish descent in the New York underworld. Barry Connors' play *The Patsy* was written in 1925 (and performed at Dundee Rep. in 1947) and the term may have been overheard in American films, but *patsy* did not come into general English usage until the 1960s-1970s, possibly popularised by the often repeated claim that Lee Harvey Oswald was 'just a patsy' in the assassination of President Kennedy.

patter   The earliest specifically theatrical usage of *patter* according to Partridge is in the mid-1870s as 'the words of a song, play etc.': 'Mozart and many other composers often introduce bits of patter into buffo solos.' (1880, J.A. Fuller-Maitland.) The common theatrical sense is more specific: *patter songs* – and there are notable

examples in Gilbert and Sullivan – and *patter acts*, involve the
rapid *delivery* of a set of comic lines. This takes us to the probable
derivation, the priest's rapid delivery in Latin of the Lord's
Prayer, *pater noster*, leading to overtones of speed, glibness and,
due to the inaccessibility of Latin to much of the congregation,
secrecy. 'Patter' has been used in this sense since C14, the transference to 'thieves' cant' (OED) occurring in mC18 – 'The master
who teaches them [young thieves] should be well versed... in the
cant language commonly called the slang patter' (1758, *Jonathon
Wild's Advice to his Successor* [in Hotten's Slang Dictionary]) –
and to performance in m-lC19 – 'He speaks admirably what is
called "patter", and he delivers a jargon in ridicule of scientific
terminology' (*Athenaeum*, 4 November 1876). The word is still
in general usage, usually used pejoratively and suspiciously of
rehearsed or often-repeated *spiel*.

pay-off 'My pay-off almost for the whole speech has been:
"...yet, to me, what is this quintessence of dust?" I come back
to this. I implore them for an answer. What is this for? I try to
squeeze it out of them' (Berkoff, 73). In comedy, a *pay-off line*,
or simply *pay-off*, is the *punch-line* of a *gag*. Above, we see it being
used in straight dramatic terms, where the aim is not the audience's laughter but a particular intellectual response. It is interesting, then, that the origins of the term may be far away in eC20
American underworld cant, where the 'pay-off' was punishment
(by death) inflicted for breaking the unspoken rules. What
remains in theatrical usage is the idea of final settlement, perhaps
an echo, too, of the comic's warning to the audience before a
good gag, 'This'll kill ya,' suggesting the borrowing has its origins
in *burlesque*, which was always close to the frontiers of legality.
An alternative, linked suggestion traces the term back to the pay-
off which was the colloquial name for the printed form an
employee received on being dismissed from work in the 1930s
and which he signed as a receipt: however, it is difficult to find
any obvious reason why this should have been adopted by comedians.

penny plain, (and) tuppence coloured   A delightful term from
C19 *children's theatre* or, as it is also known, *juvenile drama*. This
was the nickname (based on actual prices) of the sheets of copy
designs printed for the child theatre enthusiast, which they were
encouraged to save as souvenirs or cut-outs to add to toy theatre
collections.

Peoria, it won't play in   An American phrase used to refer to a
show which is too *avant garde*, arty, intellectual etc. to appeal to
general, unsophisticated theatre audiences. Not *commercial*.

Peoria is a conservative mid-Western town in Illinois, south-west of Chicago. 'It won't play in Harrogate' might be an English translation, though it lacks the alliteration.

Pepper's ghost   A stage *illusion*, rather like a primitive hologram, discovered by John Henry Pepper and first demonstrated at the Royal Polytechnic Institution in London in 1862; it was later used with much success in both music halls and straight theatre. Pepper discovered that the image of a man walking across the *pit* could be projected on to a correctly-angled piece of glass onstage, giving the insubstantial impression of a ghost. Ever the showman, Dickens used the technique in readings. Unfortunately for directors of *Hamlet*, it was difficult to give the impression that the ghost passing over the stage was speaking.

perambulatory theatre   An alternative name for *promenade theatre* – a form of staging which requires the audience to walk back and forth from *set* to set, following the action. From L. *per-*, 'through, all over' + *ambulare*, 'to walk': literally, 'walking-around theatre'. Not the kind of staging to endear itself to a Saturday *matinée* in *Peoria*. See also *multiple set*.

perch   A position inside and to the side of the *proscenium* arch, often a platform fixed to the wall above and behind the opening, from which *lanterns* can be hung and from which they used to be operated. *Perch* is also used to refer to the lights placed there, which used to include a *perch lime* and can still include a *perch spot*. The term has been used in hawking, church architecture (where, perhaps significantly, it is a bar to support a candle such as an altar light) and more generally, since eC14 for 'a bar on which something can alight or from which it can be hung', from OF *perche*, from L. *pertica*, 'a pole'.

perform   *To perform* has been used in English with a range of senses including 'to complete, carry out, make, construct etc.' since C14, (interestingly pinpointing the performer's function, at the very end of a process). From OF *parfourmer/perfourmer*, with similar meanings. Whilst the theatrical sense of 'to act a part', is found in eC17, initially it is only used transitively: 'Brauely the figure of this Harpie hast thou Perform'd (my Ariell)' (1612, Shakespeare, *The Tempest*). Most of the theatrical developments of performance-related terms appear to be C18, making it a relatively late addition to theatrical language, one which has gradually grown in significance over the last two centuries. Although the transitive form is not attested in OED until mC19, one suspects that the development must have occurred earlier, with the establishment of the term *performer* in C18: 'In Theatrical Speaking, if the performer is not entirely proper and graceful, he is ridiculous'

(1711, Steele, *The Spectator*, No. 141). The distinction between *actor* and performer, of course, is that the latter covers a much broader range of skills and artistic pursuits, the term being equally applicable to a *musician* or a *juggler*. *Performance* is also first attested theatrically in OED in C18 – 'I saw a French play represented here with some degree of performance' (1777, Dalrymple, *Travels through Spain and Portugal*). The two most common contemporary uses of 'performance' as 'a single presentation of a piece of theatre' and 'an individual performer's presentation of their skills' would appear to be C19 developments. (I have found a much earlier usage by Jonson [quoted in Nagler, 145]: 'Such was the exquisite performance...that alone...was of power to surprize with delight' (1606). Jonson is referring to the Inigo Jones's design for a *masque*, however, and I suspect the term is used in a more general sense than we are concerned with here.)

One of the most significant lC20 developments is the use of the phrase *performing arts*, first in educational drama, and then more generally, an exploitation of the term's broadness. One suspects that it may, as a generic term, denote a significant movement towards the integration of *drama*, *music*, *dance* and *technical* aspects of *production* in the minds of both performers and audience.

periaktoi Painted triangular prisms which were used to the sides and rear of the Greek and Roman stage like three-dimensional *flats*: each, by being revolved, was capable of depicting three *settings*, and several were probably used in unison to create the *backdrop* to a scene. Adapted and refined in Renaissance Italy where, renamed *telari*, they became a central feature in scenic design, they were certainly in use in England by the eC17 in Inigo Jones's *masque* designs and possibly at the indoor Blackfriars theatre; there is some evidence that they may have been used as early as eC16 at Westminster School, where the Italian ambassador reported 'a very well-designed stage'. The use of the term, however, is historical rather than contemporary to this period. See also *acoustics*.

peripeteia, peripety *Peripeteia* is *Aristotle's* term in the *Poetics* for the *reversal* in fortunes central to the *tragic plot*, from Gk *peri-*, 'round, about' + *piptō*, 'fall'. The anglicised version, *peripety*, is occasionally, but rarely found, and may equally be applied to a plot reversal in a comic context.

persona Latin *persona* was 'a mask worn by an actor'. It was transferred by extension to 'the character assumed by an actor' (as in *dramatis personae*, the character list for a play, found at the front of English texts from C16 onwards). Much later, but still in the classical period, it was further extended to mean 'an individual human being', hence *person*. It is thus one of the earliest examples and perhaps the most significant of a theatrical term being borrowed for general usage. It demonstrates very effectively the powerful influence of the theatrical experience and, consequently, theatrical language, on the way individuals perceive themselves and their role and demonstrates clearly how society is prepared to adopt theatrical terms to signify fundamental aspects of identity. However, whilst 'person' has been in use from C13 in both the dramatic and individual senses, (the former dying out quite rapidly), 'persona' was only reintroduced as 'that aspect of personality shown to and perceived by others', in contrast to 'anima', in the psychological terminology of eC20. Since then, it has become re-established with a sense of 'role, perceived character' in general speech.

personal prop   Sometimes abbreviated to *a personal*, this is a *hand* prop, such as Desdemona's famous handkerchief in *Othello*, which, because it is carried or worn about the actress' person, would be in her personal charge and care prior to her entrance.

photo-call   An abbreviation of *photograph call*, a call to the cast and possibly some crew members, to be present for the taking of publicity and press shots. Usually, *photo-calls* for a production would require the cast to appear in full costume and make-up, unless the call was for rehearsal shots.

physical theatre   A m-lC20 term adopted for theatre which places a special emphasis on *movement* skills and visual expressiveness. *Physical theatre* in Britain has developed in reaction to the perceived tendency for mainstream theatre to emphasise textual analysis, vocal delivery and scenic display at the expense of other performance possibilities, and is part of the current trend against unadventurous, strangled *realism*. Although still regarded as an *alternative* movement, leading and some might say token proponents such as Steven Berkoff and the Théatre de Complicité have performed with great success in establishment venues.

piano wire   Very strong wire, almost invisible to an audience, used instead of *flying lines* to *fly* in *scenery* etc. where the use of visible lines might be distracting to an audience. So-called because of a similarity in strength to the taut strings inside a piano.

pick up   In acting, to speed up a performance. The term is used particularly in relation to *cues*, where the instruction *pick up (on) your cues* means to come in on them quickly: failure to do so greatly slows the pace of a production and is usually a sign of lack of concentration on the part of the performers.

The phrase *to pick up an audience* is still occasionally used for a successful performance which totally captivates and involves the audience; it is claimed by Bowman and Ball to be an abbreviation of a C19 phrase 'picking up an audience into their arms'.

picture-frame stage   '[W]ith the advent of the picture-frame stage ...supporting scenes have been trimmed and single moments exploited' (Brook, 71). Sometimes abbreviated to *picture stage*, a *picture-frame stage* is a descriptive way of referring to the *proscenium arch stage* developed in eC17. The term reflects the enormous influence of the visual arts in the development of European *stage pictures*.

piece   'Although the second draft had made great strides, the piece required constant work. In a six-week rehearsal period, I spent evenings and weekend on rewrites...' (Branagh, 194). *Piece* is a term for a play used particularly in the *business* and amongst experienced *theatre-goers* and *critics*. It can be applied both to a *production* and, as above, to a *text*. It is derived from an abbreviation of 'piece of theatre', itself a literal translation of the most common French term for a play, *une pièce de théâtre*. Like many such continental borrowings, its common usage probably dates back to the Restoration and the return of exiles steeped in over a decade of immersion in French theatrical culture, although it is attested earlier in OED: 'In the last scene, all the Actors must enter to compleat and make up the Catastrophe of this great peace' (1643, Sir Thomas Browne, *Religio Medici*). It is sometimes still used in its full form: '[*Oedipus*] seems the opposite pole from *US* and yet to me the two pieces of theatre are strangely related' (Brook, 63).

pièce bien faite   The original French which was directly translated into English *well-made* play. It is still occasionally used in the original, which seems to me fine when applied to French drama or French-influenced plays, but slightly pretentious if used to refer to an indigenous *piece*.

pierrot   Based on the clown-like *commedia dell'arte* character, Pedrolino, *Pierrot* entered the C18 English *harlequinade* via French *Comédie Italienne*, retaining his French name and his traditional white hat, baggy white costume and white make-up. The term rapidly became used as a common noun: 'He was one of the oddest characters I ever saw...and in all his gestures extremely like a pierrot' (1741-70, Elizabeth Carter, *Letters* [1808]). He disappeared from the stage for a century or more, only to make a spectacular comeback in the 1891 *dumb-show*, *L'Enfant Prodigue*, in a new French incarnation which was so popular that the character was appropriated by numerous *end-of-the-pier* concert parties. Pierrot troupes were formed, specialising in song, dance and comedy.

pilots   *Pilot lamps* or *lights* are alternative names for *working lights* or *workers*, so-called because they guide actors and crew in the relative darkness when full *stage lighting* is not being employed. A *nautical* term.

pin spot   A descriptive term for a *spotlight* focused into a very small beam. Probably its most celebrated – and daring – use is in Samuel Beckett's play *Not I* (1972), in which only the mouth of one actress is lit as she performs a monologue on an otherwise pitch black stage.

Pinteresque   It is rare for a dramatist to have an adjective descriptive of his style used early in his career and also to see it spread rapidly into general usage. This was the case, however, with *Pinteresque*, coined in the early 1960s to describe the characteristics of the style of Harold Pinter (b.1930) whose work became highly influential after the production of his first full-length play, *The Birthday Party* (1958). His early subject matter was characterised by an undefined menace just below the surface of banal reality, and his style by his use of pauses, silence, and an elusive *subtext*. Whilst many people have taken his language to be characterised by meaningless non-sequiturs and comic breakdowns in communication, which is probably the most common general usage of Pinteresque, and whilst he was initially categorised as an *absurdist*, the dialogue is in fact very carefully and quite realistically orchestrated around a subtext of confrontation and avoidance. *Pinterese* is also occasionally used to describe this language.

pit   It has been ventured by some that the yard area in front of the *forestage* occupied by the standing *groundlings* in Elizabethan outdoor theatres was known as the *pit*, but to the best of my knowledge there is no evidence to support this. On the contrary, a special Prologue to Shirley's *Doubtful Heir*, written specifically for delivery in a performance at the outdoor Globe (whereas the full play was written for the indoor Blackfriars theatre) suggests that the audience should sit 'as you were now at the Black-Fryers' pit'. As Leacroft explains: 'As a result of the more cramped conditions at the Blackfriars the audience in the equivalent of the "yard" are known to have been seated on benches in what was now called the "pit", an arrangement necessitated by the need for the audience seated in the lower side galleries and in gallery facing the stage . . . to see over the heads of the occupants of the "pit".' In other words, the audience in the pit was slightly lowered in order to improve others' *sightlines*. The choice of the word 'pit' for this depressed area surrounded by seating would probably be from its resemblance to the pits used for cockfighting and bullbaiting and may owe something to the origins of the buildings chosen to be converted into theatres; certainly, the Phoenix in Drury Lane is known to have been an adapted cockpit, as was the Cockpit itself. The word can be traced back from OE *pytt*, through the Scandinavian and Germanic languages to L. *puteus*, 'a well'.

The term stuck, and when new theatres were built after the Restoration, the entire area we would now call the *stalls* was known as 'the pit': 'The house is made with extraordinary good contrivance, and yet has some faults, as the narrowness of the passages in and out of the pit, and the distance from the stage to the boxes' (8 May 1663, Pepys, *Diary*). The change of terminology from pit to stalls occurred on the turn of C18-C19 and reflects a change to more comfortable and expensive seating: 'Nash...provided eight rows of stalls adjoining the orchestra, with fourteen rows of pit benches behind' (Leacroft, 170). Ironically, the pit got pushed further and further back until, in many theatres, it has vanished out through the foyer, leaving its only vestigial echo as an abbreviation of *orchestra pit*.

plant   To *plant* an idea is to introduce an idea which will later become significant in the play. Characters, business, props etc. can all be referred to as being *planted*. The noun *planting* is also in use.

In addition, *a plant* is an actor, or any other person in collusion with the performers in a show, placed in an unwitting audience. It is almost certainly from Standard English *plant*, 'a spy, detective', itself possibly from underworld cant: 'He sold forged notes to a plant [a person sent for the purpose of detecting him]' (1812, *Sporting Magazine*, XXXIX). The use of plants by conjurers is almost as notorious as that alleged against (and equally strenuously denied by) spiritualists and clairvoyants. Plants are also a feature of *straight* theatre: Francis Beaumont's *Knight of the Burning Pestle* (1607) is one of the earliest examples of a play text which seems to call out for this trick to be played, and it is also used to effect in Thornton Wilder's *Our Town* (1938).

platform   A raised, usually wooden *playing area*. *A platform stage* (also known as an *end-stage*) is one which extends into the auditorium without a *proscenium arch*. (See also *rostrum*.) Surprisingly, 'platform' in its theatrical (or any other related) sense is not found until eC18, which gives strength to the theory that the term has a nautical origin, a *platform* being 'a division of the orlop of a man-of-war, between the cock-pit and the main mast': 'The Lieutenant...was about half an houre after wounded in both leggs, and carried down to the platform' (1667, *London Gazette*).

plaudit   Applause, from L. *'Plaudite!'* the habitual command

meaning 'Applaud!' issued by Roman actors at the end of a performance, which to modern ears would appear to smack of desp-
eration. *Plaudit* is little used now, only remaining in such twee
phrases as 'the cast received the plaudits of the audience' etc. For
derivation, see *applause*.

play, player, playing   *Play* is probably the oldest indigenous English theatrical term, the noun, meaning 'a dramatic representation
of an action' being traceable to the C9: 'Wearþ eft Godes wracu
Romanum þa hie æt hiora theatrum wæron mid heora pleyan'
(*c.*893, King Ælfred, *Orosius* [tr]). The noun is still used both as
a *play-text* and as a synonym for *production, performance* to the
present day.

The choice of *play* for dramatic presentation is interesting. One
might expect it to be in contrast to *drama* and *act*, whose etymol-
ogies emphasise real action in the world; one might suppose that
'play' emphasises fun, sport and recreation. It is true that these
associations are there; they provide a refreshing contrast with
drama and act; equally, 'play' does not imply the presence of an
audience as *theatre* does. According to OED, however, the older
senses of the noun relate to 'free movement or action' (C8) and
the root meanings of the verb also include 'to exercise (oneself or
a craft', 'to move briskly'. 'Play' is a vigorous word. It also
suggests the mimetic activities of children, the sense of learning
in safety, of rehearsing for life, in the way that animals also learn
to survive through practising killing. More than any of the other
key theatrical terms, it implies assuming a role.

With the sense of 'to perform, act', the verb is not attested in
OED until C14, though its use doubtless antedates this, (not least
because OED also has a figurative usage from Chaucer's *Troilus
and Criseyde* from about the same period, and it is impossible that
a figurative usage should precede the following literal one): 'Som-
tyme to shewe his lightnesse and maistrye/He pleyeth Herodes
vp on a Scaffold hye' (*c.*1386, Chaucer, *The Miller's Tale*).
Throughout C16 and C17, the verbs 'play' and 'act' were both
used in relation to dramatic performance (compare 'player' and
'actor', below), 'act' gradually becoming more frequent, though
'play' has remained in great use, particularly transitively: one is
far more likely to play *Hamlet* than to act *Hamlet*, though one is
far more likely to act than to play . 'Play' is also found in phrasal
verbs, such as *to play (oneself) in*, to become accustomed to and
grow in a role through playing it (which may well be a borrowing
from cricket): 'I myself knew how much the great parts benefited
from a period of playing in' (Branagh, 172). *To play straight, to
play for laughs, to play up, to play down, to play to the gallery* are all

theatrical verbs. A strange, quasi-tautological form of the verb is
to play-act: 'I have ranted, screamed, play-acted and generally
indulged in my part' (Berkoff, 147).

Player is an indigenous term for a dramatic performer, first
attested in OED in eC15 in the sense of a general entertainer: 'He
maketh a þilke þat pleyen with hem, and doon it, hiss principal
pleyeres and hise special jogeloresses' (*c*.1430, *Pilgrimage of the
lyf of the manhode*). 'One who plays a character on stage' follows
thirty years later: 'That...Pleyers in their Enterludes, be not
comprised of this Acte' (1463, *Rolls of Parliament*). 'Player' and
'actor' were synonymous terms throughout C16 and C17. From
the Restoration onwards, 'actor' gained favour and 'player' while
still known, is almost obsolete in everyday usage.

Playing, too, is used synonymously with 'acting' from C16 to
the present day, though again, its usage with this sense is dwindl-
ing: 'This filling-in by highly charged facial expressions and gestures of human detail seems to have been the characteristic of
nineteenth century playing...' (Brook, 17).

There are a variety of terms which include 'play', such as
playbill, playhouse, playscript etc. For a discussion of these, see
bill, house, script etc. except for the terms which are discussed
specifically below.

play doctor   A professional improver or toucher-up of plays:
'Shakespeare...knew all, and more than all, about the technique
of play-writing that is known by the most efficient "play-doctor"
in Broadway, New York' (*Observer*, 10 June 1928).

playgoer   An lC18-eC19 term, synonymous with *theatregoer*: 'The
present generation of playgoers' (1822, Lamb, *Elia*).

playing area   'The playing area is a square tending to a rectangle'
(Berkoff, 3). *Playing area* is a *performance space*, a C20 term
increasingly preferred to *stage* since the development of more
flexible staging techniques.

playlet   A C19 term for a short *play*; sometimes, a *one-act play*:
'In these beautiful and witty playlets there is but a ghost of an
action' (1881, *Century Magazine*, XXVIII).

play reader   Someone employed to read plays for a *theatre company, agent* etc.

play within a play   A device, such as that used by Shakespeare
in *A Midsummer Night's Dream* and *Hamlet*, whereby some or all
of the actors in a play represent actors, thereby allowing illusion
and reality to be further confused as they exchange the role of
offstage actor for *onstage* actor. (See also *backstage drama*.)

playwright   The indigenous term for *dramatist*. A term first
attested in OED in lC17. Shakespeare would have been known as

an 'author' or, the preferred Elizabethan and Jacobean term, a 'poet': 'Wherein you may...thrive better than in this damn'd Trade of a Playwright' (1787, M. Clifford, *Notes upon Mr Dryden's poems*).

plot   From C12, *plot* has referred to 'a small piece of ground for cultivation etc'. In mC16, by extension, it came to mean 'a ground plan', taking on, also, the verbal sense *to plan*. By further extension, it was transferred to 'the outline of a literary work', and from this in mC17, 'the structure of the *action* of a play:

> Notice...that there is a difference between the plot and the 'story' – [the latter] a mere synopsis of the temporal order of events incorporated in a work of literature. As we usually summarise a work, we say that first this happens, then that, then that...It is only when we say how this is related to that, and in what ways all these matters are rendered and organised so as to achieve their particular effects, that a synopsis begins to be adequate to the actual plot. (Abrams)

'This information can befuddle the audience, since at this stage of the game – [*Hamlet*, I.i] – they pay rapt attention to the plot because they are witnessing "Shakespeare"; they feel that anything they miss will be like dropping some valuable thread which plays a vital part in the grand design' (Berkoff, 6). Despite these critical terms, however, the audience's awareness of the plot is achieved through their attention to the *narrative* line of the play.

The 'plot' is also a plan of tasks to be performed before and during a show by each grouping within the production team (from C16 sense, *to plan*); it (e.g. *props plot, sound plot* etc.) is generally presented schematically and chronologically, listing *cues*, actions to be taken on those cues and so on. Preparing this is called plotting.

poached egg   An imaginatively descriptive term for a particular *light filter*. Here is the recipe: a *poached egg* is made by cutting the centre out of a frosted *gel*, discarding that centre, combining the remainder with a coloured gel and placing them both in a colour frame in front of a lantern. (This process is done in order to give the resulting beam of light a diffused edge, with the purest colour at the centre.) The poached egg effect is probably at its most effective with a rich amber gel.

point   In an actor's vocal *delivery*, to *point a line* or *point a speech* is to draw the audience's attention to certain features of it – as one does to an object with the physical *gesture* of pointing – by careful use of pacing, by pausing and by giving words added stress etc. 'Why, after all, should the curtain come down at a "strong" moment, why should a good line be "pointed"...?'

(Brook, 26). *Pointing* is a vital element in communicating the actor's interpretation of a role and one of the basic considerations in good verse-speaking. The word is also less frequently used in relation to dramatic construction, *movement* and *gesture*, again to denote the addition of emphasis.

pong A verb now largely obsolete in its theatrical sense, dating from the 1890s: it had two meanings, one roughly equivalent to *pad out* in both its senses of *ad libbing* to cover for forgotten lines and extending a role by supplying extra lines, the other meaning to deliver a role with exaggerated emphasis. The usage probably comes from *pong*, 'to stink', used as an expression of disgust and disapproval, itself from Romany *pan*, 'to stink'. The Romany connection suggests it may have entered theatrical usage via *parlyaree*.

poetic drama Generally, a play written in *verse* – in C16-C17, playwrights were most frequently referred to as *poets* – although the term *can* also be used for prose drama which has a 'poetic quality', whether in the language or in the visual images it creates, in which sense the use begs the awesomely large question, 'What is poetry', which I shall sidestep with the observation that the figurative usage of the word has been common in English since mC19. It is also interesting to note the etymology of *poetic*, from *poet*, which can be traced back to Gk *poiētēs*, 'a maker', from *poieō*, 'to make', another primary verb of practical action giving its name to an art form – compare *drama*.

political theatre Theatre which concerns itself with political events, issues or ideas. Whilst a great deal of drama from the Greek *tragedy* onwards might fall into this definition, it should be noted that in practice the term is used for theatre which has a self-consciously political intention, and in this sense is a C20 term which can be traced back to the influence of Marxist-Leninist *agitprop* groups such as the Blue Shirts founded in the postrevolutionary USSR in 1923, a trend spread in the West through the influence of Erwin Piscator in the 1920s and most influentially by Bertolt *Brecht*. These origins have meant that the term is nearly always used with left-wing connotations: *political theatre* challenges the *establishment* in both content and form and, as such, has tended to be anti-*commercial* and a genre firmly rooted in the *fringe*.

poor theatre A term coined by the Polish *practitioner* and founder of the highly-influential Theatre Laboratory, Jerzy Grotowski (b.1933) in his book *Towards a Poor Theatre* (1968). *Poor theatre* (where '*poor*' is used in its sense of 'destitute') is essential theatre, a theatre in which all the 'non-essentials' such as a conventional theatre building with stage, lighting, sound etc. are stripped away and one is left with what Grotowski considers the essence of theatre: the actor (whose training Grotowski claims should be one of monastic self-denial and dedication) and, occasionally, when they are invited, an audience. Poor theatre has influenced other Western practitioners, including Peter Brook: 'no one else in the world, to my knowledge, no one since *Stanislavsky*, has investigated the nature of acting, its phenomenon, its meaning, the nature and science of its mental-physical-emotional processes as deeply and completely as Grotowski...In his theatre, there is absolute concentration by a small group and unlimited time' (Brook, 37). It has to be said that this influence is thought-provoking but limited and more often than not in the working theatre, the term 'poor theatre' is used ironically with reference to contemporary funding or the quality of productions mounted.

portrayal   'Nicky Henderson broadens his already considerable range to create a memorably portrayal' (*The Stage*, 23 April 1992). An actor is said to *portray* a character, a term borrowed from the visual arts, where *portayal* is the action of producing a graphic *portrait*. From OF *portraire*, from *por-* = *pro-*, 'forth' + *traire*, 'draw': 'to draw forth', 'portrayal' has been used in art since mC19.

poster   'We were building a small library of information about printing and posters, budgets and publicity...' (Branagh, 161). In England *posters*, with only the barest details on them, first appeared in the mC17 as advertisements for performances; they were hung on street-posts, hence the term (from Fr. *poste*, from It. *posta*, a contraction of *posita*, the feminine past participle of L. *ponere*, 'to place'). The earliest poster on record, also by its appearance designed for distribution by hand (hence the origin of the term *hand-bill*), advertises a *variety show* 'at the Booth at Charing Cross' in 1672. The earliest poster for an established theatre is for Drury Lane in 1687. Posters gradually developed to include most of the detail we would expect on a modern *programme*, and in fact they doubled in this role for some time, but by the mid-C19, following the introduction of colour posters in France, they had become too large, lavish and expensively-produced to be handed out in quantities, hence the development of the programme. Whilst artistic posters are still produced, they achieved their apotheosis in the 1890s in the work of Toulouse-Lautrec.

practical   A *practical prop* or item of *scenery* is one which actually functions rather than just being on stage for scenic effect: hence, *practical door*, *practical staircase*, *practical lights*: 'He [a lighting designer] made use of what are known as "practicals" – wall lights, table lights or overhead lights, which appear to the audience to cast light naturally' (*Observer*, 3 May 1992). The word is commonly abbreviated to *prac*. in daily usage, but *practical* is itself an abbreviation of *practicable*, which Bowman and Ball (1963) list as an alternative, now largely obsolete, from the Standard English word in the sense of 'that can be used'. The *b* sound was presumably dropped because of the sheer awkwardness of saying it.

practitioner The Standard English sense of *practitioner* (which appears to derive from the obsolete *practitian*, or *practician*) is 'professional or practical worker', which can be traced back via Fr. and L. to Gk *praktikos* (from root word *prasso*, 'do', 'act'). However, 'practitioner' is an abbreviation of *theatre practitioner*, from *theatre practice*, a C20 English coining to directly translate Fr. *pratique du théâtre*, 'theatre experience, knowledge', where *pratique* has its French sense of 'the application of theory'. A practitioner is thus a working man of the theatre who is also schooled in theory. (The word can be likened to *dramaturge*, and it is significant that, like so many words that relate to theoretical and intellectual approaches to theatre, English borrows from continental usage, so deep, perhaps, is the native mistrust of philosophising.) The current AEB 'A' level examination in Theatre Studies prescribes four practitioners on the syllabus, *Stanislavski*, *Brecht*, Artaud (see *Cruelty*) and Craig (see *über-marionette*), all men who worked in theatre but also wrote extensively about theory and practice.

pratfall *Prat* (or *pratt*) has been in use as 'bottom, arse' since at least the C16, apparently being exported to the United States before it developed its secondary, sexual sense which Partridge coyly terms 'the female pudend'. A *pratfall* was originally an American stage term, from *knockabout* comedy, for a fall on to the buttocks, usually exaggerated. It can be used generally for any behaviour which makes the perpetrator look foolish. It is recorded in use in Canada by 1935; by 1950 it was common in Britain.

première 'The world *première* of John Osborne's new play *Déja Vu* will take place at the Thorndyke Theatre, Leatherhead, from May 5-21.' (Ad. in *The Stage*, 23 April 1992). A *première* is the first showing of a new play, although it is possible for a show which has had a *provincial try-out* to have a *London première*, a first London showing. A C19 borrowing from Fr.: 'It was a pleasant sight on the *première* of "King Arthur" to see . . .' (*Punch*, 26 January 1895). Fr. *première* is itself an abbreviation of *la première d'une pièce*, in the feminine to agree with either *nuit*, 'night' (compare *first night*), or *représentation*, 'performance'. The verb *to première* also exists, and, of course, the term has been borrowed by cinema. Premières can be very glitzy affairs attended by 'anyone who is anyone', especially if they are *gala* premières. In C19-eC20, the word was also used of the leading lady (*première actrice*), with *premier* for the leading man (compare *principal*).

preparation   '[I]f it's a director I trust then maybe I won't do anything like as much work, but if it's a director I don't know, or I'm not sure I can totally trust, I will do a great deal of preparation' (Alec McCowen, interviewed in Barkworth, 168). *Preparation* is the work done by an actor outside rehearsals in order to create his character and prepare himself for the physical, vocal and psychological demands of a role. Techniques and approaches are myriad and very from actor to actor, but common methods of preparation beyond learning the *lines* include background reading and research, *study* which might include work on *subtext* and filling in the character's biography by imagination and visualisation, work on the actor's own personal experiences and *emotion memory*.

presence   What constitutes *stage presence* is hard to define: it is often an intangible quality like charisma which allows certain actors to hold the audience's attention more than others. Olivier's description (p.158) of his friend Ralph Richardson in the role of Falstaff, which mentions *presence* in passing, also goes some way to giving a flavour of the word's meaning:

> The voice and above all the diction, like a great music-hall comedian, had every consonant hitting the back wall of the pit like a whip-lash; the richness and the detail of his characterisation, the presence, bearing, walk, voice, humanity, wicked loveableness, the dictionary of the man's humours, the sharp salt of his wit and the sudden blinding sadness of 'Peace, good Doll . . . Do not bid me remember mine end' – it may be guessed that this mighty performance is strongest amongst my favourites.

Perhaps, in the end, presence is merely the impression communicated by an especially good actor in a role they relish.

preset   Sometimes found as *pre-set*, but less and less frequently: the *lighting state* on stage prior to the opening of a performance, used particularly in *theatre-in-the-round* and with other forms of staging which dispense with *house tabs* or alternative means of masking the *set* from the audience. *Presetting* is also sometimes used as a term for programming *lighting cues* into a *memory board* ('*plotting*') prior to a show, a term from the *pre-set switchboard* used before the introduction of modern computerised *lighting* *desks*. Props placed in position on the set prior to a performance are also *preset*, and this, as the oldest use of the term, is also likely to be its origin. From *set¹*

press As a general term for newspapers the term *press* meaning 'printing, publication' dates back to C16. Many theatres, producers, and name performers etc. employ a *press agent* to issue *press releases* in order to ensure that they receive the maximum (appropriate) publicity for their projects. Favourable cuttings may be kept for future reference in a *press book*, especially those which give evidence of a successful *press night*: 'A local press night was followed swiftly by a national press night' (Branagh, 211). The aim at such events is to receive *rave notices*.

preview 'By the time I got to the first preview I thought I had built up a convincing tragic hero...' (Branagh, 96). *Previews* are *try-out performances* given in front of invited audiences, or audientes paying reduced prices, prior to the official *opening* of a show. Not all shows *preview*; those which do may preview for one night only or for several. The term is not used theatrically until C19.

prima donna 'The contemporary musical has bred up a school of shrill, strident *prima donnas*' (*Plays and Players*, October 1990). *Prima donna* was the term given to the *lead* female singer in Italian *opera*, (from *prima*, 'first' + *donna*, 'lady'), borrowed by English in mC18. Not only did the term transfer to *operetta*, but also, as the above quotation shows, it can be employed in all *musical theatre*: however, as the tone implies, outside its specific operatic use, *prima donna* has developed a decidedly censorious ring. Traditionally, the *prima donna* was a temperamental star who demanded great devotional attention and could fly into great rages at the slightest provocation: this usage became general by lC19 if not before: 'lights should not be allowed to behave like prima donnas. They should never distract an audience from the production' (Mark Henderson, lighting designer, quoted in the *Observer*, 3 May 1992).

principal The term *principal*, an abbreviation of *principal actor* or *actress*, can be dated back at least to the eC17 and probably to Elizabethan theatre. Then, 'principal', (ME, from OF, from L. *princeps principis*, 'first, chief, sovereign' [from *primus*, 'first' + *cipere* = *capere*, 'to take']), referred specifically to a *member* of a *company* as opposed to a *hireling*, and could also be applied to an apprentice playing a leading female role: 'Burt was a Boy first under *Shank* at the *Blackfriars*, then under *Beston* at the *Cockpit*; and *Mohun* and *Shaterel* were in the same Condition with him, at the last Place. There *Burt* used to Play the principal Women's

Parts, in particular *Clariana* in *Love's Cruelty'* (1699, *Historia Histrionica*, a reflection on the Jacobean and Caroline stages, quoted at length in Nagler, 158-64).
It is from this usage that the name for the traditional *pantomime* role of *principal boy* was derived in C18. A principal boy is the dashing, thigh-slapping hero of the panto, conventionally played, just to confuse matters, by a woman. (*Principal girl*, the sweet, innocent heroine [also played by a woman], does exist as a term but has not the same popular currency.) See also *dame, drag, breeches part.*

problem plays   Shakespeare's *problem plays* was a term first coined in 1896 by F.S. Boas for a group of his plays which had previously been known as the 'dark comedies', considered to fall in between the classifications of *comedy* and *tragedy*, e.g. *Measure for Measure*. Boas appropriated the term for Shakespearian criticism from a contemporary critical term describing the moral, psychological and social probings of writers such as Ibsen and Strindberg, otherwise known as 'drama of ideas'.

producer   'Very few people outside a dramatic production know what a producer is – or care' (*Daily Mail*, 25 July 1928). From L. *producere*, 'to lead or to bring forth', *producer* has been used for the person responsible for realising a work of art since lC17-eC18; in English theatre in lC19, it became used for the role we would now term, since the formal adoption of the American term in the late 1940s, the *director*. To complicate matters, the American term 'producer', which is now used in theatre, means *manager*: 'Miss Galgan, producer, Cameron Mackintosh Ltd., was this week prosecuted for failing to safeguard three of its technicians working on a West End show' (*The Stage*, 28 March 1991).

production   A term first attested in OED in lC19, derived from the verb 'to produce' (above), the most common usage of *production* today is as 'the staging of a dramatic performance', in all or some of its financial, technical and artistic aspects. 'When I did *Titus Andronicus* there was a lot of praise for this production being better than the play' (Brook, 75). Productions are *staged* or *mounted*, the final week leading up to and including the *first night* being known as a *production week*: 'Final fight call before production week' (Tim McInnerney, *Guardian*, 24/25 August 1991).

profession/pro/professional   Whereas the *business* is an abbreviation of 'show business', and those employed in it may include anyone who works in any branch of the *entertainment* industry, actors who use acting as their means of gainful employment refer to it as *the profession*. From this is derived the term *professional*, frequently abbreviated to *pro*, as in the admiring phrase 'He's a real pro', for someone dedicated to the profession and its values: 'A former actress herself and an indisputable pro, [Pat Marmont] made my mind up [about taking a first professional job]' (Branagh, 80). The approval inherent in the term is a C20 development: ironically, in C19, the age of the gentleman, professionals were looked down as being rather distastefully mercenary, (though theatre, not being respectable, has never employed this usage). From this sense also comes the affectionate term for a veteran actor, an *old pro*: 'Cockles, a young man, appears in the guise of an old pro who reminisces aptly and amusingly about his career' (*The Stage*, 28 March 1991). (See also *old trouper, old stager*.) To be praised for *professionalism* is the highest accolade: 'A mark of McKellen's professionalism [as Richard III in a production emphasising the military aspects of the play] is the way he has learned to fasten his uniform with one hand' (*Plays and Players*, October 1990). The term *amateur*, by contrast, is highly pejorative when used of a pro.

As an adjective, 'professional' stands in many phrases, most of them self-explanatory. One which may not be familiar to all is *professional matinée*, a show which starts at a time other members of the profession are unlikely to be working, so that they can see it. (See also *midnight matinée*.)

profile A two-dimensional cut-out made of plywood etc., simulating in outline an element of scenic design such as a rock, a column etc., from the obsolete Italian *profilo*. Also, an occasional American alternative to *gobo*.

From the same source, an actor assumes a *profile position* when standing side-on to the audience. Profile, a busy little word, is equally an abbreviation of *profile spot(light)*, a *spotlight* which gives a hard-edged beam of light. Contrast *fresnel*.

programme Printed information. Varying in size from a single duplicated sheet to a thick, glossy magazine, given out free or sold before a performance. *Programmes* generally include a *cast-list* and *credits* for the show about to be performed and may also include *programme notes* about the play and production, potted biographies of the cast, publicity for forthcoming attractions and a welter of advertising material. 'In his program [sic] note to that production, George Devine wrote "We're trying to show with timeless costumes and timeless sets the timelessness of the play"' (Brook, 88). For the introduction of programmes, see *poster*.

projection Although *projection* once meant 'the means by which an actor, through voice, movement, and gesture, reaches an audience effectively' (Bowman and Ball), in practice it is only used to refer to *vocal projection*. From L. *projectio*, from *projectum*, the past participle of *projicere -ject* 'to throw outwards, forwards', projection is the effective transmission of vocal sound from the actor to the furthest reaches of the *auditorium*, a feature of performance which may be enhanced by a *voice coach*: 'There was also a great deal of technical work to accomplish, and it was a great pleasure to work with the legendary Cis Berry, the RSC's voice supremo...I remember from my own experience of watching shows from the balcony that projection could be a problem, and I had to be on top of it' (Branagh, 140). See also *acoustics*.

From the same derivation comes the sense of projection as the throwing of silhouetted, photographic or cinematic images onto a set. Entertainments using the silhouetted images of puppets (created by placing the puppets between lighted candles and a translucent screen) developed in the Far East and were popular in France by m-lC18, from whence they reached England where they were known as *shadow-shows* or *ombres chinoises*. However, the projection of images onto a screen or *cyclorama* as a form of *backdrop* to a show was a later development associated with the eC20 *avant-garde*, a development appropriated from cinema and associated first with *political theatre*. Probably the first person to seize on the opportunities of employing new technology in the theatre, later also exploited by Piscator and Brecht, was the *Dadaist* Ywan Goll: 'Goll had broken out of the accepted stylistic conventions of the theatre as early as 1920...by dovetailing photography into the stage action. *The Immortal* made use of film and the projection of placards, newspaper cuttings and photographs – as Piscator was to do increasingly...' (Innes, 17). *Back-projection* – projection from behind a screen or cyc. – came to be favoured, as its use avoided unwanted shadows cast by scenery and performers onstage.

prologue   In L., *prologus* already meant the verbal introduction to a play and its speaker, a sense accepted into Engllish as early as 1300: Now o þis proloug wil we blin/In crist nam our bok begin' (*c*.1300, *Cursor Mundi* [E.E.T.S., 1874-92]).

promenade   A *promenade* production is a *perambulatory* one, in which the audience walks round from one *set* to another: 'In the large space, one is able to promenade in a relaxed and easy manner' (*Plays and Players*, October 1990). See also *multiple setting*.

prompt   Theatrically, *to prompt* is to supply an actor, from offstage, with lines which he has forgotten. From Fr., or directly from med. L. *promptare*, ultimately from *promptus*, 'readiness', 'prompt' has been in use in English since C14 as 'to incite (someone to action)' and since C15 as 'to assist a speaker who is at a loss'. The first theatrical attestation in OED is from 1679 – 'to stand behind the Scene, and prompt both Parties, to Act the bloody Tragedy' (*The Established Test*) – though it is known that in Elizabethan theatre the *book-holder* acted as *prompter* and that the term was in use at that date: 'Were it my cue to fight, I should have known it/Without a prompter' (1604, Shakespeare, *Othello*, I.ii). The *book-holder* brings us to the *prompt copy* of the text of a play being performed, *the book*. 'The person on the book is the most important of all. For example, there are ways of giving prompts: somebody can give you a prompt and at the same time manage to make you feel like an idiot for drying; somebody else might withold a prompt for a little while because they know you really know it, and then they might give you a key word or something' (Wyn Jones, interviewed in Barkworth, 189). Olivier describes his experiences as prompter in 1925: 'In "my" prompt corner (downstage left, of course)... [with] its brightly lit prompt book shelf and my own glorious array of light switches all around the top of me, there were cue switches to the switchboard, the orchestra, the prop room and seemingly every part of the house. There were two small lamps above each pair of switches – a red for warning, a blue for go' (p.57). As he testifies, the *prompt corner*, which is on the *prompt side* of the stage, which has traditionally been *stage left* since at least C18 (see *PS*, *OPS*). The shelf he mentions would probably have been on the *prompt desk*, the switches a replacement of earlier bells which the C18 prompter would have used for *calls* to actors etc.

props An abbreviation of *stage properties*: any article essential to the action of a play which does not come under the heading of *scenery*, *costume*, furniture etc. A *prop* whose appearance on stage is the responsibility of the actor is known as a *personal prop*, and if carried, a *hand prop*. The latter, but not the former, might be collected by the actor from a *prop(s) table* in the *wings*, their placement there being the responsibility of the *props man* (1633, OED) or an *ASM*, in accordance with the *prop plot*. The person responsible for the props held by a theatre or company is the *prop(s) master* or *mistress*, their bolt-hole and storage space being known as the *prop room*. A *hand-prop* is any prop taken onstage by the actor in the course of a show, usually taken from and replaced on a *prop(s) table*.

Most of these terms are very old. *Property* itself dates back at least to Elizabethan and Jacobean theatre: 'then it is time, as though you were one of the *Properties*, or that you dropt out of the *Hangings*, to creep from behind the Arras...' (1609, Dekker, *The Gull's Hornbook*). It is from Fr. *proprieté*, ultimately from L. *propriatatem*, from *proprius*, 'own, proper'.

A joke which depends on *business* involving a prop is known as a *prop gag*. Interestingly, *property boy* was an early term for a *supernumerary*, dating back to at least m-lC17: 'The Saints advance To fill the Dance, And the property boys come in' (1685, Dryden, *Albion & Albion*, III.ii).

proscenium Now commonly used as an abbreviation of *proscenium arch* or *opening*, the *proscenium* was in fact a key feature of the Greek theatre, where the *proskēnion* was the space in front of the *scene (skēnē)* and behind the *orchestra (orkhēstra)*: 'the acting area, stage'. It has never been widely employed with this sense in English, *proscenium* (from L.) being used to describe the wall and the opening in it which divide the stage from the *auditorium* in theatres built since the late Renaissance, the first proscenium arch (see *picture-frame stage*) having been erected in the Teatro Farese in Italy in 1618. 'Proscenium arch' is commonly abbreviated to *pros arch* or even *pros*, (often pronounced *proz*). Inigo Jones in his *masque* designs is generally credited with importing it to England. Naturally, the presence or absence of a barrier such as the pros arch vitally affects the relationship between actor and audience, not only in their own style of playing but also in terms of the writing that dramatists can attempt for the stage.

In Restoration theatre, *proscenium doors* were set into the arch to allow access to the *apron* in front of it. Gradually, as the stage retreated, they fell out of use, only to remain vestigially in some theatres as *call doors*.

prosthesis From Gk, from *pros-*, in this sense 'in addition', + *tithēmi*, 'place': something added in addition'. Grammatically, *prostheses* (the plural) are letters or syllables added to words as in the case of the prefix *be-* in *beloved*; in surgery and dentistry, from lC17-eC18, the term has been used for false limbs, teeth etc. Theatrical prostheses, embellishments of character *make-up*, include members as vital to the plots of celebrated plays as Cyrano de Bergerac's nose. Modern materials and make-up techniques have made the addition of pre-purchased prostheses far simpler, even for the enthusiastic amateur.

PS The standard abbreviation for the stage direction *prompt side*, or *stage left*. See *OPS*.

protagonist Gk, from *prōto-* (from prōtos, 'first'), + *agōnistēs*, 'actor'. Thespis (see *thespian*) is generally given credit for being the actor who first stepped out of the *chorus* to present a major character in the Athenian Festival of *Dionysus*. This actor was later joined by a second (the *deuteragonist*) and a third (the *tritagonist*). The term has been used in English as 'the leading character in a drama' since C17 – '’Tis charg'd upon me that I make debauch'd Persons ... my protagonists ...' (1671, Dryden, Essay) – and, by extension, as 'the leading figure in any general activity' since eC19, often with a sense of someone involved in a conflict or contest (see *agony*).

provincial   Or or pertaining to the provinces: i.e. outside London (see *out-of-town*). Used theatrically in terms such as *provincial tour, provincial rep* etc. Ultimately from L. *provincia*, 'an office, charge, province', of uncertain origin, though possibly related to *pro-*, + *vincere*, 'to conquer'.

psychodrama   A C20 term developed in *drama therapy*, from *psycho-*, 'of or pertaining to the mind' (from Gk *psukhē*, 'mind, soul', + *drama*). *Psychodrama* employs the techniques of *improvisation, role-play* and *simulation* in order to explore areas of individual personality, behaviour and inter-personal relatinships, to achieve some therapeutic effect on the individual or group. Clearly, it is an extremely dangerous technique and one which should only be undertaken by trained individuals in a controlled situation with ample time for feed-back and debriefing.

psychotechnique   Translated from the Russian, *Stanislavski*'s term for the elements of his system which concentrate on the internal preparation of an actor for his role. For details of elements of *psychotechnique*, see *emotion memory, motivation, objectives (creative)* etc. See also *Method, the*.

Punch and Judy   *Punch* is a sadistic little glove-puppet, a hunchbacked, hook-nosed Richard III in wood. He is based on Pulcinella of the *commedia dell'arte* and made his first appearance in England as Polichinello (later Punchinello, abbreviated to Punch) in the 1660s. The popularity of the character was such that he began to appear in *puppet-plays* throughout the country, acquiring two wives – Judy was the second after Joan was divorced – a dog called Toby, a crocodile, a baby and, since the end of last century, a regular job on the beaches of holiday resorts.

punchline   'Used to be a fellow lived near to me used to sell horse manure for gardens. Colourful character – red nose, big hat ... he used to go round going "Get your manure from me – hand-picked manure" ... somebody said to his wife, "Why don't you get him to say fertiliser?" She said, "It took me ten years to get him to say manure"' (Les Dawson, quoted in Wilmut, 222-3). The final sentence of that *gag* is the *punchline*, the *pay-off*, what a *straight* actor might call the *laughline*. From C20 *variety*, it is a descriptive term in that it *punches* its point over or *socks it to 'em*.

punishing roles   An actor's term: 'The intensely suffering characters, which we describe as the Punishing Roles – Lear, Othello,

Macbeth, Titus, Oedipus – are not there to be enjoyed any more than a marathon is' (Olivier, 190).

punters 'This...brought a little titter from the punters...' (Berkoff, 18). From Fr. *ponter*, 'to bet, (especially in card games etc.)', *punter* has been used since eC18 for 'one who lays a bet', and later, more generally, as 'a customer'. It tends to be an insider's term, used rather smugly and disparagingly, and is commonly found in the underworld: prostitutes, for example, refer to their clients as 'punters'.

puppet(ry) *Puppet* is a variant of the earlier *poppet*, equatable with It. *pupa, puppa*, 'a girl, a doll [note the continued popular usage of this term of endearment], a puppet', ultimately from L. *pupa*, 'a girl'. It is probably via Fr., although Fr. *poupette* appears to succeed it. Both 'puppet' and 'puppetry' are found from eC16: 'Let not oure most holy father make them moare dronken with vayne names...and like babels, as it were popetry for children' (1528, Tindale, *The obedience of a christen man*). Puppets, particularly *hand-puppets*, or *glove-puppets*, have been popular in England since early medieval times, creating one of the few theatrical traditions that seems to have continued unbroken to the present day, although it has to be said that there is evidence in lC20 that their popularity is on the wane. Compare *marionette*.

push and pull A descriptive actor's term for additional money paid (according to fixed *Equity* rates) when they are required to *scene-shift* above and beyond the demands of the role.

Quarter *The quarter* is the time – twenty minutes before *the up* in *theatre time* – for the *cue-call*, 'Quarter of an hour, please'.

quarto The name given to early, often hurriedly-published versions of Elizabethan and Jacobean plays. From the ablative of L. *quartus*, 'fourth', *quarto* was the printers' term for a sheet of paper that was folded twice, to give four sheets. See *folio* for a more detailed explanation.

queen As in *drag queen*, an artist specialising in *camp drag acts*. The accepted spelling probably hides the origins of *queen*: a lC19 borrowing of *quean*, 'a harlot' (compare *gay*). In general usage it tends to refer to effeminate gays and there is a tendency for it to be used more frequently for older homosexuals as in *you old queen*. There is also an adjective *queeny*, perhaps influenced by the woman's name, Queenie. This can often imply an hysterical emotionalism: 'He knew how provocative he was being and this was clearly meant to test what an arty Pom I really was, but I suppressed the queeny outrage in me and decided to credit him with being nervous' (Branagh, 123).

quick change A rapid change of *costume* in the course of a show, often of necessity performed in the *wings*. A *quick-change room* is sometimes provided near the stage for this purpose, otherwise a makeshift enclosure, which can also be aggrandised by the term, can be improvised from *flats* etc. A *dresser* may be on hand to help, although this would be an affront to the skill of some *quick change artists*, performers specialising in such changes. 'Quick change artist' can be met with in general use, not only for someone with a large and regularly-visited wardrobe, but also for someone given to rapid changes of opinion, mood or relationship.

quick study A *quick study* of the text is made when, for whatever reason, an actor is required to learn his *lines* quickly. The term can also be applied to actors who have a facility for learning *parts* quickly.

RADA   The abbreviation by which the Royal Academy of Dramatic Art is generally known. *RADA* is arguably Britain's – certainly the *establishment*'s – leading *drama school*, founded by Beerbohm Tree in 1904, and the only one widely known to the general public. Situated in Gower Street, London, and boasting a string of the most famous alumni including Sir John Gielgud, its prestige is reflected in the following extract from Branagh (pp. 44/5):

> when I came home there was an envelope still on the mat, with the words *Royal Academy of Dramatic Art* set out in red letters across the bottom. My heart started pounding, and I stood for ten minutes just holding the letter. I finally opened it. My eyes swam and I could read nothing while I searched for the magic words, '. . . and so I would like to offer you a place.' They were there . . . My parents were thrilled and greatly relieved. RADA was the one drama school they had heard of and the 'Royal' tag seemed to bestow an acceptably conventional status on it. If I had got into one the more avant-garde drama schools, they would have been terrified. And RADA gave you a diploma – if I didn't make it as an actor I could perhaps teach.

RADA-trained, a *RADA voice* etc. are all commonly found.

rag   A term for the *act curtain* or the *tableau curtain*, according to Partridge in use since about 1875, interestingly, about the date another similar usage of *rag*, in the phrase the *rag trade*, is attested with reference to the clothing industry. Both are familiar trade terms, using 'rag' colloquially for 'material, cloth', and affectionately depreciatory. From the Standard English sense of 'a torn piece of woven material', itself probably a back-formation from *ragged*. ME from Old Norse *roggvathr*, 'tufted'.

rail   Possibly a word derived from the nautical connection (as in *over the rail*, 'over the side of the ship'), *rail* has numerous theatrical usages: i) one of the horizontal cross-pieces on the frame of a flat – the *top rail* and *bottom rail*; ii) a *counterweight* track; iii) *balcony front lighting* – lighting attached to a *rig* on the balcony is referred to as the *rail*; iv) a *safety* handrail, either *onstage* or *front of house*.

All these terms, whether via the nautical connection or not, ultimately derive from Standard English *rail*, 'a horizontal or

214

inclined bar': ME, from OF *reille*, 'an iron rod', from L. *regula*, 'a rule'.

rain barrel (US: *rain-pipe*). A metal container perforated on the underside to allow water to be sprinkled onto the stage to simulate rain. This is not to be confused with a *rain machine*, also known as a *rain box* or *rain drum*, a wooden or metal container of peas or other pellets which, when rotated, creates a sound effect to simulate falling rain.

rake The slope of both the auditorium or the stage (as in *raked stage*) can be referred to simply as the *rake*: 'Back at 4.45 to rehearse fight on main stage. Despite the angle of the rake this is really encouraging' (Tim McInnerny, *Guardian*, 24-25 August 1991). Any sloping or slanting scenery piece can be referred to as a *raking piece*. The general English usage of 'rake' as 'slope' derives from the C17 nautical term, found as both *rake* and *rack* (probably from G. *ragen*, 'project', of unknown origin). The OED quotes 'The lengths, breadthes, depthes, rakes, and burdens' (1626) and '55 Foote...for the length by the keel,...16 foot... for the Rack forward' (1690), with the following definition: 'The projection of the upper part of a ship's hull at stem and stern beyond the corresponding extremities of the keel (distinguished as forerake and sternrake). Hence, the slope of the stern or stern-post, or of the rudder'. The OED's earliest general usage is from 1802, a theatrical attestation not occurring until 1893; I would expect, however, following the nautical clues, that theatrical usage dates back at least to the eC18.

rant 'At Drama School I had fallen into the trap of ranting through [the closet scene in *Hamlet*] and running out of steam early on...' (Branagh, 210). *To rant* (from the Dutch *ranten*, 'to rave') is to deliver lines in a manner the OED defines as involving both 'turgid declamation' and 'magniloquent and empty declamation'. *Rant* was also in use as a noun by mC17: 'Tis a brave Costly Rant th' Hesperian King vtters with many Titles' (1649, OED). Dr Johnson, quoted in Boswell's *Life of Samuel Johnson* (1791), explains its theatrical usage in mC18: 'The players, sir, have got a kind of rant, with which they run on, without regard either to accent or emphasis.'

raspberry/razz As in the phrase *to get the raspberry*. One of the rare theatrical terms derived from rhyming slang (*raspberry tart* = 'fart'), a *raspberry* is a fart-like sound made by blowing through closed lips to express disapproval. The phrase appears to have entered straight theatrical usage from music hall in lC19, and now denotes any rejection of a performance by the audience, not necessarily accompanied by sound effects.

rave 'The major critics had already visited the comedies and been warmly enthusiastic. With the usual cavils, we seemed to get away with *Hamlet*, too. There were raves, and, as always, there were those for whom I could never be Hamlet in a million years...' (Branagh, 211). A *rave review*, or simply *rave*, is a highly enthusiastic one. From ME verb, *to rave*, 'to behave or talk with frenzy or great excitement', probably from Old Norman French *raver*, with a similar meaning. The earliest use of the noun in relation to the theatre appears to be in 1896 in *My Long Life* by Mrs C. Clarke: 'She concluded amid a rave of admiring plaudits.' 'Rave' found a new sense in the dance/music craze of the late 1980s-early 1990s: *rave music*, electronic music with an insistent beat, was played at *raves* – illegal parties at ad hoc venues – which also did a brisk trade in drugs such as Ecstacy (E).

read Specific theatrical senses of the standard English verb *to read* include *to read well* or *badly*, phrases which comment on an actor's ability to **sight-read** at **audition**, when they *read for a part*: those who 'read well' are usually able to add characterisation to literal sense on first glimpsing a text.

To *read in* for an actor is to **stand in** and perform the role of another actor in their absence using a book, so that a rehearsal – or, occasionally a performance – can go ahead regardless.

A *read-through* is a term generally applied to the first get-together of cast and text, although read-throughs at later stages of the **rehearsal** process are possible: 'And if you have done your homework you will not let nerves wreck the day for you, but will use the read-through as it ought to be used: it is, after all, your first opportunity to talk and listen to the people you are going to be with in the play' (Barkworth, 21).

A *reader* is a common abbreviation for **play-reader**, either someone employed by a company, **literary agent** etc. to read and assess new plays or, historically, in C19-eC20, someone employed by the Lord Chamberlain to assist with **censorship**.

Reading has four specifically theatrical senses. Firstly, it can be applied to a public performance of a play using books – a *play-reading*. It is also an alternative to 'read-through': 'Everyone will know that it is just the first reading and not to be taken too much notice of' (Barkworth, 156). 'After the first reading I began to be aware of the rare possibilities...that the role might offer' (Olivier, 215). It can also be used for the author's initial performance of the entire text of a play to director, cast etc., but its most interesting sense is synonymous with **interpretation**. 'A director can treat a play like a film and use all the elements of theatre...to communicate to the rest of the world what he has to say. In France and Germany, this approach is much admired, and it is called his "reading" of the play' (Brook, 5). 'Invention is important to an actor if he can bring it off because it suggests that his mind is volatile and capable of taking the most bizarre reading of the text and still not only making it make sense, but actually by the wit of the actor illuminating something of the text' (Berkoff, 104).

realisation A director's *realisation of a play* or an actor's *realisation* of their role is a term translated from Fr. *réalisitation* from the verb *réaliser*: the latter's general meaning is 'to achieve an abstract idea in actuality', hence its transference in French cinema and theatre meaning 'to produce', carrying with it the sense of intellectual interpretation, as well as performance. A C20 borrowing which, like other continental terms, brings the grey area between *production* and *direction* to the fore again. For further complications, see *mis-en-scène*.

realism A complex word, frequently confused with *naturalism*, with which it is often used synonymously. (For a detailed analysis of the development of both words beyond their theatrical contexts, see Raymond Williams, *Keywords*.) 'A term to describe a method or an attitude in art and literature (and hence theatre) – at first an exceptional accuracy of presentation, later a commitment to describing *real* events and showing them as they actually exist' (Williams).

In brief, *realism* is etymologically related to *real*. (from OF *realis*, from LL, from L. *res*, 'thing'). From its first usage in C15, *real* was applied legally to things which actually existed, such as property (still echoed in the term *real estate*), and by C18 was used in contrast to things imagined and the appearance of things.

The term *réalisme* was coined in France in the early C19 and appropriated and anglicised in subsequent decades. It was first applied retrospectively to the philosophical school led by Thomas Aquinas, opposed to nominalism and akin to Platonic idealism in that it held that absolute, objective, universal essences exist independent of the objects in which their qualities are perceived. However, to complicate matters, because of a confusion with the meaning of 'real', it also began to be used for 'a tendency to regard things as they actually are; any view or system contrasted with Idealism [!]' (OED).

In theatre, in the second half of C19, realism was appropriated by the movement (led by key writers such as Ibsen and Shaw, and *practitioners* such as Stanislavski) which favoured making social and psychological reality the basis of both the subject matter of theatre and its methods of presentation. Whereas naturalism was concerned with accurate observation and presentation, and carried with it overtones of scientific objectivity, realism was concerned with attitude and presentation, and still carried with it the echoes of a search after philosophical and political truth. It included or emphasised 'hidden or underlying forces or movements which simple "naturalistic" observation could not pick up but which it is the whole purpose of realism to discover or express' (Williams, op. cit.)

Despite the nice distinctions outlined above, it must be admitted that in practice, 'realism' and 'naturalism' and their associated adjectives and adverbs are used virtually synonymously. The word is, even after all this time, highly controversial and there is a strong *anti-realistic* movement at work in theatre today: 'My interest is in the possibility of arriving, in the theatre, at a ritual expression of the true driving forces of our time, none of which, I believe, is revealed in anecdote and characterisation by the people and situations in so-called realistic plays' (Brook, 31).

recall   'Afterwards, he said that if there were a recall it would be in three days' (Barkworth, 154). A term developed from the theatrical *call*, formerly used when an actor was called back onto the stage to take an *encore*. 'He escaped behind the scenes as soon as Miss Bretherton's last recall was over' (1884, Mrs H. Ward, *Miss Bretherton*). *Recall* is encountered in other general senses from eC17. Today, its main theatrical use is found in relation to *audition calls*. After having once *read* for a part, an actor may later *get a recall* if the casting director wishes to rethink in the light of having heard others read. In some circumstances, a recall may be a signal that one has got the part, or at least stands a good chance of getting it.

receiving house   The term used for a theatre (or *house*) which does not mount its own productions but *receives* those of *touring companies*. A *venue*. The term has been used since C18 (see *circuit*).

recital   ME, from OF *reciter*, from L. *recitare*, 'to set moving again'. Originally used as 'an account, description' (see *rehearsal*) – 'A lasiuious disposed person, whom the recital of sinnes ... will not staie' (1586 OED) – the word began to be applied to specific kinds of musical performance in C18: 'Recital, formerly the general name for any performance with a single voice, but at present only applied to a recitative' (1811, Busby, *Dictionary of Music*). However, its present senses of 'a performance by one musical artist', occasionally 'a performance of the works of one composer', or occasionally 'an uncostumed performance of operatic works given by a number of artists', would appear to date from later in C19: 'Liszt's Pianoforte Recitals. M. Liszt will give at Two o' clock on Tuesday morning, June 9th, Recitals on the Pianoforte' (*John Bull*, 31 May 1840).

recitation   Related in origin to *recital*, a *recitation* is the public delivery of a speech or, more usually, verse which has been learned by heart: '*Recitation*, a reading with a loude voice' (1623, Cockeram, *The English dictionarie*).

reflector   A reflecting surface, usually of metal or glass, placed behind a light source, to diffuse the light but increase its intensity. The term is also commonly used as an abbreviation of *reflector lamp*, a lamp with a built-in reflector, working on the principles outlined above.

Regie-buch   A German term, (literally 'direction book'), borrowed in C20, sometimes anglicised to *regie-book* or abbreviated to *regie*. A notebook in which a director jots down production notes prior to or during rehearsals. In this sense, it has affinities with *the book*, the *prompt-copy*.

régisseur   An alternative French term to *metteur en scène*: *artistic director*. Occasionally used in English in m-lC20, the *régisseur* has overall control of the artistic unity of a piece. The term was also once used in French for with the overtones of *actor-manager*, having the additional general historical senses of 'manager, agent, steward', from the verb *régir*, 'to govern, rule; to manage an estate or govern an undertaking', from L. *rex, regis*, 'king, ruler'. Compare *metteur en scène*.

rehearsal   Like *recital*, *rehearsal* was first used in English to refer to the act of recounting or repeating words, or giving an account of events which had occurred in actuality: 'Forgat I to maken rehersaille of watres corosif, and of lymaille' (*c*.1386, Chaucer, *Canon Yeoman's Prologue*). The ME verb *rehearse* comes from Anglo-French *rehearser*, from OF *reherc(i)er*, perhaps from *re-*, 'again', + *hercer*, 'to harrow', i.e. 'to harrow over' and hence 'go over'. Its theatrical usage – 'the practising of a play or other artistic performance prior to public showing' – appears to be C16, though it may well be earlier: 'Rehearsinge of divers plaies . . . and their sondry Rehersells' is first attested in OED in 1579-80 and Shakespeare uses the term in *A Midsummer Night's Dream* (*c*.1594): 'Here's a maruailous conuenient place for our rehearsall' (II.i).

Because rehearsal is so central to the performance process, it has generated a number of associated phrases such as *rehearsal period*, the days and weeks spent rehearsing: 'We had a very long run-up to the rehearsal period because we didn't have a play to start with' (Edward Petherbridge quoted in Barkworth, 175). Much of the work, due to frequent unavailability of the main stage, has to be undertaken in *marked-out rehearsal rooms*: 'Feel strangely dislocated leaving rehearsal room' (Tim McInnerny, *Guardian*, 24-25 August 1991). Rehearsal may not always merely involve laborious *run-throughs* of the play, but inventive *rehearsal exercises*: 'the most eclectic use of rehearsal exercises – to develop rhythm, listening, tempo, pitch, ensemble thinking or critical awareness – is most valuable provided none of them is considered a method' (Brook, 66). Actors are notified of rehearsals by *rehearsal calls*.

In addition, there is the well-known and generally-used *dress rehearsal*, the term for the final rehearsal prior to the first *preview*, or, if there are no previews, prior to the *opening night*, when the show is performed in full performance conditions but without the presence of an audience; if an audience is present at rehearsal, it is referred to as an *open rehearsal*.

relief   A lessening of dramatic tension in a play or production by the introduction of a scene or business which allows the audience to relax momentarily – although, of course, as with other techniques of building *suspense*, such relief can often make the succeeding return to dramatic tension even more effective. Also sometimes known as *release*. From the ME verb, *relieve*, 'to alleviate from pain, distress, anxiety etc.', from OF *relever*, from L. *relevare*, ultimately from *levis*, 'light', 'to lighten' as in the sense of lightening a load or burden. *Comic relief* is by far the most common form of relief, and the Porter's Scene in *Macbeth* (a brief respite at the opening of II.iii) is frequently cited as an example of this in an otherwise unremittingly harrowing drama. The term *Comic Relief* was appropriated for its appositeness and punning value in the late 1980s by an ad hoc collection of British comic actors giving their services free to raise money for a variety of charitable causes.

remote control (board)   Formerly formally-known as a *remote control switchboard*, this term can be used for any lighting board which controls the main circuits of the house via *pilot* controls. See also *memory board*.

rendition   'Drama students who are learning how to speak verse would do well to record [Peter] Jeffrey's rendition. He uses the rhythms, relying on their variety of emphasis' (Review in *The Stage*, 28 March 1991). From the obsolete French *rendition*, from *rendre*, 'to render, surrender, give back, give up', *rendition* has been used in English since eC17 with the senses derived from the original French verb. A further sense of translation developed in America in lC17 and it is here too that its usage as 'verbal delivery' developed in C19: 'On the rendition of the verdict, the large audience manifested enthusiastic approbation' (1858, OED), with the developing sense of 'performance': 'In their rendition of *Hamlet* by the Messrs Devrient' (1877 OED). It is falling into disuse now, although it can still be found, as in the quotation at the head of this entry, with a slightly archaic feel; also in phrases such as 'the rendition of a song'.

rep.   See *repertory*.

repartee   From *repartie*, the feminine past participle of Fr. *repartir*, 'to set out again', and hence 'to reply promptly', *repartee* is 'a witty reply, a quick or clever retort', thus much used in comic drama and *variety* for a conversation or *routine* composed of quick-witted statements and replies. It is attested in use before the Restoration: 'He would pass by any thing with some repartie, som witty strain' (*c*.1645, Howell, *Letters*), appropriately mentioning in the sentence the word with which it is still generally associated, the phrase *witty repartee* being commonly used to the present. Initially a fencing term, its theatrical usage at the Restoration, when such wit was in vogue in comedy, is attested in this quotation from Villiers' *Rehearsal*, (1672): 'First one speaks, then presently t' other's upon him slap, with a Repartee' (III.i), and its use can probably be accounted for by the large French influence on those returning from exile. A noted example is Mirabel and Millament discussing their impending marriage in Act IV of *The Way of the World* (1700, Congreve). See also *stichomythia*.

repertoire   'The name of the Gate Theatre has long been synonymous with an adventurous repertoire' (Michael Coveney, *Guardian*, 3 May 1992). From Fr. *répertoire*, from LL *repertorium*, from L. *reperire repert-*, 'to find'. In part synonymous with *repertory*, but only in the sense of 'a stock of dramatic and musical pieces which a company or player is accustomed or prepared to perform; one's stock of parts, songs, tunes etc.' (OED). *Repertoire* came into use in the 1840s as a direct borrowing from French with its acute accent still intact (although it had been dropped well before the end of the century): 'The part... with the exception of the renowned... Robert Macaire, is the best character in his répertoire' (*Illustrated London News*, 16 January 1847).

repertory   After the introduction of *répertoire* in 1840s, *repertory*, which had existed in English since mC16 in a variety of senses such as 'index, list, catalogue, magazine, storehouse and repository', began to be used synonymously in one particular sense, outlined above. However, it developed its own distinct theatrical usage in the related phrase *repertory system*, denoting a system whereby a theatre or company maintained a selection (or *stock*) of plays in constant readiness for performance in any one season, plays which were rotated in a constantly changing programme.

Small *reps.*, as theatres which employed this system were known as from about 1920, flourished throughout the country well into the middle of the C20: most towns of a reasonable size could boast one and many of today's older performers gained their training there: 'I had to learn by watching and doing my time in the reps.' (Julia McKenzie, *Plays and Players*, October 1990). The rep. system is still employed by some large companies like the RSC – 'the "up" side of the repertory system is that each time you get back to a play it is fresh' (Tim McInnerny, *Guardian*, 24-25 August 1991). However, the small provincial reps. have either gone over to a system of limited *runs*, become *receiving houses* or, as is the case with most, closed due to competition firstly from cinema and, more fatally, from television.

reprise   'She was an adenoidally definitive Miss Adelaide in *Guys and Dolls* and is expected to reprise that role for a charity performance' (of Julia McKenzie in *Plays and Players*, October 1990). From *repris*, the past participle of Fr. *reprendre*, 'to take back, resume'. *Reprise*, which can be used as noun, verb and adjective, has been in existence in English since the C14, but its first artistic employment was in dance, where it signified a repeat step: 'A repryse alone ought to be made with the ryght fote in drawynge the ryght fote bakwarde a lytyll to the other fote. The seconde repryse ought to be made . . . with the lyft fote in reysynge the body in lyke wyse' (1521, R. Copland, Introduction, *Frenche Maner of dauncynge*). A further development occurred in lC17-eC18, when 'reprise' began to be used for a musical repetition, initially in one piece only: 'La Reprise (le Refrain) des Ballades, des Chansons, the Reprise, repetition, upholding, or burden of Ballads and Songs' (1702, Boyer, Dictionary Royal). Since then, the use of the word has broadened as the quotation at the head of this entry attests, so that it can be used for any repetition of artistic activity.

resident   In phrases such as *resident company, resident dramatist* etc., *resident* (ME, from Fr. *résider*, or from L. *(re)sidere = sedere*, 'to sit') signifies an artist or group of artists attached to a particular *venue*: 'the No 1 Tour spent two weeks at the Royal Court Theatre in London to give the resident company there a summer holiday' (Olivier, 63).

resolution   From L. *re(solvere)*, where *solvere* means 'to solve', an alternative term for *dénouement*, to signify the unravelling of the complex threads of a dramatic plot.

responsibles   A slightly ironic term formerly used in *rep.* and *on tour* to describe small but vital acting roles: the actor who specialised in playing them would be known as *a responsibles*, a *responsible man* or a *responsible player*.

resting The euphemistic actors' term for being out of work, dating, according to Partridge, at least from lC19. 'Resting actors and actresses with their own car, van or motorbike required for parcel delivery. Plenty time off for auditions' (ad. in *The Stage*, 28 March 1991). According to *Equity* statistics, in the 1980s it had roughly 30,000 members, 20,000 of whom were actors, (the remainder comprising 6,000 *variety artists*, and 4,000 assorted stage managers, directors, designers, broadcasters etc.). On any given day, Equity calculated that 60-70 per cent of those acting members were *resting*. Alternative euphemisms, less frequently used, include *at leisure, at liberty, available*, and *between engagements*.

Restoration drama A term applied to the drama produced from 1660 (when Charles II was *restored* to the English throne) to a date of the user's choice, generally around the turn of C17. Whilst the period did produce the tragedies of Otway and the heroic verse drama of Dryden, it is largely associated in the popular mind with *comedies of manners*, hence the term *Restoration comedy*. The term *Restoration* was coined in 1660; 'The Happy Restoration of His Majesty to his People and Kingdoms' (*Journals of the House of Commons*).

returns By far the commonest use of *returns* is for unsold tickets, returned to the *box office* for re-sale, hence the term *queuing for returns*. 'There was a packed house and a large returns queue' (Branagh, 210). The term is sometimes also used, especially in America, for reviews. A *return* can also be used for a flat or downstage curtain used to mask the off-stage view between the *tormentor* and the rest of the set.

revels A term given to court entertainments of various types, including *pageants, masques* etc. from the accession of the Tudor monarchy until the eC18. From ME verb *to revel*, from OF *reveler*, 'to riot', (developing into the sense 'to make noisy mirth' [OED]), from L. *rebellare*, 'to rebel'. (Compare *misrule*.) The earliest instances of the use of the noun are C14: He made fare on þat fest . . . With much reuel & ryche of þe rounde table' (*c*. 1375, *Sir Gawain and the Green Knight*). Such entertainments were looked after by the Master of the Revels who, in 1558, was also given the post of theatrical censor – an irony given the source of his title – which he and his successors were to fill until that role passed to the *Lord Chamberlain* in 1737: 'The Revelles together with the Tentes and Toylles was made an office' (1558 in Feuillerat, *Revels of Queen Elizabeth*).

revenge tragedy A critical term, probably lC19, for one of the most popular *genres* of the Elizabethan and Jacobean theatres.

Revenge tragedy flourished over a forty-year period from the 1580s, when Kyd wrote the seminal *Spanish Tragedy*, until the late 1620s and Ford's great study of obsessive and destructive passion, *'Tis Pity She's a Whore*. The genre is characterised by certain types such as the wronged hero or heroine and the *malcontent*, by a strong vein of veiled political and social satire, an obsession with death and the macabre which gives rise to powerful, sometimes highly lyrical dramatic verse and, almost without fail, a violent and bloody dénouement. The first attestation of the noun *revenge* is from mC16: 'Euribates, Can not remembraunce of reuenge out of thy breast be reft?' (1566, Studley, *Agamemnon*). It is derived from the ME verb, from OF *revenger, revencher*, from LL *re(vindicare*, 'to lay claim to').

reversal 'In many plots the dénouement involves a reversal, or in Aristotle's term, peripety, in the hero's fortunes, whether to his failure or destruction, as in tragedy, or to his success, as in comic plots. The reversal frequently depends on a discovery (in Aristotle's Greek term, anagnorisis)' (Abrams). The first English usage of *reversal* occurs in C15 legal terminology, the more general sense of 'a complete turn-around' not appearing until lC17. I suspect, although I do not have any direct attestation for this, that the first literary use of the term occurred in the succeeding century.

review 'I was in a tiny minority, but, for the first and only time, I was completely unaffected and unworried by the reviews... The first night faces told the story' (Branagh, 131). 'My reviews from *Zoo Story* were quite the best I have had – then or ever' (Berkoff, 63). *Reviews*, or *notices* as they are also known, are journalistic criticisms of a given production. Whilst the word (from the obsolete French *reveue*, from *revoir*, literally 'to see again') had earlier legal and military senses, its first critical use is attested in mC17: 'A Review of Doctor Bramble... his Faire Warning,' a title used by R. Baillie in 1649. Naturally, the journalistic employment of 'review' developed with journals and newspapers in the lC17-eC18. See also *revue*.

revival 'Joachim Hertz produced *Salome* for the National Opera 15 years ago and returned to supervise its revival last week' (*The Stage*, 28 March 1991). A *revival* is the production of a piece after a lapse of time, be it as little as a few weeks or several centuries, from the ME verb *to revive*, from OF *revivre*, from LL *revivere*, 'to live again': 'Besides, it [*Richard III*] had been revived only eighteen months ago by Donald Wolfit with great popular and critical success' (Olivier, 145).

revolve Used to describe an item of stage *machinery*. *Revolve* is sometimes used to refer to a turntable or is alternatively used as an abbreviation of *revolving stage*. 'A revolve which regularly eclipses [the actor] from the view of the audience elevates clever-dick technology over feeling and even sense' (*Plays and Players*, October 1990). A revolving stage is one equipped with a turntable, operated either electronically or, as was formerly always the case, by winch or castors, allowing two or more sets to be permanently constructed and quickly exchanged, or, when turned in mid-scene, as in the quotation above, allowing the set as well as the actor to move, thus opening up potentially interesting changes of perspective. The most advanced revolve in Britain is in the Olivier auditorium at the National Theatre. The term is clearly descriptive, from ME verb, from L. *re(volvere)*, 'to roll'. Although the Japanese had revolving stages in C18, the first British example was constructed at the London Coliseum in 1904.

Revox *Revox* is the brand name (compare *Leko*, *Tannoy*) of a reel-to-reel tape recorder commonly used by theatre *sound* departments. However, Revox is to tape recorders what Hoover is to vacuum cleaners, the term frequently being employed even when machines of a different make are in use.

revue 'By the time the war started in 1914, music-hall was already under threat from a new style of presentation called "Revue"' (Wilmut, 17). The word was taken directly from the French, where the theatrical usage had developed from the word for military inspection, from the same root as English *review*. 'In style, [*revue*] tended to be something between music-hall and the spectacular musical comedies of the period (in which the costumes and scenery were often more impressive than the music); the artists appeared throughout in different scenes, rather than being confined to their own act, and there was sometimes a pretence of a plot' (Wilmut, 17). Later revues diversified, some following the tendency of the *intimate revues* developed in the 1940s, emphasising sophistication or satire or wit (see *footlights*), others following the direction that was to culminate in the Raymond Revuebar. As Paul Raymond, the impresario, describes his earlier touring efforts, 'I was the first person to do one where the whole show was built as a nude revue, and all my revues did very well and packed the theatres out...' (quoted in Wilmut, 215). The difference between Raymond's revues and the famous *non-stop revues* such as those at the Windmill Theatre with its motto 'we never close', was at the latter the girls were forced by the *Lord Chamberlain* to stand in frozen *tableaux*: 'By not having any sketches in the show, but just a series of speciality acts... I didn't come under the jurisdiction of the Lord Chamberlain' (ibid.).

rhubarb   Traditionally, when the offstage noise of a crowd was called for, or a hum of background conversation, the actors in the wings would congregate and, in the words of Partridge, 'intone the sonorous word "rhubarb".' This habit is said to date back at least to the time of Charles Kean's tenancy of the Princess Theatre (1850-59), its earliest attestation being *c*.1852. Any such nonsensical muttering can now be referred as *rhubarbing*. 'I dislike intensely fake stage disapproval – gasps of the spectators, etc. So we emphasised and almost choreographed the reaction as extra huge. An orchestration of mass disapproval... This went on during the repartee with the alternate sighs of relief and shock and was exceedingly funny. So, by orchestrating them, we absolved them of the need of fake "rhubarbing" which was so familiar to me in rep.' (Berkoff, 122).

ride a laugh   See *laugh*.

rig   One of the many *nautical* loan words used in technical aspects of theatre. *To rig* is a ME verb, like much nautical language probably of Scandinavian origin: there is, for example, the Norwegian *rigga*, 'bind or tie up', which fits nicely with the English sense, 'to furnish a ship with all the necessary ropes, spars etc, for sailing'. Thus, in theatre, *to rig* is to set up all the necessary *lines*, *bars* etc. for both scenery and lighting in readiness for running a show. The result of this activity is the *rigging*, often itself abbreviated to the *rig*. In the upper levels of the stage space is the *rigging loft*, the same term which used for the gallery in a dockyard from which rigging is fixed; its alternative name, *grid-iron*, is the term for the frame of parallel beams which supports a ship in dock. To this are attached the ropes or *rigging lines*.

right   A stage direction, often abbreviated in texts to *R.*, designating the right hand of the stage from the actor's point of view, the left to the audience. Also found in combinations such as *up right*, *down right* etc., these also in varying forms of abbreviation: 'The ceiling slopes down quite sharply from L. to R. Down R. are two small low windows... Up R. is a double bed...' (1956, Osborne, *Look Back in Anger*, stage directions for Act I).

ring   A verb which, in a range of largely obsolete phrases such as *ring down/up the curtain* and *ring in the band* recalls the former habit of using a bell to signal *cue-calls* to *flymen*, *musicians* etc. See *prompt*.

The *ring* is also an abbreviation of *circus* ring, as a performance space the unintentional model for many of today's *theatres-in-the-round*. This space may also be seen as a direct though less grandiose version of the *arenas* used in Ancient Rome for gladiatorial displays etc. Normally, a circus ring is 42 feet in diameter, a size

established by the ex-soldier Philip Astley in lC18 in his design
of Astley's Amphitheatre in London, chosen because of his pre-
dilection for *equestrian acts*: it has remained standard because,
apparently, it is the ideal size to allow riders to exploit the effects
of centrifugal force to best advantage in performance.

The *ringmaster*, the *master of ceremonies* of the ring, is traditionally dressed in red coat and top hat, a fashion not developed until
eC19, in imitation of masters of the hunt.

rise   *The rise* is an abbreviation of *curtain rise*, sometimes also
known as *the rising*, a phrase identical in construction and meaning
to *curtain up* (or *the up*). A simple descriptive term in use since
at least the C19 for the *opening* of a performance.

riser   An occasional term for a wide stage *platform*, generally used
for one of larger than average size. However, the word is also
encountered in a development of its Standard English usage as
'the vertical backing of a step' meaning 'a flight of stairs', that
sense of *riser* probably also accounting for its use as 'platform';
it is also by transference from these that a third sense has developed: the step portion of a *spotlight lens*.

rise-and-sink   A descriptive term for a means of changing the
scenery at the rear of a set, because of its speed and *trompe l'oeil*
effect frequently used in *transformation scenes* in pantomime: the
upper half of the scene is swiftly raised into the *flies* whilst the
lower half is dropped into the *cellar*.

rites and **rituals**   Two theories contend to explain the origins of
drama and *theatre* – one stresses the importance of games and
sport, the other, to my mind stronger theory, stresses the importance of *rites* and *rituals*. 'In the history of ritual, repetitive themes
insist on their assertion. Archaic rites suggest a strong link
between vegetation and sexuality, the harvest and birth. Life had
a precarious hold on the surface of a stony world: to strengthen
what sustained it meant performing ceremonies of invocation,
and if they succeeded, of joyful celebration' (Harwood, 21). The
reason for mentioning these origins here is to stress the importance
of this kind of thinking on many current, *anti-naturalistic* and
highly influential theatre *practitioners* whose theories of the importance of ritual affect their approach even to the classics. *Rites* and
rituals inform the language and the approach to language of many
people in theatre today: 'The strength and the miracle of Shakespearian texts lie in the fact that they present man simultaneously
in all his aspects . . . Because deep roots are sunk beneath the everyday, poetic language and the ritualistic use of rhythm show us
those aspects of life which are not visible on the surface' (Brook,
57).

roadie   Since the early 1950s, the road managers and members of the road crew of pop (and later rock) stars have been referred to as *roadies*, and this term has been transferred to technical theatre workers *on the road*. 'The roadies are the hired mercenaries of the music business, a tough and self-sufficient group of men whose duties are to care for the equipment, get it arranged and set up for concerts, and to anticipate the wishes of their masters' (*Daily Telegraph Magazine*, 17 November 1972, quoted in Beale).

road show, company   A touring *show* or *company*. See also *on the road*.

rodomontade   An interesting term in so far as its general if infrequent English usage has outlived its theatrical significance and its meaning in its language of origin. *Rodomontade*, used as noun, verb and adjective, is applied to characters, actions and situations which are characterised by bragging and what would now be called 'big talk'. The word is taken from the name of a character in the *Orlando* epics, itself based on the now-obsolete Italian word *rodomontada*. 'Ophelia here giggles at the absurd rodomontade of his [Hamlet's] speech – his evasiveness and his absurd euphemism for what she and Hamlet have probably been having twice daily for months – and that is a good wholesome screw' (Berkoff, 21).

role   Also found in the French form, *rôle*, an actor's *part*. 'The Euangelist from God, hath received such a rowle, it being inioyned him, to prepare the way of the Lord' (1606, Gardiner, *A booke of angling or fishing*). Oddly, despite the attestation above, *role*, unlike other French words adopted by theatre in lC16-eC17, has not been anglicised other than by the loss of its circumflex. It is ideal for anglicisation, too, coming from *rôle* meaning 'a roll of parchment' on which an actor's *part* would have been written. The probable explanation is that until C20 the word was hardly ever used in a theatrical context, its rare occurrences being figurative, as in the attestation above.

It is now found much more frequently, especially in phrases like *leading role*, from Fr. *premier rôle, in the role of, staying in role* etc. It is also found in *role-play*, a technique used in *drama therapy* and educational drama, whereby an individual plays out a familiar or unfamiliar social role in a familiar or unfamiliar situation and is encouraged by a teacher, counsellor, therapist etc. to explore their experiences in that role under controlled circumstances.

roll   From OF *rol(l)er, rouler*, via Romanic from L. *rotulus*, a diminutive of *rota*, 'wheel', the verb *to roll* and associated phrases have a range of technical senses in theatre. In its pure form it means 'to clew': to hoist up a cloth from the audience's view by means of a metal device called a 'clew'. *Roll ceilings* and *roll curtains (roll drops)* are attached to a *batten* (or *roller*) around which they roll themselves when drawn across or up respectively, hence the term *roll drop hooks*, which are attached to them. A canvas flap on a piece of scenery, through which an actor can roll to make a surprise or clandestine entrance is, descriptively, known as a *roll(-)out*. Stage castors are known as *rollers*. The most generally-known use of the word is in the phrase *rolling 'em in the aisles* – making an audience laugh uncontrollably.

romantic comedy, actor etc *Romantic comedy* was a term applied retrospectively in C19 to those Shakespearian and Elizabethan plays which concern themselves with an amorous liaison which, though fraught with initial difficulties, ends happily. It is now applied to any light play whose subject matter is love. As an adjective, however, the history of *romantic* is complex. Its first usages in C17 qualified things which had the qualities of the literary genre, *romance* – 'Your friend Mr. Boyle...was saying that he had thoughts of making a short Romantick story,' (1665, *Occasional Reflections*) – or things which were fictitious to the point of incredibility: 'These things are almost romantique, and yet true' (Pepys, *Diary*, 10 March 1667). Diverse meanings related to sentiment, romantic love, crass sentimentality, imaginative appeal and, finally the concepts which distinguish a Romantic from a Classical approach to art, music and literature all developed during the course of the C18. As a result, the word can now be used in a range of ways which can only be gleaned from context.

rope-house A descriptive term for a *house* (or theatre) using *ropes* which were hauled manually. The term must have been devised after the large-scale introduction of the *counter-weight system* in the early 1800s to distinguish the two styles of scenic management. See also *hemp house*.

rostrum In theatre, used to describe a platform which can be placed in a performance space to give added elevation to an area of the stage. (The plural is *rostra*, though inevitably, *rostrums* is often heard.) *Rostrum* has an unlikely but fascinating history: its original L. sense is 'beak', (from *rodere ros-*, 'to gnaw'); by transference it came to be applied to the aggressively-shaped, beak-like prow of a warship. After the Romans seized ships from the Antiates in 338 BC, their prows were used as celebratory decorations on the stand for public speakers in the Forum in Rome, (also giving their name to that area of the Forum). By a further transference which appears to have occurred in mC18, 'rostrum' began to be used for any platform constructed for public speaking: 'It is built of brick...with a Steeple and Galleries, in which are three rostra for public Orations, Disputations &c.' (1766, OED). Some time later – certainly by the eC19 – it was often applied, as it is in the theatre, to temporary or improvised elevations: 'Mr. Tappertit mounted on an empty cask which stood by way of rostrum in the room' (1840, Dickens, *Barnaby Rudge*).

routine   With this word, from *music hall* and *variety*, the Standard English sense of 'a regular course of procedure' is applied to performance, giving the meaning of 'a set sequence': an *act*. In comedy, therefore, it equates to the ordering of a comic's *material* and *business*: 'In a way, doing a routine on a Variety stage which consisted simply of jokes without much of a linking theme took more skill and nerve than doing the older kind of routine – after all, a comedian was only as good as his last gag' (Wilmut, 118). In dance, a *routine* is the fixed *choreography* which accompanies a *number*, in the following usage transferred, as is the common pattern with variety terms, to another genre of performance: 'Sikulu is a celebration of Black South Africa with enchanting voice harmonies and powerful routines influenced by a range of tribal dances' (*The Stage*, 24 April 1992).

row   The standard use of row as 'a line of persons or things', (ME, from OE *rāw*), is found in phrases such as the *front row* (of the auditorium), but there is a more specialised usage of *row* as an abbreviation of *ground row*, *sea row* etc., the long, low *flats* positioned *upstage* in front of the *backcloth*.

Royal Court   The *Royal Court Theatre* in Sloane Square, London is included in this book because, from 1950s onwards – and, in addition, since 1969 in its converted attic Theatre Upstairs – it has been responsible for encouraging new work by a range of talented young writers, so that its name is synonymous with in English theatre circles with innovative playwrights. Those whose early careers have been given impetus by the Royal Court include John Osborne, John Arden, Edward Bond, David Storey, Christopher Hampton, Timberlake Wertenbaker and Jim Cartwright.

royalties   The sum a playwright, author (or other *copyright* owner) receives on the performance or publication of a play, or adaptation of a novel, story etc. I lean across to one of my research books and copy out the *Caution*: 'All material in this book, whether text or illustration, is protected by copyright and no reproduction in any form whatsoever is permissible without the consent of the copyright holders. All enquiries should be directed in the first instance to . . .' – I choose to quote no further as this is a standard form of words and I wish to incur no further royalty payments for this quotation. The term *royalty* (ME, from OF *roialté*, from the adjective *roial*, from L. *regalis*, 'of or pertaining to a king or ruler') was transferred from the office of kingship to a right granted by the king to an individual or corporation in eC16 and from there to an author's rights in lC19, from a slightly earlier usage 'a payment made to a landowner for the privilege of working his land'.

RSC The abbreviation of Royal Shakespeare Company. The *RSC*, a name assumed under reorganisation by the company playing at the Shakespeare Memorial Theatre, Stratford in 1960, was the heir to proposals for a national Shakespeare theatre in the dramatist's twon of birth, originally mooted as early as C18. The first theatre to be built in Stratford with the purpose of facilitating such an enterprise opened in 1879 (although it had to be replaced in 1932 due to a fire). The present company's aims, first stated in the first decade of C20 by the director of the theatre at that time and still paid lip-service to today, were 'to train a company, every member of which would be an essential part of a homogenous whole, consecrated to the practice of the dramatic arts and especially to the presentation of the works of Shakespeare' (1909. F.R. Benson). To this end, the company is organised around a group of 'associates', including actors, directors, designers etc.

The present company, alongside the *National* Theatre one of the two most prestigious in Britain, is based in Stratford (where there are three available venues) and the Barbican in London (where there are two). It has toured nationally and internationally since 1939. Although it has gone through periods of innovation and retrenchment, its world-wide profile remains high. The associations of the name depend on attitude, ranging from 'epitomising the best in English classical theatre' to 'oversubsidised and unadventurous'.

run From the Standard English verb and noun, *run* has a range of theatrical meanings.

To run a show, as in the phrase *it ran for six years*, refers to keeping a show in production, hence phrases such as *out-of-town run*, a *provincial* tour. This is a C19 term according to OED: 'Having, on its first appearance, run, in the theatrical term, near thirty nights' (1808, Mrs Inchbald, *The British Theatre*).

In 'I cut it. And it runs quite well...' (Berkoff, 47), the verb refers to the performance flow of a speech or show, (see *run-through*, which can also be abbreviated to *run*), hence *running time*, the length of time a particular scene or show runs on the night, the duration of its performance. I suspect that this and the following usage, if not the previous one too, are from a *nautical* sense of 'run', 'to sail swiftly or easily' (a term which dates from C11): 'As in a full sea, I hoyse up sayles, and run at large' (1649,

S.J. Camus, tr. Du Verger, *Admirable events selected out of his foure bookes, and his morall relations*).

In *to run a board* or to run any other piece of technical equipment, the verb is used with the Standard English sense 'to operate', except in the phrase *to run a flat*, where it refers to the action of sliding the object across the stage floor, or, more professionally: 'A flat is moved or "run" by holding the forward stile, i.e. the stile facing the direction in which the flat is to be moved, with one hand at the toggle and gripping the stile about three feet higher with the other hand. The flat is lifted from the stage and, by balancing it, can be moved easily' (Baker, 333). It does not sound particularly easy to me.

In addition, 'to run' is used to refer to things which move along a track or groove. Hence, a *running tab*, often abbreviated familiarly to *runner*, is a curtain which moves horizontally along a track, rather than one which raised or lowered. (However, there are alternative meanings of *runner*: it can be used for any matting or other material laid down in the *wings* to deaden *offstage* noise, or for the grooves in a *colour* frame which allow the *gels* to be inserted.)

The phrase *to run away with the show* is used of a performer who succeeds beyond expectations in a given performance, 'run away' here being used synonymously with *steal* as in 'stealing the scene' etc.

A *run-down* (or *run down*) is used for a pause or complete halt resulting from an actor *blanking*, or forgetting his lines, probably descriptive of the slowing down of the performance pace, just as the workings of a clock or any other machine run down before they stop.

Rundhorizont   The German term for *cyclorama*: 'curved horizon'. It is only rarely used in English, generally synonymously with *cyc.*, though Bowman and Ball suggest that it refers specifically to 'a cyclorama which is semicircular'.

run-through   From the sense of *run* referring to the flow of a performance, a *run-through* – often abbreviated to *a run* – is a rehearsal which is allowed to continue uninterrupted by comments from the director, stage manager etc. Discussing Gielgud's direction of *Twelfth Night* at Stratford in 1954, Olivier (p.211) comments 'at the risk of hurting his feelings I asked him to leave the company at the point we had got to and let us go over and over it for a couple of days until we knew the moves well enough to do a run-through without a stop; then at least he himself would be able to see his own mistakes if there were any...' See also *stagger-through*, *walk-through*.

runway A *cat-walk*, or narrow projection of the stage across the *orchestra* or even further out into the *auditorium*. *Runway* is a C19 American term which, according to OED, appears to have first been used for a wild animal track: 'We passed the runway where the deer and pack had passed' (1873, *Forest and Stream*). The transference of meaning would appear to follow this route: it is next applied to pathways constructed for factory-farmed animals – 'The incubators, hatching houses and runways have a capacity to keep 5,000 eggs in process of hatching all the time,' (1886, *Pall Mall Gazette*) – and so to theatre: 'If there is a "runway", which is an elevation like the rocky ascent in the second act of *Die Walküre*..., it is "built" by the stage-carpenters' (1888, *Scribner's Magazine*). Whilst this 'runway' is still not the C20 use of the term, we have arrived in the right building and only need one more slight transference of sense to arrive at the 'cat-walk'.

S **andbag** A canvas bag filled with sand used as a counter-weight for hanging scenery, *flying* lines etc. The word has been in general usage since lC16 but is first cited as 'ballast' (with reference to balloons) in OED in eC19; however, the theatrical use has a possible nautical origin: '*Sand-bags*, small square cushions made of canvas and painted, for boats' ballast' (1867, Smyth, *Sailors' Word-book*).

satire A literary genre which presents a critical or derogatory view of persons, groups of persons, issues etc. by holding its subjects up to ridicule. The earliest celebrated dramatic *satirist* is Aristophanes and his successors in the English theatre include Henry Fielding and John Gay. *Satire* is derived from L. *satira* (also found as *satura*), first applied to discursive verse compositions which dealt with a range of topics. This term was probably derived from *lanx satura*, 'a full dish', used for a meal put together from a wide variety of ingredients. (For another culinary source for a theatrical genre see *farce*.) The first OED attestation is from 1509 – 'Therefore in this satyre suche wyll I repreue' (Barclay, *Shyp of Folys*) – includes a spelling which points to the common misconception that the term derives from the *satyr-play*.

saturation rig A lighting *rig* with no spare capacity, all lanterns being used to their maximum potential. *Saturation* has been used in similar contexts, derived from the chemical state of saturation, since lC17.

satyr-plays *Burlesque* entertainments which followed the presentation of a *tragedy* in the Athenian Festival of *Dionysus*, generally written by the same author as the tragedy. From the remaining fragments and from pictorial evidence, they can be deemed worthy of X-rating. *Satyrs* were mythological creatures, half-man, half-beast, associated with the rites of the god, Dionysus (also known as Bromius and Bacchus). They were generally represented by the Greeks as having a horse's ears and tail, though later Roman depictions of them as goat-like link more graphically with the *Aristotelean* suggestion that the origins of tragedy (literally 'goat-song') are linked with the *satyr-play*. 'Satyr' is first used in English in C14, rapidly becoming erroneously confused with *satire*; it also carries with it associations of priapic lust and wantonness.

234

save your lights   An instruction traditionally given to the electrician, meaning 'switch off your lights'. Clearly, it derives from a time before electrical lighting, when whatever source of light was being used – e.g. tallow, *limelight* etc. – was expensive and worth conserving.

scatter   A lighting term – used as either a noun or verb – referring to light which *spills* outside the main beam of a *spotlight*.

scenario   '[A]n Italian term, meaning a sketch of the scenes and main points of an opera libretto, drawn up and settled preliminary to filling in the detail' (1883, Grove, *Dictionary of Music*). It does not appear to have been used in English until C19. It is particularly worthy of note because it has become a vogue word in lC20, very loosely used to mean 'series of events', as a synonym for that equally vague term 'situation', or even for 'state of affairs' or 'set of conditions': 'in theatre... each performer learns his role and respects it down to the last word. But this scenario does not prevent him from improvising when the event occurs' (Brook, 8).

scene   In C5AD Athens, the *skēnē* was the equivalent of the Elizabethan *tiring-house*: a wooden building behind the *orkhēstra* (or open playing-area), probably about four metres high and twelve metres long, with a large double door. It housed the actors' dressing-room, but the exterior was also decorated with designs representing palaces, forests etc., probably on painted backdrops. Significant to its wide range of meanings in English is the fact that the original Greek word (and Latin *scena*) could be used to signify either the building, the acting space or its decoration.

　　Arriving in English via Fr. *scène*, most of the current theatrical senses of the word appeared during the great burgeoning of the English professional theatre in m-lC16. The ancient sense of decorative devices to create the illusion of a specific place – later *scenery* – can be deduced to have been in use as early as 1540 from Palsgrave's use (in the Prologue to his *Comedye of Acolastus*) of the now obsolete *scenyshe* in the phrase 'scenyshe apparaylynge' – 'the settying forth or trymming of our scenes, that is to saye our places appoynted for our players to come forth of).' The term is used more clearly by Jonson in *The Masque of Blackness* (1605): 'First, for the Scene, was drawn a Landtschap, consisting of small woods... which falling, an artificiall sea was seene to shoot forth.'

　　Also in mC16, the term is employed for the sub-division of an act, as seen in Heywood's *Proverbs & Epigrams* (1562): 'In volewmes full or flat,/There is no chapter, nor no seane,/That thou appliest like that.' This separation of a *piece* into scenes is referred to as *scene division*.

　　The earliest figurative usage of the term is found as early as

1577: 'His sean is played, you folowe on the act' (Whetstone, *A remembraunce of the wel imployed life of G. Gaskoigne*). All the major theatrical usages of the term have since passed into general usage, perhaps the most famous being *behind the scenes*.

In the 1580s and 1590s, two other senses are shown to be current: those of 'setting' – 'Well doon, Balthazar, hang up the Title: Our scene is Rhodes' (1592, Kyd, *Spanish Tragedy*) – and 'stage performance or action' – 'A Kingdome for a Stage, Princes to Act,/And Monarchs to behold the swelling Scene' (Shakespeare, *Henry V*, Prologue). Later C17 theatrical developments of the word have not lasted: the term was once used for both 'dramatic writing' and for 'the theatrical world' (compare *drama* and *theatre*).

Beale charts the major C20 development of *scene*, citing an article entitled *Basic Beatnik: A Square's Guide to Hip Talk* (*The Daily Colonist*, 16 April 1959), where 'scene' is defined as 'something that's happening or the place where it's happening – (the verb here relating to the noun *happening*). This sense developed in American jazz and drug culture in e-mC20, reaching Britain by the 1950s and has spread outwards to refer to any enclosed or esoteric culture or world, as in *the literary scene* or *the political scene*.

scene bay, scene dock (also abbreviated to **dock**) Alternative names, both of *nautical* origin, referring to the place in a theatre where *scenery* is stored: 'Once in the theatre, his first proceeding is to hide himself in the scene dock, where nobody can find him' (Tom Robertson in an 1850's article entitled 'The Stage Carpenter', from *The Illustrated Times*, [quoted in Nagler, 496]). Another term for the dock is the *scene room*, mentioned in the Covent Garden Inventory (1743).

scene change '[Judi Dench] hated sloppiness in production or acting, and the actors and stage managers rallied, with everyone in the eighteen-strong team making themselves available for scene changes' (Branagh, 206): a self-explanatory *change of scene* or *scenery* during a performance, (frequently abbreviated to *change*), which can also be referred to (especially in the United States) as a *scene shift*, hence the term *scene-shifter*, frequently used of *stagehands*.

scene cloth An alternative term for either a painted *curtain* or a *backcloth/backdrop*. By contrast, a *scene curtain* is also a curtain used to hide a *scene change* from the audience's view.

scene designer See *design*.

scene painter '[U]sually one of the pleasantest men in the theatre' according to Tom Robertson (1850's article in *Illustrated Times*, [quoted Nagler, 495]), the *scene painter's* job is self-explanatory and obviously dates back to ancient theatre (see *scene*). 'In these present days of scenic display, when even no poor ghost [*sic*] can walk undisturbed by scientific satellites, lime-lights, mirrors, and the like, the Scene-painter is a far more important person in the theatre than the Tragedian' (ibid). See also *paint shop*.

scene plot   Diagrams showing both the physical arrangement of *scenes* in a show and the order in which they are *set*. See *plot* (and compare *lighting plot*).

scene-rat   No longer current, this term from the lC19 for a *super-numerary*, particularly one employed in *pantomime*, musical theatre etc., seems to me worth quoting as one of the rare examples of cruelty inherent in a theatrical term. (Compare *matinée dog*.)

scenery   The first OED attestation of *scenery* in its modern theatrical sense of 'stage décor' is in lC18: 'It has been said that the scenery only, which has been painted on purpose for *The Maid of the Oaks*, cost 1500l' (1774, *London Magazine*). However, it appears to be a variation developed from the adjective *scenary*, used in 1730s and included in Johnson's dictionary with both the broader senses of *scenic* and *theatrical*. 'Scenery' gained its much more specific nominal sense during mC18. The word is now found frequently in general usage with the sense of 'picturesque natural landscape', a sense which appears to have developed alongside the theatrical – 'He looks abroad into the varied field/Of Nature and. . ./Calls the delightful scen'ry all his own./His are the mountains and the vallies his' (1784, Cowper, *The Task*) – perhaps demonstrating the theatricality of early Romantic tendencies. From this sense, the further common meaning of 'physical appearance of an area' developed.

scene shifter   'It was impossible to see what was going on and there was a terrible noise from the scene shifters during the changes.' (Geilgud, 88). This descriptive term for a *stagehand* has tended to be used with slightly disparaging overtones since its first OED theatrical attestation in eC18, possibly due to an echo of the C16 sense of *shifter* – 'idle, thriftless fellow' – from which 'shifty' derives, or because the job is one of the most menial, though vital, in the theatre. 'Two or three shifters of scenes with the two candle-snuffers, make up a compleat body of Guards upon the English stage' (1711, Addison, *Spectator No. 42*).

scene-stealer   The phrase *to steal the scene* and the resultant *scene-stealer*, are often used unflatteringly, but not always: 'Talking of scene-stealers brings us to the delectable Carole Steward' (*The Stage*, 29 March 1991). This is true also in common parlance where both the above terms are current. The verb 'to steal', which can additionally denote *lifting* (plagiarism) – 'This is an audacious steal from *In a Gondola*' (1890, *Saturday Review*, cited in Partridge) – is used in 'scene-stealer' for a performer or performance which attracts special attention, the positive aspect of the term, but, conversely, also deflects attention, sometimes unfairly, from others on stage.

scenic   Now used most commonly in phrases such as *scenic design* and *scenic background*, this adjective, with the sense of 'of or belonging to scenery or stage effects', is prefigured by the use of *scenyshe* (1540, Palsgrave, *Prologue to Acolastus*) mentioned under *scene*. The modern sense does not appear to have been used, however, until mC19: 'It is the great scenic triumph of the play, and a burst of grand music appropriately heralds its exhibition to the audience' (1868, Whyte Melville, *White Rose*). Previous usages were all with senses such as 'of or belonging to the stage, dramatic, theatrical etc.', (also the sense of the then common form, *scenical*), as in this instance of a poetic eulogy by H. Holland printed in the First Folio of Shakespeare's plays (1623): 'Upon the Lines and Life of the Famous Scenick Poet, Master William Shakespeare'.

sciopticon   A means of *projection* developed in C19, used particularly to produce scenic effects such as cloud movements and flickering fire. A compound formed from Gk for 'shadow' and 'of or pertaining vision', the adjective *scioptic* is found in C18 defined as 'belonging to an instrument found in the camera obscura' (OED, 1775). A *sciopticon*, as 'a magic lantern adapted for the exhibition of photographed objects', is advertised for sale in *Nature* in 1879.

scissor cross or **move**   A *cross* is a *stage direction* indicating a movement (or *move*) of an actor from one side of the stage to the other. *Scissor cross* is a descriptive stage direction, indicating that two actors should cross simultaneously in opposite directions. Sometimes it indicates that each should take up the position vacated by the other.

scissor stage   A descriptive term for an arrangement of two *boat trucks* pivoted *downstage* in such a way that they can be swung on or off stage on their castors as required.

score   This term is now often used in the loosest of ways to refer to the music in a musical show, whereas its initial sense (it is first attested in OED in 1701) was quite specific, as later defined by Charles Avison in *An essay on musical expression*, (1752): 'Music is said to be in Score, when all the Parts are distinctly wrote and set under each other, so that the eye, at one view, may take in all the various contrivances of the Composer.' It derives ultimately from the verb *to score*, 'to cut a notch or a line'; the nominal sense of 'a drawn or written line' had developed by eC16.

the Scottish play   *Macbeth* is considered to be an unlucky piece to the extent that it has become traditional amongst the more superstitious members of the acting profession to refer to it as *that play, the unmentionable*, or, most popularly, *the Scottish play*. It is also considered bad luck to quote from it or use any elements of its set, costume etc. in any other production. There are several suggested sources for this tradition. One dates it back to the play's *première* in 1605 or 1606 (an uncertainty that already gives cause for doubt), when Hal Berridge, the boy actor playing Lady Macbeth, is said to have died in the *tiring-house*. Another suggestion is that C19 companies who were in financial difficulties would stage the play, as it was good *box office*; when they subsequently went bust for the same reasons that caused them to mount it, the play took the blame.

scrim   The origin of this word is obscure, but it appears to have been first used in lC18 to denote a thin canvas. This can be used theatrically, as it is in upholstery etc., as backing material or, particularly in America, where the term is sometimes used synonymously but inaccurately with the thinner *gauze*, as a *drop*. A *scrim* can thus be hung across the stage to create a dreamlike effect of mist or haze. The verb *to scrim* can be used in America for employing such a drop; in Britain it means to attach the material to scenery, props etc., often to provide a better surface for painting.

script   A term for the text of a play which, like *text* itself, can be used either for the words of a play or the book which contains them. 'There's only one person who wrote more on her script than me and that was Edith Evans' (Patience Collier, interviewed in Barkworth, 211). It might be supposed that *script* is derived from L. *scriptum*, the past participle of *scribere*, 'to write', used for a written document as early as eC14, but the theatrical usage appears, from the form of its first OED attestations, as recent as lC19, to be an abbreviation of *manuscript*: 'Hearing of the success of the play from a friend, Macready wrote asking to see the 'script' (1897, *Westminster Gazette*), and 'Mrs. Campbell has had the 'script of *"Tess"* on her hands for quite a while' (1900, *ibid*). This handwritten source of the term is backed up by a reference in John Aye's *Humour in the Theatre* (1932-3): 'Sir Frank Benson told how, in his early days, certain actors never studied any parts but their own, and that only from mysterious bits of paper called "scrip". The sight of a book was anathema to them. "Text, text? I've never heard of it," they would say. "What the hell is text? All I want, laddie, is first the bizness, then the cues...".' *Unscripted*, as in *unscripted comments* for 'impromptu remarks' is particularly common in the media.

scruto   A *trap*-door in the stage floor or a secret, curtained opening in the walls of a set, through which surprise exits and entrances can be made. It is usually constructed of strips of wood or, originally, whalebone, attached to *canvas*. The origin of the term is uncertain although it appears to be C19: 'The working of various mysterious engines called "sloats" and "scruto-pieces"' (1853, *Punch*).

sea row   See *groundrow*.

season   '[Thomas Weston's] debts increased, and before even the summer season was over he could never show his head in public unless on a Sunday' (1831, Galt, *Lives of the Players*) *Season* is used theatrically to denote a series of productions designed to run over a predetermined period. The *summer season* in *variety*, for example, traditionally referred to mid-July to early September, when the majority of British holiday-makers would be making their way to the coastal resorts where such seasons flourished. The term, developed obviously from the seasons of the year, has been used in a variety of businesses and pastimes for a period of peak activity since lC17, possibly influenced by legal seasons, a term in use from C14. 'He bound himself to give them two plays every season' (1740, Cibber, *Apology*).

second   A *second* is a now largely-defunct term from the days of *stock* and *rep*, used to refer to the *second man* or *woman*, performers who habitually played roles next in importance to the *principals*. It is still used today in the phrase *second cast*, however, denoting those performers who, in a show with a long *run*, are brought in either to entirely replace the originals, or to give them a much-needed rest.

segue   Originally a musical term – ('it follows' in Italian) – *segue* denotes a piece which flows straight into another without a pause. It has been appropriated in the last two decades by a variety of other presentational arts: in theatre it is used particularly in *lighting* and *sound plots* for a rapid sequence of cues. The BBC Radio 1 disc jockey, Noel Edmonds, was particularly influential in popularising the term in the 1970s when he used it for a sequence of pop records played without interruptions of mindless babble.

sell-out   The verb *to sell out* – 'to dispose of all one's available stock' – came into use in lC18. The noun, a back-formation of the verb, appears to be an eC20 sporting term – 'The interest in McAvoy's fight with Doug Tunero...is so great...the match is a sure sell-out' (1934, *Daily Mail*) – borrowed swiftly by *variety* and then *straight* theatre.

send up   Used both as noun and verb as a colloquial synonym for *parody*, in common usage in theatre for over-the-top *satirisation*:

'So we got on with it and did the right sounds and "sent up" Osric' (Berkoff, 196). Lyell, in *Slang, Phrase and Idiom in Colloquial English* (1931). suggests that it is a public-school term meaning 'to mock', initially transferring into upper- and upper-middle-class speech in eC20; Beale adds that it had become established as 'to burlesque or parody' by the 1950s: 'So you're very fond of me. So why are you always needling me, sending me up, taking the mickey out of me?' (1958, Rattigan, *Variations on a Theme*).

set¹ The verb *to set* is used for the action of building or arranging a set – performing a *set-up* – or simply for placing furniture and props on stage: *setting them*. This usage is of nautical origin, as in the phrase *to set a sail*, 'to hoist a sail', a usage dating back at least to eC17 (though *set up* is used from 1300): 'Set your foresaile' (1627, Captain Smith, *The Seaman's Grammar*). Just as ex-mariners employed in theatre had previously set sails with ropes and *lines* (or had *flown* them), so they now performed the same tasks with *cloths* in the theatre. (Compare *rig*, and contrast *strike*, especially as in *strike a set*). A *set-piece* is a two- or three-dimensional scenery unit which has been set to stand independently on stage, an independently-standing *property* is referred to as a *set prop*.

set² 'When I begin to work on a play...I start making a set, destroying it, making it...Then work starts with the actors' (Brook, 3). Now commonly used as a noun denoting the entire arrangement of scenery, furnishings and large props assembled onstage for a production, *set* is probably an abbreviation of *set scene* or *set scenery* (where *set* is used as a past participle of the verb, *set¹*). However, there is also an argument (see below) that points to it being an abbreviation of *stage setting*. Both terms probably contributed to the development of set³.

'Set scene' is defined in OED as 'an apparatus built-up and placed in position upon a theatrical stage before the rise of the curtain; a collection of side scenes, "skies" etc. depending upon one another for a particular effect', the latter point emphasising the importance of *set design* in the overall effect of a piece of theatre. 'Set scene' and 'set scenery' would appear from OED to be relatively late, C19 terms, although the verb *set¹*, from which they derive, suggests the usage might be rather earlier than attested. 'The scenery...was entirely of the nature of what is now termed *set-scenery*, regularly built up by carpenters before the curtain rises, to be taken to pieces again when it falls' (1854, Fairholt, *A Dictionary of Terms in Art*). Since C19, the importance and cost of the *set* in the structuring of the theatrical experience must not be under-emphasised: 'Theatrical speculators now spend such vast sums on the upholstery of their set scenes' (1887, *The Spectator*) *Set* is also found in the phrases *set design*, *set model*, and *to dress* a set.

set³ In phrases such as *set-piece* and *set speech*, the past participle of the verb *set* is used differently from *set¹*. A *set-piece* (contrast 'set-piece' under *set¹*) refers to a formulaic performance situation decided on in advance which gives an opportunity to the performer to demonstrate certain characteristic skills. A *set speech* is one carefully prepared in advance, possibly because it has been requested for an *audition*, or because it is one of those great, classy monologues of the theatre, the performance of which is used as a yardstick of an actor's ability: in classical theatre, one of Hamlet's *soliloquies*, for example.

setting Arguably a contributory factor in the development of the term *set²*, *setting*, an abbreviation of the phrase *stage setting*, appears to be a C19 coining, not directly related to the precise theatrical sense of the verb *set¹*. Before its theatrical sense developed, 'setting' referred either to the fictional location in which a literary work was set or to the literary framework through which it was expressed. The first theatrical attestation in OED is from *The Manchester Examiner* in 1885: 'The setting of the piece is charming, and it is quite wonderful how much has been made of a little stage.'

shadow play or **show** A descriptive term for *ombres chinoises* or for certain *galanty* shows, performances originating in the Far East, created by the manipulation of two- or three-dimensional characters between a light source and an image screen. Alternative terms include *shadow pantomime, shadow theatre* and *shadow-graph*.

Shakespearian Of or pertaining to William Shakespeare or his works. Unlike other formulations – *Chekhovian* or *Pinteresque*, say – it is extremely difficult to summarise what is implied by this term out of context: the 'infinite variety' of interpretations and attitudes towards the man and his works require a book to themselves. Like many such terms – compare Elizabethan and Jacobean – an eC19 coining.

Shavian Of or pertaining to characteristics of the criticism and the dramatic works of George Bernard Shaw (1856-1950). An Irish journalist-reviewer of music and theatre who later settled in England, under the influence of Ibsen and Fabian socialism, Shaw set about creating a canon of successful plays with characteristic traits which give rise to the adjective *Shavian*. The term suggests work which appeals to the intellect rather than to the emotions and which, despite its eloquence and satirical wit (and occasional lapses into narrative interest and involvement with character) has a tendency to be dominated by the didacticism of the soapbox, as demonstrated by the detailed, sometimes eccentric prefaces to his plays and his prescriptive, novelistic stage directions.

shelf A descriptive term for a *balcony* – frequently the upper circle. Perhaps more common in America (see Bowman and Ball); Beale also cites its use as the *dress circle* in a cinema from 1945 in Australia. Compare *gods, paradise*.

show Now commonly used to signify any form of dramatic presentation or performance, *show* has been used in English since lC13 for the actions of exhibiting, displaying, demonstrating and representing, but, as the adjective *showy* emphasises, it can at times carry hints of ostentation and falseness. It has tended to fall on the illusory side of the divide between appearance and reality: 'But I have that within which passeth show' (1602, Shakespeare, *Hamlet*, I.ii).

The earliest theatrical uses from C16 relate to spectacle and pageant: 'The King would have me present the Princess with some delightful ostentation, or show, or pageant' (*c*.1590, Shakespeare, *Love's Labours Lost*, V.i). This distinction is underlined by Burke in one of his *Letters on proposals for peace with the regicides in France* (1797): 'It is a shew, and a spectacle, not a play, that is exhibited.' The broader, modern usage was clearly developing, though, by mC19: 'It has been my vocation to see shows. First nights of new pieces; private views of picture exhibitions...' (1863, Sala, in *Temple Bar*). 'Show' began to be used for all forms of professional theatrical entertainment – *music hall* and *legit* theatre – from about this time, giving rise to the famous phrase *show business*, originally coined in America. From about 1870, according to Partridge, theatre was known to insiders in London as *the show-box*, a term found earlier in America (see *vaudeville*), and this usage of the term spread rapidly so that in the first years of C20, it was common in all branches of society *to do a show*: to go to the theatre.

The verb *to show*, still used in terms such as *now showing*... is in early use: 'My lord Chamberlens players did show the history of Phedrastus' (1574, ed. Feuillerat, *Documents relating to the office of the revels in the time of Queen Elizabeth*).

Probably the most famous and widespread related phrase is *the show must go on*, referring to the stoical, professional attitude of the *trouper* who goes on stage regardless of interruptions or the vicissitudes of private life. Further colloquial developments of 'show' to mean 'the entire affair, concern, or matter', as in 'he thinks he can run the show', seem to be developments from the idea of a public event involving a group of people.

showbiz   Commonly abbreviated to *the biz*, this originally American contraction of *show business* epitomises the slang of the professional, commercial C20 entertainment industry, encapsulating the interlinking worlds of *vaudeville* and *variety*, *straight theatre*, film, radio and television: '[My neighbours] ran their business empire from the hall payphone which, of course, was my crucial link to the world of showbiz' (Branagh, 87). Beale suggests that term dates from the early 1930s, transferring quickly to Britain and into general usage by 1960 at the latest, along with its adjective, *showbizzy*.

showboat   An eC19 American term, usually for a riverboat on which shows would be performed, immortalised in the musical *Show Boat* by Jerome Kern and Oscar Hammerstein, and made even more famous by the 1936 film of the same, starring Paul Robeson and Irene Dunne, with its *show-stopper*, 'Ol' Man River'. The first recorded showboat dates from 1817. The general intention was to bring theatrical entertainment to pioneer settlements via the great rivers such as the Ohio and Mississippi. The term is now also used by truckers for an eight-wheeled van and, as a verb, for 'to swagger around swankily'.

show-box   By 1870 (see *show*) a colloquial term for the theatre, although used earlier in America (see *vaudeville*). The original *show-boxes*, however, were travelling booths containing such curiosities as *peep-shows* etc.: 'But were you to present me with the Views of the Leasowes, I own I should not put them into my show-box without pain' (1748, Lady Luxborough, *Letter*).

showcase   'Attention singer and bands! . . . a West End Showcase at one of London's Top Nightspots' (Ad. in *The Stage*, 28 March 1991). A *showcase* is a display vehicle for the talents of a given performer or group of performers, sometimes used generally if a performer suits a role but also, as above, as a specific opportunity designed for performers to gain employment: a *talent show* for *agents* etc.

showfolk, show people   Late C19 American and British terms respectively for those who earn a living from a branch of *show business*. Compare *theatre people*.

showgirl   A term used primarily in musicals and variety, dating from lC19-eC20: a female performer who dances or appears in ensemble pieces but who does not act or even sing in the chorus. *Casting* for such roles tends to be based on looks, therefore *showgirl* has risqué overtones and can be used as a euphemism for stripper, or worse. It is the stuff of tabloid headlines, a fact alluded to in the title of Terence Rattigan's 1957 screenplay, *The Prince and the Showgirl*.

showman 'It was the time of Liberace's rhinestone-laden capes. But the journalist who remarked that the showman was "fruit-flavoured" ended up in court' (*Observer*, 3 May 1992). In C18 when the term was coined, as now, a showman was either the proprietor of a show or a performer in one, and from that period onwards the term has carried with it suggestions of exoticism, ostentation and a life on the fringes of the respectable: 'There are constant exhibitions from rope-dancers, mountebanks, jugglers and show-men' (1787, Cutler, from *Life, journals and correspondence* [1888]).

There is a further, British use of *showman*, however, quite at odds with the glamour of the above: a member of the *stage crew* employed to work only during *shows*. Contrast *dayman*.

Showmanship is used to describe the skills and attitudes which make someone a showman, not least among them exhibitionist risk-taking and a desire to be *in the limelight*.

show-stopper An artist, performance, song etc. creating such a great impact on audiences that the applause prevents the continuation of the show for a period of time. Generally used now with reference to songs in musicals, e.g. 'Sit Down, You're Rockin' the Boat' in *Guys and Dolls*.

showy 'There was great heart in the writing, and it read as if Douglas was exorcising some demon. In the process he had written a wonderfully showy part' (Branagh, 111). In general usage, *showy* means 'ostentatious', perhaps even 'self-indulgently ostentatious'; theatrically, as in the quotation above, it means 'highly *theatrical*'. As with all such terms relating to *show*, can one sense a faint whiff of self-indulgence in the *subtext*?

shutter A *lighting* device, most commonly a hinged metal plate, used to trim and direct the *beam* of light from a lantern. *Shutters* are commonly employed in pairs, (see *barn doors*). The term was appropriated with the mass introduction of electric lighting in the 1880s, either from camera shutters, developed in mC19 to control the exposure of photographic film by controlling the opening and closing of the lens aperture, or directly from the origin of that term, the shutters on a window which control the entry of light into a room. Shutter is an occasional alternative to *trap* and *shutters* was the C17 name for pairs of adjustable *flats* which ran in fixed grooves along the side of the *set*.

sight-line (alternatives *sightline* and *sight line*) '[A]lthough we had rough re-blockings in the last week at Birmingham, we were faced with immediate adjustments which dealt with sight-line problems which had been impossible to predict in advance' (Branagh, 212). A *sight-line* is a term borrowed in C20 from

architectural and graphic design for an imaginary line drawn from
the eyes of a viewer to the object viewed: i.e. from any member
of an audience to any point on the performance space. Unimpeded
sightlines should be respected by directors, designers etc. when
considering set design and *blocking*, as the audience's ability to
see the show has some bearing on its enjoyment of it, a minor
practicality often overlooked.

sight-read   The ability of an actor at first sight of a text to deliver
the words not only with mechanical accuracy, but also with sense,
feeling etc., is known as *sight-reading*. 'Do it whenever you feel
like it, and go on with it until you make no mistakes of either
diction or meaning . . . until it feels like talking, not reading: personal and natural' (Barkworth, 103). See *read*.

signpost   'Signpost each word – like a warning' (Berkoff, 99). An
actor's term, akin to *telegraph*. To signpost a word or action is to
point it, to emphasise it to the audience, making them more conscious of it than they would be in the normal course of playing.
Surprisingly, the common noun *signpost* did not develop until
mC19, the verb, meaning 'to provide with signposts' first being
attested in use in the *Daily Mail* in 1923: 'Where the road is not
so good and badly needs signposting.' The figurative use of the
word is a mC20 development.

silence   Like the use of the choreographed pause, one of the
trademarks of the writing of Harold Pinter is his use of *silence*,
marked in his *scripts* as a *stage direction*:

> BETH: I knew there must be a hotel near, where we could get
> some tea.
>
> *Silence*
>
> DUFF: Anyway, luck was on my side for a change. By the time
> I got out of the park the pubs were open.
>
> (1968, Pinter, *Landscape*)

Of course the idea of silence in the theatre is hardly new. The art
of *mime* exploits it, the absence of language emphasising movement, and in English theatre there is the early tradition of the
dumb-show. It is also used to great effect by *circus artistes* to
heighten dramatic tension. Silent characters in very verbal pieces
– Katrin in Brecht's *Mother Courage*, for example – can be used
to great effect. As all actors know, the importance of a role is not
measured in dialogue inches. As Coriolanus greets his wife (II.i):
'My gracious silence, hail!' For an interesting discussion of the
function of silence in C20 literature, see George Steiner's *Language
and Silence* (1967).

simulation   One of the prime techniques used in mC20 *drama
therapy*, *psychodrama*, vocational training, educational drama etc.

is the *simulation*, often grouped together in the phrase *role-play and simulation*. Simulation, used as a learning strategy or as a means of re-orientation, awareness development etc., places non-actors in a circumstance or situation which they encounter in real life, but, importantly, in a controlled environment where responses can be analysed, feedback given etc. Perhaps the difference between the two terms is that simulation focuses on the whole activity and role-play on the individual's role within it. From the verb *to simulate* (from L. *simulare*, from *similis*, 'like'), used since C17 with the senses of 'to counterfeit, feign, or imitate'.

singspiel 'That best and truest form of German Opera, "the singspiel"' (1883, Grove, *Dictionary of Music*). *Singspiel* (from G. *singen*, 'to sing' + *spiel*, 'play') began as a lC18 German genre (related to the English *ballad opera*) in which song and dialogue alternated, but with the music subordinate to the vocal parts, a style which was later to be drawn on heavily by *Brecht*. Despite English versions of German works in C18, the word itself does not appear to have been appropriated for English use until lC19, the quotation from Grove above, being the first OED attestation.

skene See *scene*.

sketch 'The next day being Monday, Ruby, Julian and I had an early start to get to Manchester to join the *Ghost Train* for one of its try-out tours, with our sketch at the beginning as a curtain-raiser' (Olivier, 52). *Sketch* entered English from Dutch (and possibly also German) in m-lC17 as 'a rough drawing' (in which sense it is still used in theatre *design*). It had an amusing variety of spellings from *schytz* through *schetse* to *scetch*, the current anglicisation being settled for by the end of that century. It also came to be used for 'a hasty or brief narrative account' before the end of C17, and it is from this that the sketch (popularised by Dickens' *Sketches by Boz* [1835-6]) developed as a literary genre, often humorous. It is recorded as 'a short play or performance of slight dramatic construction and usually of a light or comic nature' (OED) by mC19, a development which may well have occurred in *music hall*: 'We always did a laughable sketch entitled Billy Button's ride to Brentford' (1861, Mayhew, *London Labour...*). Certainly, the sketch is now well-and-truly associated with *variety* and *revue*, although there was an attempt in lC19 to develop a slightly up-market dramatic presentation of the same name: '"Sketches" – the new name for small or condensed, and in some cases, mutilated stage plays, the acting time of which shall not be more than 40 minutes, and the performers in which shall not be more than six' (1892, *Daily News*).

skin act The costume worn by an animal impersonator in *panto-*

mime or children's play is known as a *skin*, hence *skin act* as a term for artistes specialising in such performances.

skip A large basket or hamper, traditionally used on tour, though still found in theatres; used as a container for *wardrobe, props* etc. A variation of *skep*, first attested in use in English around 1300 and found in variant forms throughout Northern Europe.

skit Used as 'a piece of harmless *parody* or *satire*' since at least the early C19: 'A manuscript with learning fraught/Or some nice, pretty little skit upon the times' (1820, Combe, *The second tour of Doctor Syntax in search of consolation*). The word has a fascinating history which can be traced back through 'a satirical remark' (eC18) to phrases like *skit-brained* (C16) which point to *skit's* far from savoury origins as, to quote OED, 'animal diarrhoea', and (figuratively) 'dirt', from a Scandinavian root related to *shit*. A whiff of this kind can be detected, as it were, in the modern phrase 'having the squitters' (or 'squits').

sky borders or **cloths** Also known descriptively in the C19 as *blues*, these were *borders* and *cloths* fashioned, self-evidently, to represent the sky.

slap A still-current theatrical term for *make-up* which was, according to Hotten's *The Slang Dictionary* (1860) obsolescent in mC19! It is possibly descriptive of the way in which oil- and fat-based make-ups (prior to *greasepaint*) were applied, or it may be a variant of *slop*, 'liquid mud or slush'. See also *slosh or splosh*.

slapstick Originally an American term (coined from a simple combination of words) for the flexible lath paddles used by *vaudeville* and *circus* comedians to make a great racket in their mock fights. The item was figuratively transferred to describe a whole genre of physical comedy – *slap-stick comedy* – alternatively *knockabout*. 'It required all the untiring efforts of an industrious 'slapstick' coterie . . . to keep the enthusiasm up to a respectable degree' (1907, *New York Evening Post*).

sleeper A term which can be used of a production in two ways: firstly, one so dull it induces sleep and secondly, one which becomes or is expected to become a *hit* after a poor initial reception, say on an *out-of-town run*.

slice of life A term taken as a literal translation of Fr. *tranche de vie*, applied in C19 to naturalistic dramas. Compare *cup-and-saucer drama, kitchen sink drama*.

sloat/slote Variant spellings for a now obsolete stage device first mentioned in 1843 – a form of trap consisting of grooved parallel rails used for raising or lowering actors, *groundrows* etc. by winch through a stage *cut*. The term is a variant of *slot*, and is originally found in C14-15 used with reference either to door bolts or other wooden bars and cross-pieces: '[The] barowe-bulles...have slotes of wood put through theym lyke rails' (1523, Fitzherbert, *The Boke of husbandry*).

slosh or **splosh**   The sloppy substance used for *custard pie routines* in *slapstick*. 'Recipe for slosh: Finely grate a stick of shaving soap into a bucket...Mix in just enough water to make a stiff "goo". Use a powerful electric drill on slow speed with an industrial beater or piece of bent metal to whip up the mixture, adding water as required. Add two tablespoonsful of cornflour in water to the mixture and remix at high speed. Colour with *Boots* food colouring for least staining' (1991, Colin Winslow, *Oberon Glossary of Theatrical Terms*).

slow burn   An acting term particularly from comedy, describing the slow build-up of frustration which precedes an explosion of anger. When *signposted* to an audience, it has a great comic effect. The term is in direct contrast to the common expression for short-temperedness, 'having a short fuse', in that it comes from a kind of slow-burning fuse used in dynamiting etc.

SM   The common abbreviation for *stage manager*.

small part   Obvious, but a term which gained strength in *stock* and *rep* from the term *small part player* as in the specialism *small parts and understudies*. Stanislavski's famous rejoinder to this concept is, however, often quoted, not least by those endlessly cast in such roles: 'There are no small parts; only small actors' (1936, *An Actor Prepares*).

smash   'Thus, despite all the predictions, *Richard III* hopped up to roost on the same branch as the others to make a record season of three equal smash hits' (Olivier, 148). An abbreviation of *smash hit*. *Hit* has been used to describe a success since eC19, possibly from a successful sporting stroke, the earliest OED theatrical example dating from 1829: 'Mr. Peel seems to have made a hit as the chief character in Shiel's play' (*Blackwood's Edinburgh Magazine*). The term 'smash hit' is undoubtedly from tennis where a 'smash' is a forceful overhead winning shot, from the verb: 'W. "smashing" a ball into the net, left the game and set in his brother's favour by six games to two' (1882, *Daily Telegraph*). The abbreviation, however, would appear to be eC20. In inimitable style, the Americans also have *smasheroo* for an exceptionally successful show.

sock it to 'em   *To sock it to them* is an American *vaudeville* term which gained widespread currency in Britain in the late 1960s after being used as a *catchphrase* in the imported American television comedy show, *Rowan and Martin's Laugh-In*. It is an exhortation to perform with great verve, the verb *to sock* being used with the sense of *to hit*, which has been Standard English since at least the end of the C17: '*Sock*, to Beat... *I'll sock ye*, I'll drub ye tightly' (*ante* 1700, *A new dictionary of the terms ancient and modern of the canting crew*). Also found adjectivally in the phrase *a sock hit* (see *smash*) and in the more descriptive variant, *a soccoboffo* hit. (For further verbal violence directed at the audience, compare *punchline*.)

soft shoe shuffle An alliterative phrase describing a form of gently rhythmic jazz dance, the antithesis of *tap*, performed by *vaudeville* artists in soft-soled leather shoes.

soliloquy Theatrically, a speech delivered by a character alone on stage (contrast *monologue*), frequently performed directly to the audience. Although Shakespeare was a great employer of this device, he never uses the term in a play and it is a moot point whether he knew it, although he may have since the OED's earliest English attestation of it other than in reference to St Augustine (see below) is from 1604: 'Soliloquie, priuate talke' (R. Cawdrey, *A table alphabeticall of English wordes*). From L. *solus*, 'alone' + *loqui*, 'to speak', the term appears to have been coined by St Augustine in C5 in his book of meditations, *Liber Soliloquiorum*. From the scansion of C17 verse examples, it would appear that the word was originally stressed on the first and third syllables.

solo 'John [Sessions] had already been developing his one-man shows and wanted to do a three minute solo improvisation' (Branagh, 65). Originally a musical term, *solo* is also used nominally or adjectivally in the contexts of dance and theatre, as above, to denote a performance by an individual player. From It. *solo*, (from L. *solus*, 'sole, alone'), the term is found in English in lC17: 'I don't much matter your Sola's or Sonata's, they give me the Spleen' (1695, Congreve, *Love for Love*).

son et lumière Fr. for 'sound and light', this term originated in France in the 1950s to describe elaborate outdoor spectacles held in the evening at places of historical and architectural interest. In a *son et lumière* show, the performers, if indeed there are any, tend to be amateur: bathed in floodlights and drowned out by elaborate pre-recorded sound effects, most commonly they re-enact in pageant a scene or scenes from local history. More recent musical developments – again originating in France, where the climate encourages such things – include Jean-Michel Jarre's laser spectaculars which have been redesigned to tour to venues such as London's docklands.

song and supper rooms The name given to the venues which spread rapidly in London and elsewhere in Britain in lC18-eC19. Developing from C18 prototypes, they offered a *cabaret* of food, drink and comic songs and were the immediate forerunners of *music hall*.

soprano   Directly from It. (from *sopra*, 'above'), *soprano* designates both a quality and range of voice – approximately covering the notes from middle C to those two octaves above it – and a performer, usually a woman or a boy, working within that range. Most commonly a term in music and *musicals*, its use in English dates from eC18: 'We must provide a Soprano man and a Contrealt Woman' (1730, in *Posthumous Letters addressed to Francis and George Colman the Elder, 1721-1820*).

soubrette   A French theatrical term originally applied from mC18 onwards to the *stock* character of the lady's maid, often a *confidante* and frequently a flirtatious intriguer; later applied to actresses specialising in such parts. 'There is a soubrette called the Niccolina' (1753, Walpole, *Letters*). Given the coquettish nature of the character, it is interesting to note its playful origins in the Provençale *soubreto*, from *soubret*, 'coy, reserved' (from *soubra*, 'to set aside'). For further use of French terms for female performers, see *comédienne*, *ingénue*.

sound   A theatrical department which grew with the development of sophisticated recording and playback techniques, replacing the *effects men* (see also *FX*) of earlier times. In the larger theatres today, this department is led by a *sound designer*. See *levels*, *Revox*, *technical/technician* etc.

space   The common theatrical abbreviation of *acting space*, which can be used to refer to the playing area of any type of stage and which, as in the phrase *it's a nice space*, can sometimes apply to performance area and auditorium combined – the entire *venue*. 'Ted drew up a set of plans in three days, virtually redesigning the space as far as was possible' (*Plays and Players*, October 1990). The use of *space* in this specific sense can be traced back at least to the eC18 but, given that this reference from Cibber's *Apology* (1740, quoted in Nagler, 343) refers to events at the end of C17, may well antedate this: 'But when the actors were in Possession of that forwarder Space [the apron], to advance upon, the Voice was then more in the Centre of the House...'

sparks   The common theatrical abbreviation for an electrician. 'Sparks were removing heavy, cumbersome lamps and everyone was talking' (Barkworth, 239). Given the properties of electricity, the origin of the term is not problematic. Beale says that *sparks* was originally a Services' term for 'wireless operator', a usage he dates back to *c.*1916, taking the more general sense of 'electrician' to be an immediate post-World War II development, presumably from the same source. The theatrical usage certainly antedates the latter but I can find no attestations to support my hunch that it also predates the Services' use.

spearbearer/spear-carrier   General actors' terms to describe *supernumerary* or *walk-on* parts – those without dialogue. Olivier quotes Lewis Casson's offer of a job to him in 1924 (p.55): '"All right," he said, "spear-, halberd- and standard-bearer, all the understudies you can undertake without looking ridiculous, and second assistant stage manager...at a salary of £3".' The term is possibly C19 in origin and self-explanatory. It can also be used derogatorily for an unsuccessful actor.

special   A *lighting* term for a lantern placed to create one specific effect in a production such as a *door special* which might come on only when a door is opened etc.

speciality act   Although *speciality* has been used in English since eC15, its use as 'a special area of knowledge or skill' does not appear to have developed until mC19: 'Even men of boundless knowledge...must once have had their speciality, their pet subject' (1858, Kingsley, *Miscellanies*). The term *speciality act* was first used in *music hall* in lC19, from whence it has been passed on into *variety*, to describe an act which demonstrates a particular performance skill less easily-classifiable than *comic*, singer etc. Conjurers and jugglers were sometimes included under this heading as were 'the comedy dancers Wilson, Keppel and Betty – who were perhaps the best speciality act in the business' (Norman Murray, quoted in Wilmut, 82). Other speciality delights included animal acts such as Vic Duncan's Collies, ventriloquists such as Arthur Prince and "Jim". No lesser star than Charlie Chaplin was once a *speciality artist* – a clog-dancer in The Eight Lancashire Lads – before going to Hollywood to become the most famous man in the world.

spectacle   From OF *spectacle*, from L. *spectaculum* (from *spectare*, 'to look'), *spectacle* is first found in English as a specially-prepared public entertainment in C14: 'Hoppynge & daunceynge of tumblers and herlotis, and other spectakils' ([ante] 1340, Richard Rolle of Hampole, *The Psalter*).

'Spectacle', like *show*, often carries with it associations of ostentation and bad taste – 'The Romaynes...were wont to put [elephants and rhinoceroses] together vpon the theater or stage, for a spectacle' (1553, OED) – and in addition, as the use of the adjective *spectacular* evidences – 'They are fond of spectacular magnificence' (1864, *Daily Telegraph*) – something visually imposing, as in '...that, which...was most taking in the *Spectacle*, was the sphere of fire, in the top of all...' (1606, Jonson, *Hymenaei*). *Spectacular* was coined as a noun in lC19 to describe a *showy* spectacle of epic proportions: 'An amphitheatre... in which spectaculars on a grand scale might be produced before a half-million spectators' (1890, *Pall Mall Gazette*).

spectator/spectatory   An observer at a play or an event in real life – thus, theatrically, a member of an audience. *Spectator* is either a direct borrowing of L. *spectator* (from *spectare*, 'to look') or taken indirectly from F. *spectateur*. The latter does not appear in F. until *c*.1540 and OED's earliest English attestation is from 1584: '[He] thought no eyes of sufficient credite in such a matter, but his owne; and therefore came himself to be actor, and spectator' (1584, Sidney, *Arcadia*), the attestation already demonstrating a theatrical use. The C18-C19 coining of *spectatory* for what is now almost universally termed the *auditorium* (see *audience*) leads to interesting speculation as to how much the selection of a particular physical sense for the word denoting the witnesses of a dramatic performance reflects the theatrical priorities of a given period.

speech[1]   The term used to denote a unit of dialogue or group of lines belonging to one actor: 'Speak the speech, I pray you, as I pronounced it to you, trippingly off the tongue' (1600, Shakespeare, *Hamlet*). The OED dates this sense of speech, admittedly outside a dramatic context – 'a certain number of words uttered by a person at one time; *esp* a more or less formal utterance or statement with respect to something' – from C9, and as the *Hamlet* attestation demonstrates, its theatrical usage is early.

speech[2]   In its sense of 'the natural expression of the vocal organs' (OED) *speech* has been used in English since at least C8. The faculty of speech, and especially the quality, *diction*, *tone*, projection etc. of the *voice*, is clearly vital to the success of an actor and the word is commonly found (often as a synonym for voice, occasionally for *elocution*) in phrases such as *speech coach*, *speech exam* etc.

Spelvin, George   The American equivalent of *Walter Plinge*, first used in a programme with reference to Charles A. Gardiner's *Karl the Peddler* (New York, 1886).

spill   A *lighting* term, which can be used as noun or verb, most frequently used for light which *leaks* from a *lantern* on to an area of the stage which should, ideally, be unlit. (It is interesting to note the frequent use of terms for liquid [and other less moist substances – see *spread*] transferred to light.) *Spill* in this sense is a C14 development, the word having been used in English since C10 with a range of senses related to destroying and injuring. See also *ghost*.

spirit gum   A liquid glue, often alcohol-based, used at least since

C19 to attach false beards etc. on to an actor's face. (*Spirit* in the sense of distilled liquor is an early C17 development from one of the highly-refined liquids which were thought in medieval times to permeate the human body, affecting its humours. It was also transferred to alchemy.)

spot/spotlight   *Spot* is an abbreviation of *spotlight* (originally *spot light*, *spot-light*), also used as a verb (as in *to spot it* [see below], 'to focus on a spot on a given area of the stage'). *Spots* are lanterns which, in contrast to *floods*, can be focused to throw a particularly sharp, intense light onto a specific area of the stage. 'Spot' as 'a specific, limited location' dates from C14. The OED's first attestation of *spot-light* is from 1922 – 'While in the warm dark seats we watch the spotlight/Dazzle upon the singer's hair and eyes' (C. Aitken, *Jig of Forslin*) – but theatrical usage is certainly earlier, the term having been used in lC19 as a synonym for *limelight*, a fact still echoed in the colloquial usage *in the spotlight* (compare *in the limelight*), 'to be the centre of attention'. The term is probably derived from a *spot line*, a *line* of rope used to hang an object at a given place where it is said to be *spotted*. Small spots are known as *baby spots* and may be found in a row on a *spotlight strip*. See also *follow spot*.

   Spotlight is also the name of the most prestigious *casting* directory in Britain, a glossy cross between *Who's Who* and the *Situations Wanted* column of a newspaper.

spread   The width of a beam of light from a lantern is known as its *spread*. Lenses used to increase the diameter of the beam are known as *spreader lenses*. (See *spill*.)

stage   From OF *estage*, from L. *staticum* (ultimately from *stare*, 'to stand'). OF developed a range of meanings revolving around 'standing, station, standing-place', many of which transferred to ME in C13-14. For the theatrical development of the noun, the sense of 'a floor raised above the level of the ground for the exhibition of something to be viewed by spectators' (OED) is significant – Ymiddez of þe temple es a stage of xxiii. grecez hie' (*c.* 1400, *The Buke of John Maundeville . . .*). The specific sense of 'a raised acting space' was firmly established by mC16 (as here, in 1551, in Robinson's English translation of More's *Utopia*): 'Whyles a commodye of plautus is playinge, . . . yf yowe shoulde sodenlie come vpon the stage in a philosophers apparrell'. About this time, the word took on added significance, by lC16 having metonymically developed the more general sense of *theatre* itself: 'There were also poets that wrote onely for the stage, I meane playes and interludes' (1584, Puttenham, *The Art of English Poesie*).

   As will be observed in many of the entries immediately following, *stage* is now frequently used adjectivally in a way similar to (and in many cases interchangeable with) 'theatre'. It is thus impossible to list all the possible usages and many, for example *stage carpenter*, can be found by looking for the relevant substantive.

The verb *to stage* is found in C16-C17 with the senses of 'to erect a stage' and 'to put a character on stage' – 'Death of Pluto, and you Stage mee, Stinkard; your Mansions shall sweate for't' (1601, Jonson, *Poetaster*, III.iv) – but its common current sense of 'to mount (a production)' is not found until lC19: 'If an... author... permits a play of his to be mounted or staged without his permission' (1879, *Theatre* [magazine]). The figurative general term, *to stage a come-back*, particularly used of sporting persons or teams who 'come back from the dead' in the later stages of competition is a development of this which Beale dates from the 1920s.

Stage, The   Now *The Stage and Television Today*, *The Stage*, as it is still generally known, is the only weekly newspaper in Britain dealing solely with theatre and variety. It was established in 1880: '[I] answered an ad in *The Stage* looking for actors to work in Ireland' (Margaret Ramsay quoted in the *Weekend Guardian*, 24-25 August 1991).

stage actor   A C20 term used to distinguish an actor who specialises in live theatrical work from one who works in cinema, television etc.

stage area   A term applied generally to the stage or, more precisely, to any one of the sections into which the acting area, particularly of a *proscenium arch* stage, is traditionally divided: *stage areas* are commonly identified in texts in *stage directions*. The areas used in modern theatre are denoted by plotting positions along two axes – one running from *upstage* to *downstage* and the other from stage right, through stage centre to stage left, (giving nine main stage areas) and giving rise to stage directions such as *move down left*. Further refinements can lead to the precision of up left centre, etc. In texts, such areas are abbreviated, so that the latter would be expressed as *ULC*.

stage cloth   '[C]upids chariot, two rain trunks and frames... The Stage cloth...' (1743, from the Covent Garden Inventory). Known in America as a *ground cloth*, this is a large sheet of material, sometimes carpet but far more usually canvas, spread over the floor of the stage and traditionally painted to represent paving stones, floor-boarding etc., although this practice is now obsolescent.

stagecraft   (Also found as *stage craft*, *stage-craft* etc.) 'Their ingenuity and knowledge of stagecraft is wonderful' (1882, *Society* [magazine]). In this combined noun, *stage* is used in its broadest sense of *theatre*, *stagecraft* being a term which can be applied to practical skill demonstrated in any area of theatrical endeavour from writing, through directing, designing and acting, to the skills of the technician.

stage direction[1] 'All through January I slaved over a hot typewriter to produce a text and detailed stage directions which would allow my conception of the piece to be visualised by others...' (Branagh, 203). In a script, the *stage directions* are instructions extraneous to the dialogue which describe production details and stage action to those working on the *text* or simply reading it. These may be the *dramatist's* own directions or, as is frequently the case in *acting editions*, the additions of a later editor. They largely confine themselves to actors' *moves* (described by the use of *stage areas*), *scenic* detail and *effects*. Perhaps the most famous stage direction of all time appears in *The Winter's Tale* (III.iii): 'Exit, pursued by a bear.'

Stage directions have been used, as this example indicates, since Elizabethan and Jacobean times, although one has to be wary, as some directions in early texts are the handiwork of later editors. Many refer to stage structures which no longer exist (see *within*, for example). Some which are still used (see *above*, *below*) were decided when most stages possessed a *rake*. Other obsolete stage directions in old texts have yielded fascinating staging and performance details to historians of theatre.

stage direction[2] The work of the *stage director* (see below).

stage director The history of *stage director* is even more complex than that of *director*, with which it overlaps. It is a term which has undergone considerable changes of meaning on both sides of the Atlantic during this century, a confusion compounded since at different times it has meant different things on 'opposite sides of the pond'. It was once synonymous in America with the present British sense of *stage manager* and in Britain with our current sense of *producer*. With post-World War II British adoption of the American sense of 'director', the fuller 'stage director' was sometimes also used. However, now, in Britain, stage 'director', following a general trend to employ the word 'director' to confer status, tends to designate an executive – (also used in the loosest sense) – who combines wider production responsibilities with overall responsibility for the stage, (including the *stage management team*).

stage door (Frequently found as *Stage Door*) 'I was so stupidly besotted with [Vivien Leigh] that although I was working with her I would wait at the Stage Door to see her leave the building'

(Alec McCowen, interviewed in Barkworth, 172). Although the term can denote an onstage door, it is far more commonly used for an entrance at the side or rear of a theatre, generally forbidden to the public. It is sometimes used metonymically to denote the whole *backstage* area: for example, theatres tend to have a *box office* phone number and a *stage door* number. This is because the stage door has been traditionally manned by a *stage door-keeper* or *doorman* who may also have additional duties as porter, messenger etc. (See *call board, notice.*) His duties also involve[d] keeping at bay the *stage-doorers* – a term first attested by Partridge in 1870 – or *Stage Door Johnnies* – an Edwardian term – who hung around the door to importune their favourite *stars*.

stage fall   A fall *choreographed* to look realistic but to avoid injury.

stage-fright   'This produced a terrible stage-fright... where all acting stopped as remembering took over. I would stare glassy-eyed at my fellow actors, thinking of my next speech...' (Branagh, 101). A debilitating form of actor's nerves, so strong as to severely detract from a performance or even prevent the actor from going on stage. The term is in common usage to denote nervousness, especially with reference to public speaking. (See also *first night nerves.*)

stagehand   Used for a theatrical worker with no particular skill; a *scene-shifter*. *Hand* has been used since mC17 for a person employed in a manual position – i.e. as a workman – but the origin of its theatrical usage is undoubtedly *nautical*. At sea, a hand referred to a general member of a ship's *crew*: 'Come aft all hands', (1669, Sturmy, *The Mariners Magazine*).

stage management, manager   *Stage managers* are the people who, during the *run* of a show, are in complete charge of the stage and backstage areas and their organisation. Performers and personnel of all the theatre's departments are answerable to them. Before and during the *rehearsal period*, the stage manager and stage management team (generally consisting of one or more *DSM*s and a variable number of *ASM*s) have a long list of organisational responsibilities. (For a summary of details, see Griffiths, 31-49). See also *prompt copy* and *on the book*.

The term is probably a lC18 one, the first OED attestation (from 1817), from a life of Kemble, referring to a person's 'appointment to the position of stage manager... in 1788.' The modern term *stage management* appears to be a slightly later, C19 development, preceded by a now obsolete form, *stage managership* (used in a letter by Coleridge in 1817).

For a fascinating insight into the role of the C19 stage manager, (which also shows that very little has changed in general terms), see the extract from Thomas William Robertson's sketch from *The Illustrated Times* (reproduced in Nagler, 403-05) from which this is the introduction:

The Stage Manager is the man who should direct everything behind the scenes. He should be at one and the same time a poet, an antiquarian, and a costumier; and possess sufficient authority, from ability as well as office, to advise with a tragedian as to a disputed reading, to argue with an armourer as to the shape of a shield, or to direct the wardrobe-keeper as to the cut of a mantle.

The verb *to stage manage* also became common in C19 – 'I have never seen them stage manage a play' (1879, *Theatre* [magazine]) – and its figurative use, 'to organise a public event with great thoroughness' is definitely in use by the beginning of C20: 'The meeting was well stage-managed' (*Daily Chronicle*, 8 May 1906). See *manager, management*.

stage name   A soubriquet. When an actor or other performer assumes a professional name, it is not always a question of vanity: no one can lay that charge on Elton John who, in order to be a credible rock star changed his name from Reginald Dwight, or on Kirk Douglas who changed from Issur Danielovitch for reasons of memorability. In fact, *Equity*, the actors' union, does not allow any new member to work under a name that is already held by one of its existing members. In addition, actors born with relatively common names such as John Roberts, for example, would naturally assume an alternative in order to increase job offers.

The habit of assuming a stage name is old. Molière, real name Jean-Baptiste Poquelin (1622-73), is thought to have assumed his name in order to spare his family embarrassment at his demeaning choice of profession.

stage plan   A *ground plan*.

stager   A rare and obsolete term for an actor. 'As for those stagers ... are they not commonlie such kind of men in their conuersation, as they are in their profession?' (1580, *2nd & 3rd Blast Against Plays & Theatres*). However, see *old stager*.

stage school   Although the term is sometimes used synonymously with *drama school* (see *RADA, training*), a stage school is more properly an educational establishment which specialises in the theatrical training of children of school age, and combines an academic with a theatrical education. Britain's first and most prestigious *stage school* was founded by Italia Conti in 1911, though it could be argued that the Children of the Chapel and the Children of Paul's, members of royal choirs who also performed at Court and elsewhere in C16, were also products of a stage school.

stagese A Victorian term, rarely used today, though one which could still possibly be applied to some of the jargon in this book; OED defines it as 'the "dialect" peculiar to the stage': 'Such phrases as... "I would have speech with thee..." may be described as accepted stagese' (1876, *The Times*) and 'The rest mopping and mowing in what was not to be called English but rather stagese' (1882, *Pall Mall Gazette*). Modern *stagese* has developed schismatically away from the mock-Shakespearian dialect implied in these attestations, (although it does still exist in pockets), towards a range of dialects one might term as *darlingese* (or *luvvie-ese*), *avant-gardese*, *fringese* etc.

stage staff A catch-all term used to refer to all the *backstage* and *front-of-house* personnel of a theatre other than director and actors.

stage-struck 'Barry Jackson was a stage-struck millionaire who ran the best professional theatre in the country, the Birmingham Rep...' (Olivier, 59). To be *stage-struck* is to have an obsessional fascination with the theatre. It is used particularly of amateurs and would-be performers of all ages.

stage weight Sometimes also known as a *brace weight*, this a heavy, metal object, used to support and make firm a stage brace, a lighting stand etc. Some weights are specially manufactured and fashioned in order to accommodate the foot of a brace.

stage whisper A form of stage *convention* akin to the *aside*: the actor whispers loudly or speaks *sotto voce* whilst the audience accepts the convention that this utterance goes unheard by certain other onstage characters. A term with a wide general usage, the main difference being that the real life *stage whisper* is heard by all.

staging 'We cannot reconstruct a Shakespearian theatre by imitation. By the time we have decided on a Shakespearian technique we are wrong... Modern staging is already as musty as the traverse curtain' (Brook, 55). A development from the verb *to stage, staging* refers to *how* a play is staged: the particular methods, techniques and style involved in transferring it from the text to the stage. Having said that, today 'staging' is most frequently used to denote the physical theatre form, the type of stage employed in a production: i.e. *theatre-in-the-round, proscenium* with *thrust, promenade* etc. It has gained this narrower sense since 1945 as the need for a term has arisen: theatres have become more flexible and the possibility of choosing an appropriate theatre form to stage a given show has become a required directorial and design skill.

stagey, stagy 'The woman... came rather hastily forth, and flung up both her arms in a stagy manner' (1862, F.W. Robinson, *Owen: a waif*). *Stag(e)y* is a synonym for *theatrical*, used in its depreciatory sense: 'artificially dramatic; *hammy*. Like *stagese*, a

C19 coining which reflects the dominant, *melodramatic* playing style of the period.

stagger-through 'Not a real "run" but a "stagger" through the whole play. This is the first time we have put any of it together' (Tim McInnerny, in the *Weekend Guardian*, 24-5 August 1991). A *stagger-through* is a descriptive term for an attempt at a *run-through* (from which it playfully takes its name), generally at a stage in the *rehearsal* process when it could not be expected to flow uninterruptedly. However, most theatre-goers have seen performances which looked like stagger-throughs (or, correctly but rarely, *staggers-through*).

stalls First used in lC18-eC19 for individual theatre seats, often expensive ones with arm-rests at the front of the *pit*, but later used for all the main blocks of *seating* at ground level in a theatre *auditorium*. This confusion about the status of the word (and the seats) may be traced to the fact that *stall* made one entry into Old English from a Teutonic root as 'cattle stall, stable', and another into Middle English, probably from OF *estal* (although from the same ultimate root), as 'seat of high status in a church', such as might be occupied by a knight or bishop. However these senses affected the associations of the word, the theatrical use was probably taken directly from mod. F. *stalle* (from It. *stallo*) adopted in eC19: 'An orchestra has been constructed [at the Lyceum]; that is, a separation of the best part of the pit to the extent of about one third; each row divided into "stalls" at about half-a-guinea each' (1828, Sala, *Journal*). Eventually, the term 'stalls' spread back through the auditorium.

stand by, stand-by *To stand by* in its sense of 'to hold to oneself in readiness for something', is a verbal phrase first attested in OED as a *nautical* term in 1669: 'Come, stand by, take in our Top-sails' (Sturmy, *Mariners Magazine*). As an imperative, the term is still used in this way, given to stage *crews* to warn them that they should be ready for an imminent *cue*. As a noun, the *stand-by* is a *call* requesting actors, crew etc. to be ready to take a cue.

Stand-by also signifies an actor who is prepared to step into the shoes of another should the need arise: usually, unlike an *understudy*, the stand-by is not a member of the *company*. Compare *stand-in*.

An extension of this is the term *stand-by tickets*, which are not for sale in advance of the night of a show, when they can be queued for. Some theatres reserve special *student stand-bys*.

stand in, stand-in *To stand in* for someone means to replace them temporarily, and is descriptive of *standing in their place* on stage, either in rehearsals or performance, giving rise to the general expression *standing in for someone*, which, according to Partridge, had been appropriated from the theatre for Services' use by the 1920s. An actor who performs this function is known as *a stand-in*.

standing room only 'The next day, we had standing room only' (Geilgud, 67). Sometimes abbreviated in America to SRO, this is a graphic way of describing a *full house*. The phrase began life as a notice or call outside a theatre to prospective theatre-goers, probably in *music hall* or *variety*.

stand-up An abbreviation of *stand-up comedian* or *comic*. *Stand-up* comedy *routines* are characterised by a solo performer delivering a *patter* of quick-fire *gags* linked by a tenuous narrative if any at all. This style, under American influence, began slowly to replace the traditional British character comedian with his *monologues* during the 1920s. The origin of the phrase, whilst clearly descriptive, is uncertain but probably American and eC20 (compare *stand-in*). (The *stand-up buffet* was also gaining vogue at this time, first attested in OED Supp. in 1920).

Stanislavskian Of or pertaining to the *naturalistic* acting theories and practice of Konstantin Sergeivich Stanislavski [real name Alexeyev], (1863-1938), actor, director and teacher, founder of the Moscow Arts Theatre, as propounded in his English-language books *My Life in Art* (1924), *An Actor Prepares* (1936), and the posthumous *Stanislavsky* [sic] *Researches 'Othello'* (1948) and *Building a Character* (1950). Stanislavski's is without doubt the most influential practical teaching about acting of the first half of the C20. See *emotion memory, tree, (be a)*, motivation, *psycho-technique, objectives (creative)* etc.

star Whilst it might be presumed from its Hollywood associations that this term meaning 'a highly successful performer with a high public profile, a *box office* attraction' is C20 in origin, it is first hinted at in this context in lC18: 'The little stars, who hid their diminished rays in [Garrick's] presence, begin to abuse him' (1779, Warner in *Jesse Selwyn & Contemp*). By the early C19 the usage is fixed: 'Carter . . . was at a loss for a star in the pugilistic hemisphere to produce him a crowded house' (1824, OED). The term's development meaning 'an illustrious figure' might have been influenced by earlier senses, from the abbreviated reference to the Virgin Mary (from *Stella Maris*, 'the star of the sea') found as early as C13, or from the non-Christian belief that the souls of the illustrious are turned into stars after death: 'For Ioues ys not ther aboute . . . To make of the as yet a sterre' (*c*.1384, Chaucer, *The House of Fame*). The astronomical origins of the term took on a new twist in 1920s' Hollywood in the punning use of the *star* *system*, referring to the film studios' methods of handling stars, but based on the scientific term first used in the 1870s. The adjectival usage as in *star billing*, originally for a *bill* advertising the appearance of a *star performer*, can be dated back to 1890s, when *star turn* also developed in *music hall*. *Stardom* for 'the condition of being a star' or 'the status of a star' appears to be an eC20 development based on a Standard English formula as in free, freedom etc.: 'Ruby[Miller]'s call to stardom had been a *Little Bit of Fluff* at the end of the Great War' (Olivier, 47). *Star* can now be found in common use (as in 'You're a star, you are') for anyone of whom the speaker particularly approves.

star trap   A descriptive term for a *trap* door with a circumference which can also be circular, hexagonal or octagonal. It is constructed of triangular flaps whose bases are hinged to the circumference, and which create a star effect as the performer disappears through them (usually on some form of counterweighted platform). As the system lends itself to sudden appearances and disappearances it is often used in *pantomime* for magical entrances. Compare *bristle trap*.

stealing a scene   To attract attention away from other performers during the course of a scene – see *scene-stealer*. Such an action is referred to as a *steal*, a term which can also be used for plagiaristic writing or performances – compare *lift*.

steal someone's thunder   This phrase, which is now in common usage meaning 'to make use of someone else's idea in a way which they consider to be unfair (or, in theatrical terms, to *steal a scene* etc.), has precise theatrical origins. The dramatist John Dennis (1657-1734), supposed inventor or first user of the *thunder sheet*, on hearing that the device had been employed in a rival play, is alleged to have said, accusingly, 'Sir, you have stolen my thunder' (*c*.1710).

step on a laugh   An actors' term meaning to throw away a *laughline* by inept *timing* or some other shortcoming in *stagecraft*. To *step on someone else's line* suggests maliciousness. See *laugh*.

stichomythia   'Take ... the passage of dialogue between Richard and Queen Elizabeth in "Richard III", as vivid a piece of stichomuthia as the English drama has to show' (1914, *Blackwell's Magazine*). 'Drama, dialogue in alternate lines, employed in sharp disputation, and characterised by antithesis and rhetorical repetition or taking up of the opponent's words. Also applied to modern imitations of this' (OED). See *repartee*.

stile   (Sometimes also found as *style*.) The vertical side pieces in the frame of a *flat*. Possibly from Dutch *stijl*, 'pillar, prop, doorpost', this term has been used generally since lC17 for the vertical bars of wainscots, windows, door-frames etc. As an early DIY manual attests: 'You must leave some stuff to pare away smooth to the struck line, that the Stile (that is, the upright Quarter) may make a close Joynt with the Rail (that is the lower Quarter)' (1678, Moxon, *Mechanick exercises, or the doctrine of handy-works*).

stock OED lists 65 separate senses of this noun, which is found theatrically in adjectival form in terms such as *stock piece, stock actor* and *stock company*. The latter is the term developed in the United States in the 1850s for a company which worked regularly together, often based in one theatre, with a changing *repertoire* of plays: 'I... being at the time one of the stock company playing at the Beverley Theatre, New York' (1864, P. Paterson, *Glimpses of Real Life*). Of course, the practice was old; only the term was new. *Stock* was, however, established much earlier in its sense of theatrical repertory: 'Time...wasted in rehearsing old Stock plays, for the Sake of the new Performers to be introduced in them' (1761, Victor, *Theatres of London and Dublin*). This sense of 'constantly recurring material' has even earlier literary attestations – 'the old Stock-Oaths' (1738, Swift, *Polite Conversation*). As the weary tone there suggests, 'stock' does carry with it overtones of the hackneyed, the clichéd and the stereotyped; consequently, *stock actor* is still used deprecatorily of a 'jobbing actor' whose work has little artistic merit and the strong savour of *ham*.

stooge In a comic pairing or *double act*, the *straight* man or *feed*. On occasions, this character can also end up as the *fall guy*. An eC20 American term from *variety*. The origin is uncertain, although it has been suggested that it is a corruption of *stool-pigeon*, 'a card-sharp's decoy', itself from shooting, or a corruption of *student*. My own preference, because I find it the most colourful, is connected to the latter: that it derives from *stoo-jus*, the American pronunciation of *studious*.

straight From ME *stregt, stragt*, from the past participle of the verb *strecchen*, 'to stretch', all the theatrical usages of *straight* in some way relate to C16 metaphorical developments of the original sense to mean 'honest, ordered, direct' (in contrast to notions of 'physical and moral crookedness and eccentricity'). To *play something straight* is to perform it faithfully, without embellishment or *parody*. Likewise, *straight make-up* is a basic make-up which does not seek to suggest age or character.

Straight can also be used synonymously with *legit(imate)*, as in the term *straight theatre*: dramatic theatre as opposed to *music hall, variety, musical comedy* etc.: 'Ours was the straight act on the bill – and the comics and the trick-cyclists, all the most brilliant talents imaginable, would gather in the wings to watch the 'legits'

(Olivier, 47). In the phrase *straight part*, and sometimes in *straight man*, the sense is similar, although the latter can also be used synonymously with *stooge*, the half of a comic partnership who delivers the *straight lines*, the unfunny ones: 'some characters are developed less organically since they are "straight men" for Hamlet's wit...' (Berkoff, 121).

street theatre   'Due to programme changes by agents in exotic foreign lands, Britain's leading street theatre company find themselves at a loose end in weeks commencing...' (Ad. in *The Stage*, 23 April 1992). Outdoor performances by groups of travelling players are a traditional element of European theatre, perhaps the form in which theatre traditions were handed down during the *dark* centuries of theatre history: however, this specific term is from the 1960s, bred from the outburst of *alternative*, *fringe* activity of the post-war years. Areas such as Covent Garden in London now provide regular pitches for street performers who make a living by passing round the hat.

strike   *To strike a set*, or to do *the strike* refers to the dismantling of the *set* for one scene, or, more commonly, for an entire production. This is almost certainly another example of the influence of nautical language on theatre terminology, for whilst this term has been in use in the sense of 'dismantling' in areas such as building (where scaffolding is said to be *struck*) since C17, the nautical usage, 'to lower sail', dates from C14: 'Thei hadden wynd at wille, tho With topseilcoile and forth thei go, And striken nevere, til thei come To Tyr' (1390, Gower, *Confessio Amantis*). If it follows the usual pattern, the theatrical usage is almost certainly C18, although the OED has no attestation until 1889 in the New York *Daily Tribune*: 'An elaborate scene is "set" when it is arranged upon the stage, and "struck" when it is removed.'

stringers   The side-pieces of a theatrical staircase to which the *risers* and *treads* are attached. The OED first attests a general usage of this term in 1883; however, not surprisingly, there is an earlier nautical definition from 1830, defined in Hedderwick's *Marine Architecture*: '*Stringers*, strakes of planks wrought round the inside at the height of the undersides of the beams [of a ship]'.

striptease   A performance art popularised in *burlesque*, but dating back at least to biblical times (e.g. Salome in the New Testament); it involves a *terpsichoreal artiste*, known as a *stripper*, slowly removing her clothing – or *stripping* – to musical accompaniment, in such a fashion as to titillate or *tease* the male members of the audience. According to Beale, the term was borrowed from America during the 1940s, becoming Standard English by about 1970.

strobe An abbreviation of *stroboscope*, (from Gk *strobos*, 'whirl-ing', + -*scope*, from Gk *skopeō*, 'look at'). The first *stroboscopes* were instruments devised in eC19 by the Viennese scientist, Stampfer, 'for observing the successive phases of a periodic motion by means of light periodically interrupted' (OED). The entertainment potential of the stroboscope as a forerunner of cinema was quickly seized on: the use of 'a scientific toy which produces the illusion of motion by a series of pictures viewed through the openings of a revolving disc' (OED) is attested as early as 1836. The major current use of *strobe* is for a *lantern*, especially popular in discos from the 1970s onwards, which can be program-med to flash at periodic intervals, at certain rapid frequencies giving the jerky impression of early cinematic movement. It can be highly dangerous to epileptics and others because of the effect of its frequencies on the brain. It is equally dangerous in the hands of poor directors, who tend to overuse it for effect.

strut one's stuff A jokey actor's term for performing in front of an audience, carrying with it suggestions of a rather *showy* perfor-mance. The verb *strut* has a long theatrical pedigree in this sense – 'Life's but . . . a poor player,/That struts and frets his hour upon the stage,/And then is heard no more' (1605, Shakespeare, *Mac-beth* V.iii) – a quotation which may, in part, have influenced the development of the phrase. *Stuff* has been used generally in Eng-lish as a term for the tools or skills of a particular trade since eC16. Compare *material*.

studio theatre A C20 term, originally from *alternative* theatre, used to designate a small, informal performance *space*, (compare *workshop* and *laboratory*), often with a flexible auditorium. '[The mid-1980s] coincided with a feeling that the Fringe should shake off the studio theatre malaise of the 1970s' (Michael Coveney, *Observer*, 3 May 1992). *Studio theatres* – commonly abbreviated to *studios* – are often found in educational establishments and drama schools or as small, experimental performance areas attached to larger theatres. Italian *studio*, 'a study, or workshop for a graphic artist', was first appropriated by English in eC19: 'The greatest work which issued from his [Cimabue's] studio, was his scholar Giotto' (1819, *Edinburgh Review*). The transfer-ence to other skill areas began in mC19 – Thackeray in *The New-comes* (1854), for example, refers to 'a dentist's studio'. The theat-rical usage of the term undoubtedly gained currency from the fame gained by the Actor's Studio in New York, founded in 1947 by Elia Kazan (see *Method*).

study '[Y]ou see I haven't studied this play as I usually do. I haven't done it nearly so thoroughly' (Patience Collier, quoted in Barkworth, 209). An actors' term for learning the *lines* of a part; it now also carries overtones of working on a *part*, researching background, developing the character's motivation etc. *To study* has been used in English with the sense of 'to concentrate on acquiring knowledge' since at least the eC14 (from OF *estudier*). The theatrical usage is very old: 'Have you the lion's part written? Pray you, if it be, give it to me, for I am slow of study' (*c.*1594, Shakespeare, *A Midsummer Night's Dream*, I.ii).

stunt, stuntman   '[T]he camera would catch the first moment when the actor pretended the stunt before the stuntman took over and the actor would come in at the end where he would be filmed falling into place' (Berkoff, 78). An American term, appropriated theatrically from film, for an act involving some physical risk: such *stunts* are often not played by the actor but by a professional *stand-in* known as a *stuntman*. *Stunt* is a term which appears to have developed in American colleges in C19, obscure in origin, though it has been conjectured that it may be from G. *Stunde*, 'hour', or a variant of *stint* or *stump*. 'Stunt: one of those convenient words which may be used almost in any connection and the exact meaning of which must be determined largely by the context... [Editor's note; Doing stunts is used in N.Y. city by boys in the sense of performing some feat of rivalry, – a long jump for instance, – one boy "stumping" or challenging another]' (1895, *Dialect Notes, published by the American Dialect Society*).

Sturm und Drang   German for 'Storm and Stress': the title of a play by Klinger (1776) which gave its name to a sub-genre of the German Romantic movement in theatre – violently-emotional depictions of individual *angst*. Such plays had some influence on the development of *melodrama*, and the term is still used for highly-charged emotional performances etc.

sub-plot   Double and multiple *plots*, the interweaving of two or more, sometimes only tangentially-related plots into the structure of a play, were a feature of Elizabethan drama. The term *sub-plot* for a secondary plot (which often broadens the audience's understanding of the themes of the main plot) was coined by C20 literary criticism: 'A programme note added that *Lear* was a perfect story ...once one had done away with the tedious sub-plots involving Kent, Gloucester, Edmund, Cornwall, Albany et el...' (review in *Plays and Players*, October 1990).

subtext   A C20 term to describe all the psychological and non-verbal information implied below (*sub-*) the written dialogue (*text*) of a play, which, according to modern rehearsal practice, it is the duty of the actor to explore and develop. *Stanislavski* explained subtext to his actors by employing the analogy of an iceberg: the text is the small fraction of text provided by the dramatist, the *lines*; the actor's responsibility is to disclose the majority of his role which, like the bulk of the iceberg, is hidden below the surface. Branagh outlines what can happen when a director takes an over-rigorous approach to *subtextual* analysis:

She also insisted that we 'headlined', or described each line that our character spoke. For instance, if Chebutkin said in the text 'Hello, Natasha', the headline would be 'The doctor greets Natasha warmly'. Then a subtext had to be written: 'The doctor appears to be greeting Natasha warmly, but in fact only slightly covers up his annoyance with her, whilst appearing to be polite for the others.' As this was done for every single sentence of the dialogue, rehearsals involved writing a short novel... (p.64).

sugar glass   A descriptive term for artificial glass made from a sugar solution and set into the shapes of window panes, bottles or any other supposedly glass object which has to break harmlessly on stage.

supernumerary   Frequently abbreviated to *super*, occasionally (in America) to *supe*. An actor employed in a non-speaking role: a *walk-on* or, in film and television terms, an *extra*. First attested in OED in 1836, this quotation from Mayhew's *London Labour and the London Poor* (1851) – 'I...sunk to be supernumerary for 1s. a night at one of the theatres' – gives a flavour of the job's status and its rewards. In fact, the word derives from LL *supernumerarius* ('surplus to numbers'), used for those soldiers who were added to a Roman legion when it was already up to its full complement. It has been used in a variety of contexts in English with the sense of an additional helper/member of staff etc. since eC17.

superobjective   The *Stanislavskian* term to denote the main theme of a production, the interpretation, expressable in a sentence or two, which should guide and unify the intellectual and artistic decisions made by everyone involved in the production: 'In a play the whole stream of individual, minor objectives, all the imaginative thoughts, feelings and actions of an actor, should converge to carry out the super-objective of the plot' (1936, Stanislavski, *An Actor Prepares*).

support   An abbreviation for *supporting actor* or *role*: 'In England a young, ambitious actor takes these minor parts in his stride. He plays Oliver in *As You Like It* or Salarino in *The Merchant of Venice*, or any of those supporting roles, and tries to find something to do with them, while waiting for the time he will be allowed to play Orlando or Shylock' (Geilgud, 70). The term suggests the status-consciousness that exists in the acting profession: the *star* carries the show, the supporting actor helps him to carry it (or, on occasions, carries him).

switchboard   Although the abbreviated term, *board*, is still used, since the advent of computerised lighting desks, this form is becoming an obsolete way of referring to a stage lighting control board. *Switchboards* were usually installed in the wings, hidden from the audience's view.

The electrical *switch*, used for connecting or breaking an electrical circuit, is a term first used in 1860s, the name being taken from larger mechanical devices (e.g. for changing railway points) which, in turn, took their name from *switches* as 'tree branches'. 'Switchboard' is first attested in OED from the *Pall Mall Gazette* in 1884 – in the midst of the period when all major theatres were equipping themselves with electrical lighting – the term *board* having been appropriated from that word's usage since 1400 for any piece of furniture resembling a table or desk.

symbolism   *Symbol*, ultimately from Gk *sumbolon*, 'mark, token', entered English in C14 meaning a summary of Christian faith or belief (as in the Apostles' Creed, for example): A transference of sense had been completed by the end of C16, *symbol* coming to designate a written or graphic sign which represents or stands for something else: 'they [ostriches] are the simplest of fowles and symbolls of folly' (1615, George Sandys, *Travels*). As such, all theatre from medieval times onwards has employed varying degrees of literal *symbolism* – for example, in the Elizabethan theatre a throne would designate a royal court, a tree a forest etc. – a word which enters English in mC17, originally in a mathematical sense (referring to algebra). With the possible exception of the German Romantic dramatists, it is not until C19, under the influence of the French Symbolist Movement in literature, that dramatists came self-consciously to employ heavy symbolism in their work in the way that Chekhov, Ibsen and Strindberg all do. The term is even more closely associated with the Belgian, Maeterlinck, and in Ireland with Yeats – writers who minimise the realistic nature of their characters in favour of their poetic and symbolic significances. This is not a common trait in the English theatre.

System, the   'My "system" will never manufacture inspiration. It can only prepare a favourable ground for it' (1936, Stanislavski, *An Actor Prepares*). *The System* is a term frequently applied to the teachings of *Stanislavski* – see also *emotion memory, motivation, psychotechnique, superobjective, tree, (be a)* – but is one, as in this reference, which he was careful to keep alive and changing: he stressed that it was not a formula for good acting – something that his American followers – see *Method, the* – were perhaps less careful about.

Tableau (Plural *tableaux*, or occasionally the anglicised *tableaus*.) 'Rosencrantz and Guildenstern approach the King. The attitudes are of a tableau. It suddenly comes to life' (Berkoff, 131). A *tableau* is a stage picture formed by a group of actors standing motionless, frozen as in a still photograph. Fr. 'painting', from OF *tablel*, a diminutive of *table*, 'table'. The word has been used in English since C17 to describe a painting with a carefully-composed group of figures: 'The History of Maria de Medicis is painted by Rubens ... The allegorical assistants in all the Tableaux are very airy and fancifully set out' (1699, Lister, *Journey to Paris*). By eC19 it had become fashionable society entertainment for individuals or groups to dress in costume and imitate the composition of famous paintings in what were known as *tableaux vivants*, 'living pictures': 'The different stories were represented in Tableaux Vivans and songs' (1817, OED). From this, the theatrical usage developed. See *tabs*.

tabs 'A good wheeze is to pretend that the next performance after a bad night is not a performance at all but a rehearsal. "Pretend the tabs are down," said Murray McDonald, "and there's no audience there"' (Barkworth, 75). *Tabs* is an abbreviation of *tableau* curtains, so-called due to the C19 fashion for actors to group for applause at the end of an act or show in *tableaux vivants* behind a pair of curtains *upstage* of the main curtain or *act-drop* (although in many theatres these curtains were eventually replaced by *tabs*, now generally synonymous, as in the quotation above, with main *curtain*). In some theatres the *tabs* divide, in others a single tab is used which rises, sometimes in festoon.

tag The last line of a speech, scene, act or, most commonly, a play (compare *curtain line*) can be referred to as the *tag* (therefore *speech-tag*, *tag-line*.). In some theatrical circles it is considered bad luck to deliver this time before the opening night. According to Partridge, the word is of C19 origin, and from 1860-1900 was occasionally used as a colloquial name for an actor. The theatrical usage is probably related to the Standard English senses of *tag* (ME, of unknown origin) which all relate in some way to appendages which dangle loosely, are tied on etc.

tail An alternative term for a *leg*: a *flat*, or more commonly a curtain, generally used to *mask* off the *wings*. (This combination of three different parts of a bird's anatomy is quite coincidental.)

269

take¹ The verb. With reference to performance, take appears in a variety of verbal phrases. Some use *take* in its sense of 'seize': *to take the corner* is to move to an attention-grabbing position at the *downstage* corner of the stage (though, for stage crew it can also mean to assume the role of *prompter* [see *prompt corner*]). *To take a scene, to take the stage* and *to take the audience by storm* etc. all suggest dominance and success, though not always with generosity: 'taking a scene' is close to *stealing* it.

In the sense of 'receive', *to take the nap* is to receive a blow when a hand-clap is given either offstage or on as a sound effect to deceive the audience into thinking that a real blow has been struck. The *nap* (probably from ME imitative verb *to knap*, 'to knock, rap' [possibly connected with Norwegian *napp*, 'a tug, pull']), has meant 'a pretend blow' since at least mC19: 'Then Pantaloon comes up..., and I give him the "nap", and knock him on his back' (1851, Mayhew, *London Labour*). Learning to receive such a blow is known as *napping the slap*.

In some instances, the word is a weaker alternative 'to perform': 'to execute': thus, *to take a call* or *bow* is to come forward to acknowledge the applause at the end of a show; 'to take three bows and an encore', now largely obsolete, was to go one stage further and repeat part of a scene. Other phrases include *take it away*, now generally used as encouragement to start the performance (in general terms of anything), but originally an instruction to the curtain operator: 'remove the curtain (for the show to begin)'. *To take (up) a cue* is to respond to it as rehearsed, another phrase which has entered general usage.

take² The noun from the verb *take¹*. In acting terminology, *a take* is a look or glance towards an onstage character, prop etc. which directs the audience's attention towards it. The actor's eyes select and control the focus of the audience's attention almost as effectively as a camera shot does in cinema. (Compare the cinematic use, and see *double take*).

take-in, take-out Alternatives to the *get-in* and *get-out* (largely American).

take off A term more frequently used by audiences than performers, meaning to *mimic* or *imitate*, or 'do an impression of'. The term dates at least from the mC18: 'He ... perfectly counterfeited, or took off, as they call it, the real Christian' (1766, attested in Partridge).

tallescope A term for an extendable metal ladder, sometimes on wheels, especially useful for making adjustments to high-hanging lamps. Whilst I can find no definitely attested etymology, I should hazard the guess that the name is a pun on *tall* and *telescope*.

Tannoy   A term for a *PA* system, from an American brand name. '"The tannoy and the video monitor were both on. We were all in the green room having a bite between shows and cheering you on"' (Branagh, 134). The origins of the trade name, are, according to all the sources I have consulted, uncertain. Those who have ever had to suffer the unwelcome commentary of a *tannoy* at the wrong moment might think it a conflation of *to annoy*.

tap, taps   Abbreviations respectively for *tap dance* and *tap shoes* (or the *tap plate* on tap shoes). *Tap*, a word descriptive of the rhythmical sound produced by this dance (from an OE and Germanic root) was the descriptive name given in C19 to a form of dance popularised in *minstrel shows* in the United States. The distinctive sound is produced by small metal plates, or *taps* which are usually nailed on to special tap shoes. 'It was good to see... the immaculate dancing in white tie and tails of the New Berry Brothers (though why they did not have taps on their shoes is beyond me)' (*The Stage*, 20 March 1991).

teaser   Part of the *false proscenium*, a horizontal *flat* or *border* curtain used to mask the *flies* and provide a frame for the inner stage opening. It is usually placed behind the front curtain and in front of the more imposing and obvious *tormentors*, from which it would appear to get its name, from a pun on the sense of a tease as a small torment.

tech.   The common abbreviation of *technical* rehearsal: a *rehearsal* held primarily for the benefit of the technical crew, focusing on *lighting* and *sound cues* and other technical aspects of production. 'The nightmare of the lighting designer is time. There is only one day – "the tech" – in which to rehearse' (*Observer*, 3 May 1992). Normally, the *tech* is *run* in conjunction with the actors, though under pressure of time the latter may *walk through* parts of a scene or *top and tail* – skip to the next major technical cue (a dangerous practice given the importance of techs to actors too [as the next quotation attests]). Here, the verb *to tech* is employed for the running of such a rehearsal: '[The dress rehearsal] terrified me, as it was so long since we had "teched" the first scenes that we were all in danger of forgetting everything' (Branagh, 145).

technical, technician, technique   *Technique* differs from *technical* and *technician* in that it can be applied to the skills of the actor and director (and artists generally), whereas the first two terms are applied as adjective and noun to the activities and functions of those involved in what might be termed the practical aspects of *production*. In some theatres, this also marks an unfortunate and counterproductive divide between company members which, if not linguistic, is clearly reflected in language. All three words derive originally from Gk *tekhnē*, 'art, craft', but they belong on different sides of a schism created from lC17 onwards, when *art* and associated words parted company with others such as *artisan, skill, craft* etc., which were deemed to belong to a separate, scientific, practical and industrial domain, by and large the world of *tekhnē*-related words.

'Technique' comes from Fr. *technique*, (ironically the F adjective for 'technical' employed as a noun [compare *die Technik* in German], but, possibly because French in origin, one which could still be applied to the artistic. It is used to signify 'the manner of artistic execution or performance; the basic skills underlying these'. 'In *Zoo Story* I had unlocked a way of seeing character and let it fill my whole body. I felt I had captured a certain technique from watching Plummer for those six valuable weeks of my life...' (Berkoff, 63). 'Technique' is first attested in OED in eC19 – 'Illogical phrases... which hold so distinguished a place in the technique of ordinary poetry' (1817, Coleridge, *Biographia Literaria*) – but still the word was employed in C19 as a poor relative to 'art' itself: 'Their [poetic] work, however curious in technique, fails to permanently impress the refined reader' (1876, Stedman, *Victorian Poets*). That is, one can have technique but still fail to be an artist. The word can also be used as 'fixed pattern, formula': 'When I begin to work on a play, I start with a deep, formless hunch which is like a smell, a colour, a shadow... I have no technique' (Brook, 3).

'Technical' and 'technician' are both derived from the now largely-obsolete *technic*, and are eC19 words. The OED defines 'technician' as 'one skilled in the technique or mechanical part of an art...' and the word 'mechanical' is most telling. A theatrical attestation (albeit using a rare sense of the word, related closely to 'technique' hammers the point over more clearly: 'The mere technician can never interest; the literary man, even if inexpert in stage technique, may do so to a high degree' (1833, OED). The implication is that technicians lack 'full' creativity.

The modern sense of 'technician' as a theatre production worker still carries with it these unfortunate overtones. They are referred to, and sometimes refer to themselves, as *techies*. Whilst it might be argued that this is affectionate (compare *chippie* for 'carpenter'), one has only to go to a first night party at many theatres and to see where the plaudits and attention are directed, to see a form of creative apartheid in operation. I think the remarks under the heading *nautical* assist in driving this point home. Perhaps the use of phrases such as *technical director*, *lighting director* etc., for people in charge of the technical aspects of a production go some way to correcting this inbalance of associations. For *technical rehearsal*, see **tech**.

telegraph   To *telegraph* (and *telegraphing*) are actor's terms for conveying information to an audience by gesture or glance prior to it being made obvious by dialogue, plot etc. The verb is also generally used, as in football, for example – 'telegraphing a pass to a defender' – for conveying information to someone by non-verbal means, a metaphorical use of the communications term (from Fr. *télégraphe*, from Gk *tele-*, 'at a distance' + *graphē*, 'writing'). It has been used in this way since shortly after the discovery of telegraphy: 'Tom Durfy... began telegraphing Biddy, who... had shoved herself well before the door' (1842, S. Lover, *Handy Andy*). A technological equivalent to *signpost*.

temperature   In lighting, used to refer to the *colour temperature* of lights: i.e. a blue *gel* creates a cold temperature, a pink gel a warmer one.

tempo   Used as a synonym for pace, the speed and rhythm at which a piece – musical or dramatic – is, or should be played. *Tempo* is a musical term developed in Italian from L. *tempus*, 'time', first used in English in eC18 and logically extended to theatrical usage. It is also generally used as in *the tempo of events* and here, Peter Brook transfers it to the rhythm at pace of thinking in rehearsals: '[Gielgud] loves "changing the moves" in rehearsals and of course he is right... But many actors have trouble keeping up with his tempo, become resentful, long to be told once and for all what they have to do and then be left alone' (p.82). A further extension of the term is made by Stanislavski in *Building a Character* (published posthumously in 1950), in his theories of *tempo-rhythm*, applicable to both the pace of an individual performance and to a scene.

tenor   Used to describe a particular quality of voice, the highest normal adult male register, just above baritone, from the octave below middle C to the A above it (and the singer who uses this register), *tenor* is also used to describe the speaking voice of an actor: 'Moissi had a curious tenor voice. He was playing, of course, in German which I could not understand...' (Geilgud, 65). The term 'tenor', from OF *tenor, tenour*, 'the general content, substance, tone of a document' had, from C14, a range of meanings revolving around the Fr. sense. It was chosen for the voice, apparently, because the tenor register tended to carry the melody of a song or piece of music.

terence-stage   Sometimes referred to as a *Terentian stage*. A form of medieval staging which was to have influence on the later

development of European theatre forms. In 1427, lost works by
the Roman dramatists Plautus and Terence were re-discovered.
In an attempt to stage them as had been originally intended, a
compromise occurred whereby contemporary theatre forms were
combined with descriptions from the writings of Vitruvius. Later
editions of these plays from lC15 show woodcuts of the results,
which came to be known as *terence-stages*.

terpsichoreal *Terpsichore* was the Greek Muse of Dancing, hence,
in true C18 heroic style, the occasional adoption of *terpsichore* to
mean a female dancer or, on occasions, the art of dance itself.
The adjective *terpsichoreal*, of or pertaining to dance, is thus
derived. Its use since the C19 has been either pompous or ironic:
'The loving couples . . . hold themselves aloof from the busy hum,
or mix it in for terpsichoreal or restorative purposes only' (*Daily
News*, 19 May 1869).

text The written version of a play; the script in both its senses
of dialogue and book. From Fr. *texte* and Old Norman French
tixte (and variations), *text* is derived from L. *textus*, what Quintilian
defined as 'the tissue of a literary work', from *text-*, the past
tense stem of *texere*, 'to weave'. That is, it is a unified piece composed
of strands taken from elsewhere. The word is first used in
C14 with the sense of the actual words written or spoken: 'Fyrst
telle me þe tyxte of þe tede lettres' (OED). It also carries with
it (as is born out in its use as 'gospel' and 'extract from the gospel')
an aura of truth and authority: 'But truly I telle as þe texte sais'
(1400, *Destruction of Troy*). Its figurative use for 'content' or 'subject
matter' was developed in C17, but its use as an edition or
book was not developed until C19: 'Our present Received Text
hath been a growth developed from many and various sources'
(1841, OED). Clearly, in theatre the text is only the starting-point
of a production and there is always a tension between the author's
(unknowable) intentions – textual authority – and a director's
reading of them (which echoes the debate over *texte, écriture* and
lecture which still rages between traditional, structuralist and post-
structuralist literary critics). Swift spotted this in 1720 in 'To
Stella': 'Say, Stella, when you copy next,/Will you keep strictly
to the text?'

It is a decision that a director *has* to make. Here Peter Brook
impales himself on the fence of that dilemma

Should we respect the text? I think there is a healthy double
attitude, with respect on the one hand and disrespect on the
other. And the dialectic between the two is what it's all about.
If you go solely one or the other way, you lose the possibility
of capturing the truth . . . What in one line doesn't matter, in

another matters like hell. One must trust one's judgement and take the consequences. (p.95)

theatre Under the entry for *drama*, the debate about the distinction between 'theatre' and 'drama' was opened. To resume: whilst I found good reason to dispute Elam's definition of *drama*, his definition of *theatre* as 'the complex of phenomena associated with the performer-audience transaction' does seem to be borne out by the word's etymology. It is significant that Gk *theatron* means literally 'a seeing-place' or 'a place for viewing', from *theaomai*, 'to behold', as it stresses not the performer nor the drama performed but the *audience*, the *spectators*. Theatre is thus, by definition, a public event, and the importance of the audience is stressed over that of the performer, although, of course, nothing can be seen without something to see.

It is this that makes me suspect that the term 'theatre', whilst more socially sophisticated than drama, is the younger concept. 'Drama', with the emphasis inbuilt in the root on the primacy of *doing*, harks back to the roots of *ritual* and of participation. With 'theatre', a separation has occurred. This is not the place for a detailed description of the ancient theatre but the outline in OED seems worth quoting for what we can deduce from its *staging*: 'It had the form of a segment of a circle; the auditorium was usually excavated from a hillside, the seats rising above and behind one another; the orchestra, occupied by the chorus, separated the stage from the auditorium.'

Whilst the precise nature of the details of Ancient Greek staging will always include aspects of surmise, I believe the structure of the *theatre site* informs the nature of the *theatrical experience*. There tends to be some separation, emotional and intellectual as well as physical, in the theatre between the audience and the performer/ performance, but at the same time, here in the form of the *chorus* which is both part of the action and part of the audience to the main plot – in a sense an intermediary – there is also a form of participation. It is this shifting balance of distance and involvement that distinguishes theatre spaces, theatre genres and individual plays and performances one from another.

It is significant that both the OED's first attestations of 'theatre' have members of the audience as subject: 'Comune strompetes of swich a place that men clepyn the theatre' (*c.*1374, Chaucer, *Boethius*) and 'Thei maden a sawt with oon ynwit, or wille, in to the teatre' (1382, Wyclif). The difference in spelling suggests a possible difference of pronunciation and also that Chaucer may have taken his word direct from L. *theatrum* whilst Wyclif's may come from Fr. *teatre*. It is worth noting at this juncture that pronunciations still differ: in England, the word tends to be stressed on the first syllable, whereas there are still those in America (and in Britain, if trying to sound ironically *actorly*, often delivering the word in *ham* fashion) who stress the second syllable.

We can possibly give credit for the use of 'theatre' (as opposed to 'playhouse' etc.) as the generic term for the purpose-built English building to James Burbage who, in 1576, built the first custom-built theatre – The Theatre, in Shoreditch, outside the boundaries of the City of London: 'Those places...which are made vp and builded for such Plaies and Enterludes, as the Theatre and Curtaine is' (1578, Northbrooke, *Dicing*). Of course, he may simply have given the building the most obvious descriptive name, as certainly the word is generally used alongside 'playhouse' from only marginally later: 'As in a Theater, the eyes of men/After a well-graced Actor leaues the Stage,/Are idly bent on him that enters next' (1595, Shakespeare, *Richard II*, V.ii). (This spelling of *theater*, now American, was prevalent alongside the current English spelling until eC18 but had been dropped by 1750.)

From lC16-mC17, it was possible to use 'theatre' as 'stage' – 'A theatre, or scaffold whereon musitions, singers, or such like shew their cunning, orchestra' (1589, OED) – but this practice died out by lC17. Significant to our definition of the word, however, are the early attestations of its use as 'a theatreful of spectators; the audience, or "house", at a theatre' (OED). 'The censure of the which one must in your allowance o'reway a whole Theatre of others' (*Hamlet*, III.ii).

Whilst 'drama' does not appear to have been extended into metaphorical use until C18, this process occurred early with 'theatre', as it did with *stage*. Whilst the *Hamlet* attestation above could arguably be seen as such an extension, the metaphorical development is made clear in Bacon's *The Advancement of Learning*, (1605): 'But men must know, that in this theatre of man's life it is reserved only for God and angels to be lookers-on.' A vast range of such usages exists to the present day, notably in the much-employed *theatre of war*, a term first attested in eC18: 'The theatre of a Civil War' (1720, tr. Ozell, *History of the Revolutions that Happened in the Government of the Roman Republic*).

Its further modern usage in terms such as *lecture theatre* and *operating theatre*, based on the fact there was an audience at both, can be dated to eC17 too, with the adoption of the term for what was to become the Sheldonian Theatre at Oxford University: 'That is now rather become a Sepulcher of sciences, then a Theater, there being not above five students' (1613, Purchas, *Pilgrimage*).

'Theatre' was not used as a general term for 'dramatic art' until after the Restoration, at the same time this development occurred to 'drama': it was a great period for abstract classification: 'By his encouragement, Corneille, and some other Frenchmen, reformed their theatre, which before was as much below ours, as it now surpasses it' (1668, Dryden, *Essay on Dramatic Poesy*). However, it could be argued that this process was occurring before the Interregnum, as in this reference to the opus of Ben Jonson: 'He was often pleas'd, to feed your eare/With the choice dainties of his Theatre' (1640, C.G., in Brome, *Antipodes to Censuring Criticks*).

'Theatre' is also commonly used with an adjectival function, e.g. 'theatre design'. As this list is practically endless, with the exception of a group of words included alphabetically below, the substantive word can be found under its own heading e.g. *design*.

theatre club   A *theatre club*, like a 'stage society', is often a closed organisation which does not open its doors to public audiences, drawing instead on a list of members or subscribers. In the past, such clubs were on occasions private expressly in order to avoid the restrictions imposed by the *Lord Chamberlain* and local Watch Committees: for example, the Traverse Theatre in Edinburgh was only able to get away with its influential experimental work involving 'bad' language, nudity etc. by dint of its somewhat bogus club status.

Theatre, Doctor   *Doctor Theatre* is a common theatrical term implying the restorative powers of theatre for those suffering from fatigue of the body, mind and soul. It is clearly modelled on the same formula as 'Doctor Brighton', a common society colloquialism dating from the 1820s. Whereas that did not survive into C20, Doctor Theatre is still practising.

theatre-goer   The term, dating at least from mC19, applied to any person who attends a theatrical performance, though more commonly suggesting an habitual visitor to theatres, someone given to *theatre-going*: 'Part of the great quest was theatre-going itself. I had seen my first Shakespeare at the St. George's Theatre, Tufnell Park, when I was fourteen...Now that I'd found my vocation, theatre-going was a wonderful adventure' (Branagh, 36).

theatre language, theatrical language   *Theatre language* can be used to refer simply to the *dialogue* of a play, but it has two further, specialised usages: firstly, the in-language of *theatre people*, the subject of this book; the second is more commonly encountered in the form *theatrical language*: 'We are adopting a different theatrical language, and we have to speak it very fluently, very quickly for the audience to get the meaning' (*Plays and Players*, October 1990). This m-lC20 term is not merely a reference to dialogue: it refers to a nexus of non-verbal language and *conventions* 'spoken' in theatrical performance which, like all languages, needs to be decoded by the audience and, like all conventions, needs also to be accepted by them. Theatrical language, like all languages, is in a state of constant evolution. The dialects most difficult for Joe Public to interpret are those of the *avant-garde*. See also *vocabulary*.

theatre-in-education See *T.I.E.*

theatre-in-the-round The term used to refer to a type of *staging* also less commonly known as *arena staging*. It is characterised by the performance area being a *ring* or (despite the apparently wild geometrical inaccuracy) some form of square or polygon: this space is entirely surrounded by the audience. Such staging goes back to Ancient times but was only reinstated in Western European indoor theatres in lC18 in the form of *circuses*. Artaud proposed its use in the 1920s, although he also suggested that the action should surround the audience, and it was adopted by Moscow's Realistic Theatre for some productions in the mid-1930s, reaching Britain in the 1940s by way of John English's Arena Theatre Company. Its adoption as one of the most common m-lC20 *auditorium* forms in newly-designed theatres, and a favourite format for *flexible staging*, has been rapid. Its popularity amongst professionals and audiences alike, reflects a significant reappraisal of the theatrical experience.

theatre people Along with *theatre-folk*, a term used for all those professionally involved in the theatrical world.

theatre-pitch '[My voice] can go on for longer, at full theatre-pitch, just as those toy cars powered by a certain battery can outlas those using an inferior sort,' Barkworth (p.96) claims of periods when he is working in the theatre and doing regular *voice* exercises. *Theatre-pitch* refers to level and control of *projection*, *diction*, pace etc. required for public performance.

theatre time Traditionally, *theatre time* is chronologically inaccurate by five minutes, at least from the *backstage* point of view. 'If a poor girl be one minute late by the Cruel Stage Manager's infallible chronometer, which, with the Green-room clock, he always keeps five minutes before the horse Guards, he directs the prompter to "fine her"' (1850s, Thomas William Robertson, *The Illustrated Times*, quoted in Nagler, 494).

theatre workshop A term which has grown in usage since the 1950s, echoing the name of the highly-influential, post-war Theatre Workshop company which eventually found a home at

the Theatre Royal, Stratford East (i.e. Stratford, East London).
See *workshop*.

theatrical   As an adjective, with its simplest sense of 'of or pertaining to the theatre', *theatrical* is in evidence from mC16, the earliest
OED attestation being from 1558: 'To dispense God's word...in
poor destitute Parishes...more meet for my decayed Voice...
than in Theatricall and great audience.' In this factually- descriptive sense it is to be found in a variety of phrases such as *theatrical
agent*, *theatrical digs*, and *theatrical family* – the latter referring to
dynasties such as the Terrys, the Mills, the Redgraves etc. In
most such senses, the adjectival use is self-explanatory and the
substantive word can be found under its own heading.

A development occurs in mC17, when 'theatrical' takes on the
sense of '...that simulates or is simulated; artificial, affected,
assumed' (OED). 'Man in businesse is but a Theatricall person,
and in a manner but personates himselfe' (1649). The affected
overtones are developed in eC17, when OED adds the more
derogatory 'extravagantly and irrelevantly histrionic; "stagy"
[*sic*]; calculated for display, showy, spectacular', quoting Steele
and Addison (1709-10, *The Tatler*, No. 136): 'His Theatrical Manner of making Love.'

theatricality   The noun developed in eC19 from *theatrical*. Whilst
there was a rare sense of the word meaning 'a dramatic performance' – 'I remember once taking her to Drury Lane Theatre...
Of the theatricality itself that night, I can remember absolutely
nothing' (1866, Carlyle, *Reminiscences*) – by far the most common
senses relates to 'theatrical', and it can be used with a range of
nuances from 'having or exploiting the qualities of a theatrical
performance' to 'the quality of being stagey and showy': 'I love
theatricality...but for me a great naturalistic performance in a
quiet part can be just as exciting as seeing someone in heavy
make-up with a physical contortion very clearly "acting"' (Branagh, 112). It can be seen from this reference that the term almost
has the overtones of '*melodramatic*'. It has been used generally
almost since being coined, here with less extreme connotations:
'By act and word he strives to do it; with sincerity, if possible;
failing that, with theatricality' (1837, Carlyle, *French Revolution*).
An alternative form, *theatricalism*, is rarely used.

theatricals   Now most commonly used as a term for 'theatrical
performances and related activities', though it is most frequently
used for amateur 'dabblings' in theatre, probably because it carries the sense of the adjective *theatrical*, 'of or pertaining to the
theatre': it is not quite the thing itself (compare *dramatics*). It is
most commonly found in the phrase *amateur theatricals*: 'My

primary school's taste for theatricals was encouraged by Beryl
Levitt, my final form teacher and a great enthusiast for drama'
(Branagh, 24). The noun is still occasionally found with its com-
mon C19 sense of *theatre-people*.

therapy   As in the phrase *drama therapy*. Along with *music* and
art therapy, a way of using the arts, in this case specifically *drama
games*, *role-plays* and *simulations*, rather than actual theatre performances, to therapeutically assist those with learning difficulties,
behavioural problems etc. In extreme circumstances, such work
might also stray into the province of *psychodrama*.

thespian   'I believed...one should...put something back into
the world through whatever work one did. I felt that as an actor
this was possible and the implication that any aspiring thespian
was an effete, money-grabbing waster galled me' (Branagh, 46).
As here, *thespian* tends to be used somewhat ironically for 'actor',
if not derogatorily at times by those outside the *profession*. It is
commonly abbreviated to *thesp*: 'Somehow we impersonate a
camp delivery if we wish to barb a comment. Fellow thesps will
know exactly what I mean...' (Berkoff, 123). It derives from
Thespis, the semi-legendary Attican poet and dramatist who won
the first *Dionysian* contest in 534 BC. None of his plays are now
extant. He was the leader of a travelling company and may well
have acted himself, in which case he would be the first actor, as
well as dramatist, known by name. Olivier expands on his significance, which also includes the role of *director*: 'Sophocles would
have been the apple of Thespis' eye had they shared the same
generation. Actors are commonly referred to as Thespians, but
it seems that Thespis himself was more producer than actor in
that he brought to the tradition regnant in the theatre up till then
– that of solo recitations at great length of religious eulogies – the
idea of a colloquy between two actors, thus instigating The Scene'
(p.46). Perhaps Thespis should really be termed a *dramaturge*.

Thespian appears to have been used sporadically and mock-
heroicially as an adjective meaning 'of or pertaining to theatre,
tragedy etc.' from C17, but only became commonly used as a
noun for an actor from eC19: 'The Thespian's outward guise of
happiness, her secret mood belies' (1827, W. Kennedy, *Poems*).

thinking part/actor   Two very contrasting terms. *Thinking part* is
an ironic C19 euphemism for a role with no lines, a non-speaking
part. A *thinking actor*, however, tends to be used as a complimentary C20 description of an actor who approaches a role in a committed, intellectual way; this too can be used ironically or disparagingly however, depending on the speaker. The thinking
actor in *Charley's Aunt* may not necessarily be ideal *casting*.

three-hander A play or scene for three actors: see *-hander*. Also known (mainly American) as a *threesome (scene)*.

through line Sometimes written as *through-line* or *throughline* – an abbreviation of 'the through line of action' from the Russian: the consistent development of a role and characterisation during the course of a play. A *Stanislavskian* term: once a *super-objective* has been established for a play, the Stanislavskian actor is expected to work on a *throughline* which is consistent with it. 'That inner line of effort that guides the actors from the beginning to the end of a play we call the *continuity* or the *through-going action*. This through line galvanises all the small units and objectives of the play and directs them toward the superobjective. From then on they all serve the common purpose' (1936, Stanislavski, *An Actor Prepares*).

throw (away) Working on a script, Barkworth (p.256) devises a personal system of annotation: 'Here it is again, with suggested hesitations (/) and bits to throw away (a line over the words).' By the verb to *throw away*, actors are denoting a line or piece of business to be deliberately under-emphasised either because they offer little opportunity to the actor, or to allow other lines to be *pointed* by contrast, or because to say certain lines in an under-emphasised manner is actually more comic or dramatically effective. Hence, a *throw-away line*, a phrase now in common usage. However, one can also *throw away one's lines* or an entire scene due to lack of concentration or a failure of *technique*. (A throwaway is also a term [largely American] for a *hand-bill* or *flyer*.) If an actor is *thrown* by an event or situation he loses his concentration in some way, possibly *blanking* as a result: 'Anyone fool enough to go out front and watch will know how completely thrown I am' (Barkworth, 157).

throwline A *line* or rope used to tie flats and other stage items together. It is also called a cleat *line* or (largely American) *lashline*.

thrust stage Now used as a descriptive term for a form of *staging*, also known as an *open stage*, which projects or *thrusts out* into the auditorium. Usually, the audience is seated on three sides of this stage. Quite when the term was first used I have been unable to ascertain, but it is certainly in keeping with C16 theatre language; there is a rare stage direction, 'thrust out', used when a heavy prop or piece of furniture had to be pushed forward onto the stage.

thunder The *sound effect* of thunder, now generally reproduced on a *sound tape*, has been produced in English theatre since C16 in a variety of fascinating ways, with equally fascinating names. Most of the following are from C18-C19. *Thunder crashes* (or *thunder-barrels*) were created by the technique of dropping stones or other weighty objects onto an iron sheet from a suspended barrel. *Thunder boxes* (also known as *thunder rollers, thunder runs, rabbit hutches* and *rumble boxes*) were either boxes with grooves along which iron balls were run or, alternatively, wagons with unbalanced wheels which were rolled along the back of the stage (in which case they might also be known as *thunder carts* and *rumble carts*). *Thunder sheets* or *thunder curtains* were suspended sheets of metal which could be rattled by a handle or hit with a stick and, finally, (although it is certain that this list contains a great many omitted devices and terms), a *thunder tank* was, as one might guess, a suspended tank which could be hit by a stick.

ticket   *Ticket* has been used in its modern sense of 'an admission slip' – i.e. a slip of paper, cardboard etc. acting as proof of payment and guarantee of service – since at least the Restoration: 'Therefore, I say, let our Gallant (having paid his half Crown, and given the Door-keeper his Ticket) presently advance himself into the middle of the Pit...' (1674, Vincent, *The Young Gallant's Academy*). The term was also used as an alternative to *poster* and *bill* at this time, a usage dating back at least a century earlier in Scotland and Ireland: 'At the suggestion of sum tikkettis affixt on the Tolbuyth dur of Edinburgh, be his lettre sent to hir majestie, [he] had desyrit James Erll Bothwell, and certane specifiit in the saisis tikkettis, to be apprehendit' (1567, in a ruling of the Privy Council of Scotland). This usage brings us to the etymology, from OF *estiquet(te)*, from *estiquer*, 'to stick, fix' (the same root as *étiquette*), the initial *e-* being lost by aphesis (the gradual loss of the initial unstressed vowel).

Associated theatrical phrases, which are for the most part self-explanatory, include *ticket agency* and **agent**, *ticket office, ticket rack* (where tickets are held until collected) and *ticket tout*, (see *tout*).

T.I.E.   An abbreviation of *Theatre-in-Education*. This is not, as might be expected, a term for the orthodox teaching of drama on the syllabus of schools and colleges: it is a term for theatre companies, some funded by Local Education Authorities, some existing entirely on bookings and grant-*funding*, which play specifically to school and college audiences in Britain. Few remain today: the great T.I.E. boom occurred during the late 1960s and into the 1970s, but lack of *funding* has killed off the vast majority of groups in the last two decades of C20. Usually T.I.E. groups were touring companies which visited educational premises, sometimes doing *straight* drama, but often performing devised shows geared to open up a social issue which would later be developed in discussion and teachers' follow-up work in the classroom.

timing   The *timing of a scene* may refer simply to its length, but a more specialised usage would be referring to its *rhythm* and pacing. A specialised use of timing by actors, most notably in the phrase *comic timing*, refers to an elusive point of *technique*. 'What most people mean by "timing" is using a beat-pause between the feed-line and the laugh-line, but of course it depends very much on the meaning of the lines' (Barkworth, p.64). Consequently, 'timing' is an extremely difficult thing to define, relying, as it does, on an instinctive feel for when to deliver a line for maximum effect and how to weight and phrase the delivery of that line, which is why most actors assert that it cannot be taught:
'I think a sense of timing, a sense of comedy, a sense of what is funny about a part, are gifts from God. God or whoever. But you can help them along in various ways, for example with rhythm or with different dynamics. To put it no higher, I think you can get laughs in the theatre by tickling the audience's ears, by surprising them. I mean loud and soft and fast and slow, really. Music can be funny in the same way.' (Prunella Scales, interviewed in Barkworth, 220)
The term may well be influenced by music, in which case, it may date back to C16-C17: 'What is the timing of a note... It is a certayne space or length, wherein a note may be holden in singing' (1597, Motley, *A plaine and easie introduction to practicall musicke*). It was certainly in use by C19 – compare 'timing' in cricket, attested in OED lC19.

tiring-house   Henslowe and Alleyne, commissioning the building of the Fortune Theatre in 1599 for the Lord Admiral's Company, specified 'a Stadge and Tyreinge howse to be made... to the manner and fashion of the saide howse called the Globe' (quoted in Nagler, 118-19). The term is a C16 aphetic version of *attiring house*, in a literal sense the Elizabethan version of *dressing-room*. It derives its name from the fact that costumes were at this time referred to as *tires*, *attires* and variations on these: 'The attyre of [the] *Masquers* was alike, in all, without difference' (1605, Ben Jonson describing *The Masque of Blackness*, quoted in Nagler, 145-6). However, the *tiring-house*, (found in various forms including *tyerhowsse*), as the main building of the Elizabethan theatre served far more functions: it probably contained most of the features one would now expect to find *backstage* in a theatre. In 1596, a visiting Dutchman, de Witt, in a valuable sketch of the Swan Theatre, designated the tiring-house *mimorum ades*, 'the house of the actors'; it certainly housed the *inner stage*, at least one *gallery*, a *machine-room* and other rooms besides.

title   'It's coming closer... the dread moment. The audience grows silent. They want to hear how the "title" of the play sounds. They are almost afraid of him' (Berkoff, 8). *Title* is an abbreviation of *title role*, (also found as *title part* and *title character*), dating back at least to C19: 'we knew what the first play was going to be: it was *Peer Gynt* with Ralph in the title role' (Olivier, 143).

toggle Abbreviation of both *toggle rail* and *toggle bar*. A toggle bar is a wooden strengthening *batten* fastened horizontally across a *flat*: the *toggle iron* is the metal device which attaches it to a *stile*. It is hardly surprising, given its function, that *toggle* turns out to be a nautical term (of unknown origin) dating from at least C18. On board ship it designated a 'device for fastening with cross-piece which can pass through hole or loop in one position but not in another; pin or other cross-piece through eye of rope, link of chain, etc., to keep it in place; pivoted barb of a harpoon' (Concise Oxford).

toi toi toi Used mainly in European theatre, though it has gained limited currency in Britain, *toi toi toi* is an explosive phrase emitted in circumstances when the staider English actor might mutter 'break a leg': a way of wishing a performer good luck before they go on stage. It is a stylised and sanitised version of spitting over one's shoulder, and another example of superstition in the theatre.

top¹ Used adjectivally in phrases such as *top lighting* to refer to the upper half of the stage. *Top lighting* is illumination provided from directly above the playing area or the equipment *rigged* there. A *top drop* is another term for a *border*.

top² In phrases such as *top of the bill*, *top billing* and *top-liner* as applied to the *star* of a show, the term was once descriptive: such performers' names literally appeared at the top of a playbill (compare American 'headliner'). All the phrases entered into general usage to denote people or things of excellence in lC19-eC20.

Phrases such as *taking it from* or *going from the top*, where *top* means 'beginning', have a related etymology, referring to the top of the page, thus the *top of a scene*. Again, in general usage. By transference, the *opening*, ('beginning') of a show becomes the *top of the show*.

top³ Actors use the verbs *to top*, *to top it* and the resultant noun *topping* to describe the *building* of a speech: an increase in its volume, pace, intensity etc. This usage is reminiscent of the colloquial imperative *Top that!*, 'exceed that', a verb only developed in C20, possibly in America, from the Standard English use of *top* as the 'highest', used in theatre in *top prices*.

top and tail A phrase used in *rehearsal*, largely at the *tech* stage. *To top and tail* is to omit long speeches, occasionally even sections of scenes, in order to leave only the vital *cues*: a method of speeding

up the teching process. It probably comes from culinary usage –
cutting the heads and tails from fish, the top and bottoms from
gooseberries etc. Interestingly, 'top and tail' is also used in nursing
for a method of bed-washing which concentrates only on the very
public and very private parts of a patient.

tormentor   Semi-permanent *wings*, either *curtains* or *flats*, used
to mask the *offstage* area from the audience's view. In C18 theatre,
they were sliding extensions of the *proscenium* wing. Whilst I can
find no corroboration for this, I should hazard a guess that the
term comes from the tormenting effect on those in the audience
who might have liked to have seen what was going on in the
wing-space more than the proceedings on stage, since the verb
has no other recorded sense. Related terms include *tormentor entrance*, an entrance made from between tormentors; *tormentor lights*,
lights positioned on a *tormentor batten* to give side-lighting to the
stage. See also *tower* and *teaser*.

total theatre   Initially a translation of the German term *Total-
theater*, a projected design by the architect Walter Gropius for
Erwin Piscator in 1926; anticipating later developments in flexible
staging and including many 'futuristic' technical effects, it was
never built. In some technical senses it can be seen as a C20
avant-garde version of Wagner's *Gesamtkunstwerk*. It did, however, have a conceptual influence, notably on Artaud (see *cruelty*):
Brook describes 'total theatre, that time-honoured notion of getting all the elements of the stage to serve the play...' (p.47).

touring   See *on tour*.

tout   In theatre terms, a *ticket tout*, 'someone who buys or otherwise obtains sought-after tickets in sufficiently large quantities to
make a living or at least a sizeable killing from their resale'. From
the verb *to tout*, 'to peep, peer, look out', in use since C15, by
eC18 *tout* had come to mean a criminal's look-out man. According
to Partridge, both the meaning of 'a solicitor of custom for tradesmen' and the word's more specialised horse-racing sense of 'one
who surreptitiously watches the trials of racehorses, so as to gain
information for betting purposes' (Hammond, *Horse Racing: a
Book of Words*) developed from mC19. The racing tout has
become respectable, as has the *ticket agent*, some of whose
activities, especially in the West End, correspond to legalised
touting: the ticket tout proper, or improper, remains a shady,
underworld figure.

tower   An abbreviation of *light tower*, a descriptive term for metal
scaffolding, often on castors, often fitted with a ladder and/or
platform, enabling *lighting men* to *rig* and *focus* otherwise inacces-
sible lights. The term is also used (as in *tormentor tower*) for a

structure on which lights can be hung. (Compare *ladder*.) Occasionally, it is even used of a single lighting bar placed in an elevated situation.

toy theatre   The name given to the model stages used in *juvenile drama*. See also *penny plain*, *tuppence coloured*.

tragedy   Were it not so crucial a word in theatre, one might feel tempted to agree with Taplin: 'two words on the origin of Greek tragedy: unknown and irrelevant' (p.23). At least in his choice of the first of those adjectives, it is hard to fault Taplin: Gk *tragōidia* is generally agreed to be a compound of *tragos*, 'goat', and *ōidē*, 'song', giving the perplexing 'goat-song'. Various explanations have been given for this name, including the widely-held theories that at the early Athenian Festivals of *Dionysus* – himself a complex deity whose ambiguities may hold some clues – a goat was awarded as prize, or that the earlier rites from which tragedy sprang involved some relic of animal worship and sacrifice. There may also be some clue to the origins of *tragedy* in the name of the *satyr-plays* which were performed alongside tragedies at the festival. 'Tragedy' must certainly antedate the first recorded tragic contest held in 534 BC – sixty years before the first extant plays – when Pisistratus invited the essentially rural genre, which was already a source of national pride, into Athens. The prize went to the semi-legendary Thespis (see *Thespian*) who is credited with introducing a *protagonist* into the *choral dithyramb*. This was also 200 years before *Aristotle* was to lay down the critical groundplan of tragedy in his *Poetics*.

The first English usage of the term as 'a literary work of a serious nature with a sorrowful or disastrous conclusion', initially, a story or narrative poem, dates from C14, arriving via OF *tragedie*, from L: 'Tragedye is to seyn, a dite of a prosperite for a tyme that endith in wrecchydnesse' (*c*.1374, Chaucer, *Boethius*) and 'Goo litel booke goo litel my tregeedie' (*c*.1374, Chaucer, *Troilus and Criseyde*). In the following century references are found to the ancient dramatic tragedies: 'The tragidés divers of unkouth and morall Senec' (1430, Lydgate). The earliest native claims to be the author of a theatrical tragedy occur in eC16: 'Companyons I want to begynne thys tragediye' (1538, Bale, *Thre Lawes*).

What is interesting, however, is that 'tragedy' is generally applied to 'an unhappy or fatal event or series of events in real life' (OED) – a sense which is still by far its most common usage – as early as the beginning of the C16. There is an OED attestation from 1509, but I choose to cite a slightly later one: 'To telle you alle this commodie, but for thabbot a tragedie, hit were to long' (1535, Layton in *Letters on the Suppression of the Monasteries*

[Camden]). Here alongside *comedy*, often regarded as its antonym and frequently accompanying it in such references, it follows the trend seen frequently in this book of a word finding a general usage after it has become established as the signifier of a literary genre: here its cue is from narrative verse rather from theatre, where it was not as yet established. The public was familiar with 'tragedy' before dramatists began to use it, so it is futile for purists to argue, as one has often heard them do, that the word is misused and has lost its pure Aristotelean meaning. In English, it is they who are the usurpers of the common meaning. This may, alongside a national predisposition to shun formulas, in part account for the English drama's cavalier attitude to the classical rules of tragedy, in such contrast to continental *neo-classicism*.

tragedian This term shadows the development of *tragedy* itself, being used in C14 for a writer of (verse) tragedies – 'A Tragedeyn, þat is to seyn a makere of ditees þat hyhten tragedies' (*c*.1374, Chaucer, *Boethius*) – and in lC16 'tragic actor': 'The Tragedian who represents his person' (1592, Nashe, *Pierce Penilesse*). This term lingers into C19, the era of Macready and the great melodramatic *hams*, by which time it smacks not a little of *stagese*.

tragic 'Witnes theyr Satyr sharpe, and tragicke playes' (1563, *A myrroure for magistrates*), is the first OED attestation of the term (although the now obsolete *tragical* was in common use a century before this). Its common use for 'unhappy events in real life' is widespread, and it is found in a number of key phrases such as *tragic error* or *flaw*, an English rendering of the Gk *hamartia*, 'error of judgement', the negative quality which contributes to the tragic hero's démise. A *tragic carpet* was a cloth of green baize traditionally placed on the stage in C17-C19 performances of tragedies, a convention which had the advantage of keeping the actors' costumes clean in the busy Act V death scenes.

tragi-comedy A term for a hybrid genre which admits the coexistence of tragic and comic elements in both its subject matter and style. It is not hinted at in OED until 1631, in the title of a play by James Mabbe, *The Spanish bawd represented in Celestina; or the tragicke comedy of Calisto and Melibea*, though it, and other hybrids, were undoubtedly known to Shakespeare: 'The best actors in the world for tragedy, comedy... tragical-historical, tragical-comical-historical...' (1601, *Hamlet*, II.ii).

training Most actors *train* in some way; they 'achieve a desired standard by instruction and practice'. However, the phrase *trained actor* suggests the formal training in acting one might acquire at a school. *Training* has been used for 'instructive development' since the mC16, (from the verb *to train*, ultimately from L. *trahere*, 'to draw along, drag'), the first OED reference allying it to school occurring in 1600: 'Schooles...freely bestowed for the training vp of youth.' (The word was not applied to physical and sporting development until C19 – 'a professional pugilist; always in training' [1854, Dickens, *Hard Times*] – though it was used for horses in eC16 [see Hammond, *Horse Racing: a Book of Words*].)

Most early actor training occurred on the job: in C16, boys were taken on in boy companies such as the Children of the Chapel or employed by adult companies such as the King's Men: '*Hart* and *Clun*, were bred up Boys at the Blackfriers; and acted women's Parts, *Hart* was *Robinson's* Boy or Apprentice: He Acted the Dutchess in the Tragedy of *the Cardinal*, which was the first Part that gave him Reputation' (1699, *Historia Histrionica*). This system continued until C19 and only in the first years of C20 – the *Central* was founded in 1906, *RADA* in 1909 – was the kind of formal training expected today established.

transformation scene   This is the name given to a highly-dramatic scenic effect developed in C18, one of the centre-pieces of *pantomime*, in which one *setting* vanishes, sometimes *in a puff of smoke* (thereby creating another phrase in general usage), to be immediately replaced by another. An example is the famous scene in *Cinderella*, where the Fairy Godmother turns the mice into footmen, a pumpkin into a coach etc. And there were other 'tricks, which were produced by the magic wand of Harlequin; such as the sudden transformation of palaces and temples to huts and cottages; of men and women into wheel-barrows and joint-stools; collonades to beds of tulips; and mechanic shops into serpents and ostriches' (1808, Thomas Davies, Memoirs of the Life David Garrick). Techniques and devices used over the centuries have included *falling flats*, the *fan effect*, the *rise-and-sink* system of scene-changing and *transparencies*.

transparency   One of the scenic devices used in lC19 *transformation scenes* whereby the backdrop was painted on canvas or linen in transparent dye. With a change from front-lighting to back-lighting, (made possible by recent developments in lighting technology), entire scenes could be made to disappear and other scenes painted on the rear of the transparency back-drop could replace them. From *transparent*, from med L. *transparens*, ultimately from L. *trans*, 'through', + *parere*, 'to appear'.

trap   An abbreviation of *trap-door* (sometimes found as *trapdoor*), originally a term from domestic joinery, primarily used in theatre for any concealed opening in the stage-floor, although it may also be applied to those in the rear or side walls or even the ceiling of a set, or in items of *scenery*: 'it appeared likely that he has fallen through a trapdoor while rearranging a cluster of lights below a gantry shortly before the show began' (*The Stage*, 21 March 1991). *Traps* vary in sophistication from flaps to flats, through hinged, wooden openings in the stage floor, to the highly complex *Corsican trap* or *ghost slide*. The term was used generally from C14: '"Which way be ye comen?..." Quod she... "Here at this secre trappe dore," quod he' (*c.*1374, Chaucer, *Troylus and Criseyde*). Traps have been used in English theatre since the *pageant* wagons of *medieval drama* if not before. The *cellar* below the stage or part of it may sometimes be referred to as a *trap-cellar* (or *-dock*, *-room*); a stage with traps as a *trapped stage*. In C19, British actors were renowned throughout Europe for the quality of their *trap-work*, including their *roll-outs*. For further details of specific traps, see *bristle trap*, *cauldron trap*, *Corsican trap*, *footlights* trap, *ghost glide*, *grave trap*, *slote*, star trap and *vampire trap*.

trapeze   An *acrobat*'s swing; a cross-bar suspended from strings, wires etc., used in *circus* or *variety* acts. From F. *trapèze*, from LL *trapezium*, the geometrical term for 'a quadrilateral with only one of its two pairs of sides parallel'. This would appear to derive from the eccentric craftsmanship of Ancient Greek joiners, coming as it ultimately does from Gk *trapezion*, from *trapeza*, 'table'. See also *leotard*.

traveller   A descriptive term used for either the track used with draw *curtains* or for curtains themselves, if, like the *traverse curtain*, they can be drawn horizontally. The word is used in this sense for a 'moving mechanism' (Concise Oxford) in other trades too: for example, a *traveller* also denotes a travelling crane.

travelling company   A term which can be employed either for a theatre company without a home base, which specialises in touring, or any other company which, at the time of reference, is *on the road*.

traverse   Now most commonly used for a form of *staging* repopularised in Britain in m-lC20 at the Traverse Theatre in Edinburgh, where its adoption was a necessity in a cramped *Fringe* theatre club: stage action *in traverse* occurs between two banks of seating. The Traverse selected the word for sound theatrical reasons: a *traverse* is an alternative name for *traveller*, much used in America: at the Restoration it was the name for a recess which could be revealed at the rear of the stage by the opening of a *traverse curtain*.

travesty   A term for a *burlesque* or parody, adopted from Fr. *travesti* in mC17: 'What think you of Romances travesti... Burlesque and Travesti? These are hard words, And may be French, but not Law-French' (1662, Davenant, *Play House to Let*). *Travesty* shares the same root as *transvestite*: from L. *trans-*, 'across' + It. *vestire*, 'to dress': i.e. 'disguise oneself'. The authors of travesties dress in other authors' literary clothes, and the word carries with it the idea of disguise and, possibly, a hint of the ridiculous. (In 1970, I learnt of an interesting American campus refinement of the term from my friend, Matt Wikander, who claimed that a travesty was a literary genre with a simple definition: it should be exactly one typed A4-page in length, be tastelessly overwritten and end in an act of unspeakable violence. He is the only exponent of the form I have ever met.)

treads   Used most commonly on the stage for a set of stairs, from *tread*, the joiner's and builder's term for the horizontal cross-piece of a step (contrast *riser*), ultimately from the same Germanic root as *trade* (which links 'footstep' with 'pathway').

tread on a line   '[Y]ou feel an actor trod on your lines or upstaged you in some way... it's difficult to express your pain realistically without sounding somehow "precious"... so you might say, "We've got our mum out there tonight, have we then?"' (Berkoff, 123). *To tread on someone's lines* is an actor's term for the intentional or unintentional interference with another actor's speech, possibly *overlapping* or by distracting with unnecessary *business*. Compare *laugh, tread on a...*

tread the boards   A traditional and, in C20, hammily self-conscious term for 'acting'. See *boards* (a term used colloquially for 'stage' from mC18 according to Partridge).

tree, be a   A mocking phrase now used colloquially both inside and outside the acting profession with reference to some of the more outrageous *improvisations* and *rehearsal* exercises an actor or student of drama might be expected to suffer: 'You don't want me to be a tree, do you?' The phrase certainly dates back to the 1950s and may have been part of the public reaction to what it read in the newspapers about *the Method*. Perhaps it is ultimately traceable to Stanislavski's chapter on Imagination in *An Actor Prepares* (1936), worth quoting for its sheer absurdity:

"I am going to choose a passive theme because it will necessitate much more work... That is why I suggest that you, Paul, are living the life of a tree."

"Good," said Paul with decision. "I am an age-old oak. However, even though I have said it, I don't really believe it."

"In that case," suggested the Director, "Why don't you say to yourself: I am I, but if I were an old oak, set in certain surrounding conditions, what would I do?..."

"On myself I see a thick covering of leaves, which rustle."

"They do indeed," agreed the Director. "Up there the winds must often be strong."

"In my branches," continues Paul, "I see some birds' nests."

The Director then pushed him to describe every detail of his imaginary existence as an oak tree. (p.65)

trestle stage Although *trestle* is a common enough word, especially in the phrase *trestle table*, that indispensible accessory to village fêtes etc., its theatrical use – for a stage mounted on a portable hinged structure – is worthy of note as another likely *nautical* borrowing: it is the word for the horizontal pieces on a lower mast which support a topmast. *Trestle stages*, because of their temporary nature, are particularly associated with the *barnstorming companies* and *gaffs* of C19. The Trestle Theatre Company is a current *touring company* which has chosen the name for its associations.

tripe In its sense of 'utter nonsense', tripe has been in slang usage since C19, especially in relation to writing and the arts, based on a play on the Standard English sense of 'the second stomach of ox etc. as food' (Concise Oxford) – i.e. inferior food. Beale suggests that it is due to the standards of its output that Broadcasting House in London has been called the Tripe Shop, especially by taxi drivers, since about 1930. To reassure devotees of the BBC, in theatre, *tripe* can be used to describe loose electric cabling in the flies and elsewhere, running to a *control board*, an equally likely derivation for the term Tripe House. Anyone who has witnessed the untidiness of yard upon coiled yard of this tripe, ineffectually secured by *gaffer tape* in the wings of some amateur *venues*, and who has also seen offal in an abattoir, might hazard a guess that the term is descriptive, especially given the alternative World War II sense of 'filth, dirt'.

troupe 'Circus impresario Peter Jay's plans for a troupe of performing pussies has put the cat among the pigeons with RSPCA officials' (*The Stage*, 21 March 1991). Fr. *troupe* (from OF *trope*, first used in C13) is used as a collective grouping for a wide range of subjects including soldiers, animals (as in *herd*, *flock*, *drove* etc.), thieves and performers, especially when they are on the move. From this usage it entered English probably via America in eC19: 'The whole troupe were equally excellent' (*New York Post*, 6 December 1825). The word is perhaps particularly associated with touring companies and, possibly via the French sense above, with dancers and animals: 'A troupe of jumping dogs' (1906, E.V. Lucas, *Listener's Lure*). The military connection is interestingly reminiscent of the usage of *company*. It is also interesting to note the existence in Fr. military jargon (cited in *Harrap's Shorter French and English Dictionary*) of the term *vieux* *troupier* for 'old campaigner', corresponding directly with *old trouper* for a seasoned theatrical performer.

truck   An abbreviation of *boat truck*.

try-out   Also found as *try out* and *tryout*. 'It was a playlet called *The Unfailing Instinct*, written by Julian Frank himself... to provide a vehicle for Miss Ruby Miller, his star for the first try-out of *The Ghost Train*, which was thought to be a little on the short side for the provinces, where audiences liked to get their money's worth' (Olivier, 46). A *try-out*, a noun clearly developed from the phrasal verb *to try out*, is most commonly used for public performances of plays, most usually *out-of-town runs*, and there is something implicit in the word which can rankle with provincial guinea-pigs as the Olivier attestation may underline. This is further emphasised in the largely obsolete *try it (out) on the dog* (compare 'try it on the *matinée* dog'), a phrase used in lC19 for try-outs or, as 'try-out' itself can be used, for any form of theatrical experimentation, including things attempted at rehearsal. The phrase is possibly derived from early forms of animal experimentation: it is one of the few theatrical phrases which clearly spell out a less than generous attitude to the audience.

tumbler   Ralegh (1614, *History of the World*) gives some description of the activities of early tumblers: 'a tricke of climing vpon mens heads, somewhat after the manner of our tumblers.' *Tumbler* as a term for an entertainer who specialises in acrobatic tricks dates from C14 (from the ME verb *tumbel*, of Germanic origin). The first two OED references to tumblers from C14 cast alarming aspersions on their morals, or at least on the company they kept: 'Hoppynge & daunceynge of tumblers and herlotis' (ante 1340) and 'Mynystrele or jogelour, tumbler and harlot' (1380). As these groupings of performers suggest, there was some confusion in the roles of entertainers at this period (compare *juggler* and *jongleur*): 'Certaine vearses like us verie well,... when we heare some tumbler or dauncer sing them to the Harpe' (1581, OED). For a dreadful pun on *tumbler*, see *acrobat*.

turn   'It was very funny for the audience who saw the joke, and they clapped each one in turn – the drummer giving, of course, a drum roll before each "turn"' (Berkoff, 78). *Turn* encompasses both *variety* performers and their *material*. Its use was once far more prevalent in Britain than that of its synonym, *act*, which was preferred in American *vaudeville* and *burlesque*. OED suggests that it is a C19 *music hall* term, from the Standard English sense of *taking one's turn* before or after other performers: 'The wire-walking of Mme. Zulia and her little girl... furnishes a clever and interesting turn' (*Evening News and Post*, 9 June 1890).

two-hander   A play or scene from a play involving only two actors. An example of a *two-handed, one act* play is Harold Pinter's *The Dumb Waiter* (1960). See *-hander*.

type, type-casting   'They're all very disparate characters, so you can't call it type-casting' (David Calder reviewing his roles in *Plays and Players*, October 1990). From Fr. *type* or L. *typus*, ultimately from Gk *tupos*, 'impression, figure' (from *tuptō*, 'strike'). Used from mC16 as 'a symbol', in the fever of classification which characterised eC19, *type* was transferred to mean both 'the general or characteristic form of a thing' and 'a person who exhibits the general qualities of a class etc.' 'The Tahitians are considered by Lesson as the type of the whole Polynesian reace' (1842, Prichard, *The Natural History of Man*). It is from this, possibly influenced by *stereotype*, that the idea of types as *stock characters* developed, although, of course, such *characterisations* have always figured strongly in theatre. (See *heavy man, woman* as an example.) *Type-casting*, equally, has always been a feature of *casting*, and, when all is said and done, it keeps many limited actors in continuous work. Actors who prefer to be *versatile*, however, have a fear of being typed: 'I hoped to prove that a really good actor need not be type-cast' (Olivier, 272).

Ü **ber-marionette** A term coined by the theatre practitioner Edward Gordon Craig (1872-1966). Craig, a prolific writer about theatre as well as a theatre historian, designer, teacher etc., rejected many elements of *naturalism* and *realism* as artless copying, seeing the actor reduced to 'an imitator not an artist'. In *The Marionette* (1918) he proposed that this should be countered by the creation of theatrical images which would 'unveil thoughts to our eyes, silently – by movement – in visions' and to this end he proposed that actor become an *über-marionette* (from G. *über*, 'over, above, superior', + *marionette*: a kind of 'super-puppet'). 'The marionette appears to me to be the last echo of some beautiful and noble art of a past civilisation'. Needless to say, whilst his ideas on design were of great international influence, he did not endear himself greatly to the average actor.

underplay *Underact* and *underplay* are synonymous terms for an understated performance of lines or business. Both words had a general sense (compare *act* and *play*) prior to the theatrical one: *underact* is first cited in OED in 1623, underplay in 1733. Both suggest below par performance in an activity: 'Faulconbridge was appointed Admirall, with Commission to take or sinke all ships he met;... who did not under act, but made many depredations along the Coasts' (1623, Buck, *The history of the life and reign of Richard the third*). None the less, on occasions an actor can underplay for effect.

understudy 'I had to understudy in *The Ghost Train*... and stand in a doorway backstage centre dressed as a policeman with a painted moustache' (Olivier, 52). An *understudy* is 'an actor or actress who studies a superior performer's part in order to be able to take it if required; also, to study a part for this purpose' (OED). See *study*.) Despite the dubious concept of the understudy's inferiority to the actor he or she is shadowing, this definition will suffice. Ill health or other acts of God do require understudies to step into the shoes of a *lead*, though nowadays it is only large companies or big *box office* shows which can afford to employ understudies who are not also cast in another role. 'Understudy' is first cited in OED from the *Slang Dictionary* of 1874, which suggests that the term came into use in the e-mC19: 'Some actors of position... have always other and inferior... artists under-

294

studying their parts' (ibid.). A further reference implies a *prima donna* attitude prevailing amongst the stars which would possibly be less tolerated today: 'She has to understudy Rose Sergeant and play her parts when that lady's temper is out of order' (1894, Crockett, *Play Actress*).

The word has had a general usage for someone who stands by or *stands in* for someone since at least C19: 'There is a tendency for gods to double their parts, or rather... for each part fo have its "under-study"' (1887, *Language of Myth, Ritual and Religion*).

unit A term with a variety of theatrical uses. Scenically, it can be used either for a piece of scenery such as a window which is inserted into a *flat* (hence, a *window unit*), or for any item of scenery which is part of a *unit setting*: a *set* which, by rearrangement of its component parts, can be used for a variety of scenes. The term is also used by adherents to the *Stanislavskian* system as an abbreviation of *unit of action*: a section of a scene which, like a paragraph in prose, seems to have a single topic. Stanislavskian actors are encouraged to break the text down into units, giving each a short title, later looking for their character's *motivation* (and the actor's *creative objective*) within it.

Unities, the From L. *unitas*, from *unus*, 'one': 'The three principles of the Aristotelian canon of dramatic composition (as adopted and expanded by the French classical dramatists), according to which a play should consist of one main action, represented as occurring at one time (i.e. in one day) and in one place' (OED). Generally, these are referred to as the *unities of action, place and time*: 'The famous Rules, which the French call Des Trois Unitez, or, the Three Unities, which ought to be observed in every regular play' (1668, Dryden, *Essay on Dramatic Poesy*). Although the *unities* were known in Britain earlier, their employment in the shaping of dramatic writing increased after the Restoration alongside other continental dramatic fashions. In fact, they are never explicitly stated as rules in Aristotle's *Poetics*, although they can be inferred, the practice evidenced in extant classical texts also supporting the idea. Fortunately for creative freedom, use of the unities went against the spirit of British playwriting. As the *tragedies* of Racine and Corneille reveal, the advantages of employing the unities are probably outweighed by their limitations.

university drama It is known for certain that drama flourished in the universities from at least C14 as, indeed, it did at Westminster School and elsewhere. In eC17, Thomas Heywood, in *An Apology for Actors* (quoted in Nagler, 124), explains why dramatic performances were encouraged: 'This it [Cambridge] held necessary

for the emboldening of their junior schollers to arme them with
audacity against they come to be employed in any publick exercise
... It teacheth audacity to the bashful grammarian... and makes
him... able to moderate in any argumentation whatsoever.' It
appears that performances were relatively sophisticated, too, as
can be seen by the reaction to an Inigo Jones *masque* in 1605: 'the
university was not impressed by what Inigo Jones had to offer in
the way of new inventions, which suggests that these were already
accepted and in use in this educational establishment' (Leacroft,
53). The fact that the *University Wits* – Marlowe, Greene, Nashe
and Peele amongst others – had been pre-eminent in the rise of
the London theatre of the 1590s argues further in support of the
relative excellence of university drama at this period.

Extra-curricular drama continued to flourish, first at Oxbridge
(notably this century in the *Footlights*, the ADC and OUDS), and
later wherever higher education was established, providing generations of playwrights, actors and critics. The academic and practical study of drama as a degree course began in the United States
in 1914 at the Carnegie Institute of Technology in Pittsburgh; in
Britain, Bristol University opened a department in 1946, to be
followed by Manchester, Birmingham and Hull in the 1960s.

unpractical   Used for any *prop* or piece of *scenery* which is not
practical, i.e. which does not work or function: thus, a door which
cannot be opened would be termed *unpractical*.

up, upstage   *Up*, frequently abbreviated in texts to *U*, is a common *stage direction*, signifying a position at or movement towards
the back of the stage. (Contrast *down* and compare *above*.) 'A
window up centre' (1957, Pinter, *The Room*, Act I), describes its
position in the middle of the back wall of the *set*. *Up* is derived
from the *rake* or incline common on C17 and C18 stages: an actor
positioned behind another was literally *upstage* of him, a term
still in common usage: 'He steps out of the square, upstage, and
begins to walk round the circle' (1973, Peter Shaffer, *Equus*). In
a totally different context, *the up*, an abbreviation of *curtain up*,
is commonly used to refer to the starting time of a show: the time
it *goes up*.

Used as a verb, actors *upstage* someone if they focus attention
on themselves (and away from other performers), generally at a
point in the production when that is not artistically desirable: 'A
happy company is based on generosity. And generosity on the
stage consists of not upstaging your colleagues any more than you
have to, of downstaging yourself whenever you possibly can, of
not distracting when the focus of attention should be on someone
else...' (Barkworth, 78). This usage is derived from the fact that

a position upstage on a raked stage was the one which attracted most attention. *Actor managers* were notorious for arranging that their entrances should occur *upstage centre* and it was common for them to assume positions throughout a performance which ensured the audience's unfaltering attention.

The verb *to upstage* has been in general usage since early this century. However, the earliest OED attestations point to its initial, obsolete use as an adjective meaning 'assuming an air of superiority, haughty, "stuck up"': 'Although Costello...had definite ideas...in connection with his art, he was never the least bit "up stage" with us youngsters' (1927, *Daily Express*). It is interesting to note that this sense, with its implications of an extreme consciousness (and abuse) of experience and status, points again at the style of the actor manager.

upper stage   Although not an Elizabethan term, the *upper stage* was coined by theatre historians, probably in lC19, to describe the acting area (known as the *tarras* or *terrace*) on the *balcony* over the Elizabethan stage. See *above*.

usher/usherette   With the exception of the odd remaining cinema *usherette*, the residual use of the title for a person who shows one to one's pew at a church wedding, a court usher and the Gentleman Usher of the Black Rod, this 'official or servant who has charge of the door' has given way in C20 to the receptionist, the bouncer and, in the theatre, to prosaically-named *front-of-house* staff. *Usher* is first recorded in OED 1386 in Chaucer's *Squire's Tale*: 'The vsshers and the sqiers been ygoon,/The spices and the wyn is come anoon.' From OF *ussier/uissier*, from med. L. *ustiarus*, ultimately from L. *ostium*, 'a door', ushers were employed in the theatres of Elizabethan London to look after and ensure good order in the audience; the usherette is a C20 cinema development, the lady with the torch who directed people to a vacant seat. Pinter, in *Old Times* (1971), given the date of the film mentioned, must be referring to the late 1940s in the following: 'and there was this fleapit showing *Odd Man Out* and there were two usherettes in the foyer and one of them was stroking her breasts...'.

utility   '[A]t one of theatres...I eventually rose to a "general utility man", at 12s a week' (1851, Mayhew, *London Labour*). *Utility* as a noun meaning 'the quality of usefulness' has been in use in English since C14 (from L. *utilis*, 'useful'). The theatrical usage is from C19. A *utility actor* in *stock companies* (also known as a *utility man* or *general utility*) was one who would play a range of smaller roles, including *walk-ons*, and also be available for other *backstage* tasks. A *utility character* in a play is one who is useful not not essential to the plot. The term is also applied to inanimate objects: an item of stage hardware which is of general usefulness can be referred to as a *utility*; a *utility truck* is a wheeled cart useful for moving props, scenery etc. (Compare the use of *utility* for functional, post-war furniture and domestic items.)

V **andyke crystals** Water-soluble crystals which contain a dye used by *scene painters* in the treatment of props and scenery which need to be broken down or otherwise texturally altered for effect. *Vandyke* (sometimes found unanglicised as *Van Dyke*) is a rich, deep brown pigment named after the Flemish painter, Sir Anthony Van Dyke (d. 1641), who was knighted in England in recognition of his portrait-painting, notably of Charles I.

vamp *To vamp* was initially a cobblers' term for mending or patching up, a *vamp* being, from C13, the part of the shoe or boot which covers the front of the foot, from OF *avantpié*, (*avant*, 'before', + *pié*, 'foot'). Interestingly, this sense is still echoed in the verb *to revamp*. Vamp was transferred to an artistic usage as early as C17: 'To th' tap-house then lets gang and rore, Cal hard, tis rare to vamp a score' (1632, Lyly, *Sappho*, II.iii), with the sense of 'patching up (or giving new *vamp* to) a work, improving on it'. The sense of composing through using old materials, common later in C17, was gradually replaced in C18 by the sense of 'to improvise', which it still carries: 'I remember very early in my musical life to have heard one of the town waits at Shrewsbury vamp a base upon all occasions' (1789, Burney, *A general history of music*).

The original meaning of the noun also led to a rare verb meaning 'to tramp or trudge' – 'We vamped the streets in the stifling air' (1896, Hardy, *Wessex Poems*) – and this, combined with the connotations of *vampire* (see *vampire trap*), ultimately from the Slavonic *vampir*, may have given rise to the sense of 'a woman of easy virtue who attracts men by blatently displaying her sexual charms', first encountered in eC20, and echoed in the *tramps' and vamps' balls* which were popular in the 1950s and 1960s. To *revamp* is to rework the writing or production of a scene or play.

vampire trap '[A] vampire is a trap used by the sprites, and is cut in the "flats", and often in the stage – the sprite falling bodily through the trap' (1886, *Stage Gossip*). According to J.R. Planche (1796-1880), this trap was so named because it was first used in his *melodrama The Vampire: or the Bride of the Isles* in 1820. Used for sudden exits and entrances by actors skilled in *tumbling* and *roll-outs*, it consisted of two spring-leaves, and was more commonly found in a *flat* than in the stage floor.

299

variety   Some confusion arises through the overlapping of the terms *music hall* and *variety* in Britain, and *variety* and *vaudeville* in the United States. In Britain, 'variety' as a term gained currency in lC19, when, through commercial developments – some might say exploitation – the music hall began to be staged with ordinary theatre seating and, often, twice-nightly *bills*: '(Cassell's) the biggest variety company ever seen at the East-end of London' (1886, *Referee*). The success of such developments led to a building explosion as Theatres of Variety sprang up across the country. The loss of the earlier, informal atmosphere of music hall was to some degree compensated for by the greater variety of acts on offer, including drama, ballet and grander spectacle, as well as traditional *acts* such as singers, comics, impersonators etc.

In the sense of 'a collection of different things', the word entered English in eC16 from Fr. *variété*. The theatrical use of the word appears to have developed in the eC19 for the American genre equivalent to music hall, which grew out of the saloons and beer halls of the American Industrial Revolution. In this light, it is significant to note that the first variety show in Britain is claimed to have been staged by Maurice de Frece at the Alhambra in Liverpool, a city which continued to import American entertainment before the rest of the country until the 1960s. What de Frece was actually importing, however, was the format of *vaudeville*, which superseded variety in America, but which many in its American audiences persisted in calling 'variety', (just as in Britain until mC20, many still referred to 'variety' as 'music hall'). Both radio and television, the latter of which delivered the final *coup de grace* to variety in the 1950s, appropriated the term and to some degree its format for their own light entertainment programmes, in which context the term is still commonly used.

Variety is also the name of one leading American show-biz trade paper, founded in 1905 and known until recently (as *The Stage* was in Britain) as 'the Actor's Bible'.

vaudeville   *Chansons du Vau de Vire*, 'songs of the valley of the Vire' in Normandy, was a name first given to *ballads* composed by Olivier Basselin, a fuller from Calvados, in C15. The development of the word in French may have arisen through a mishearing as *chansons des voix de villes*, 'songs of town voices'. The term had the sense of 'a popular satirical ballad' in England as early as the lC17, but its meaning was developing still further in French: *pièces en vaudevilles* – plays and dumb-shows with popular music, similar to English *ballad operas* – became the mainstay of the Opéra-Comique. It is with this sense that it was used in England in the C19: 'Fanny was inimitable in vaudeville, in farce, and in the lighter comedy' (1833, OED). The term took a stronger hold, however, in Francophile eC19 America: 'The third, the Olympic, is a tiny show-box for vaudevilles and burlesques' (1842, Dickens, *American Notes*). Here, a discrete form of entertainment is being referred to. It is interesting to note its use in tandem with *burlesque*, as the two were to be clearly distinguished in the following century, vaudeville becoming respectable family entertainment in a string of well-organised, purpose-built theatres which replaced the saloons and beer halls of *variety*. Comedians, singers, dancers and a whole range of *speciality* and *novelty acts* provided entertainment until the 1930s, when cinema and radio, which were already poaching many of its major *artistes*, led to the demise of vaudeville. As with many other theatrical terms, once current it began to be used figuratively, in this case for a brief period only: in 1876, George Eliot writes in *Daniel Deronda*, 'Is this world . . . only like a farce or vaudeville, where you find no great meanings?'

vehicle   'I put it on [*The Damascus Blade*] as an excellent vehicle for Johnnie Mills and Peter Finch and sent them to Brighton' (Olivier, 179). The modern *show-biz* sense of *vehicle*, 'a showcase for the talents of a given performer', is an e-mC20 development. None the less, it is etymologically exact (ultimately from L. *vehere*, 'to carry'), and close to earlier senses such as the C17 'medium of expression or utterance' and 'means by which ideas are communicated and made known'.

ventriloquism/ventriloquy   From med. L. *ventriloquium*, from L. *venter*, 'belly' + *loqui*, 'speak' – literally, 'belly-speaking'. The modern notion of *ventriloquy* as an entertainment in which a performer speaks without moving his lips and 'throws his voice' so that it appears to be coming from a *dummy*, appears to date from the lC18. In earlier centuries, when those with this knack were also known as *engastriloques*, it was far more commonly believed to be 'diabolicall witchcraft' (1584): 'some have questioned whether it can be done lawfully or no' (1642, OED). Clearly, when death at the stake was a likelihood, few were keen to try to use the skill to earn their livelihood. However, in *variety* and *vaudeville, vent. acts*, as they were known, were very popular, especially in England. In fact, in a text-book on the subject in 1893 it was noted: 'It is curious that ventriloquists are nearly all English.' As is the case with *prestidigitation*, *legerdemain* etc., the term is an example of a rather bizarre *novelty act* aggrandising itself with a fine, latinate name.

The earliest figurative usage in OED dates from 1819 and this example, whilst it mixes its theatrical metaphors, is typical of the way in which it is still used: 'The Ventriloquist of Varzin who can pull the strings of three Imperial Chancelleries' (1885, *Pall Mall Gazette*). It is also common to use the image of the ventriloquist's dummy with reference to someone who is suspected of merely echoing another's words.

venue Theatrically, this word is commonly used in lC20 as a synonym for 'theatre', from a *fringe* usage as any place where a performance is scheduled to be held: 'By the late sixties... [fringe theatre] had arrived in London, where a multiplicity of venues, often in pubs, blossomed and usually just as swiftly died' (*The Stage*, 28 March 1991). *Venue* derives originally from OF *venue*, 'coming'. Adopted as 'arrival' in eC14 (and also used in specialist senses in the military and fencing), by eC16 it had come to designate the place to which a jury was summoned to attend a trial: 'The venew must nedes be of Stevenage aforsed' (1531, *Star Chamber Cases*). By mC19, it was also in use for the appointed place at which meetings, sports events etc. were to be held: 'A steeple-chase in which both Universities were to take part... The venue was fixed at B' (1857, George Lawrence, *Guy Livingstone*). It is from this development that its theatrical sense has developed, probably greatly influenced by the *Edinburgh* Fringe, where it is now also the Official Festival term for all places where events are to be held. The demand in the 1950s and 1960s for performance spaces as the Fringe grew rapidly led to the use of a range of unlikely *venues* for shows, the term becoming generally adopted.

verfremdungseffekt Although *verfremdungseffekt* is commonly held to be a complex of techniques for distancing an audience, or achieving its emotional *alienation* from the action during a performance, its etymology suggests a slightly subtler meaning. *Verfremdung* is a term almost uniquely associated with Brecht. *Entfremdung*, also translated as 'alienation', already had a long philosophical pedigree in German, used by Hegel and later by Marx to describe the proletariat's alienation under capitalism. Brecht avoided this term and used *verfremdung* for the first time after a visit to Moscow in 1935, possibly in an attempt to translate a Russian phrase, *priyom ostranyeniya*, 'a way of making strange', used by the *formalist* critic Victor Schlovsky. *Verfremdungseffekt*, he says, in an essay on Chinese acting, was an 'effort to make the incidents on stage appear strange', so that 'acceptance or rejection ... was meant to take place on a conscious plane, instead of... in the audience's sub-conscious' (1935, Brecht, 'Alienation Effects in Chinese Acting').

So, *Verfremdungseffekt* is a theatrical device designed to make the audience pay critical attention to the strangeness of social situations they might otherwise take for granted: thus, in writing *The*

Good Woman of Setzuan, Brecht sets the action in a 'half-westernised city' so that the dialectic between familiar western conditions and the unfamiliar Chinese setting allows the strangeness of his heroine's plight to be highlighted. Other techniques to prevent the audience from empathising with the situation on stage and encourage them to analyse it include breaking up the flow of the plot by using commentaries and songs as interruptions, and a variety of staging techniques: e.g. using placards to anticipate later events and making the workings of the theatre apparent, so that the audience are always aware that what they are witnessing is a theatrical illusion. Another important element is the *Gestus*.

verse drama   From OE *fers*, later reinforced in ME by OF *vers*, both from L. *versus*, 'a line or row', + *drama*. Originally the turn of a plough or furrow, *versus* was applied to a line of writing for obvious figurative reasons.

Verse drama – that is, drama written in metrical lines – is the form we find in the earliest extant Greek texts and as such is central to western drama. In English, the rhymed iambic couplet and *blank verse* became standard choices for the composition of drama in C16 and C17, which is why the dramatists of those eras, in line with the classical tradition, are often referred to as 'poets'. Although gradually superseded by prose as a dramatic medium, periodic attempts have been made since the lC18 to reintroduce verse drama, most notably in this century by Auden and Isherwood, Eliot, Fry, and, among contemporary writers, Ted Hughes, Seamus Heaney and Tony Harrison.

verse-speaking   A notoriously difficult art for the actor and one which, through *training*, has become more consciously studied in C20. The technical demands of *verse-speaking* are markedly different from those required in the *delivery* of prose: 'I . . . had to come to terms with the verse-speaking problem by reaching the truth behind the text *through* the verse – never ignoring it, never singing it (natural speech is essential), but working in harmony with the inherent fabric, rhythm, beat, with full awareness of all the poetic values and nuances' (Olivier, 213). Verse-speaking competitions, some of which draw on dramatic verse extracts, have been popular since the C19 and external examinations are set by bodies such as LAMDA. See *elocution*.

villain   'The fact is, you do not believe in such characters as Surface – the villain of artificial comedy – even as you read or see them' (1822, Lamb, *Elia*). The term *villain* used for an evil character around whose actions the plot of a play (or novel) revolves – *the villain of the piece*, (now a general term for a guilty party) – appears to have been used more frequently from eC19, much popularised by the central role of that character in *melodrama*. Of course, the word is much older, first attested as 'a low-born, base-minded rustic' (OED) in 1303. It comes ultimately from L. *villanus*, someone dwelling in a *villa*, 'a country estate', and as such is very much an urban word, equating the country-dweller with a lack of both culture and morals.

virtuoso   Whilst the noun *virtuoso* has been used in English as a musical term meaning 'a great artist' since mC18, the word tends to be used adjectivally in theatre: 'With virtuoso histrionics you can be accused of going over the top, but at least you'll be noticed' (Branagh, 112). It is from the Italian adjective meaning 'full of learning, skilled, skilful'.

voice   The voice is one of an actor's two principal performance tools, and as such needs to be developed, trained and cossetted. The first attestations in English of *voice* (from OF *voiz, vois, voix*, from L. *vox*, 'voice, sound') as an instrument, without an article, are from C14: 'Among alle thingis vois is a freel thing' (1380, Wyclif, *Sermons*). The expressions *to be in (good) voice* or *out of voice* date from mC18: 'You know very well...that I am not in voice for singing to-day' (*c*.1760, Goldsmith). For an actor to be *in voice* is to be vocally *warmed up*: 'How important is it for you to be in voice, and do you do any work on it before you go to the theatre?' (Barkworth, 167). Specific voice training for actors, rather than merely for choristers or professional singers, would appear to date from the beginning of C20 with the development of *drama schools* and the introduction of professional *voice coaches*: '[I was] introduced to her, I believe, by Elsie Fogarty, the famous voice coach who was such an invaluable help to so many young players – Laurence Olivier, Peggy Ashcroft and myself' (Geilgud, 98).

vomitory (vom.)   An ancient term which had almost passed out of currency but gained renewed usage with the arrival of *theatre-in-the-round*. A *vomitorium* (from L. *vomere*, 'to vomit') was originally one of the many passages for access to and from the seats in a Roman *amphitheatre*, presumably descriptive of the way in which spectators suddenly burst in when the gates opened, (or, given the nature of the spectacles on show there, their demeanour as they rushed out). As *vomitory*, the term has been used occasionally in English from eC18 in historical references – 'He had made the number of the Vomitories in the Middle full in the second Line' (tr. 1730, Gordon, *Maffei's Compleat History of the Ancient Amphitheatres*) – but only rarely has it been used of modern theatres. However, generally abbreviated to *vom*, it is now sometimes used for an entrance passage for actors situated below the *auditorium*, leading on to the *arena* stage of a theatre-in-the-round.

Wagnerian   An adjective formed from the surname of the German composer Richard Wagner (1813-83). It is generally applied to works which contain some of the characteristic qualities associated with either his subject matter, based on Teutonic myth, its presentation, which was *epic*, emotive and grand, or its staging, which was ambitiously innovatory, especially at Bayreuth in his own, custom-built theatre, where he tried to create the *Gesamtkunstwerk* – the complete work of art: vocal and orchestral music, dance, drama, spectacle, stage tableaux, epic sets and complex stage machinery. Along with Dickens, Wagner appears to be one of the first beneficiaries of a custom which began in mC19, the adjectival immortalisation of writers in their own lifetimes. 'The Wagnerian opera . . . presumes that the singer of average ability shall be capable of doing justice to the music' (1873, *All Year Round*). *Wagnerian* was eventually preferred to *Wagneresque*, cited in OED in 1884.

wag(g)on stage   A development or elaboration of the *boat truck* system of scene-changing, based on a system of rails and lifts. The same term is also used for the carts used in *medieval pageants*.

wait   An abbreviation of *stage wait*: waits can be either unintentional delays in a performance or, as in *Hamlet wait*, protracted periods of time when a character remains offstage. *Wait* is also occasionally used to refer to an interval.

walk a flat   A *scene-shifters*' term with a probable *nautical* origin: to move a *flat* by carrying it upright. Flats can be *walked up* – when the bottom is placed against a fixed object and the flat is raised manually to an upright position, raising it *stile* by stile – or they can be *walked down*, a slightly more precarious process. OED attests the nautical use of the verb: 'the men . . . walked the anchor up to the bows' (1836, Marryat, *Pirate*).

walk down   The *walk down* is that magical moment remembered from childhood visits to *pantomimes* (although it can also be applied to *revue, variety* etc.) when one by one, in order of *billing*, the entire cast comes back onstage to receive their applause, often making their entrances by *walking down* a staircase, *up centre*.

walk-on   A *supernumerary* whose dramatic function and significance is described in his name. A C19 term, probably from *stock*: 'The part just now is a walk-on, with an understudy of one of the

305

principals' (1907, H. Wyndham, *Flare of the Footlights*). Occasionally, *walker-on* is found. Compare the slightly more expansive *walking ladies and gentlemen*.

walk(-through)   The noun *walk-through* is used either when a scene in rehearsal is *run* with less than full performance intensity or for early rehearsals when the director is first 'getting the play on its feet' – starting to add movements (*blocking*) after the first *read-throughs* of the text: 'In these brief walk-throughs of the scenes I found myself being dangerously dogmatic' (Branagh, 222). *To walk* or *walk through* a scene are related verbs which can also be used when actors move through the *blocking* of a scene so that, for example, the *lighting designer* can check that they are appropriately lit or so that other technical details of a production can be checked. Often, *stand-ins* from the stage crew may be used at this stage. Compare *run-through*, *stagger-through*.

walking ladies and gentlemen   'I had heard that Mr. Beverley of the Tottenham Street Theatre was about to open the Croyden Theatre for a brief season. I applied to him for a walking gentleman' (Benjamin Webster, quoted in Miles, *The New Anecdote Book*, [1906]). A term from *stock* for actors in minor parts, a politer though hardly less patronising version of the contemporaneous *walk-on*. See also *bit part*, *extra*, *spear-carrier*, *supernumerary*.

Walter Plinge   Dating from around 1900, this is a name used in *programmes* etc., when, for whatever reason, it is considered best to conceal the identity of the true performer. In America, *George Spelvin* is preferred.

wardrobe   i) The department of a theatre that takes care of, fits, and often makes the *costumes* for productions; ii) the items of costume needed for a particular show. The modern domestic wardrobe, a small piece of furniture or a built-in unit in a bedroom, is usually a far cry from 'A room in which wearing apparel (sometimes armour) was kept; esp. a room adjoining the chamber or sleeping apartment; hence a dressing-room... In C16-18, often applied to a room for keeping costly objects generally' (OED). The word comes from OF *warderobe*, a variant of *garderobe*, (from *garder*, 'to keep, take care of' + *robe*, 'a fine, outer garment', ultimately from Germanic *raubh*, 'booty', from the same root as *rob*). It entered English in lC14: 'After euensang, sir Arthure hyme selfene Wente to hys wardrope, and warpe of hys wedez, Armede hym in a actone...' (1400, Malory, *Morte d'Arthure*).

The theatrical use of *wardrobe* developed directly after the Restoration, probably as a direct translation of theatrical Fr. *garderobe*: in the plan for Covent Garden (1731-2), C.P.M. Dumont

marks 'les garderobes ou sont serrés les habits d'hommes'. At the
same period, a contemporary states that 'wardrobes and other
coneniencys' were to be constructed 'in the roof of the said
intended Theatre', (Leacroft, 107), making it clear that the wardrobe had become a separate department and a costume workshop,
run by the *wardrobe mistress* or *master*.

warm-up Nowadays it has become commonplace for actors to
undergo *ensemble* exercises in voice, movement, concentration
and focus immediately prior to a performance in order to *warm
up* for a show. The earliest OED attestation of the phrasal verb,
warm up, albeit in a different sense, is from 1879: 'He warmed
up as he went along' (McCarthy, *Own Times*), suggesting 'to
acquire zest' (OED). The development of the term at this period
may well derive from engineering or electricity, where generated
heat leads to greater efficiency of performance. This sense is also
found implied in the term *warming up the audience*: 'Laughter is
largely a matter of audience temperature, hence the phrase
"warming them up"' (Barkworth, 63). *Warm-up* used as at the
head of this entry probably comes from an eC20 sport and dance
terminologies, where the muscles need to be literally warmed for
maximum effectiveness in performance.

warning The *call* given to an actor or *crew* member to prepare
them for a *cue* is known as the *warning*. If someone misses a cue,
the caller may well defend themselves by saying 'Well, I did warn
them'.

water row A long, low, painted flat used on a *proscenium arch*
stage to suggest the presence of water. Often, the top edge would
be cut into a wave formation. The rather unnaturalistic effect this
created led to its obsolescence by mC20, except in pantomime
and other stylised productions.

well-made play A direct translation of Fr. *pièce bien faite*, a term
initially used in eC19 France to praise the ingenuity of a dramatist's plotting and construction. This very neatness was to turn
the phrase's sense back-to-front. The patness of the *well-made
play* appeared grossly unnaturalistic to lC19 writers and critics –
notably Zola (see *Zolaesque*) in France and Shaw (see *Shavian*)
in England – and came to be used disparagingly of works that
were considered to be life-defyingly well-constructed, and graced
with appropriate rather than realistic *dénouements*.

West End London's major *commercial* theatre district, west of
the City of London (contrast East End), the equivalent of *Broadway* in New York. The West End is centred around Shaftesbury
Avenue, Aldwych, the Strand and Charing Cross Rd. The term
seems to have been first used geographically in eC19 – 'As you're

staying with a relation at the west end...there's no harm making
a genteel acquaintance' (1815, *Zeluca*) – and was soon to carry
overtones of wealth, high fashion and privilege: 'that West-End
view of the realities of life which Englishmen of a certain class
feel it proper to take' (1889, OED). Theatres had flourished in the
region since lC17, Lincoln's Inn Fields Theatre (1656) and Drury
Lane (1663) being the earliest establishments. The connotations
of the phrase *West End theatre* have changed during the century,
the latest, perhaps, being of a theatre predominated by *musicals*
and *box office* concerns at the expense of experimentation and
vigour.

Whitehall farce   A genre of risqué *farce* which came to promi-
nence at the Whitehall Theatre during the period that it was
actor-managed by Brian Rix – 1950-67.

whisper   i) An abbreviation of *stage whisper*; ii) an actor's term
for a vocal performance which lacks confidence and commitment:
'I whispered for all the rehearsal period' (Judi Dench, interviewed
in Barkworth, 165).

whistling in the wings   It is generally regarded as very bad luck
to *whistle in the wings* of a theatre, or on stage, for that matter,
unless required to do so in the script. Whilst it might be thought
that is yet another example of theatre superstition, (see *leg, (break
a)*; *Macbeth*; *toi, toi, toi*), it had originally been a commonsense
arrangement. The ex-sailors who *crewed* in the *flies* in lC17-C18
still communicated to each other at times in whistles as they had
done at sea to counter the sound of wind and waves. Any other
whistling, clearly, might lead to a false instruction, and consequent injury or annoyance.

whodun(n)it   A theatrical genre that developed and took its name
from a class of C20 crime and detective novels in which the major
interest lies in the plotting and in the reader/audience attempting
to guess who *done* [*sic*] the crime. The most notable author (in
terms of *box office* receipts) to have turned her hand to *whodunnits*
was Agatha Christie (1890-1976), whose sixteen plays formed the
backbone of the repertoire of many post-war amateur groups,
and whose blockbuster *The Mousetrap* (1952) still holds the record
for the longest single run in the *West End*. The term appears to
have gained currency in America in the early 1930s, 'who done
it', obviously, being a dialect form of 'who did it' which mildly
satirises both the form and its readership. It first appears in English usage in the early 1940s.

wig   An abbreviation of *periwig*, itself a development of pronunciation and spelling from *peruke*, from Fr. *perruque*, from It. *per-
rucca/parrucca*, of unknown origin. The fashion for wearing wigs,

which began on the Continent as the etymology attests, was imported to England at the Restoration. The first OED attestation is from 1675: 'He...looks down with Contempt on every body, whose Wig is not right Flaxen' (*Character of a Town-Gallant*). Clearly, however, given the use of *boy actors* on the English stage from C16, wig-wearing and wig care (the latter now performed by the *wig mistress* and *wig master*) are traditions which predate the fashion. Related terms include *wigband*, 'the cloth strip holding the wig to the head', *wig line*, 'the join where the wig meets the face', and *wig paste*, 'an adhesive *make-up* used to attach the wig, which also masks the wig line.

wind machine   A wooden drum which, when rotated, causes wooden slats to rub against a stretch of canvas, producing a *sound effect* like the wind. In most modern theatres, taped effects have now made the machine obsolete.

wing it   'It's such a tight, anal little group. You can't wing or busk anything. It's always "Get it right, get it right"' (Eric Idle, *The Listener*, 28 June 1979). *To wing* is now generally used with a sense akin to 'improvise' or 'to try out without benefit of full rehearsal', from the major theatrical sense of *wing* below. It is a C19 term which OED defines as 'to study (a part) in or about the wings, having undertaken it at short notice': 'In the event of an artiste being suddenly called upon to play a part of which he knows nothing...he frequently has to "wing" the part' (1886, *Stage Gossip*).

wings   The term now generally designates the areas to either side of an *end-stage* or *proscenium arch* stage which are obscured from the audience's view by *flats*, *curtain tabs* etc. These are the natural places for performers to stand prior to making an entrance on to the stage, hence the generally-used term, *waiting in the wings*, which describes a person ready (and generally able) to take their place in an on-going action.

The Roman architect and engineer, Vitruvius (fl. 1 BC), in the fifth book of his work *De Architura* states that 'beyond [the periaktoi and machinery] are the projecting wings which afford entrances to the stage, one from the forum, the other from abroad.'

Wing, in its earliest sense, is an abbreviation of *wing flat*. LC16 and eC17 English *masques* used forms of *book-flat* or *periaktoi* to create such wings, although the term does not appear to have been used until the end of the century at the earliest. Cibber (in his *Apology* of 1740), in referring to Rich's alterations at Drury Lane in 1696, states that 'where the doors of Entrance now are, there formerly stood two additional Side-Wings, in front of a full Set of Scenes, which then had almost a double Effect, in their

Loftiness, and Magnificence.' When the term was transferred
from the structures to the space behind them remains unclear.
The first OED attestation of the term: 'the technical modern term,
wings, or side scenes' (1790, Malone, ed. *Shakespeare's Works*)
is ambiguous. The first usage resembling the modern sense is not
attested until 1847: 'the frantic stage manager in the wing' (OED).

within Like *above*, an Elizabethan/Jacobean stage direction
which is descriptive of the physical structure of theatres of the
period. In *Othello* V.ii we find:

> OTHELLO. It is too late. *(Smothers her [Desdemona])*
> *Emilia at the door.*
> EMILIA.   *(Calls within.)* My lord! My lord!

Within means out of view of the audience. Whilst there is still
dispute as to the precise structure of lC16/eC17 theatres, it seems
likely that this stage direction could have been complied with in
one of two ways. If the actor playing Othello were on the main
forestage of the first Globe Theatre, Emilia would be *upstage* of
him, probably curtained off within the *inner stage* which was set
into the main structure of the *tiring-house*. Alternatively, if the
inner stage were used for Desdemona and Othello's chamber,
Emilia would be offstage inside the tiring-house.

wooden 'As Albany and Cornwall, Richard Brenner and Richard
O'Callaghan are wooden and unimaginative. These actors look
exposed; they need props, furniture, a world to inhabit before
they can make us believe in the play' (*Plays and Players*, October
1990). *Wooden* meaning 'mentally dull ... unintelligent, blockish'
(OED) has been Standard English since C16: 'Who have .../...so
wooden wits as not that worth to knowe' (1586, Sidney, *Astrophel
and Stella*, Sonnet vii). Theatrically, it is a term used to describe
the awkward, inhibited performance of a weak actor. It may have
gained its specific theatrical usage in mC19, from which period
Partridge cites the adjective being used metaphorically in thirteen
slang phrases. It may well also have involved an unflattering comparison with the acting skills of *marionettes* and *puppets*.

word '[T]he actor at last, in despair, called out: "Barry, give me
the word, will you?" To which Barry replied, loud enough for
the audience to hear: 'What word, my boy?"' (1914, Englebach,
Anecdotes of the Theatre). To *give the word* (or *line*) is another term
for *to prompt*.

words A common term for an actor's *part* or *lines*: 'having a good
knowledge of the words in advance ... enables you to assess more
clearly the rightness or the wrongness of the moves a director
may suggest' (Barkworth, 19). *Word rehearsal* is a less common
alternative for *line rehearsal* – one in which the emphasis is placed

on knowing and delivering the text rather than on the *moves*. When actors are fully *au fait* with their lines, they are said to be *word perfect* (see **DLP**): 'Noel Coward had a disconcerting habit of turning up at a first rehearsal absolutely word perfect, even if it was not his own play' (Hay, *Anecdotes of the Theatre*, 60). This phrase has entered common usage and was appropriated in the 1980s as a punning brand name for a word processing software package.

work a show A *technical* term for carrying out all the processes of production, lighting, sound etc. necessary for the running of a show. A *nautical* usage: sailors *worked* a sailing ship, especially when they were tacking or involved in other manoeuvre which required rope-work: 'The shipping... had direction to worke about to another Creake' (1633, Sir Thomas Stafford, *Pacata Hibernia*).

working 'I attempted to give mime classes when not "working". I always felt a terrible guilt when unemployed...' (Berkoff, 112). The question 'Are you working?' is all to frequent in the acting profession, where at any given time more than 95 per cent of paid-up, full *Equity* members are unemployed, or, euphemistically, *resting*. The phrase *working actor* is used for someone in regular work.

working (lights) Commonly abbreviated to *workers*. These produce a lighting state dimmer than normal production intensity but adequate for safe working. A working light may be used for rehearsals or technical work or may be used in a production as a *convention* understood by the audience as the equivalent of an *act-* or *scene-drop*: during this time the stage may be reset, actors leave or take up new positions, etc. 'Kill the workers...' is a common but politically-dubious theatrical pun, often followed by the equally dubious '...and hang the blacks'.

   Working is also found in a variety of theatrical contexts – *working border, working line, working flies* etc. – to denote a piece of equipment which is active during a production. See *work*. Occasionally, the *prompt side* is referred to as the *working side*.

workshop In its primary contemporary usage, *workshop* designates i) a small theatre or studio where often works of an exploratory, *experimental*, educational or political nature are staged; ii) a group session, usually practical, collaborative and improvisatory, often awareness-raising or educational, devised to allow intensive exploratory work on a given topic. The word is also used adjectivally in sense i) in the phrase a *workshop production*: 'Here the skill of workshop production lies in the fresh emphasis lent to the entire action' (*The Stage*, 28 March 1991). In sense ii) it is found verbally, as in *to workshop an idea*, 'to explore it through workshop exercises'. All senses of the word suggest work in progress rather than completed work and hint at the socialist ethic which lay behind its adoption. Intensively used in lC20 English-speaking theatre, the workshop ethos was popularised by Joan Littlewood's *Theatre Workshop* founded in 1945 and heavily influenced by the subject matter, performance styles and theories about the actor/audience relationship inherent in the political theatres of Appia, *Brecht* and, to a lesser degree, Meyerhold.

However, in English, *workshop* has signified, since its first usage in C16, a place where industrial and manual work is carried out, and this is the sense that it carried until the mC20. *Workshops* were areas of the theatre set aside for *painting* and the manufacture of *scenery* and *props*. In the sense above, however, it is used with an appropriation of the sense of Fr. *atelier*, 'workshop': 'an artist's place of work'. It is as if the modern usage of the term is a partial attempt to bridge and heal the linguistic divide between artistic and technical cultures which was opened up in C18.

See also *activism, alternative, community theatre, laboratory theatre, T.I.E.*

wow   A *wow* is an American term for a *hit show*. It appears to have been used first in the 1920s, and was in use in Britain by the end of that decade. It has been suggested that it comes from the barking of a dog, an approximation of the sound of a wildly-appreciative audience. Beale compares it with the phrase 'a howling success'.

Z **anni** This was the name given to the comic servant characters of *commedia dell'arte*, such as Arlecchino (see *Harlequin*), Columbina, Pulcinella (Polichinelle – see *Punch*) and Pantalone (see *Pantaloon*), who in England were to form the major characters of the eC18 *harlequinade*, and, later, *pantomime*. The word is from Venetian *Gianni*, from It. *Giovanni*, 'John'. The nature of the stage humour of these characters led to the development of the word *zany*.

zany From its origins as a clown-like figure, one of the *zanni* in the *commedia dell'arte*, the anglicised *zany* originally meant 'an attendant clown'. The adjective formed from it suggests the anarchic end of the comic spectrum: *zany* is 'farcical, ridiculous, madcap, crazy'.

Zolaesque Of or pertaining to the works and style of Emile Zola, (1840-1902). Primarily a novelist, Zola also wrote several plays, most notably the stage adaptation of his own novel, *Thérèse Raquin*. Due to his uncompromising naturalism and open-eyed, committed attitude to a range of subjects, many considered taboo in C19, *Zolaesque* suggests painful and unmitigated *naturalism and realism*. Theatre *practitioners* influenced by him include Antoine in France and Ibsen and Strindberg in Scandinavia.

References

Abrams, M.H. (1957) *A Glossary of Literary Terms*, 5th edn, Orlando, Florida: Holt, Rinehart and Winston, Inc.

Baker, Hendrik (1988) *Stage Management and Theatrecraft: A Stage Manager's Handbook*, New York: Theatre Art Books.

Barba, Eugenio and Savarese, Nicola (1991) tr. Richard Fowler, *The Secret Art of the Performer*, London: Routledge.

Barkworth, Peter (1991) *The Complete About Acting*, London: Methuen Drama. Based on *About Acting* (1980) and *More About Acting* (1984), both published by Secker & Warburg.

Beale, Paul, ed. (1989) *A Concise Dictionary of Slang and Unconventional English*, London: Routledge. Entries are alphabetical. Based on Partridge.

Bentley, Eric (1981) *The Brecht Commentaries*, London: Eyre Methuen.

Berkoff, Steven (1989) *I Am Hamlet*, London: Faber and Faber Limited.

Bloomsbury Theatre Guide see Griffiths.

Bowman, Walter Parker and Ball, Robert Hamilton, (1962) *Theatre Language: A Dictionary of Terms in English of the Drama and the Stage from Medieval to Modern Times*, New York: Theatre Art Books.

Branagh, Kenneth (1989) *Beginning*, London: Chatto and Windus.

Brook, Peter (1987; 1988) *The Shifting Point: Forty years of theatrical exploration: 1946-1987*. New York, Harper & Row; London: Methuen.

Elam, Keir (1980) *The Semiotics of Theatre and Drama*, London: Methuen.

(1980) *Truly Yours: One Hundred and Fifty Years of Play Publishing & Service to the Theatre*. London: Samuel French Ltd.

Geilgud, John (1979) *An Actor in his Time*, London: Sidgwick and Jackson. (I have used the 1981 Penguin edn.)

Green, Michael (1964) *The Art of Coarse Acting*, London: Hutchinson.

Griffiths, Trevor, ed. (1982) *Stagecraft: The Complete Guide to Theatrical Practice*, Oxford: Phaidon Press Ltd.

Griffiths, Trevor R. and Woddis, Carol, eds. (1988) *Bloomsbury Theatre Guide*, London: Bloomsbury.

315

Hartnoll, Phyllis, ed. (1967) *The Oxford Companion to the Theatre*, Oxford: Oxford University Press.

Harwood, Ronald (1984) *All The World's A Stage*, London: Secker & Warburg/BBC.

Hay, Peter (1987) *Theatrical Anecdotes*, Oxford: Oxford University Press.

Innes, C.D. (1972) *Erwin Piscator's Political Theatre*, Cambridge: Cambridge University Press.

Leacroft, Richard (1973) *The Development of the English Playhouse: An illustrated survey of theatre building in England from medieval to modern times*, London: Eyre Methuen Ltd.

Leacroft, Richard and Helen (1984) *Theatre and Playhouse: An illustrated history of theatre building from Ancient Greece to the present day*, London: Methuen.

Menear, Pauline and Hawkins, Terry (1988) *Stage Management and Theatre Administration*, Oxford: Phaidon Press Ltd.

Nagler, A.M. (1952) *A Source Book in Theatrical History*, Toronto, Ontario, General Publishing Company Ltd. (I have used the New York, Dover edn.)

Needle, Jan and Thomson, Peter (1981) *Brecht*, Oxford: Basil Blackwell Publisher.

Olivier, Laurence (1982) *Confessions of an Actor*, London: Weidenfeld & Nicholson Ltd

Partridge, Eric (1948) *A Dictionary of Slang and Unconventional English*, 8th edn, London: Routledge & Kegan Paul.

Pickering, David, ed. (1988) *Dictionary of the Theatre*, Market House Books. (I have used the Sphere Reference edn.)

Stanislavski, Constantin (1936) tr. Elizabeth Reynolds Hapgood, *An Actor Prepares*, New York: Theatre Arts Inc. (I have used the Eyre Methuen edn, 1980).

Stein, Charles W., ed. (1984) *American Vaudeville As Seen by Its Contemporaries*, New York: Da Capo Press Ltd.

Taplin, Oliver (1978) *Greek Tragedy in Action*, London: Methuen & Co. Ltd.

Williams, Raymond (1976) *Keywords: A vocabulary of culture and society* London: Fontana. (I have used the revised and expanded 1983 edn, London: Flamingo.)

Wilmut, Roger (1985) *Kindly Leave the Stage: The Story of Variety 1919-1960*, London: Methuen.

Winslow, Colin (1991) *The Oberon Glossary of Theatrical Terms: Theatre Jargon Explained*, London: Oberon Books Ltd.